THE IMPERIAL JAPANESE NAVY

OSPREY
PUBLISHING

Dedication

To my mother, Louise, who gave me the love of reading and writing.

Acknowledgements

I would like to thank the many people over the years who have contributed in ways large and small to my work on the Imperial Japanese Navy. Among the most gracious with their time were John Lundstrom, Allyn Nevitt, and Alan Zimm. This book would not have been as appealing without the outstanding collection of photographs which come from many sources. In particular, I would like to thank Robert Hanshew at the Naval History and Heritage Command, Tohru Kizu, editor of *Ships of the World* magazine, and the Yamato Museum.

THE IMPERIAL JAPANESE NAVY

IN THE PACIFIC WAR

MARK E. STILLE

OSPREY PUBLISHING
Bloomsbury Publishing Plc

Kemp House, Chawley Park, Oxford OX2 9PH, UK
1385 Broadway, 5th Floor, New York, NY 10018, USA
Email: info@ospreypublishing.com

OSPREY is a trademark of Osprey Publishing, a division of Bloomsbury Publishing Plc

First published in Great Britain in 2013 by Osprey Publishing

A CIP catalogue record for this book is available from the British Library

ISBN: 978 1 4728 0146 3
ePub ISBN: 978 1 4728 0925 4
PDF ISBN: 978 1 4728 0924 7

Index by Mark Swift
Typeset in Trade Gothic and Adobe Garamond Pro
Originated by PDQ Digital Media Solutions Ltd, Suffolk
Printed and bound in India by Replika Press Private Ltd.

20 21 22 23 24   10 9 8 7 6

Editor's note
This work is an edited and expanded compilation of several Osprey books. All books used are listed below:

NVG 109 Imperial Japanese Navy Aircraft Carriers 1921-45
NVG 135 Imperial Japanese Navy Submarines 1941-45
NVG 146 Imperial Japanese Navy Battleships 1941-45
NVG 176 Imperial Japanese Navy Heavy Cruisers 1941-45
NVG 187 Imperial Japanese Navy Light Cruisers 1941-45
NVG 198 Imperial Japanese Navy Destroyers 1919-45 (1)
NVG 202 Imperial Japanese Navy Destroyers 1919-45 (2)

The following maps and artwork have appeared in previous Osprey books:
Map page 26 (RAID 26); maps pages 30, 33, 40 (CMD 26); maps pages 36, 37 (CAM 226); map page 41, artwork page 44 (CAM 255); map page 48 (DUE 48); map page 49 (CAM 163).

Osprey Publishing is supporting the Woodland Trust, the UK's leading woodland conservation charity, by funding the dedication of trees.

www.ospreypublishing.com
To find out more about our authors and books visit our website. Here you will find extracts, author interviews, details of forthcoming events and the option to sign-up for our newsletter.

Front cover top: *Myoko* in March 1941 after her second modernization. (Yamato Museum)
Front cover bottom: *Ryujo* pictured on its full speed trials in April 1933. (*Ships of the World*)
Back cover top: Port-quarter view of *Mogami* in August 1935. (Yamato Museum)
Back cover bottom: *Arashi* in December 1940 before final completion. (Yamato Museum
Contents page: *Sendai* in 1939 acting as a destroyer squadron leader. (Yamato Museum)

CONTENTS

INTRODUCTION

At the start of the Pacific War in December 1941, the Imperial Japanese Navy (IJN) was the third most powerful navy in the world. This was an impressive achievement for an organization which had only been in existence since 1868. The meteoric rise of the IJN was due to a combination of factors, not the least of which was an accepted imperative to modernize in the face of a visible foreign threat, accompanied by able administration and willingness to adapt and innovate, and the assistance of first Great Britain and then other foreign countries. So quickly did the IJN modernize that it was able to defeat China in a war from 1894 to 1895, and then, to the astonishment of the world, vanquish a major European power in the Russo-Japanese War of 1904 to 1905.

The war against Russia culminated in a decisive battle in which the outnumbered Japanese battle fleet prevailed through its superior training and fighting spirit. This became a template for the IJN's next war, which would be fought against an even more daunting opponent – the United States Navy (USN). The USN had gone from being a hypothetical adversary in 1907 to the only force able to block Japan's imperial ambitions in 1941. The IJN had spent the entire interwar period preparing for war against the Americans and in 1941 went to war at the height of its powers and even enjoyed a numerical advantage over the USN, which had to devote resources to the Atlantic theater. In 1941, the balance was as favorable as it would ever be for Japan with the IJN honed to a fine edge and the USN not yet reinforced by the ships from its "two-ocean navy" building program which, if realized, would swing the naval balance drastically against the IJN.

The opening of war in December 1941 showed the IJN to be more than a match for the USN and Allied navies for the first six months of conflict. Not only did the IJN possess superior ships in most categories, but the training of their crews under virtual wartime conditions made them decidedly more combat ready than their enemies. As a result the IJN was virtually unchecked during the first phase of the war, during which it accomplished all its objectives for the loss of no ship larger than a destroyer.

The run of Japanese victories was stopped at Coral Sea and Midway in May and June 1942, but the IJN remained a formidable adversary as shown by its ability to outfight the USN during the Guadalcanal campaign from August 1942 until February 1943. This was the true turning point in the Pacific War since it inflicted severe attritional losses on the IJN in ships and aircraft, and, more importantly, in highly trained personnel, for no strategic benefit since the Japanese proved eventually unable to stop the first American offensive of the war. The campaign also indicated another Japanese weakness as tactical excellence proved to be no substitute for lack of strategic insight.

Into 1943, the IJN girded its strength for another decisive battle to turn the tide of the American advance. This occurred first in June 1944 at the Battle of the Philippine Sea, and again a few months later in October in the climactic Battle of Leyte Gulf. Both resulted in catastrophic defeats and by the end of October the IJN was no longer a viable force, which opened the Japanese home islands to the prospect of direct attack. From its initial sweeping victories in 1941 and early 1942 in the Pacific and Indian Oceans, the IJN was reduced in 1945 to mounting effective resistance only with suicide aircraft. The final gesture of committing the superbattleship *Yamato*, which symbolized the IJN and the Japanese nation, against overwhelming USN air power in April 1945 effectively marked the end of the short life of the IJN.

IMPERIAL JAPANESE NAVY STRATEGY AND DOCTRINE IN THE PACIFIC WAR

Mutsu, *Ise*, and *Fuso* in line-ahead formation, prior to the Pacific War. Like all navies of the interwar period, the strength of the IJN's battle line defined its status. (Naval History and Heritage Command)

DECISIVE BATTLE STRATEGY

Going into the Pacific War, the strategy of the IJN was underpinned by several key assumptions.

The most fundamental assumption was that, just as the Russo-Japanese naval war had been decided by the Battle of Tsushima on May 27–28, 1905, the war against the USN would be decided by a single great naval clash. The nature of this battle was also believed to be certain, and this conviction was shared by both the IJN and the USN: the battle would be decided by the big guns aboard battleships. All other arms of the IJN were dedicated to supporting the dreadnoughts when they met the USN in battle. The place of the great clash between dreadnoughts was also sure, at least for the IJN. The Japanese assumed that at the start of any conflict, they would quickly seize the largely unprotected American-held Philippines. This would force the USN to mount a drive across the Pacific to retake them. Accordingly, the great clash would take place somewhere in the western Pacific when the IJN decided the time was right to stop the American advance.

Furthermore, it was clear to the Japanese that in order to win the decisive clash they would have to make up for a numerical disadvantage. The Japanese realized that they would never have the industrial capacity to create a navy equal in size to the USN, but, since they were planning on deriving the benefits of being on the defensive, they calculated that they had to have only 70 percent of the strength of the USN to be in a position to prevail in the great clash. This assumption was built on two pillars. Both became driving forces in IJN naval construction, tactical development, and training between the wars. The first was that the IJN had to have the weapons and tactics to inflict severe attrition on the USN before the decisive battle, which would bring the IJN to at least parity. Once at rough parity, IJN units with superior speed and capable of hitting at ranges beyond the reach of the USN, crewed by superbly trained personnel, would win the day.

THE WASHINGTON AND LONDON NAVAL TREATIES

The Washington Naval Treaty of 1922 was one of history's most effective arms reduction programs, since it froze the construction of battleships for the next 14 years and affected the composition of all the world's major navies. Because no major power was in a position to execute a large battleship-building program in the wake of the ruinous World War I, an agreement was relatively easy to reach. A system of ratios was set up between the five signatory powers. The United States and Great Britain were each allocated 525,000 tons of capital ships – Japan had to be content with 60 percent of this at 315,000 tons (a ratio of 5:5:3). Italy and France were each restricted to 175,000 tons. A 10-year moratorium on battleship construction was agreed to. Replacement of battleships was allowed after they had reached 20 years of service, but none could be bigger than 35,000 tons or carry guns larger than 16in. Carriers were also restricted with the same 5:5:3 ratio, with Japan's allocation being 81,000 tons.

The Washington Treaty did not restrict the building of ships other than battleships and carriers, so what ensued was a building race for heavy cruisers. In 1927, the five signatories convened the Geneva Naval Conference in an attempt to limit heavy cruiser proliferation, but failed to reach agreement. However, the Washington Treaty had set a limit on the size of these ships (10,000 tons) and the size of their guns (no larger than 8in).

The London Naval Conference, resulting in the London Naval Treaty of 1930, was called to complete the system of naval limitations. This was a much more contentious convention, and within the Japanese government there was a divide on what terms were acceptable. Some within the IJN were insistent that, unlike at Washington, Japan needed an allocation of 70 percent for other types of warships to ensure the nation's defense. In the end, they were forced to accept 60 percent of the US and Great Britain heavy cruiser allocation, or 108,400 tons. Japan was allocated 70 percent for light cruisers (100,450 tons) and destroyers (105,500 tons). Submarine tonnage was set at 52,700 tons, or parity with other naval powers.

Attempts to extend the London Treaty were unsuccessful. Preliminary meetings for a second London Treaty were held in 1934, but Japan's notice in December of that year that it intended to withdraw from all naval treaties meant the collapse of the system to restrict naval construction. As of January 1937, the IJN would be free of all treaty restrictions. Throughout the period of naval treaties the IJN had found ways to circumvent the strict letter of the treaty restrictions, but had adhered to their spirit. Now it faced the uncertain future of a naval race with the United States.

The USN was also now free of limitation, and as war loomed in Europe, a series of naval expansion plans were authorized which threatened to move the IJN well below its required 70 percent comparative strength. In response, the IJN did the only thing open to it – it placed an even more intensive reliance on quality. This was marked by even more realistic and demanding training, but more dramatically by the introduction of super weapons like the Yamato-class battleship and the Shokaku-class carriers.

NAVAL CONSTRUCTION PROGRAMS

Like other navies, the IJN received yearly authorizations for construction of naval units. From 1907 to 1920, these were formulated with the goal of achieving the cherished '8-8' fleet plan, which would have resulted in the balanced battle fleet of eight battleships and eight battlecruisers which IJN planners thought necessary for the defense of Japan. Such a plan proved beyond the capabilities of a relatively poor country like Japan to pay for, but pressures to keep up with the United States brought large and unsustainable naval appropriations. In response to a 1916 US Navy Bill, the IJN received authorization in the 1916 and 1917 programs for 63 ships including four battleships and 10 cruisers, two of which were to be battlecruisers. In 1918, another two battlecruisers were authorized which, if completed, would have brought the 8-8 plan to fruition. In 1919, the US announced another large navy bill with an astounding 10 battleships and six battlecruisers which would have left the IJN far behind. In response, the IJN gained approval of its 1920 building program which would have provided four battleships and four battlecruisers by 1927. These ships were never finished and the 8-8 program never realized since they were superseded by the 1922 Washington Naval Treaty. IJN construction during the 1920s focused on heavy cruisers, which were not restricted numerically by the Washington Treaty.

In response to the London Treaty of 1930, a series of Naval Replenishment (construction) programs were devised which were known unofficially as Circle Plans. Circle 1 was approved in 1931 and provided for 39 ships to be laid down between 1931 and 1934; this program again focused on cruisers. Circle 2, approved in 1934, was delayed by the need to modify many ships already in service to correct stability problems, but included the last two large cruisers and two fleet carriers. The end of the naval reduction treaties brought Circle 3 in 1937 which included the two Yamato-class superbattleships, the two Shokaku-class carriers and 64 other ships. Circle 4 was a six-year program approved in September 1939 which included two more Yamatos, carrier *Taiho* and a massive expansion of the naval air arm. Even more massive was Circle 5, approved in June 1941, which was an attempt to respond to the US Two-Ocean Navy Act of 1940. Circle 5 included three more improved Yamato-class ships and two battlecruisers. Few of these ships were completed and it was cancelled after Midway and replaced with the revised Circle 5 which gave priority to carriers and submarines. In 1941, three special Circle plans were also approved to provide for needed smaller ships and auxiliaries. When the war began in December 1941, almost all Circle 3 ships had been completed and work on Circle 4 and the special plan ships were underway. Despite this great progress, it would be inadequate for a war with the United States.

CARRIER DOCTRINE

In the infancy of naval aviation, carriers were seen as valuable only in that they could provide support to the battle line. This equated to reconnaissance, spotting for gunnery, and providing antisubmarine protection and fighter protection against enemy aircraft attempting similar support functions against the Japanese. Gradually, as the associated technology became more mature, naval aviation took on offensive functions and these were folded under the attritional strategy before the decisive battle. The main target of Japanese carrier aircraft was now determined to be enemy carriers. Destruction of the enemy's carrier force would then allow Japanese carrier aircraft to weaken the enemy's battle fleet. Because carriers were seen to be very vulnerable to attack, the essential precondition for carrier combat was that the IJN strike first. This accounts for the great Japanese emphasis on large carrier air groups composed of aircraft uniformly lighter than their opponents, giving them greater range.

The four Takao-class cruisers on display in October 1935. *Chokai* is the closest ship. Note that all four ships are as originally built, with their massive bridge structures. Beyond the Takao ships are three of the 7,500-ton scout cruisers and a carrier. The second row consists of three light cruisers and a Fuso-class battleship. (Yamato Museum)

One important advantage exercised by the Japanese at the start of the war was their ability to mass carrier air power. In April 1941, the Japanese brought all their fleet carriers into a single formation, the First Air Fleet. The Kido Butai (literally: "mobile force" but better rendered as "striking force") was the First Air Fleet's operational component. At the start of the war, three carrier divisions made up the Kido Butai. Unlike in the USN where carrier divisions served only in an administrative capacity, the carrier divisions of the Kido Butai were operational entities. The two carriers in a division fought together, often exchanging aircraft squadrons and commanders on strikes. The commander of the Kido Butai could wield the aircraft of its three divisions as a single entity bringing masses of modern aircraft crewed by highly trained and brave aviators onto a single target.

BATTLESHIP DOCTRINE

Japanese naval tactics centered on the battle line. Early Japanese tactics favored forming the battle line into a line-ahead formation. The Japanese formation would maneuver to cross the enemy's T (aligning the ship's broadside to the enemy's bow) and deal devastating blows by concentrating fire on selected targets. Japanese destroyers would launch night torpedo attacks on the enemy battle line should a decisive result not be reached after the first day. The battle line was too valuable to risk at night, with the exception of the fast battleships, which were tasked to support the breakthrough of lighter units delivering torpedo attacks. The battle line would maneuver to be in position to engage the weakened enemy at dawn and finish them off. The desired number of battleships to execute these tactics was 16. This was considered the maximum number of ships that could be controlled by a single commander, and would be broken down into two *sentai* (divisions), each consisting of eight ships.

A critical component of Japanese tactics was the concept of outranging the enemy, an advantage calculated to allow the Japanese to strike the enemy before they could effectively retaliate. This range requirement applied in particular to the big guns of the battleships. The concept was first put into practice with the 14in guns aboard the *Kongo*, and continued up through the deployment of 18.1in guns on the superbattleship *Yamato*. The development of greater gun elevation and specially designed shells led the Japanese to assess in the mid-1930s that their battleships out-ranged USN battleships by 4,324–5,468 yards. Naval Staff College studies indicated that the Japanese could track targets at 44,000 yards and open fire at 37,000 yards. This capability gave the Japanese the opportunity to cripple their targets before they could retaliate. In 1939, the Japanese claimed 12 percent main battery accuracy at 35,000 yards, using spotting aircraft (claims which proved totally unfounded during the war).

The Revised Battle Instructions of 1934 stated that "battleship divisions are the main weapon in a fleet battle and their task is to engage the main force of the enemy." Other elements of the fleet, including carrier aircraft, submarines, cruisers, and destroyers, would conduct torpedo attacks to cripple the enemy, but it was up to the battleships to deliver the decisive blows. In these intricate tactical scenarios, the main battle force consisted of the two battleships of Battleship Division 1 (the Nagato class), and the four battleships of Battleship Division 2 (the four Fuso- and Ise-class units). The fleet vanguard included the four fast battleships of the Kongo class. The Kongos were assigned the mission of opening lanes for the cruisers and destroyers to allow them to deliver massed torpedo attacks. Once the torpedoes had done their work, the battleships would assume a parallel course some 38,000 yards distant from the enemy battle line and begin to fire with the aid of spotter aircraft. The Japanese assessed that the combination of massive torpedo attack and battleship gunnery would cause extensive damage to the American fleet. In the battle's final stages, the Japanese battleships would close to between 21,000 yards and 24,000 yards to deliver the final blows. Interestingly, while these complex plans looked viable in the halls of the Naval Staff College and to the Naval General Staff, they were never tested in their entirety in fleet exercises.

CRUISER DOCTRINE

Heavy cruisers were an integral part of the IJN's pre-decisive-battle operations. After 1934, the heavy cruisers were seen as the IJN's principal night-fighting unit. Under the revised Night Battle Tactics of that year, the heavy cruisers were intended primarily as a component of the Night Battle Force to attack the US battle fleet with long-range torpedoes, inflicting heavy attrition before the Japanese battleships closed for a climactic daylight gunnery action. The Takao-class heavy cruisers were to combine with the four Kongo-class fast battleships to open a way through the defensive ring of the US battle fleet. Supporting the attack, and slated to deliver massed torpedo fire, were four night battle groups, each composed of a cruiser squadron formed around a class of heavy cruiser and a destroyer squadron of 14–16 ships led by a light cruiser. This concept was modified just before

Sendai in 1939 acting as a destroyer squadron leader. An unidentified destroyer is on its starboard beam and a Hatsuhara-class destroyer is steaming off its starboard quarter. (Yamato Museum)

the start of the war so that two battle groups attacked each side of the US battle fleet. While the massive fleet engagement desired and planned for by the Japanese never happened, this concentration on small-unit tactics paid off handsomely for the Japanese, as shown by the success of cruiser and destroyer units during the first part of the war.

Light cruisers were seen as supporting ships to enhance the effectiveness of the torpedo attacks by destroyer and submarine squadrons. Japanese light cruisers were designed as flagships for destroyer squadrons. The light cruisers were required to provide accommodations for the admiral leading the destroyer squadron and his staff. The extra space offered by a light cruiser was required to exercise proper command and control of the squadron. This included expanded space for the staff and additional communications gear. In battle, light cruisers were tasked to lead the attack of the destroyer squadrons. With their heavier firepower, they were to protect the attacking destroyers from gunfire from enemy destroyers and cruisers. Though Japanese light cruisers were equipped with a comparatively light torpedo armament, these also would contribute to any massed torpedo attack. A special squadron of three modified Kuma-class torpedo cruisers, each with a broadside of 20 torpedoes, was developed to increase the effectiveness of the planned massed torpedo attacks.

DESTROYER DOCTRINE

Before the war, Japanese destroyers were organized into divisions of three or four ships, each almost always equipped with ships of the same class. Three or four divisions composed a squadron, which was led by a light cruiser. Destroyer squadrons were expected to attack en masse during night combat to deliver shattering blows to the enemy. In the 1934 battle instructions, each destroyer squadron was supported by a division of heavy cruisers, which provided combat power to permit the destroyers to penetrate the enemy's screen to attack his battle line. If all went according to the carefully choreographed and rehearsed sequence, the heavy cruisers would open the night battle with a massed torpedo assault, followed by a massed attack by the destroyer squadrons at close range. The destroyers would fire their first torpedo load, then disengage, reload, and fire a second barrage. The tactics practiced by Japanese destroyers proved devastating on a number of occasions during the Pacific War.

SUBMARINE DOCTRINE

The IJN's submarine force became an important part of its decisive battle strategy. Accordingly, the Japanese became the leading proponents of large, ocean-going submarines. In order to contribute to the decisive battle concept, submarines were tasked to perform extended reconnaissance of the enemy battle fleet (including while in port), shadow and pursue it, and, most importantly, attack and wear it down before the decisive engagement.

Beginning in 1938, the IJN finally decided to test how its submarine force was able to execute the various tactical aspects of this mission. The results of these exercises revealed how impractical the entire Japanese submarine doctrine was in reality. Two key lessons were the difficulty in conducting close surveillance of well-defended fleet units, and the vulnerability of large submarines to detection. The difficulty of conducting command and control of submarines acting in concert with the battle fleet was also amply demonstrated.

Another disconcerting lesson was the extreme difficulty submarines had in executing the attack phase of their doctrine. The Japanese believed that the best position for a torpedo attack was at a distance of some 1,500 yards off the bow of the target. To achieve such a position, the submarine would have to gain contact on the enemy force and then use its high surface speed to place itself across the enemy's path of movement. Unless the enemy's line

Destroyer Squadron 1 at anchor sometime in the 1930s. A Sendai-class light cruiser is the flagship, with nine Kamikaze and Minekaze destroyers anchored behind. The destroyer squadron was the basis for massed night torpedo attacks. (Naval History and Heritage Command)

of advance could be clearly predicted, a picket line of submarines was deployed across the possible lines of advance. During exercises in 1939 and 1940 it was found that the enemy force usually transited the submarines' operating area unscathed as it was hard enough just to maintain contact with an enemy force, much less to speed ahead and wait submerged for the enemy to come cruising by. Torpedo attacks on the surface were found to be impracticable because of the likelihood of detection.

The port auxiliary engine room on *I-14*. Despite their large size, habitability on Japanese submarines was largely ignored. This meant that, especially in tropical conditions, on any long deployment Japanese submarine crews tired quickly. (Naval History and Heritage Command)

All of the lessons gained from these prewar exercises had great impact on wartime operations; for example, the emphasis on concealment translated during the war into extreme caution. Overall, the prewar exercises demonstrated the basic unsuitability of Japanese submarine doctrine; however, the Japanese chose to relearn this lesson during the war under the penalty of heavy losses.

Japanese submarine doctrine clearly focused on the enemy's battle fleet at the expense of developing the strategy and tactics required to attack the enemy's commerce and sea lines of communication. Curiously, when Japanese submarines were exercised against merchant targets, they were found to be effective. However, not only was this lesson not heeded with regard to the employment of Japanese submarines, but neither was the converse possibility, that enemy submarines could cripple Japan's sea-going commerce. The Japanese did consider attacks on US shipping to be an important part of a Pacific war, but only if such operations did not interfere with the primary mission of attacking the enemy's battle fleet.

THE IMPERIAL JAPANESE NAVY IN THE PACIFIC WAR

The primary operational entity of the IJN was the Combined Fleet. Virtually all combat elements of the IJN were under its control except forces operating off China and local defense forces of key bases. At the start of the Pacific War, the Combined Fleet allocated significant forces to the Pearl Harbor operation. This included the Kido Butai with its six fleet carriers; escorting the carriers were two Kongo-class battleships and the two new Tone-class heavy cruisers, supported by one light cruiser and nine destroyers. The IJN's primary objective during the initial phases of the conflict was to seize the lightly defended oil resources in the Dutch East Indies and British possessions in the Far East, which offered Japan a way to escape the effects of the Allied trade embargo. To accomplish this, the Second Fleet (with the majority of the IJN's heavy cruisers) and Third Fleet were sent to the southern areas, supported by powerful land-based air units. The First Fleet, with seven battleships after the commissioning

The Japanese carrier force gave its best performance of the war during the Battle of Santa Cruz on October 26, 1942. In this view, a well-coordinated strike of Japanese dive- and torpedo bombers cripples the carrier *Hornet*, which later sank. (Naval History and Heritage Command)

The driving force behind the Pearl Harbor attack was the commander of the Combined Fleet, Admiral Isoroku Yamamoto. Against almost universal skepticism he achieved his goal of opening the war against the United States with a daring attack against the heart of American naval power. (Naval History and Heritage Command)

of *Yamato* in December 1941, remained in Japan as a strategic reserve. These were being held back for the anticipated decisive battle. The Fourth Fleet based at Truk defended the Central Pacific and was tasked to seize several Allied-held islands. The Fifth Fleet was tasked to defend Northern Japan. Most of the IJN's modern submarines were assigned to the Sixth Fleet based in Kwajalein in the Marshall Islands, and most of these were allocated to support the Hawaiian operation.

This wartime force allocation reflected a very different strategy from the one for which the IJN had been planning and training for the past 30 years. This was due to the views and actions of a single man – Isoroku Yamamoto, who assumed command of the Combined Fleet in August 1939. Yamamoto changed the IJN's passive wartime strategy to a much more aggressive forward strategy almost overnight. According to his chief of staff, Yamamoto first discussed an attack on Pearl Harbor in March or April 1940. After the completion of the Combined Fleet's annual maneuvers in the fall of 1940, Yamamoto directed that a Pearl Harbor attack study be performed under the utmost secrecy. By December, Yamamoto had decided to conduct the Pearl Harbor operation. Not only was this a risky operation which exposed the IJN's most powerful striking force to early destruction, but it obviously changed Japan's strategic calculus by bringing the US into the war. A war which could have been fought for the limited goal of seizing Dutch and British possessions in the East Indies and Malaya was instantly transformed into a total war against the most powerful nation on Earth. Yamamoto's decision was fateful for the IJN and Japan since it condemned both to a prolonged and bitter war that neither was capable of conducting nor even fully understood.

It is impossible to understate the impact of the Pearl Harbor attack for the IJN. Yamamoto was convinced that war with the United States was inevitable once the Japanese began hostilities. He believed that, since a traditional victory against the US was not possible, he had to shatter American morale and force a negotiated peace. For this reason, he scrapped the IJN's traditional passive strategy of creating a decisive battle in the western Pacific in favor of an initial blow so crippling that it would undermine American morale. What happened was actually the reverse. The attack so enraged the Americans that any hope of a negotiated peace was removed. With the benefit of hindsight, there is little doubt that had Yamamoto kept to the IJN's basic strategy of defending against an American drive across the Pacific, the IJN would have been much better off. Yamamoto sold the attack to the Naval General Staff on the basis that it would provide the time required to complete the conquest of the East

Tora Tora Tora – Pearl Harbor 1941

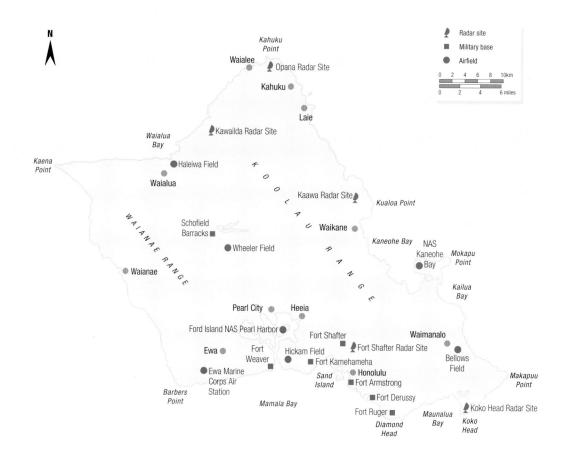

Haleiwa Field
47th Pursuit Squadron (subordinate to 15th Pursuit Group based at Wheeler)

Bellows Field
44th Pursuit Squadron (subordinate to 18th Pursuit Group; 10–12 fighters present on December 7)
86th Observation Squadron
2x OA-9, 7x O-47B, 1x B-18
Note: prior to December 7, the 47th Pursuit Squadron (Fighter) and the 44th Pursuit Squadron (Interceptor) were deployed to Haleiwa and Bellows Field, respectively, for gunnery practice. Because aircraft may have flown back and forth to Wheeler over the weekend preceding the attack, the exact number and types of aircraft actually located at Haleiwa and Bellows cannot be determined.

Wheeler Field
14th Pursuit Wing with 15th and 18th Pursuit Groups
12x P-40C, 87x P-40B, 39x P-36A, 6x P-26A, 6x P-26B, 3x B-12A, 4x AT-6, 3x OA-9, 1x OA-8

Ewa Marine Corps Air Station
Marine Air Group 21 (VMF-211, VMSB-232, VMJ-252)
8x SB2U-3, 23x SBD-1/2, 10x F4F-3, 1x SNJ-3, 2x J2F-4, 1x JO-2, 1x JRS-1, 2x R3D-2

NAS Kaneohe Bay
Patrol Wing 1 (VP-11, VP-12, VP-14)
36x PBY-5 (3 absent on patrol), 1x OS2U

Hickam Field
18th Bombardment Wing (Heavy) with 5th and 11th Bombardment Groups
58th Bombardment Squadron (Light)
19th Transport Squadron
12x B-17D, 32x B-18, 12x A-20A, 2x P-26A, 2x A-12, 2x C-33, 1x B-24A
Note: additionally, 8x B-17E and 4x B-17C from 38th and 88th Reconnaissance Squadrons arrived during the attack.

NAS Pearl Harbor
Patrol Wing 2 (VP-22, VP-23, VJ-2)
13x PBY-3, 12x PBY-5, 4x PBY-1, 1x SOC-1, 1x SU-3, 7x J2F-1/2/3/4
Note: additionally, there were a total of 77 other US Navy aircraft on Oahu. Many (27) were liaison, scout, and transport aircraft based at Pearl Harbor but the majority (50) were battleship and cruiser floatplanes and reserve carrier aircraft based on various ships and at Ford Island.

Indies. In fact, since the Combined Fleet held a numerical advantage over the USN's Pacific Fleet in every category, and since the Japanese-held islands in the Central Pacific provided a barrier, the Pacific Fleet did not have the military or, even more importantly, the logistical means to interfere with the Japanese attack south. In the final analysis, the Pearl Harbor raid was militarily unnecessary.

THE PEARL HARBOR OPERATION

Yamamoto had great difficulty getting his risky plan to attack Pearl Harbor approved by a skeptical Naval General Staff. Among other things, the Naval General Staff was responsible for directing operations and exercised supreme command over the IJN. This is not how Yamamoto viewed the situation. In a series of meetings on October 17–18, 1941, Yamamoto threatened to resign unless his plan was approved. This threat brought final approval, since Yamamoto was viewed as too valuable to lose. This was not the last time that Yamamoto would use this tactic.

Making the whole scheme possible was the Kido Butai with its six carriers with over 400 embarked aircraft. In Yamamoto's mind, the purpose of the raid was to sink American battleships since this, he believed, would shatter American morale. In fact, Yamamoto was expecting to lose at least a third of the Kido Butai in the operation, meaning that he was content to trade his modern carriers for outdated American battleships. The staff of the Kido Butai saw things differently and planned to use the weight of its attack aircraft against any American carriers present.

The results of the attack of December 7, 1941 are well known, but the impact of the attack is less well understood. The two waves of 350 aircraft gained complete surprise and successfully hit their intended targets. The attacks against airfields were very successful and crippled any possibility of the Americans mounting an effective airborne defense or launching a retaliatory strike on the Japanese carriers.

With total surprise gained, the well-trained Japanese aircrews dealt a series of heavy blows against the Pacific Fleet. The 40 torpedo bombers were the most important part of the plan since they were targeted against the American battleships and carriers. Of the eight battleships present, five were exposed to torpedo attack. Japanese torpedo aircraft accounted for battleships *Oklahoma* and *West Virginia* sunk, two torpedoes into battleship *California* which eventually sank, and a single hit on *Nevada* which started a chain of events that led to its sinking. In addition, torpedoes damaged two light cruisers, and sank a target ship and a minelayer. All this cost only five torpedo bombers.

The efforts of the torpedo bombers were complemented by 49 level bombers armed with 1,760lb armor-piercing bombs. Dropping from 10,000ft, the Japanese scored ten hits. One of these penetrated the forward magazine of battleship *Arizona* and completely destroyed the ship. The other hits slightly damaged battleships *Maryland*, *West Virginia*, and *Tennessee*.

The 167 aircraft of the second wave accomplished much less. This part of the attack included 78 dive-bombers with the IJN's best crews. However, against stationary targets, they scored only some 15 hits including five on battleship *Nevada* as it slowly moved down the channel to the harbor entrance. The battleship was beached to avoid blocking the channel. A single bomb hit was scored against battleship *Pennsylvania* located in dry dock but caused only light damage. Light cruiser *Honolulu* suffered a near miss that caused moderate damage.

American losses were heavy, but were ultimately insignificant when placed in the context of subsequent naval production. The IJN sank or damaged 18 ships. Of most importance to Yamamoto, five battleships were sunk or beached. All but two (*Arizona* and *Oklahoma*) returned to service; one (*Nevada*) returned in 1943 and the other two (*West Virginia* and *California*) returned in 1944. The three other battleships damaged in the attack were all back in service by February 1942.

JAPANESE EXPANSION

The IJN thought that it was fighting a limited war in which it would seize key objectives and then use the power of the defense to defeat American counterattacks, which in turn would lead to a negotiated peace. The initial period of the war was divided into two "operational phases." The First Operational Phase was further divided into three separate parts. During these, the major objectives of the Philippines, British Malaya, Borneo, Burma, Rabaul and the Dutch East Indies would be occupied. The Second Operational Phase called for further expansion into the South Pacific by seizing eastern New Guinea, New Britain, the Fijis, Samoa, and "strategic points in the Australian area." In the Central Pacific, Midway was targeted as were the Aleutian Islands in the North Pacific. Seizure of these key areas would provide defensive depth and deny the Allies staging areas from which to mount a counteroffensive.

First Operational Phase

Much to the surprise of the IJN, the First Operational Phase went according to plan with extremely light losses – no ship larger than a destroyer was sunk. The invasion of Malaya and the Philippines began in December 1941 and a notable success was scored on December 10 when Japanese land-based long-range bombers operating from bases in Indochina sank British capital ships *Prince of Wales* and *Repulse* in the South China Sea.

The American island of Guam was seized on December 8 after token resistance. The British Gilbert Islands were seized on December 9 and 10. The only temporary setback was the failure of the first attempt to seize Wake Island on December 11. In response to this failure, a carrier division from the Pearl Harbor attack force was added to the forces allocated for the second attempt, which was mounted, this time successfully, on December 22. The bastion of British power in the Far East, the fortress of Singapore, surrendered on February 15.

Allied naval opposition to the IJN during the First Operational Phase was sporadic and ineffective. In the first major surface engagement of the war on February 27 at the Battle of the Java Sea, an Allied cruiser-destroyer force was defeated by a Japanese force of similar size. Following its debut at Pearl Harbor, the Kido Butai supported the capture of Rabaul in January 1942 and the Dutch East Indies in February. The only problem during the First Operational Phase was the failure to occupy the Philippines on schedule. However, with no prospects of reinforcement, the fall of the Philippines was only a matter of time and the last American and Filipino forces surrendered in early May 1942.

The last major operation of the First Operational Phase was the Combined Fleet's raid into the Indian Ocean. This large operation included five carriers of the Kido Butai to neutralize the RN's Eastern Fleet and a task force built around heavy cruisers to attack shipping in the Bay of Bengal. The operation began in April with the Kido Butai delivering heavy attacks against RN bases at Colombo and Trincomalee. The Japanese also caught and sank a British light carrier and two heavy cruisers at sea, but were unable to locate and destroy the main British fleet. The Japanese cruiser raiding force wreaked havoc with British shipping in the Bay of Bengal. The entire operation was a strategic dead end

This poor-quality photo from a Japanese wartime magazine shows the British carrier *Hermes* under attack by Japanese dive-bombers. The carrier was sunk on April 9, 1942, as it withdrew south following the Japanese attack on Trincomalee on Ceylon. (Courtesy of Michael A. Oren)

Initial Japanese successes in the Pacific, Dec 1941 – May 1942

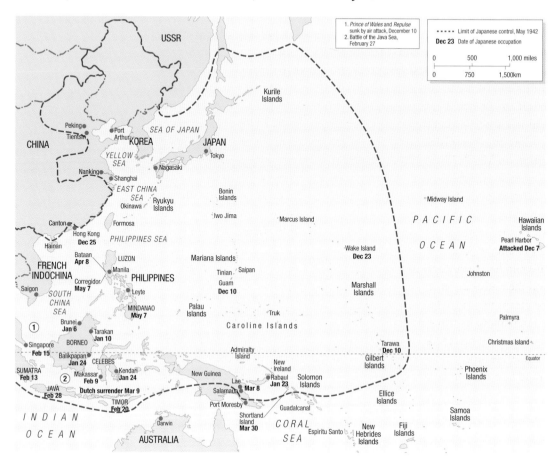

since it was only a temporary projection of power that could not be sustained, and only served to put more strain on the Kido Butai.

Second Operational Phase

The ease with which the IJN accomplished its First Operational Phase objectives created a phenomenon called "Victory Disease." This led to the IJN's severe underestimation of the enemy and the resulting failure to concentrate the IJN's superior forces at key places and times. As a result, the critical months of May and June 1942 saw the IJN lose both its offensive power and the initiative. The Second Operational Phase was planned to expand Japan's strategic depth by adding eastern New Guinea, New Britain, the Aleutians, Midway, the Fijis, Samoa, and "strategic points in the Australian area." However, the Naval General Staff, the Combined Fleet, and the Imperial Army, which had to contribute troops for some operations, all had different views on the sequence of operations.

The Naval General Staff advocated an advance to the south to seize parts of Australia. The Imperial Army declined to contribute the forces necessary for such an operation, which quickly killed the concept. The Naval General Staff still wanted to cut the sea links between Australia and the United States by capturing New Caledonia, Fiji, and Samoa. Since this required far fewer troops, on March 13 the Naval General Staff and the Imperial Army agreed to operations with the goal of capturing Fiji and Samoa.

The Second Operational Phase began well when Lae and Salamaua on eastern New Guinea were captured on March 8. However, this was to be the last of the uninterrupted victories for the IJN. On March 10, American carrier aircraft struck the invasion forces and inflicted considerable losses. This raid had major operational implications since it forced the Japanese to stop their advance in the South Pacific until the Combined Fleet provided the means to protect future operations from USN carrier attack.

Yamamoto had an entirely different strategy in mind. In his view, it was essential to complete the destruction of the USN, which had begun at Pearl Harbor. He proposed to do this by attacking an objective that the Americans would be certain to fight for. His choice was Midway Atoll since it was close

The *Shokaku* at Coral Sea under attack by American carrier aircraft. The carrier was struck by three bombs and could not be repaired in time for the Midway operation. Its sister ship, the *Zuikaku*, was also unable to participate in the Midway operation after its air group suffered crippling losses. This removed one third of Yamamoto's heavy carriers from his would-be decisive battle. (Naval History and Heritage Command)

enough to Hawaii that he assessed the USN would be forced to contest a Japanese invasion there.

In a series of meetings from April 2–5 between the Naval General Staff and representatives of the Combined Fleet, a compromise was reached. Yamamoto got his Midway operation, but only after he again threatened to resign. However, in return, Yamamoto had to agree to two demands from the Naval General Staff both of which had potential implications for the Midway operation. To cover the offensive in the South Pacific, Yamamoto agreed to allocate one carrier division from the Kido Butai to the early May invasion of Port Moresby on New Guinea. Yamamoto also agreed to include an attack to seize selected points in the Aleutian Islands concurrent with the Midway operation. These were enough to remove the IJN's margin of superiority in the coming Midway attack.

THE BATTLE OF CORAL SEA

The attack on Port Moresby, codenamed the MO Operation, was divided into several phases. In the first phase, Tulagi would be occupied on May 3. Then the carriers borrowed from the Kido Butai would conduct a wide sweep through the Coral Sea to find and attack Allied naval forces. The landings on Port Moresby were scheduled for May 10.

As was typical in IJN operational planning, the MO plan was overly complex and depended on close coordination of widely separated forces. Another hallmark of the plan and of IJN planning in general was the almost complete disregard for the actions of the enemy. By committing only a portion of the Kido Butai, Yamamoto not only jeopardized the success of the MO Operation, but also imperiled Yamamoto's decisive Midway operation if those ships were lost or damaged.

The MO Operation featured a force of 60 ships led by carriers *Shokaku* and *Zuikaku*, one light carrier (*Shoho*), six heavy cruisers, three light cruisers, and 15 destroyers. Additionally, some 250 aircraft were assigned to the operation including 140 aboard the three carriers.

The actual battle did not go according to the IJN's tightly scripted plan. Tulagi was seized on May 3, but the following day aircraft from the American carrier *Yorktown* struck the invasion force. For the next two days, both the American and Japanese carrier forces tried unsuccessfully to find each other. On May 7, both carrier forces went into action, and both achieved disappointing results. The Japanese carriers launched a full strike on a contact reported to be carriers. The report turned out to be false, and the

The Battle of Coral Sea, May 1942

N

PACIFIC OCEAN

New Ireland

Rabaul

Green Island

New Britain

Bougainville

Solomon Islands

Solomon Sea

Shortland

Choiseul

To Rabaul May 8

To Rabaul May 8

May 7, 2400hrs

Trobriand Island

May 7, 2400hrs

Woodlark Island

Tulagi

Malaita

May 7, 0000hrs

May 8, 2400hrs

Guadalcanal

PAPUA

May 7, 0000hrs

May 7, 1100hrs

May 7, 0630hrs

Shoho sunk

May 7, 2400hrs

San Cristobal

China Strait

Long Reef

Misima Island

Jomard Passage

Deboyne Island

Tagula Island

Rossel Island

May 8, 0530hrs

Calvados Reef

Louisiade Archipelago

May 8, 1100hrs

May 7, 2400hrs

Rennell Island

May 7, 2400hrs

Shokaku damaged

May 8, 1045hrs

May 7, 0000hrs

May 7, 1800hrs

May 7, 1945hrs

May 7, 0625hrs

May 7, 0000hrs

May 7, 0740hrs

May 7, 1045hrs

May 7, 2400hrs

May 8, 0625hrs

Lexington and **Yorktown** damaged

May 8, 2000hrs

May 8, 1100hrs

Lexington sunk

May 8, 2000hrs

CORAL SEA

May 8, 2400hrs

⬅	MO Main Force
⬅	MO Carrier Striking Force
⬅	Covering Force
⬅	MO Invasion Force
⬅	Task Force 17
⬅	Support Group

0   50   100   150 miles

0   100   200km

strike force found and struck only an oiler and a destroyer. The American carriers also launched a major strike on incomplete reconnaissance. Instead of finding the main Japanese carrier force, the Americans were forced to settle for an attack against *Shoho*, which was quickly sunk. This was the largest Japanese ship lost so far in the war.

Finally, on May 8, the opposing carrier forces found each other and exchanged strikes. The 69 aircraft from the two Japanese carriers succeeded in sinking carrier *Lexington* and damaging *Yorktown*. In return, the Americans damaged *Shokaku*, but left *Zuikaku* undamaged. However, aircraft losses to *Zuikaku* were heavy, and the Japanese were unable to support a landing on Port Moresby. As a result, the MO Operation was canceled.

The battle was a disaster for the IJN. Not only was the attack on Port Moresby stopped, which constituted the first strategic Japanese setback of the war, but all three carriers committed to the battle would now be unavailable for the Midway operation. In fact, after the Pearl Harbor attack the six carriers of the Kido Butai never again acted together as a single group. Had this force been kept together, it would have been very difficult for the USN to handle.

THE BATTLE OF MIDWAY

Yamamoto saw the Midway operation as the potentially decisive battle of the Pacific War which could open the door for a negotiated peace favorable to Japan. Unfortunately for the IJN, the Combined Fleet's plan for the MI Operation (as the attack on Midway was codenamed) was flawed. It took the Japanese penchant for complexity and using far-flung forces to a new height, and, most importantly, it ignored the actions of the enemy.

For this operation, the Kido Butai had only four carriers. Assuming strategic and tactical surprise, these would knock out Midway's air strength and soften the atoll for a landing by 5,000 troops. Following the quick capture of the island (which was another faulty assumption (this time untested) as the combat elements of the landing force were not much larger than the well entrenched American defenders), the Combined Fleet would lay the foundation for the most important part of the operation. Midway was nothing more than bait for the USN which would dutifully depart Pearl Harbor to counterattack after Midway had been captured. When the Pacific Fleet arrived, Yamamoto would concentrate his scattered forces to crush the Americans.

An important aspect of Yamamoto's decisive battle scheme was Operation AL, the plan to seize two islands in the Aleutians concurrent with the attack on Midway. Despite persistent myth, the Aleutian operation was not a diversion to draw American forces from Midway. Yamamoto wanted the Americans to be drawn to Midway, not away from it. The forces directly engaged in this operation constituted a considerable drain on the IJN's resources. These included two carriers, six cruisers, and 12 destroyers. Distant cover for Operation AL was provided by another four battleships, two light cruisers, and 12 destroyers. The positioning of these forces made them useless in the upcoming battle.

The ultimate result was that the Japanese were actually outnumbered at the point of contact where the battle would be decided. An American force of 26 ships faced the 20 ships of the Kido Butai with an aircraft count of 233 (348 if Midway is included) against the Kido Butai's 248.

The battle opened on June 3 when American aircraft from Midway spotted and attacked the Japanese transport group 700 miles west of

A view of *Hiryu* taken by one of *Hosho*'s Type 96 carrier attack aircraft on the morning of June 5. Based on this sighting, a destroyer was ordered to the scene, but *Hiryu* finally sank before it arrived. (Naval History and Heritage Command)

The approach to contact by forces of both sides at Midway, June 1–3, 1942

Kamchatka

Attu

Kiska

Aleutian Islands

Dutch Harbor

Adak

0740hrs/5

0200hrs/4

Paramushiro 2200hrs/3 2200hrs/4

Kiska Invasion Force

Kurile Islands

1000hrs/4 0900hrs/5

1000hrs/3

1000hrs/2

Attu-Adak Invasion Force

HOKKAIDO 1100hrs/1

1100hrs/31

2nd Kido Butai (Kakuta)

Ominato 1100hrs/30

PACIFIC OCEAN

HONSHU

Guard Force (Takasu) 0700hrs/5

1st Kido Butai (Nagumo)

KOREA

Tokyo 1000hrs/4

0300hrs/4 1000hrs/2

1000hrs/1 1000hrs/4

Bungo Strait 0700hrs/5 0900hrs/4

1200hrs/2

Task Force 17 (Fletcher)

1100hrs/31

Main Body (Yamamoto)

1100hrs/30 1000hrs/1

1100hrs/29 2300hrs/4

Ryukyu Islands

1200hrs/28 1000hrs/1

Okinawa Midway Invasion Force (Kondo) 1100hrs/2 1000hrs/3 1000hrs/4

Midway Island

Task Force 16 (Spruance)

Iwo Jima 1000hrs/2 0300hrs/5

Transport Group (Tanaka) 1000hrs/4

1000hrs/1 1000hrs/2 1000hrs/3

1000hrs/1

1100hrs/31 Minesweeping Group

Mariana 1100hrs/31 Wake Island
Islands

Japanese forces | US forces

1100hrs/30

0 500 miles Close Support Group (Kurita)

1100hrs/29

0 500km

Guam

Midway. At 0430hrs on June 4, the Kido Butai launched a 108-aircraft strike on the island. The attackers brushed aside Midway's defending fighters at about 0620hrs, but failed to deliver a decisive blow to the island's facilities. Most importantly, the strike aircraft based on Midway had already departed to attack the Japanese carriers, which had been spotted at 0530hrs. This information was passed to the three American carriers, and soon 116 carrier aircraft, in addition to the aircraft from Midway, were on their way to attack the Kido Butai.

The aircraft from Midway attacked bravely, but they failed to score a single hit on the Kido Butai. In the middle of these uncoordinated attacks, a Japanese scout aircraft reported the presence of an American task force. Unfortunately for the Japanese, it was not until 0830hrs that the presence of an American carrier was confirmed. This put the Japanese commander, the timid Vice Admiral Chuichi Nagumo, in a difficult tactical bind in

Duel of the carriers: tracks of the opposing forces on June 4, 1942

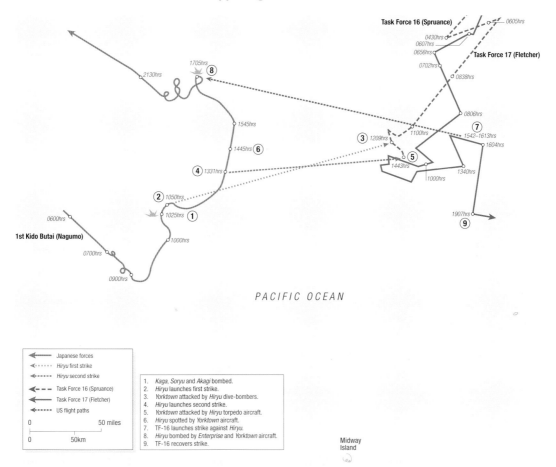

Japanese forces

Hiryu first strike

Hiryu second strike

Task Force 16 (Spruance)

Task Force 17 (Fletcher)

US flight paths

0   50 miles

0   50km

1. *Kaga, Soryu* and *Akagi* bombed.
2. *Hiryu* launches first strike.
3. *Yorktown* attacked by *Hiryu* dive-bombers.
4. *Hiryu* launches second strike.
5. *Yorktown* attacked by *Hiryu* torpedo aircraft.
6. *Hiryu* spotted by *Yorktown* aircraft.
7. TF-16 launches strike against *Hiryu*.
8. *Hiryu* bombed by *Enterprise* and *Yorktown* aircraft.
9. TF-16 recovers strike.

which he had to counter continual American air attacks and prepare to recover his Midway strike, while deciding whether to mount an immediate strike on the American carrier or wait to prepare a proper attack. After quick deliberation, he opted for a delayed but better-prepared attack on the American task force after recovering his Midway strike and properly arming aircraft.

This plan was flawed since the American carrier dive-bombers were already in the air. Beginning at 1022hrs, these surprised and successfully attacked three of the Japanese carriers. With their hangar decks strewn with fully fueled and armed aircraft, all three were turned into blazing wrecks. A single carrier, *Hiryu*, remained and it launched an immediate counterattack. Both of its attacks hit *Yorktown* and put the carrier out of action. Later in the afternoon, the two remaining American carriers found and destroyed *Hiryu*. The striking power of the Kido Butai had been destroyed and the battle lost. Early on the morning of June 5, the IJN canceled the Midway operation. Yamamoto's decisive battle had in fact turned the tables on the IJN and, with the blunting of Japan's offensive power, the initiative in the Pacific was up for grabs.

THE GUADALCANAL CAMPAIGN

On August 7, the US Navy landed on the islands of Guadalcanal and Tulagi in the Solomons. Now the IJN was on the defensive for the first time.

The local Japanese naval commander, Vice Admiral Gun'ichi Mikawa, commander of the new Eighth Fleet at Rabaul, reacted quickly. He gathered five heavy cruisers, two light cruisers, and a destroyer, and ordered an attack on the Allied invasion force for the night of August 8–9. Mikawa's bold response resulted in a brilliant victory during which four Allied heavy cruisers (three American and one Australian) were sunk. No Japanese ships were lost. It was one of the worst American naval defeats of the war, only mitigated by the failure of Mikawa to attack the defenseless transports. Had he done so, the first American counterattack in the Pacific could have been stopped dead in its tracks.

The Japanese originally deemed the American landings as nothing more than a "reconnaissance in force." A fatal pattern of piecemeal commitment by the Japanese now began.

The IJN was slow to respond to the first USN offensive of the war. By the middle of August, it had assembled a force of four battleships, five carriers, 16 cruisers, and 30 destroyers to dislodge the Americans. On August 24–25, the IJN launched an operation to move a small transport convoy to Guadalcanal and to crush any American naval units in the area. The ensuing clash, known as the Battle of the Eastern Solomons, included the third carrier battle of the war. The IJN achieved neither of its goals – the American carrier force was not destroyed and the reinforcement convoy failed to reach the island. Japanese losses were heavy with 75 carrier aircraft lost, a light carrier, a transport, and a destroyer sunk. In return, carrier *Enterprise* was damaged, but managed to elude Japanese attempts to complete its destruction. With the American-held airfield on Guadalcanal now operational, convoys of slow transports could not be run to the island. Until the airfield was suppressed, Japanese reinforcements could only be delivered by inefficient nightly destroyer runs to the island.

The Japanese continued to underestimate the number of US Marines on the island. By the time some 6,200 Imperial Army personnel had been delivered by destroyer for an attack on the Marine perimeter, Japanese estimates were that only 2,000 marines were on the island. With the number closer to 20,000, the attack launched on two successive nights from September 12–14 failed. Meanwhile, the struggle for control of the waters around Guadalcanal was going better for the Japanese. A Japanese submarine sank carrier *Wasp* on September 15. This left a single American carrier, *Hornet*, active in the Pacific. During the same period, the Japanese possessed up to six operational carriers, but the IJN failed to recognize or grasp this opportunity.

The Battles of October 1942

By October, it was obvious even to the Japanese that the Guadalcanal campaign was becoming a major test between the IJN and the USN. But the battle could only be won if the Japanese garrison on the island was dramatically reinforced. For the next attack, an entire Japanese division would be employed. Efforts were intensified to get the required force to Guadalcanal by October 13 or 14 so that the offensive could be launched by October 20. To do this, the Combined Fleet promised to step up night runs by destroyers and high-speed seaplane carriers (carrying heavy equipment) to Guadalcanal, to increase air bombardment of the airfield, and to run a large convoy of transports directly to the island. The IJN also decided to use battleships to suppress the airfield allowing the convoy to arrive safely. Yamamoto now defined the Combined Fleet's primary mission as supporting the recapture of the island; the destruction of the Pacific Fleet was reduced to secondary importance.

On the night of October 13–14, two battleships bombarded the airfield on Guadalcanal with 918 14in rounds, destroying 40 aircraft and putting the airfield temporarily out of commission. Despite all the IJN's prewar preparations for a titanic clash of battleships, this was the most successful of any Japanese battleship operation during the war.

The Japanese convoy arrived on Guadalcanal on the night of October 14–15, preceded by two heavy cruisers again shelling the airfield. Aircraft from two carriers flew air cover over the transports. American aircraft did succeed in sinking three of the six transports, but not until 4,500 men had been landed along with two-thirds of their supplies and equipment. The IJN kept up the pressure with another cruiser bombardment on the night of

The campaign for Guadalcanal

N

PACIFIC OCEAN

Solomon Islands

Solomon Sea

New Ireland

Rabaul

New Britain

Green Island

Buka

Bougainville

Shortland

(16)

Choiseul

New Georgia

Santa Isabel

(12)

Woodlark Island

Malaita

Maramasike

San Cristobal

(10)

(4)

Tulagi

(7) (8) (11) (13) (14)

(6) (2)

(15)

(1) (3) (5) (9)

Guadalcanal

0 — 100 miles

0 — 100km

1. August 7: 1st Marine Division lands on Tulagi and Guadalcanal.
2. August 9: Battle of Savo Island. A Japanese cruiser force inflicts heavy losses on the Allied surface force covering the invasion in a night engagement but fails to attack the defenseless transports.
3. August 21: first Japanese land offensive against the Marine perimeter fails.
4. August 24: Battle of the Eastern Solomons. The third carrier battle of the war ends indecisively, but Japanese suffer heavier losses and fail to get a convoy through to Guadalcanal.
5. September 12–14: second Japanese land offensive fails.
6. October 11–12: Battle of Cape Esperance. An American cruiser force defeats the IJN in a night action for the first time in the war.
7. October 14: battleship bombardment of Henderson Field. Two Japanese battleships temporarily neutralize the airfield.
8. October 15: Japanese convoy with three merchant ships reaches Guadalcanal.
9. October 24–25: third Japanese land offensive fails.
10. October 26: Battle of Santa Cruz. The fourth carrier battle of the war results in a Japanese victory. Heavy losses prevent Japanese from following up their success.
11. November 13: First Naval Battle of Guadalcanal. An American cruiser force intercepts a Japanese battleship force attempting to bombard the airfield. The bombardment is stopped; both sides suffer heavy losses.
12. November 14: air attacks on an 11-ship Japanese convoy sink or force back seven transports. Only four reach Guadalcanal where they are beached and later destroyed.
13. November 14–15: Second Naval Battle of Guadalcanal. In the Pacific War's first battleship duel, two American battleships sink a Japanese battleship to stop another Japanese attempt to bombard the airfield.
14. November 30: Battle of Tassafaronga. A Japanese destroyer force inflicts heavy damage on an American cruiser force in a night action.
15. February 1–7, 1943: Japanese evacuate remaining troops on Guadalcanal by destroyer.
16. April 18, 1943: Admiral Yamamoto shot down over Bougainville and killed.

The Second Naval Battle of Guadalcanal, November 14–15, 1942

November 14

1. 2313hrs – Japanese lookouts aboard *Shikinami* spot TF-64. *Ayanami* dispatched to scout the channel west of Savo Island and the rest of the Sweeping Unit is ordered to clear the channel east of Savo.

November 15

2. 0001hrs – TF-64 gains radar contact on Sweeping Unit at 18,000 yards.

3. 0012hrs – Americans gain visual contact on Sweeping Unit; Lee orders battleships to engage, thinking this was the Japanese bombardment force.

4. 0015hrs – Kondo orders Screening Unit led by *Nagara* to engage Americans; Japanese heavy units turn to the northeast to give his light forces time to clear the way.

5. 0017hrs – *Washington* is ordered to clear the channel east of Savo.

6. 0022hrs – *Ayanami* detected by radar south of Savo; Americans engage her with gunfire.

7. 0027hrs – The Screening Unit is detected west of Savo. American destroyers engage with no effect; Japanese return fire and cripple *Preston*. Her captain orders the destroyer abandoned at 0032hrs.

8. 0033hrs – *South Dakota* loses electrical power.

9. 0037hrs – *Benham* and *Walke* hit by torpedoes; *Walke* sinks almost immediately. *Gwin* damaged by gunfire. Lee's destroyer screen is out of the fight.

10. 0054hrs – Kondo, thinking the American force has been destroyed, orders his heavy ships to approach Guadalcanal to commence the bombardment. He immediately receives reports of American battleships which he dismisses.

11. 0100–0104hrs – Japanese engage *South Dakota* and score heavily with gunfire destroying the battleship's radar and fire control systems forcing her from the fight at 0110hrs. However, no Japanese torpedoes find their target and *South Dakota* is in no danger of sinking.

12. 0100hrs – Undetected *Washington* given permission to engage *Kirishima*. At a range of only 8,400 yards, the Japanese battleship is crippled by a torrent of well-aimed 16in. and 5in. shells.

13. 0113hrs – *Atago* and *Takao* each engage *Washington* with eight torpedoes from only 4,000 yards; again, no hits are scored.

14. 0132hrs – Kondo cancels bombardment; three groups of Japanese ships concentrate on *Washington*.

15. 0240hrs – After several additional unsuccessful torpedo attacks, the Japanese lose contact on *Washington*.

16. 0425hrs – *Kirishima* sinks.

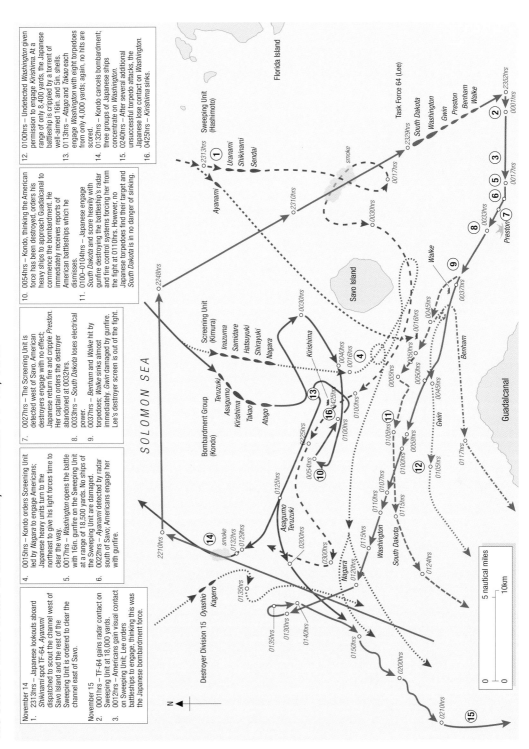

Yamamoto watches an A6M "Zero" fighter take off as part of his air offensive against Allied targets in the South Pacific, which featured four major attacks. The operation achieved little except to highlight the growing impotence of the IJN's airpower. (Juzo Nakamura via Lansdale Research Associates)

October 15–16 and more reinforcement destroyer runs.

After several delays, the Imperial Army started the offensive on October 24. The main Japanese attack finally commenced on the night of October 25–26. Despite claims of victory, all attacks were repulsed with heavy losses. Concurrent with these attacks, the IJN planned the largest naval operation yet to counter and defeat any American naval forces operating in support of the Marines. The Combined Fleet departed Truk on October 11 with a force of four battleships, four carriers, nine cruisers, and 25 destroyers. In addition, Mikawa's Eighth Fleet added four more cruisers and 16 destroyers. After the series of false starts, Yamamoto ordered the Combined Fleet to engage the Americans on October 25.

The Battle of Santa Cruz which followed on October 26 was the fourth carrier clash of the war. It was IJN's greatest victory over the Pacific Fleet since Pearl Harbor. The Japanese sank carrier *Hornet* and again damaged *Enterprise*. Yamamoto ordered his subordinates to seek a night battle to finish off the fleeing Americans, but their fuel situation forced the IJN to return to Truk by October 30. American losses had been high, but the Japanese had been turned back and their carrier air groups had been decimated and two carriers heavily damaged. These losses made Santa Cruz a pyrrhic victory for the IJN and prevented it from exploiting success.

The Battles of November 1942

The Guadalcanal campaign came to a climax in November. The Combined Fleet planned another massive effort to reinforce the island. A plan identical to the October offensive was outlined with a larger convoy preceded by another battleship bombardment to neutralize the airfield.

The scope of the operation suggests that the Japanese had finally determined that this was a decisive battle and were prepared to employ sufficient forces to guarantee success. The Combined Fleet was sure that the naval balance had swung in its favor after the great victory at Santa Cruz. The mission to neutralize the airfield was given to a force of two battleships, one light cruiser, and 11 destroyers which departed Truk to execute the bombardment on the night of November 12–13. This attempt was thwarted by a smaller American force of five cruisers and eight destroyers, which intercepted the Japanese and forced a vicious night action at close range. Losses were heavy on both sides, but the critical bombardment did not occur. Battleship *Hiei* was damaged and when daylight came was helplessly circling in the waters off Guadalcanal. It succumbed to air attack, becoming the first IJN battleship lost in the war.

The Combined Fleet assembled a new force to attempt another bombardment. This was centered on a single battleship with two heavy cruisers and two destroyer squadrons. Additional battleships were available, but were not employed. This renewed attempt was met by the last major American surface assets in the Pacific – two modern battleships. In another savage night battle on the night of November 14–15, the Japanese were again turned back. In the first battleship duel of the Pacific War, the Japanese lost battleship *Kirishima*.

These two night battles, known as the First and Second Naval Battles of Guadalcanal, were the decisive events of the campaign. While the Americans had delivered large numbers of additional troops to the island, the Japanese only delivered 2,000 troops and a meager amount of supplies. The large Japanese convoy had ended in disaster with all ten transports sunk since American aircraft from the undamaged airfield were able to intervene. Naval losses were heavy for both sides. The Americans lost two cruisers and seven destroyers sunk and many ships damaged. The Japanese lost two battleships, a heavy cruiser, and three destroyers. The IJN had been defeated more by a failure to mass its forces than by being out-fought.

The battle of attrition was too much for the IJN. On January 4, the Navy Section of the Imperial General Headquarters instructed Yamamoto to prepare to withdraw the remaining troops from Guadalcanal. The evacuation of Guadalcanal was codenamed the "KE" Operation. The Americans detected the preparations for the KE Operation and believed they were actually for another Japanese attempt to reinforce the island. The evacuation operation was carefully planned to take place in three destroyer lifts and would begin in late January.

On the night of November 12–13 1942, a large Japanese task force including two battleships headed toward Guadalcanal to conduct a bombardment of Henderson Field. In order to save the airfield from devastation, the Americans were forced to intercept the Japanese with a smaller force of cruisers and destroyers. Both sides closed until the formations were almost intermingled. At 0148hrs, the lead Japanese battleship, *Hiei*, used its searchlights to illuminate targets for the rest of the fleet. These lights settled on the lead American cruiser, *Atlanta*. This scene shows the opening moments of the most vicious night battle of the war.

The first evacuation run was conducted on February 1 with 20 destroyers. Another run with 20 destroyers was conducted on February 4. A third run on February 7 was conducted with 18 destroyers. The operation was successful and the best sources indicate that 10,652 men, most severely emaciated, were rescued. Japanese losses were a single destroyer. The Japanese attributed the success of the operation to careful planning, boldness on the part of the evacuation forces, and good air cover. It is fair to wonder why this level of commitment was not displayed when the battle was still in the balance.

AFTER GUADALCANAL

With Guadalcanal lost, the focus shifted to the Central Solomons and New Guinea. In another sign of declining Japanese fortunes, in the Battle of the Bismarck Sea on March 2–4, Allied air attack destroyed a convoy attempting to move troops from Rabaul to Lae on New Guinea. To redress Japan's declining position in the Solomons, Yamamoto devised a major air offensive to suppress the growing Allied strength in the region. He moved the air groups of the Combined Fleet's four carriers, about 160 aircraft, to Rabaul to join the 190 aircraft of the Eleventh Air Fleet bringing Japanese air strength to some 350 aircraft. The air offensive was codenamed the "I"

Operation and consisted of four major attacks conducted on Allied positions on Guadalcanal (April 7), Buna (April 11), Port Moresby (April 12), and Milne Bay (April 14). Japanese pilots claimed great success against Allied shipping and defending fighters which prompted Yamamoto to declare the operation a success and ordered its conclusion on April 16. In fact, little had been achieved. Japanese losses were heavier than those suffered by the Allies and resulted in further attrition to IJN's precious carrier aircrews.

During 1943, the IJN attempted to preserve its strength in the face of two attack avenues by the Americans. In the Solomons, the action turned to the Central and Northern Solomons between March and November. During this time, the two contestants fought seven surface engagements of which all but one on the Japanese side were conducted by destroyers and light cruisers. All of these actions were fought at night during which the IJN still enjoyed an advantage. Twice, Japanese destroyers defeated an Allied cruiser-destroyer force, demonstrating to the Americans that it was not wise to use large light cruisers to chase Japanese destroyers at night.

The failure of the Japanese to reinforce Guadalcanal in November 1942 was decisive. Shown here is one of the ten transports lost in the large November convoy. (Naval History and Heritage Command)

Four of these engagements were duels between destroyers. In the first, the Battle of Vella Gulf in early August, three out of four Japanese destroyers were sunk by American destroyers using radar and a new doctrine which highlighted torpedo attacks. It was the first time in the war that the IJN's destroyers had been beaten at night. The next action, fought on August 18, was indecisive. On October 6, the two sides met again. Japanese torpedoes shattered the American formation, but the Japanese did not follow up their advantage. The final tally of one destroyer sunk from each side was not a long-term recipe for success by the IJN.

On November 2, the IJN committed two heavy cruisers, two light cruisers, and six destroyers to attack the American beachhead on Bougainville Island in the northern Solomons. In another night action, called the Battle of Empress Augusta Bay, an American force of four light cruiser and eight destroyers intercepted the Japanese and defeated them, sinking a light cruiser and a destroyer. American losses were limited to a single destroyer damaged. It was obvious that the Japanese had lost their tactical advantage in night engagements. Adding to the IJN's misery, when the Second Fleet arrived at Rabaul on November 5 with six heavy cruisers to "mop up" American naval forces off Bougainville, they were immediately subjected to carrier air attack. Four were damaged and forced to return to Japan for repairs and the operation ended as a complete fiasco. This marked the end of major IJN operations in the South Pacific and the end of Rabaul as a major base.

The verdict that the IJN had lost its edge in night combat was confirmed later in November at the Battle of Cape St George when a well-handled USN destroyer force intercepted five Japanese destroyers, sinking three of them at no loss. The USN now had all the requirements for victory in place – aggressive leadership, tactics which played on their superior technology, and an ever-growing number of modern ships.

INTO 1944

As the Allies drove relentlessly north through the Solomons to neutralize and eventually encircle Rabaul, the USN was beginning a major offensive in the Central Pacific. This kicked off in November 1943 with landings in the Gilbert Islands. The IJN was forced to watch helplessly as Japanese garrisons in the Gilberts and then the Marshalls were crushed. The fallacy of the Japanese strategy of holding overextended island garrisons was fully exposed. In February 1944, the USN's fast carrier force attacked the IJN's

Central Pacific bastion of Truk. The Combined Fleet moved its main forces out of the atoll in time to avoid being caught at anchor, but two days of air attacks resulted in significant losses to Japanese aircraft and merchant shipping. The power of the American attack on Truk far surpassed that of the Kido Butai against Pearl Harbor.

Forced to abandon Truk and unable to stop the Americans on any front, the IJN husbanded its remaining strength in preparation for what was hoped would be a decisive battle. This came in June 1944 when the Americans landed on Saipan in the Marianas, which was inside Japan's inner defense zone. The Japanese reacted with the sortie of a nine-carrier force, led by *Shokaku*, *Zuikaku*, and the new armored-deck carrier *Taiho*. The resulting clash, the Battle of the Philippine Sea, was the largest carrier battle in history. Though this was the largest IJN carrier force of the war, the carrier clash did not turn out as the Japanese had planned; in fact, their decisive defeat resulted in the virtual end of the IJN's carrier force. A series of Japanese carrier air strikes on June 19 were shattered by strong American defenses. On the same day, *Shokaku* was hit by four torpedoes from a submarine and sank with heavy loss of life. The *Taiho* was also sunk by the effect of a single torpedo.

The next day, the Japanese carrier force was subjected to carrier air attack, and suffered the loss of carrier *Hiyo* to air-launched torpedoes. The Mobile Fleet returned with only 35 aircraft of the 430 with which it had begun the battle. The IJN's ultimate effort had resulted in total defeat.

FINAL GAMBLE AT LEYTE GULF

After Philippine Sea, the IJN was still a formidable force, at least on paper. Of the 12 battleships commissioned before or during the war, nine still remained operational; of 18 heavy cruisers, 14 were also available. Efforts to rebuild the carrier force were unsuccessful since the training given new aviators was of an abysmally low standard. The new Unryu-class carriers never went to sea with a full air group. This left the IJN with a collection of converted carriers, led by the last Pearl Harbor survivor, *Zuikaku*.

The IJN was faced with an unenviable choice: to commit its remaining strength in an all-out attack, or to sit idly by as the Americans occupied the Philippines and cut the sea lanes between Japan and the southern resource areas in the Dutch East Indies and Malaya. The plan devised by the IJN attempted to play to its last remaining strength – the firepower of its heavy

The Battle of Cape St George, November 25, 1943

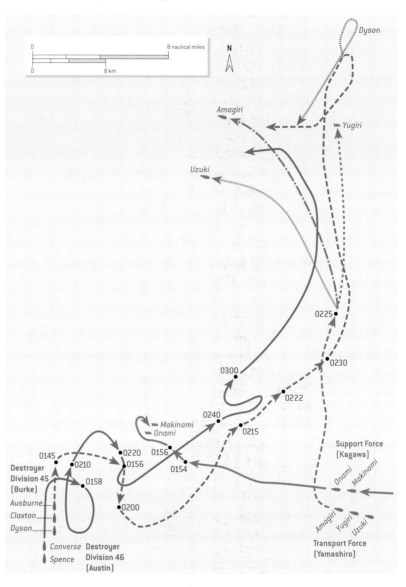

cruisers and battleships. In a final attempt to create a decisive battle, these were all committed against the American beachhead at Leyte Island. The only hope that this would be successful was the decision to use the remaining carriers as a lure to draw the USN's carrier force away from Leyte Gulf long enough for the heavy units to enter and destroy any American shipping present.

The Japanese effort was expansive with five major groups totaling four carriers, nine battleships, 14 heavy cruisers, seven light cruisers, and 35 destroyers. However, the carriers only embarked just over 100 aircraft (equal to those on a single US fleet carrier) and the land-based air fleets were hollow shells which would soon begin suicide attacks as the only method to inflict losses on the Americans. In contrast, the USN brought 17 fleet and light carriers, 18 escort carriers, 12 battleships, 25 heavy and light cruisers, and 162 destroyers to the fight. The Japanese were risking annihilation.

The battle revealed the weakness of the IJN by 1944. After departing from Brunei Bay on October 20, the main battleship force (Force "A") was attacked by two American submarines in restricted waters and suffered two heavy cruisers sunk and another crippled; both subs escaped. After entering the Sibuyan Sea, this force was assaulted by a full day of American carrier air attack. Another heavy cruiser was forced to retire, but the Americans concentrated their attentions on superbattleship *Musashi* and sank it under a barrage of 20 torpedo and 17 bomb hits. Many other ships were struck, but continued on.

Convinced that this pummeling had made Force "A"

Leyte Gulf: the Japanese plan of attack

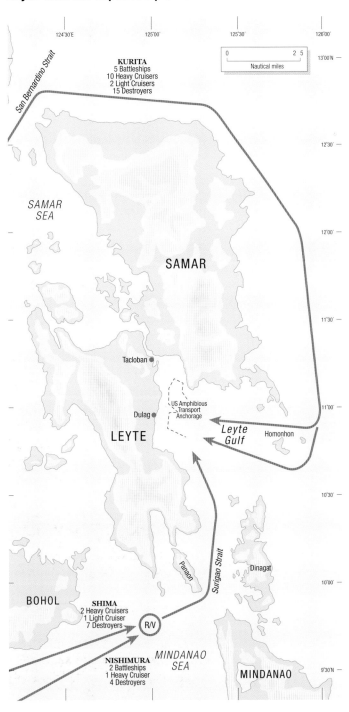

ineffective, the American carriers headed north to address the newly detected threat of the nearly empty Japanese carriers. So weak was Japanese naval aviation at this point that the last air strike of the war launched from the carriers against their American counterparts went unrecognized as a carrier strike. In an action known as the Battle off Cape Engano on October 25, the Americans threw over 500 aircraft sorties at the Japanese force, followed up by a surface action group of cruisers and destroyers. All four Japanese carriers were sunk, but at least this part of the Leyte plan had gone something like according to plan for the IJN.

The final major surface action fought between the IJN and the USN occurred off Samar on October 25 when Force "A" fell upon a group of USN escort carriers escorted by only destroyers and destroyer escorts. Both sides were surprised, but the outcome looked certain since the Japanese could still bring to bear four battleships, six heavy cruisers, and two light cruisers leading two destroyer squadrons. In perhaps the most unlikely action of the Pacific War, the Japanese failed to even recognize, much less press home their advantage, and were content to conduct a largely indecisive gunnery duel before breaking off. In exchange for the loss of three heavy cruisers, Force "A" sank a single escort carrier and three escorts. After this clash, the on-scene Japanese commander decided not even to attempt to execute his orders to storm into Leyte Gulf.

Just before the final action off Samar, another group (known as Force "C"), consisting of the two Fuso-class battleships escorted by a heavy cruiser and four destroyers, attempted to enter Leyte Gulf from the south through Surigao Strait. This action was fought at night, unlike the action off Samar, and was more of a maritime execution than a battle. An American force of six battleships (two sunk at Pearl Harbor and salvaged), eight cruisers, and 26 destroyers waited in ambush. Conducting a radar-guided torpedo attack, American destroyers laid waste to the Japanese, sinking one of the battleships, damaging the other, and sinking three destroyers. Naval gunfire finished off the second battleship. Only a single Japanese destroyer survived, and only a single American destroyer was heavily damaged in return. Another IJN force built around two heavy cruisers failed even to coordinate its movements with Force "C" and arrived at Surigao Strait in the middle of this slaughter. It made a desultory torpedo attack and retreated down the strait.

At the conclusion of the Battle of Leyte Gulf, the IJN was finished as an effective force. Losses were extremely heavy with four carriers, three battleships, and six heavy cruisers sunk. Most of the remaining ships suffered some level of damage, and many never returned to Japan.

THE FINAL SORTIE

Survivors of the defense of the Philippines gradually returned to Japan where almost all were virtually immobilized for lack of fuel. Following Leyte Gulf, there were only minor surface skirmishes between the IJN and USN. The last major surface engagement involving the IJN was actually fought between the heavy cruiser *Haguro* and the RN on May 16, 1945 near the Andaman Islands. The action resulted in the loss of the cruiser for no loss to the British. In April 1945, the Americans landed on Okinawa as a preliminary to landing on the Japanese home islands. For reasons linked more to pride than to operational necessity or value, the IJN decided to send its last surface force to attack the Americans off Okinawa. For this last effort, only a few ships remained operational – superbattleship *Yamato*, a light cruiser, and eight destroyers. The force departed Japan on April 6, and was attacked the following day by hundreds of American carrier aircraft. In this symbolic end, *Yamato*, the light cruiser, and four destroyers were sunk and over 3,600 of their crews lost before even getting close to their target. The USN lost ten aircraft in return. For the final months of the war, the USN hunted the IJN's remaining units in port. At the time of Japan's surrender, the once-mighty IJN had been reduced to insignificance.

This towering column of smoke marks the death of superbattleship *Yamato* on April 7, 1945. The demise of *Yamato* not only symbolized the death of the IJN's battleship force, but also marked the end of the entire IJN. (Naval History and Heritage Command)

AIRCRAFT CARRIERS

During the opening period of the Pacific War, the IJN possessed the most powerful carrier force in the world. By virtue of a potent combination of excellent ships, well-designed aircraft, and unsurpassed aviators, the IJN's carrier force recorded a string of victories from Hawaii to the Indian Ocean. Even after the crushing defeat at Midway, the Japanese carrier force remained a force to be reckoned with as shown by its excellent performance at Santa Cruz in October 1942. Only with the virtual elimination of the last of their highly trained aircrews were Japan's carriers rendered powerless to interfere with the USN's march to the Japanese homeland.

JAPANESE CARRIER DEVELOPMENT

The IJN's aviation program developed in broad parallel with those of the RN and the USN. By 1913, the Japanese were impressed enough with the potential of naval aviation that a naval transport, *Wakamiya Maru*, was fitted to carry two seaplanes and was used in fleet maneuvers. In 1914, after Japan's entry into World War I, aircraft from *Wakamiya Maru* took part in the Japanese seizure of German territories in China. During the war, Japanese naval observers with the RN allowed Japan to keep abreast of developments in the world's leading aviation navy.

A well-known shot of *Zuiho* under attack during the Battle of Leyte Gulf. Note the flight-deck camouflage; though dramatic it was ineffective. No. 13 radar can be seen on the lowered mast on the port side. Also note the buckled flight deck aft, the result of a bomb explosion on the hangar deck. (Naval History and Heritage Command)

Through their own experience with *Wakamiya Maru* and their observation of the RN, the Japanese realized the importance of aircraft carriers and the requirement for a modern navy to incorporate naval aviation. Accordingly, the construction programs of both 1918 and 1920 provided for the construction of carriers. In 1920, the Japanese asked their British ally for technical assistance in developing their naval aviation program. Between 1921 and 1923, the RN mission sent to assist the Japanese proved indispensable in the development of the IJN's carrier force. All aspects of naval aviation were advanced, from training and design details for the first Japanese carrier to design and construction of naval aircraft.

The Washington Naval Treaty of 1922 greatly affected Japanese carrier design and construction, as it imposed a limit on the size and number of aircraft carriers allowed. The treaty limited newly constructed carriers to a displacement of 27,000 tons. Conversion of two existing capital ships into carriers was permitted and these could be up to 33,000 tons. Under the treaty, the total carrier tonnage allowed to the IJN was 81,000 tons; this meant that the Japanese were placed in a position of inferiority, as the US and Royal Navies were each permitted 135,000 tons. Until the restrictions were lifted at the end of 1936, the Japanese were continually working to maximize the utility of their allotted tonnage while also attempting to maintain numerical parity of carriers with the USN.

AIRCRAFT AND AIRCRAFT OPERATIONS

By the start of the Pacific War, the Japanese had six fleet carriers in service supported by three smaller units. Also in service was a world-beating carrier fighter (the Mitsubishi A6M2 Type 0 carrier fighter plane Model 21, with the Allied codename "Zeke" but more commonly known as the "Zero"), the world's best carrier torpedo aircraft (the Nakajima B5N2 Type 97 carrier attack plane Model 12, Allied codename "Kate"), and a very accurate carrier dive-bomber (the Aichi D3A1 Type 99 carrier bomber Model 11, Allied codename "Val"). These aircraft, along with well-trained and experienced aircrews and deck crews, combined to make the IJN's carriers into formidable striking platforms.

The aircraft capacity of Japanese carriers was determined by hangar space. Unlike on USN carriers, all aircraft servicing, refueling, and weapons reloading was done in the hangar. Japanese carriers did not maintain a deck park of aircraft. This practice, and the fact that only the Kate had folding

wings, meant that Japanese carriers did not usually possess the aircraft capacity of US carriers.

When launching aircraft, operations were directed by the air operations officer positioned on a platform on the rear of the island. To launch aircraft, the carrier turned into the wind and steamed at full speed. Between 20 and 30 seconds were needed for each aircraft launch. Lighter aircraft were spotted forward to take off first, as they needed less of a flight-deck run to become airborne. A Zero could take off in a mere 230ft in the right wind conditions; heavier aircraft needed twice that distance. Unlike USN and RN carriers, Japanese carriers were never equipped with catapults to assist in aircraft launching.

A proficient Japanese carrier could recover an aircraft every 25–45 seconds. Japanese pilots were not guided down to the ship's deck with the assistance of a landing signals officer, as was the case for American and British carrier pilots. Japanese carriers were equipped with a system of approach lights that assisted the pilot in judging his angle of approach. Though it was not stabilized to compensate for the movement of the ship

The A6M fighter was a formidable air-superiority fighter, but was less well suited for fleet air defense. Here, A6Ms are ready to launch during the Hawaiian operation. (NARA)

in a heavy sea, it proved successful and was used throughout the war. Japanese fleet carriers had up to nine arresting wires placed in the rear portion of the flight deck. By the start of the Pacific War, carriers were equipped with the Kure Type 4 arresting system that used an electric engine and could stop an 8,000lb aircraft in about 130ft. Forward of the arresting wires was a crash barrier. This protected any aircraft parked on the forward part of the deck from an aircraft that failed to catch one of the arresting wires. This innovation greatly speeded up aircraft recovery. Once aboard, aircraft had to be moved quickly down to the hangar deck for maintenance, refueling, and re-arming; the size and placement of elevators was a key factor in aircraft handling. Japanese carriers used aircraft elevators driven by electric motors. On fleet carriers, there were usually three elevators, all located on the ship's centerline (or just off centerline).

Hangars on Japanese carriers were unarmored, as was the flight deck. Most fleet carriers featured two hangars, each usually between 13 and 16ft tall and placed one above the other. Outboard of the hangars were areas dedicated to aircraft maintenance. The sides of Japanese carrier hangars were designed to vent the force of a bomb exploding on the hangar deck outwards instead of upwards, which could render the flight deck useless. In practice, the opposite frequently occurred, and the result of a bomb hit on the hangar deck was a ruptured flight deck. This design flaw was apparent throughout the war. Only the introduction of two late-war carriers with armored flight decks addressed this key vulnerability.

This faulty hangar design was worsened by the fact that hangars were not flash or vapor tight. To ventilate the hangar, Japanese carriers used intake and exhaust fans. Fires on the hangar deck were an obvious danger that the Japanese planned to combat with a foam spray system using rows of pipes and nozzles on the hangar walls. In addition to the faulty hangar design, aviation fuel handling arrangements on Japanese carriers were dangerously inadequate. Fuel tanks were part of the structure of the ship, which meant that shocks to the hull were also absorbed by the tanks, creating possible leaks. Combined with the inability to vent these fumes from the hangar, the potential for disaster was obvious.

To make things worse, damage-control training on IJN ships was generally poor. Organizationally, damage control was not given proper priority. These factors, combined with the design flaw of enclosed hangars and a vulnerable fuel system, meant that Japanese carriers could be characterized as ships with great striking power but with limited ability to take damage.

The torpedo-armed B5N was a potent ship-killer. It was also used in a horizontal bomber role. (Naval History and Heritage Command)

CARRIER SHIPBOARD WEAPONS

As the Pacific War developed, the IJN was increasingly exposed to air attack. In response, the Japanese greatly augmented the antiaircraft protection of their surface ships, carriers included. However, in spite of the increased number of guns on board the carriers, the vulnerability of Japanese ships to air attack increased and proved a decisive weakness as the war progressed.

Two primary guns were mounted on Japanese carriers for air defense. The primary heavy antiaircraft gun was the Type 89 5in/40cal dual mount that was successfully tested for fleet use in 1931. It was a respectable weapon and was used on a variety of other surface ships and also as a coast defense gun in both antiaircraft and antisurface roles. The weakness of this weapon was not its performance, but its fire-control system. The Type 94 high-angle director was very reliant on manual inputs and control and thus was generally unsuitable for tracking fast targets. The older Type 91 high-angle director had similar problems. Adopted in 1932, the system took 11 men to operate and the manual operation was slow in both elevation and training. The system was not designed to handle high-speed targets. In 1940, the Japanese calculated that the Type 91 director could achieve a hit rate of 0.9 percent under battle conditions, but this proved far from reality under combat conditions. Compounding the ineffectiveness of the Type 89 was the fact that the Japanese never developed any sort of proximity fuse, as used with great effectiveness by the USN against Japanese aircraft.

> **Type 89 5in/40cal High-Angle Gun**
>
> **Shell weight:** 51lb
> **Muzzle velocity:** 2,379ft/sec
> **Max elevation:** +90 to -8 degrees
> **Max range:** 16,075yd/30,970ft max ceiling
> **Rate of fire:** 14 max; 8 rounds sustained per minute

> **Type 96 25mm Antiaircraft Gun**
>
> **Shell weight:** 0.6lb
> **Muzzle velocity:** 2,953ft/sec
> **Max elevation:** +85 to -10 degrees
> **Max range (against aircraft):** 3,815yd (effective range 1,635yd)
> **Rate of fire:** 130 rounds per minute

As undistinguished as the Type 89 proved to be in service, the IJN's selection of its light antiaircraft gun proved to be a disaster. The standard light antiaircraft gun of the Pacific War was the Type 96 25mm. Initially, the Type 96 was introduced as a double mount; the triple-mount version entered service in 1941 and was followed by a single gun mount. The 25mm gun was an adaptation of a French Hotchkiss design. Unfortunately for the IJN, it was a weapon with a relatively low rate of fire and which used a projectile with insufficient hitting power to destroy increasingly rugged American aircraft. Though it had a nominal rate of fire of 200–260 rounds per minute, the reload system that required ceasing fire when a 15-round clip was exhausted reduced the actual rate of fire to approximately 130 rounds per minute. Additionally, the weapon had a slow training and elevating speed. The Type 96 could be controlled manually or by the Type 95 director, which was considered state of the art when it was adopted in 1937. It had a theoretical maximum range of 4,155 yards. The triple and double mount also had a back-up sight, and the single 25mm mount only had an open-ring sight that proved inadequate for high-speed targets. Despite the growing profusion of 25mm guns on all Japanese ships during the war, the IJN grew ever more vulnerable to the increasing scale of American air attack. The lack of effective antiaircraft protection and a faulty doctrine for the use of escorting ships in defending the carriers meant that the best hope for survival of a carrier under air attack was usually the maneuvering skill of its captain.

CARRIER RADAR AND FIGHTER DEFENSE

The IJN's radar program was far less developed than that of the Allies. The tardy introduction of radar and its ineffective use was perhaps the single biggest weakness of the IJN during the Pacific War. While the use of radar greatly strengthened the air defense of American ships, the lack of effective radar was devastating to Japanese aircraft carriers.

No Japanese carrier or any other ship began the war fitted with radar. This made the task of controlling defending fighters very difficult. In the early-war period, IJN fleet carriers embarked a fighter squadron with 18 aircraft. These aircraft were usually divided into a nine-aircraft division to accompany outgoing strike aircraft and another nine-aircraft division to provide air defense for the ship and its escorts. With no radar, air defense was accomplished by conducting standing patrols. However, only a few aircraft (usually a section of three) would be airborne at any time, with the remaining aircraft standing by to be scrambled if adequate warning was gained. Adding further difficulty to the fighter defense problem was the inferior quality of Japanese aircraft radios which made it virtually impossible to control aircraft already airborne. Even when carriers received radar late in the war (the first carrier to receive radar was *Shokaku* in 1942), the Japanese were never able to maximize their fighter assets by integrating all incoming information into what the USN called a Combat Information Center.

Two primary types of radar were used on Japanese carriers; however, the first carrier did not receive any radar until after the

Japanese Carrier Names

Japanese carriers were given poetic names based on flying creatures. There were several exceptions, but these were ships that were converted into carriers and retained their original names.

Akagi – Red Castle – an extinct volcano in the Kanto area near Tokyo
Amagi – an extinct volcano
Chitose – a city in Hokkaido
Chiyoda – a city near Tokyo
Chuyo – Heaven-bound Hawk
Hiryu – Flying Dragon
Hiyo – Flying Falcon
Hosho – Flying Phoenix
Junyo – Peregrine Falcon
Kaiyo – Sea Hawk
Kaga – an ancient Japanese province
Katsuragi – a mountain near Osaka
Ryuho – Dragon Phoenix
Ryujo – Heavenly Dragon
Shinano – an ancient Japanese province
Shinyo – Godly Hawk
Shoho – Happy Phoenix
Shokaku – Flying Crane
Soryu – Deep Blue Dragon
Taiho – Great Phoenix
Taiyo – Great Hawk
Unryu – Heaven-bound Dragon Riding the Clouds
Unyo – a Hawk in the Clouds
Zuiho – Lucky Phoenix
Zuikaku – Lucky Crane

disastrous Battle of Midway. The first set developed and fitted on carriers was an air-search radar known formally as the Type 2 (1942) shipboard search radar Model 1 Modification 2, or abbreviated as No. 21 (2). The No. 21 (2) radar had a mattress antenna. On carriers with an island, it was mounted atop the island; on other ships it was placed on the flight-deck edge and the control room and radar antenna were lowered flush with the flight deck when aircraft operations were under way. Performance was mediocre, with the ability to detect a group of aircraft at approximately 60 miles and a single aircraft at about 45 miles. Another air-search radar was introduced later in 1943 and designated as the No. 13 (Type 3, No. 1, Model 3). This had a long ladder antenna. The No. 13 air-search radar was mounted on many Japanese ships, including carriers, as approximately 1,000 were built. Performance was similar to the No. 21, with the capability to detect a group of aircraft at 62 miles and a single aircraft at 31 miles. The No. 13 was mounted on the mainmast or radio masts of carriers.

Junyo was equipped with both No. 21 and No. 13 radar. The No. 21 is the mattress spring antenna forward of the stack, and the No. 13 is mounted on the mainmast aft of the stack. (Naval History and Heritage Command)

Japanese Carrier Radars		
	No. 21 (2)	No. 13
Peak power output	5kW	10kW
Maximum range	93 miles	93 miles
Effective Range single aircraft group of aircraft	 43 miles 62 miles	 31 miles 62 miles
Accuracy	1,094–2,187 yards	2,187–3,280 yards
Bearing accuracy	5–8 degrees	10 degrees

PREWAR-BUILT CARRIERS

Hosho

Design and construction

The IJN's first carrier was not the first ship to be designed as a carrier from the keel up, as is often stated. *Hosho* was laid down as a mixed seaplane carrier/aircraft carrier employing both seaplanes and deck-launched aircraft. The ship was modified during construction and was completed as a full-deck aircraft carrier based on a light cruiser hull. With a narrow beam and a 300ft hangar, only 21 aircraft could be carried. This was later reduced to 11 as aircraft got larger.

Hosho Construction				
Ship	Built at	Laid down	Launched	Completed
Hosho	Tsurumi	12/16/19	11/13/21	12/27/22

Armament and service modifications

When *Hosho* was completed in 1922, little consideration was given to antiaircraft defense, and the ship was equipped for defense primarily against surface attack. Accordingly, four 5.5in guns were mounted outboard of the hangar and two 3in antiaircraft guns were positioned on the flight deck. As war neared, only the 3in guns remained; these were removed at the start of the war, and eight 25mm antiaircraft guns were fitted. The number of 25mm guns was increased to 30 by 1944. When surrendered in 1945, only six 25mm guns remained.

Hosho Specifications

Displacement: 7,470 tons standard*
Dimensions: Length 579ft (1944) / beam 59ft / draft 20ft
Maximum speed: 25kt
Range: 8,680nm at 12kt
Crew: 550

* Standard displacement was adopted by the Japanese in response to the Washington Naval Treaty. It was the weight of the ship with a full load of stores and ammunition, but with no fuel, lubricating oil and reserve feed water.

Hosho in October 1945 after its surrender. The widened and lengthened flight deck is evident and now extends well over the ship's bow and stern. The landing-light system can be seen on both sides of the stern. Camouflage of both the hull and the flight deck can be faintly made out. (*Ships of the World* magazine)

The most obvious modification occurred early in *Hosho*'s career. A small starboard-side island was found to impede aircraft operations on such a narrow deck and was removed. Navigation was now accomplished from two platforms mounted on either side of the forward edge of the hangar. During the Pacific War, *Hosho* was relegated to secondary duties in home waters and was therefore only slightly modified. The flight deck was lengthened and widened in 1944 to facilitate its role as a training carrier.

Wartime service

During the Sino-Japanese War of 1937–40, *Hosho* was active in operations off the China coast. Of marginal usefulness by the opening of the Pacific War in 1941, *Hosho* was employed in a few minor operations before it participated in the Battle of Midway as an escort to the battleship-heavy Main Body. Afterwards, *Hosho* returned to the Inland Sea and was used as a training carrier for the remainder of the war. *Hosho* survived the war and was used for repatriation duties before being scrapped in 1947.

Akagi

Design and construction

After their experience with *Hosho*, the Japanese decided that they needed carriers with a larger aircraft capacity that had the speed to operate with the fleet. As a result of the Washington Naval Treaty, a number of incomplete battlecruisers were slated for scrapping. Their large hulls and high speed made them ideal platforms for conversion into carriers. In 1923, conversion began on battlecruiser *Akagi*. What emerged in 1927 demonstrated the evolving nature of Japanese carrier design. *Akagi* possessed a flight deck of 632ft but no island. There were two hangars; each had its own flying platform forward. This arrangement allowed 60 aircraft to be carried.

Akagi Construction				
Ship	Built at	Laid down	Launched	Completed
Akagi	Kure Navy Yard	12/6/20	4/22/25	3/25/27

Armament and service modifications

Completed with a total of ten 8in guns, after the 1937–38 reconstruction *Akagi* still retained six 8in guns mounted in casemates. Placed low to the water, they were virtually unusable in any kind of sea. Antiaircraft protection was strengthened and now totaled 12 4.7in antiaircraft guns in dual mounts *Akagi* was the only fleet carrier not to receive the newer Type 89 5in antiaircraft guns) and 14 twin 25mm guns. *Akagi* maintained this configuration until its loss. No radar was ever fitted.

Not surprisingly, *Akagi*'s multi-level flight-deck arrangement proved impractical and it was removed from service in 1937 for modernization. This was extensive and saw the removal of the two lower flight decks and the lengthening of the main flight deck to 817ft. The hangars were also lengthened (aircraft capacity being increased to 66 plus 15 reserves) and a third elevator was added. A small island was also added. The formerly complex stack arrangement was reduced to a single downward-facing stack on the starboard side, a common design feature on most subsequent Japanese carriers.

> **Akagi Specifications (after 1938 reconstruction)**
>
> **Displacement:** 36,500 tons standard
> **Dimensions:** Length 855ft / beam 103ft / draft 29ft
> **Maximum speed:** 31kt
> **Range:** 8,200nm at 16kt
> **Crew:** 1,630

Akagi in 1939 after modernization. (Naval History and Heritage Command)

The top view shows *Akagi* as it appeared at the start of the Pacific War. Note the small port-side island. The middle view is of *Kaga* in December 1941. As with *Akagi*, its non-carrier origin is obvious. The bottom view shows *Soryu* as it appeared at the start of the war. Its sleek lines suggest that it was the first IJN ship designed from the keel up as a fleet carrier.

Wartime service

The wartime exploits of *Akagi* made it the most famous Japanese carrier. *Akagi* served as the flagship of the First Air Fleet and led the Kido Butai during the war's first six months. During this time, *Akagi* and its elite air group devastated Allied forces at Pearl Harbor, Rabaul, the Dutch East Indies, Port Darwin, and Ceylon. At Midway, American dive- bombers caught *Akagi* with fully fueled and armed aircraft on its decks. Hit by a single well-placed bomb, the resulting fires raged out of control and resulted in the ship being scuttled the following day.

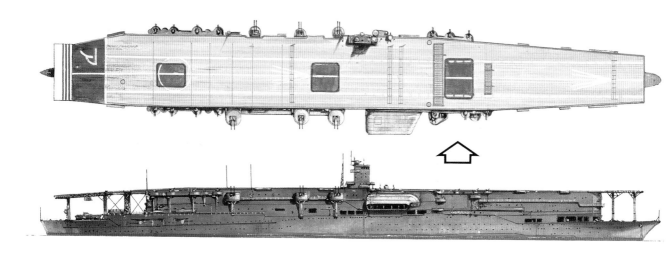

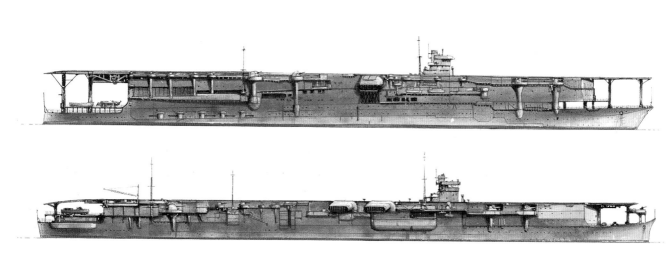

Kaga

Design and construction

Earmarked for scrapping under the Washington Naval Treaty, *Kaga* received a new lease of life when the battlecruiser *Amagi*, earlier slated for conversion to a carrier, was damaged in the 1923 Tokyo earthquake. *Kaga* was substituted and work began in late 1923. Though the hull of the battleship was over 60ft shorter than *Akagi*'s, upon completion *Kaga* possessed the same general layout as *Akagi*. Because the hangars were extended and were wider, the same number of aircraft could be carried as on *Akagi*. However, the larger beam and less powerful machinery on *Kaga* resulted in a slower speed than any other IJN fleet carrier, only 28.3 knots.

Kaga in 1936 after modernization. (Naval History and Heritage Command)

Kaga Construction				
Ship	Built at	Laid down	Launched	Completed
Kaga	Kobe by Kawasaki and Yokosuka Navy Yard	7/19/20	11/17/21	3/31/28

Armament and service modifications

Kaga's original armament was similar to that of *Akagi* but was significantly upgraded during its 1934–35 modernization. The carrier retained its ten 8in guns, but all were mounted in casemates only 15ft above the waterline, drastically reducing their effectiveness (assuming an 8in gun on a carrier had any utility at all, which was clearly not the case by 1941). Antiaircraft protection surpassed that of *Akagi* and included eight Type 89 dual mounts. A total of 30 25mm antiaircraft guns were also fitted in twin mounts. *Kaga* did not carry radar.

As with *Akagi*, the multi-level flight-deck arrangement proved impractical. After just over four years in service, *Kaga* returned to the yards for a major reconstruction. This work actually occurred before *Akagi*'s and was even more extensive. The hull was lengthened by 34ft and underwater protection increased. The two lower flight decks were removed and the main flight deck rebuilt so that it extended up to the bow for a total of just over 812ft. As with *Akagi*, a third elevator and a small island were added and the former stack system was reduced to a single downward-facing stack. Aircraft capacity was increased to 72 plus 18 reserves. *Kaga* returned to service in mid-1935 and retained this configuration until its loss.

Wartime service

Together with *Akagi*, *Kaga* formed the IJN's Carrier Division 1, the elite unit of the First Air Fleet. *Kaga*'s wartime exploits were similar to *Akagi*'s except that *Kaga* missed the expedition into the Indian Ocean in April 1942 because of a grounding incident in February 1942. Repaired on time for the Midway operation, *Kaga* was struck by four bombs from American dive-bombers on June 4, 1942. The resulting fires could not be brought under control and it sank the same day.

Ryujo

Design and construction

After the construction of *Akagi* and *Kaga*, only 30,000 tons remained for additional carriers under the Washington Treaty. With this remaining tonnage, the IJN wanted as many ships as possible, each with a useful number of aircraft and the speed to operate with the fleet. The treaty

Ryujo under way in September 1938 after its second major refit to correct stability problems. Though designed to carry 48 aircraft, in service many fewer were embarked. At the Battle of the Eastern Solomons, only 24 A6Ms and nine B5Ns were carried. The ship's small flight deck, small elevators, and unfavorable elevator placement made aircraft operations difficult and greatly reduced the ship's effectiveness. (Naval History and Heritage Command)

exempted carriers under 10,000 tons from treaty tonnage calculations. *Ryujo* was designed to make use of this exemption. Originally it was to be an 8,000-ton ship carrying 24 aircraft in a single hangar. However, before construction was begun, it was determined that such a small air group would not be effective, so a second hangar deck was added which brought aircraft capacity up to 48. The resulting design resulted was a ship of some 12,500 tons, well over treaty restrictions.

> ### *Ryujo* Specifications (after 1936 refit)
>
> **Displacement:** 10,600 tons standard
> **Dimensions:** Length 590ft / beam 68ft / draft 23ft
> **Maximum speed:** 29kt
> **Range:** 10,000nm at 14kt
> **Crew:** 924

Ryujo Construction				
Ship	**Built at**	**Laid down**	**Launched**	**Completed**
Ryujo	Yokohama	11/26/29	4/2/31	5/9/33

Armament and service modifications

Ryujo entered service with a heavy armament including six Type 89 mounts and 24 12.7mm machine guns. Two of the Type 89s were removed in *Ryujo*'s first refit. By the outbreak of the Pacific War, the machine guns had been replaced with 22 25mm guns in a mix of double and triple mounts. No radar was fitted before the ship was lost.

After a year in service, *Ryujo* was returned to the yards in August 1934 to address stability problems. These were largely corrected by the addition of larger bulges, more ballast, and the removal of two of the six Type 89 mounts. After it re-entered service, additional problems were found, again related to the ship's stability. *Ryujo* again entered the yard in May 1936 to have an additional deck built on its forecastle to prevent shipping water in heavy seas.

Wartime service

Despite its limitations, *Ryujo* was employed extensively during the initial period of the war, mostly on secondary operations. *Ryujo*'s aircraft covered the landings in the Philippines in December 1941 and later the invasion of Java in February 1942. The ship was also part of the Indian Ocean raid in April 1942. It was also present at the Battle of Midway, but was assigned to the Aleutians diversionary attack, thus avoiding the disastrous defeat inflicted on the main carrier force. Committed to counter the American seizure of Guadalcanal in August 1942, *Ryujo* was subjected to attack by aircraft from USS *Saratoga* during the Battle of the Eastern Solomons and was quickly destroyed by four bombs and one torpedo.

Soryu Class Specifications

Displacement: 15,900 tons standard
(*Hiryu* 17,300 tons)
Dimensions: Length 746ft / beam 70ft
(*Hiryu* 73ft) / draft 25ft (*Hiryu* 26ft)
Maximum speed: 34kt
Range: 7,750nm at 18kt (*Hiryu*
10,330nm at 18kt)
Crew: 1,103

Soryu Class

Design and construction

Soryu has the distinction of being the first Japanese fleet carrier designed as such from the keel up. It epitomized Japanese carrier design philosophy with a relatively large aircraft capacity on a fast, light hull. With some modification, *Soryu* served as a template for the remainder of the IJN's fleet carrier designs. Two hangars were provided, giving *Soryu* the capacity to operate 63 aircraft with another eight in reserve. Three aircraft elevators were carried. Exhaust gases were vented through two downward-venting stacks on the starboard side, and a small island was built well forward on the starboard side. Powerful machinery and a cruiser-type hull, combined with a high beam-to-waterline ratio, gave a very high speed, but protection over machinery and magazine spaces was entirely inadequate.

Hiryu was a near sister of Soryu and was laid down to an improved design. With an extra 1,400 tons in displacement, some important improvements were made. The hull was strengthened and the beam increased for added stability. Additional armor was also fitted, rectifying one of the design defects on Soryu, but it was still inadequate against attack by aircraft bombs. The single biggest difference between the two ships was the portside island mounted amidships on Hiryu. Like the portside island on Akagi, it proved a failure in service because of the generation of dangerous wind currents aft of the island and the fact that the placement of the island adversely affected aircraft recovery and parking space. This experiment was never repeated after the completion of Hiryu. A total of 57 aircraft were carried with another 16 in reserve.

Soryu projecting an image of speed and power during sea trials in January 1938. *Soryu's* air unit included 18 A6M fighters, 18 D3A dive-bombers, and 18 B5N attack aircraft. (*Ships of the World* magazine)

Soryu Class Construction				
Ship	**Built at**	**Laid down**	**Launched**	**Completed**
Soryu	Kure Navy Yard	11/20/34	12/23/35	12/29/37
Hiryu	Yokosuka Navy Yard	7/8/36	11/16/37	7/5/39

Armament and service modifications

Both ships carried six Type 89 mounts, three on each side just below the flight deck. Short-range antiaircraft protection was provided by a mix of double and triple 25mm mounts. *Soryu* carried 14 double mounts while *Hiryu* carried a mix of seven triple mounts and five twin mounts. Of note, *Hiryu's* one Type 89 mount and three 25mm mounts aft of the stacks on the starboard side were provided with full shields, another design feature repeated on carriers with downward-venting stacks. No armament was added before their loss and neither ship carried radar.

Both ships proved very satisfactory in service and neither saw any significant modification during their relatively short service lives.

Wartime service

The two ships formed the Kido Butai's Carrier Division 2 and saw extensive service before their loss early in the war. Both participated in the Pearl Harbor operation and then were detached to support the invasion of Wake Island in December 1941. Operating with the rest of the Kido Butai, both supported the invasion of the Dutch East Indies and participated in the

Hiryu on trials in April 1939. The ship carried an identical air unit to *Soryu*: 54 aircraft in three equal squadrons. (Naval History and Heritage Command)

This plate shows *Hiryu* preparing to launch a torpedo plane strike against the American carrier task force during the Battle of Midway on June 4, 1942. This was *Hiryu*'s second strike of the day. In this scene, ten torpedo planes escorted by fighters are preparing to take off. This strike succeeded in hitting carrier *Yorktown* with two torpedoes which led to its eventual loss. In the inset is an A6M Type 0 fighter and a B5N Type 97 carrier attack plane with markings indicating that they are part of *Hiryu*'s air group.

devastating attack on Port Darwin. In April 1942, Carrier Division 2 took part in the Japanese raid into the Indian Ocean, striking Colombo and Trincomalee in Ceylon. Both ships met their end at Midway. *Soryu* was caught by dive-bombers and was hit by three bombs from *Yorktown* aircraft. The ship was soon ablaze as the fire spread from fueled and armed aircraft, and only 20 minutes after the attack the ship was abandoned. It sank the same day with a heavy loss of life. *Hiryu* escaped the initial attack and immediately retaliated against the American carriers with torpedo and dive-bomber strikes. These eventually resulted in the loss of *Yorktown*. Later on June 4, *Hiryu* was attacked by dive-bombers, resulting in four hits. Although initially able to maintain power and fight the resulting fires, the ship could not be saved and was abandoned early on June 5.

Shokaku Class

Design and construction

With the expiration of the Washington Naval Treaty in December 1936, the IJN was free to pursue its first fleet carrier without any design restrictions. The Japanese desire for a ship with a high aircraft capacity, high speed, a superior radius of action, and good protection was realized in the Shokaku class which was laid down in 1937 and entered service just in time to be included in the Pearl Harbor operation. The success of the design was evidenced throughout an eventful wartime career, and the class can be easily considered the most successful Japanese carrier design. The Shokaku class was superior to all its foreign contemporaries and was not surpassed until the introduction of the USN's Essex class in 1943.

The class was essentially an upgraded *Hiryu*, being almost 100ft longer and approximately 8,500 tons heavier. In spite of this increased size, the ships retained a very high speed. This was due to the fitting of the most powerful machinery ever on an IJN ship and a new bulbous bow that reduced underwater drag.

As with the Soryu class, two hangars were provided, which gave an aircraft capacity of 72 with room for another 12 spare aircraft. Unlike on earlier carriers, these reserve aircraft were not stored in a state of disassembly and could be readied for operation in a short time. Three elevators were installed. A small island was placed forward on the starboard side.

Armament and service modifications

The Shokaku class carried a heavy antiaircraft suite. A total of eight Type 89 mounts and four Type 94 fire-control systems were fitted. The short-range antiaircraft fit was continually increased throughout the war. When commissioned, each ship carried 12 25mm triple mounts. In June 1942,

Shokaku after completion in August 1941. When commissioned, the ship had an air group of 18 A6M fighters, 27 D3A dive-bombers, and 27 B5N attack aircraft. (Naval History and Heritage Command)

Shokaku Class Construction				
Ship	Built at	Laid down	Launched	Completed
Shokaku	Yokosuka Navy Yard	12/12/37	6/1/39	8/8/41
Zuikaku	Kobe by Kawasaki	5/25/38	11/27/39	9/25/41

another four triple mounts were added, two forward and two aft. By July 1943, another two triple mounts were added with another 16 single mounts for a total of 70 guns. *Zuikaku* received additional protection after the Battle of the Philippine Sea; 26 more single mounts were added for a total of 96. Of these, ten were portable mounts positioned on the flight deck during periods of no flight operations. Before *Zuikaku*'s final action, it received six 28-barrel 4.7in rocket launchers for short-range antiaircraft defense. These weapons were designed to deter dive-bomber attack as they had a vertical range of only 3,300ft. In service, they proved of no value.

During their very eventful service lives, neither ship received a major refit. After *Shokaku* was lost at the Battle of the Philippine Sea, due to an aviation fuel fire, *Zuikaku* had the capacity of its fuel tanks reduced and concrete blisters fitted for added protection. Both received No. 21 radar, which was mounted on the island; in fact *Shokaku* was the first carrier to

Zuikaku after completion in September 1941. After Midway, the composition of the ship's air unit was altered. The number of fighters was increased to 27 and the number of attack aircraft was reduced to 18. (Naval History and Heritage Command)

receive this equipment. On *Shokaku*, a smaller antenna was used which allowed the radar to be placed on top of the Type 94 fire-control director; on *Zuikaku*, the island director was removed and a No. 21 mounted in its place. In 1944, *Zuikaku* received a second No. 21, placed on the portside aft area of the flight deck. Both ships also received a No. 13 radar mounted on the mainmast.

Shokaku Class Specifications

Displacement: 26,675 tons standard
Dimensions: Length 845ft / beam 85ft / draft 29ft
Maximum speed: 34kt
Range: 9,700nm at 18kt
Crew: 1,800

Wartime service

Zuikaku joined *Shokaku* in October 1941 to form Carrier Division 5 of the Kido Butai. Together, both would participate in every carrier action of the Pacific War, except Midway. Both were present during the Pearl Harbor attack and then in raids on Allied forces in New Guinea and Rabaul. Having missed the Kido Butai's attack against Port Darwin and the East Indies, their next operation was the April 1942 Indian Ocean raid. The two ships were next assigned to cover the Japanese invasion of Port Moresby in New Guinea. This resulted in the first carrier action in history in May 1942 in the Coral Sea, where, as already described, the two sisters acquitted themselves well. With *Shokaku* under repair and *Zuikaku*'s air group unfit for action following Coral Sea, the IJN's two most modern carriers missed the fateful Battle of Midway.

Following Midway, the Shokaku class was at the center of attempts to wrest control of Guadalcanal from the Americans. At Eastern Solomons, the two sisters again engaged USN carriers on August 24, 1942 in an inconclusive clash. *Shokaku* was hit again, suffering light damage from bomb fragments. In the October carrier clash at Santa Cruz, the two sisters were again at the center of the battle. *Shokaku* took the brunt of the damage, taking six bomb hits, which nearly sank her. In exchange, the Japanese sank carrier *Hornet* and damaged *Enterprise*, mostly due to the efforts of aircraft from *Shokaku* and *Zuikaku*. Repairs to the heavily damaged *Shokaku* prevented it from returning to service until March 1943.

The next action for the two sisters was not until June 1944 during the Battle of the Philippine Sea. Both carriers contributed aircraft to the large and ineffectual Japanese air strikes on June 19. On the same day, *Shokaku* was hit by four torpedoes from the submarine *Cavalla*, all in the forward area of the ship. After hours of flooding, the bow was submerged to the point where the sea washed over the flight deck. As the crew gathered on the aft portion of the flight deck to prepare to abandon ship, the water reached the forward elevator well and poured into the hangars. The ship quickly upended and plunged into the depths with a loss of 1,272 crewmen. The

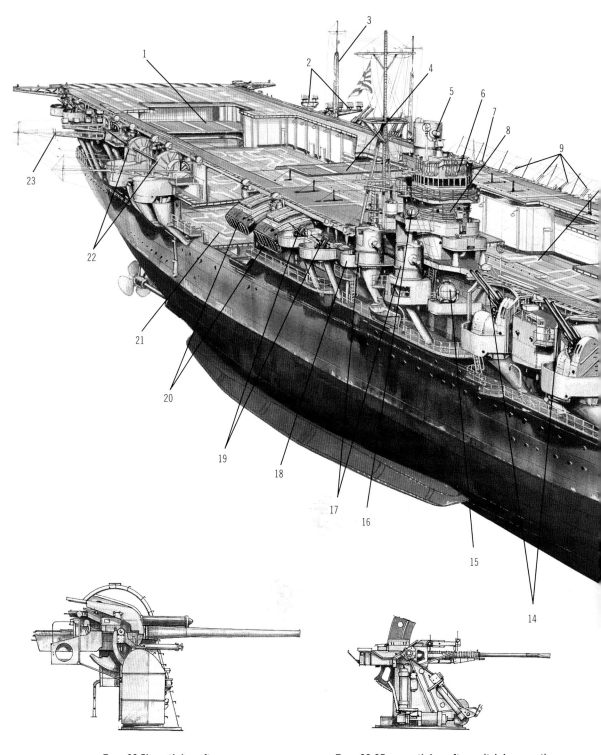

Type 89 5in antiaircraft gun

Type 96 25mm antiaircraft gun (triple mount)

Zuikaku: 1941

This plate shows *Zuikaku* in its original configuration as it appeared during the Pearl Harbor attack and the Battle of the Coral Sea. *Zuikaku* was the second ship of the Shokaku class that was ordered in the Third Naval Replenishment Program in fiscal year 1937, the same plan that authorized the two battleships of the Yamato class. These carriers were designed without treaty restriction, and, like the *Yamato*, were intended to have no foreign equal.

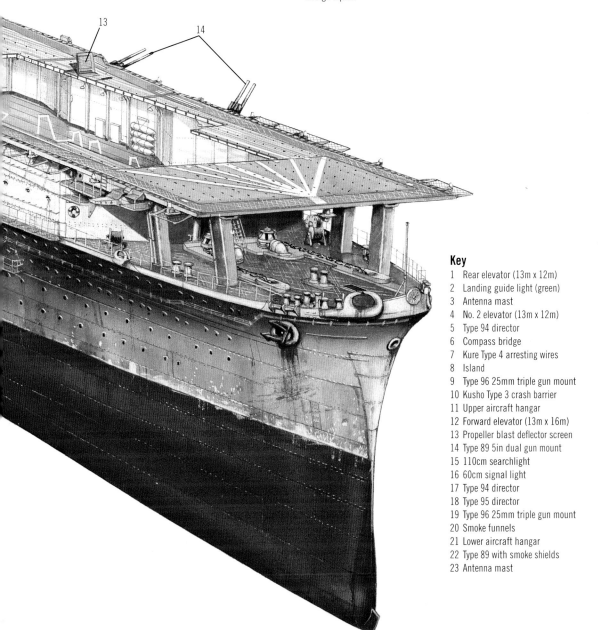

Key

1 Rear elevator (13m x 12m)
2 Landing guide light (green)
3 Antenna mast
4 No. 2 elevator (13m x 12m)
5 Type 94 director
6 Compass bridge
7 Kure Type 4 arresting wires
8 Island
9 Type 96 25mm triple gun mount
10 Kusho Type 3 crash barrier
11 Upper aircraft hangar
12 Forward elevator (13m x 16m)
13 Propeller blast deflector screen
14 Type 89 5in dual gun mount
15 110cm searchlight
16 60cm signal light
17 Type 94 director
18 Type 95 director
19 Type 96 25mm triple gun mount
20 Smoke funnels
21 Lower aircraft hangar
22 Type 89 with smoke shields
23 Antenna mast

next day, the Japanese carrier force was subjected to carrier air attack, and *Zuikaku* was moderately damaged by one bomb that penetrated the flight deck and started a fire in the hangar.

Zuikaku returned to service in August 1944. In October, it led the IJN's hollow carrier force into action at Leyte Gulf. This was intended as a sacrificial mission, and *Zuikaku* paid the price. On October 25, it was attacked and sunk by carrier air attack after receiving seven torpedo and nine bomb hits.

THE LIGHT CARRIER CONVERSIONS

Shoho Class

Design and construction

During the 1930s, the IJN created a shadow fleet of merchant ships and auxiliaries designed to be easily converted into carriers during war. This was another guise to avoid treaty restrictions and was an attempt to alleviate the problem of inadequate shipyard space should war come. The first result of the program was a class of two ships laid down in 1934–35 originally as high-speed oilers, *Shoho* and *Zuiho*. Both were to have their hulls strengthened to facilitate conversion to light carriers. Plans were changed and the ships were built as submarine tenders. The first joined the fleet as such in 1939, but the second was never completed as a submarine tender. With war clouds looming, conversion of the second ship into a carrier commenced in January 1940.

When completed in December of that year, *Zuiho* became a template for other auxiliary-to-carrier conversions to follow. The original diesels were removed and replaced by destroyer turbines. No armor was fitted. The flight deck was fitted over the existing structure and two elevators served a single hangar deck that could hold 30 aircraft. No island was fitted, navigation being accomplished from a position forward of the hangar. Conversion of the sister ship, *Shoho*, took only a year and was completed in January 1942.

Shoho Class Construction				
Ship	**Built at**	**Laid down**	**Launched**	**Completed**
Shoho	Yokosuka Navy Yard	12/3/34	6/1/35	1/15/39
Zuiho	Yokosuka Navy Yard	6/20/35	6/19/36	12/27/40

Armament and service modifications

A total of four Type 89 mounts were carried, two on each side, with their own Type 94 fire-control system. The short-range antiaircraft fit originally consisted of an inadequate four triple 25mm mounts. *Shoho*'s weapons fit was not modified before its loss. During 1943, *Zuiho* received an additional six triple mounts and four double mounts. In July 1944, *Zuiho*'s antiaircraft guns were increased to 68 with the addition of numerous 25mm single mounts. Six 28-barrel 4.7in rocket launchers were also shipped. *Zuiho* also received a No. 21 and a No. 13 radar. In 1943, the flight deck was extended forward from 590ft to 631ft.

Shoho in December 1941 before its conversion was complete. Part of the ship's company can be seen mustered on the flight deck aft of the wind screen. Note the downward-facing stack. Just forward of the stack is a Type 89 antiaircraft mount and a Type 94 fire-control director. (*Ships of the World* magazine)

Wartime service

Shoho had a very short service life and was the first Japanese carrier sunk during the war. Commissioned in January 1942, its first combat action was to escort the invasion fleet during the Port Moresby operation in May. In the opening stages of Coral Sea, *Shoho* was struck by a reported seven torpedoes and 13 bomb hits by aircraft from *Lexington* and *Yorktown*. Only 203 crewmen survived.

Zuiho participated in a number of actions and survived well into 1944. The ship took part in the Midway operation. Its next operation was at Santa Cruz; in this engagement,

Shoho Class Specifications

Displacement: 11,262 tons standard
Dimensions: Length 712ft / beam 59ft / draft 22ft
Maximum speed: 28kt
Range: 9,236nm at 18kt
Crew: 785

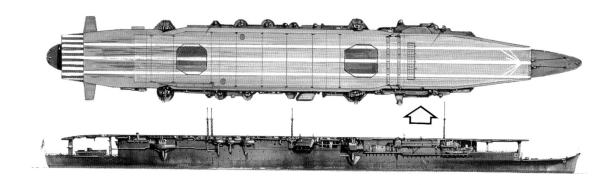

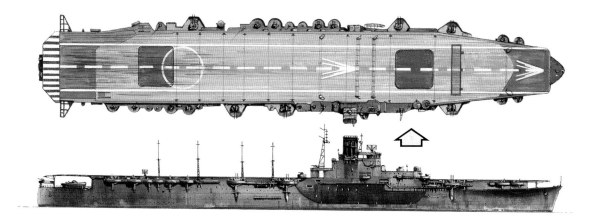

The top two views show *Shoho* in May 1942 just before its loss. Note the typical light carrier flush-deck appearance with the downward-facing stack on the starboard side. The bottom views are of *Hiyo* as the ship appeared in June 1944 before its loss at the Battle of the Philippine Sea. The mercantile lines of the *Hiyo* are clearly evident as is the large island with the slanted stack.

Zuiho suffered moderate damage when it was hit by a single bomb aft. *Zuiho* was present at Philippine Sea where its group was almost annihilated but the ship was undamaged. Assigned to accompany *Zuikaku* as part of the diversionary force at Leyte Gulf, it was subjected to extensive air attack and suffered two torpedo hits, several bomb hits, and innumerable near misses. Progressive flooding resulted in its loss on October 25 with a relatively small loss of life.

Hiyo Class

Design and construction

In addition to several auxiliary ships that were designed to be quickly converted into carriers, the IJN also subsidized the building of passenger liners that could be converted into carriers. The largest of these merchant conversions became the Hiyo class. The *Kashiwara Maru* and *Izumo Maru*,

Hiyo Class Construction				
Ship	Built at	Laid down	Launched	Completed
Hiyo	Kobe by Kawasaki	11/30/39	6/24/41	7/31/42
Junyo	Nagasaki by Mitsubishi	3/20/39	6/26/41	5/3/42

the largest passenger liners in the Japanese merchant fleet, were laid down in 1939. However, in response to growing American naval appropriations beginning in 1938 and a desire to maintain carrier parity with the USN, the two liners were requisitioned in February 1941 and work began on their conversion into carriers.

The Hiyo class represented a different direction for Japanese carrier design. The largest island to date was provided, and for the first time the stack was combined with the island. The stack was sloped outward at 26 degrees to keep exhaust away from the flight deck. During conversion, a minimum of protection was provided so as not to reduce the already borderline 25.5 knots top speed. Only some 2in of steel was provided around the machinery spaces and 1in around the magazines. Some additional watertight subdivision was incorporated.

In an attempt to increase speed, a hybrid propulsion system was provided with destroyer-type boilers being mated to merchant turbines. The result was machinery that proved troublesome and provided a marginal speed for

Junyo shown after the war. The two ships of the Hiyo class were the most elaborate merchant conversions completed during the war. Initially, a typical air unit for these ships was 12 A6M fighters, 18 D3A dive-bombers, and 18 B5N attack aircraft. By 1944, this was modified to 27 fighters (nine of which were fighter-bombers), 18 dive-bombers, and six attack planes. (Naval History and Heritage Command)

fleet use. Two elevators were installed to service two hangars. Aircraft capacity was rated at 48 with another five in reserve.

Armament and service modifications

Six Type 89 mounts were positioned three per side. When commissioned, eight triple 25mm mounts were also carried. In early 1943, *Hiyo* received an additional four triple 25mm mounts. *Junyo* received the same increase during the summer of 1943. Before Philippine Sea, both ships received an additional four triple 25mm mounts and 12 single mounts. After the battle, *Junyo*'s antiaircraft armament was increased by an additional three triple, two double, and 18 single 25mm mounts for a total of 79 25mm guns. *Junyo* also received the standard Japanese carrier late-war addition of six 28-barrel 4.7in rocket launchers mounted three per side along the forward part of the flight deck.

Junyo received a No. 21 radar in July 1942 mounted on the island; similar work followed on *Hiyo* in the autumn of 1942. Both ships received a second No. 21 in 1943 and a No. 13 in 1944. In June 1944, following the loss of *Hiyo* to an aviation fuel explosion, *Junyo* had the spaces around its fuel tanks filled with concrete.

Wartime service

Junyo was commissioned in May 1942 and *Hiyo* in July 1942. *Junyo* quickly saw its first action as part of the Northern Force assigned to occupy two islands in the Aleutians as part of the Midway operation. Its next action was at the Battle of Santa Cruz, where its air group helped sink *Hornet* while *Junyo* suffered no damage in return. *Junyo* remained active in the South Pacific throughout July 1943. Off the Japanese coast in November 1943, a USN submarine hit the carrier with two torpedoes but *Junyo* was towed to port. At Philippine Sea, *Junyo* was bombed on June 20, taking two hits around the island. After repairs, it conducted two transport missions to the Philippines area. While returning to Japan after the second, it was hit by three submarine torpedoes. Despite heavy flooding, the ship made it back to Japan but was never fully repaired. *Junyo* was surrendered and scrapped after the war.

Hiyo was active in the South Pacific early in its career but missed Santa Cruz because of engine problems. In June 1943, it was torpedoed by a submarine off the Japanese coast but survived. During Philippine Sea, it was hit by two aircraft torpedoes. Leaking fuel vapors were the probable cause of massive internal explosions, resulting in the loss of the ship.

Hiyo Class Specifications

Displacement: 24,140 tons standard
Dimensions: Length 718ft / beam 88ft / draft 27ft
Maximum speed: 25.5kt
Range: 10,000nm at 18kt
Crew: 1,224

Ryuho

Design and construction

Another member of the IJN's shadow carrier fleet, *Ryuho* was the least successful of the five light carriers converted from auxiliary ships. It originally entered service as a submarine tender in 1934. Conversion to a light carrier began in December 1941 and was completed in November 1942. Of note, while undergoing conversion in Yokosuka Navy Yard, it was lightly damaged by aircraft from the Doolittle Raid in April 1942.

Ryuho Construction				
Ship	**Built at**	**Laid down**	**Launched**	**Completed**
Ryuho	Yokosuka Navy Yard	4/12/33	11/16/33	3/31/34

When completed, the ship presented the same flush-deck appearance as the Shoho class. The customary two elevators were fitted, but aircraft capacity was only 24, with another seven in reserve. The original diesels were removed and replaced by destroyer turbines during conversion, but top speed was a relatively slow 26 knots. With its small flight deck, insufficient speed, light construction, and small air group, *Ryuho* was considered a second-line unit.

Ryuho shown after the war at Kure. The ship's only combat service was at the Battle of the Philippine Sea, during which it embarked an air group of 21 A6M fighters and nine attack aircraft. (Naval History and Heritage Command)

Armament and service modifications

The standard four light-carrier Type 89 mounts were carried, two on each side with their own Type 94 fire-control system. The number of 25mm guns upon completion was 26 (eight triple and two single); this was increased in 1943 to 42 and again in 1944 to 61. The final configuration was ten triple, four twin, and 23 single 25mm mounts.

In 1943, the flight deck was extended forward from 607 to 660ft to allow the use of heavier aircraft. In 1944, a No. 21 radar was fitted.

Wartime service

Ryuho's career confirmed the low opinion held of it by the Japanese. For most of its life it was used as an aircraft ferry or training carrier.

The ship was torpedoed off Tokyo Bay in December 1942 but survived. *Ryuho*'s only combat action was as part of the IJN's carrier force at Philippine Sea in which the ship suffered light damage from bomb near misses. *Ryuho* did conduct the last voyage of an IJN carrier beyond home waters when it transported 58 Ohka suicide rocket bombs to Formosa in December 1944–January 1945. In March 1945 the ship was attacked and severely damaged by USN carrier aircraft in Kure Navy Yard. The ship was put into dry dock to repair flooding, but was never fully repaired. *Ryuho* survived the war to be scrapped in 1946–47.

Ryuho Specifications

Displacement: 13,360 tons standard
Dimensions: Length 707ft / beam 64ft / draft 22ft
Maximum speed: 26kt
Range: 8,000nm at 18kt
Crew: 989

Chitose Class

Design and construction

The two ships of the Chitose class were the final two auxiliaries to be converted to light carriers. Both were built originally as high-speed seaplane carriers and saw service early in the Pacific War in this capacity. After Midway, with the need for carriers becoming pressing, it was decided to convert both into carriers.

Chitose's conversion began in January 1943 and was completed in January 1944; *Chiyoda*'s was completed in only ten months.

Chitose Class Construction				
Ship	Built at	Laid down	Launched	Completed
Chitose	Kure Navy Yard	11/26/34	11/29/36	7/25/38
Chiyoda	Kure Navy Yard	12/14/36	11/19/37	12/15/38

During conversion, large bulges were added to maintain stability. These ships were the only light carriers to have two hangars, but aircraft capacity remained the same as the Shoho class – 30 aircraft. In all other respects, the class was very similar to *Zuiho* in its late-war configuration. The relatively high speed of this class combined with the ships' long radius made them suitable for employment in fleet service, working with *Zuiho*.

A ship of the Chitose class pictured in the Inland Sea in late 1943. The simplicity of the conversion from its seaplane carrier origin is evident. Designed for a capacity of 30 aircraft, these ships carried 21 A6M fighters and nine attack aircraft during the Battle of the Philippine Sea. (*Ships of the World* magazine)

Armament and service modifications

Four Type 89 mounts were carried, two on each side in the usual light-carrier arrangement. Thirty 25mm guns were carried in ten triple mounts. In July 1944, another six triple mounts were added for a final total of 48 25mm guns.

Wartime service

During March and April 1944, *Chiyoda* conducted two urgent aircraft ferry missions. Both ships were assigned to the "Van Force" during Philippine Sea, where they were escorted by the IJN's most powerful surface units in an attempt to draw US carrier strikes away from the main carrier force. Despite this, only *Chiyoda* was damaged during the battle, suffering a single bomb hit on June 20. Both ships were available for the last sortie of the IJN's carrier force during the Battle of Leyte Gulf. Both ships were attacked by USN carrier aircraft on October 25. *Chitose* was hit by what were probably three torpedoes and sank within an hour. *Chiyoda* was hit by four bombs. Escort ships were unable to rescue the crew and, later on the 25th, *Chiyoda* came under fire from USN surface forces. The ship sank with no survivors.

Chitose Class Specifications

Displacement: 11,190 tons standard
Dimensions: Length 631ft / beam 68ft / draft 24ft
Maximum speed: 29kt
Range: 11,000nm at 18kt
Crew: 1,470–1,505

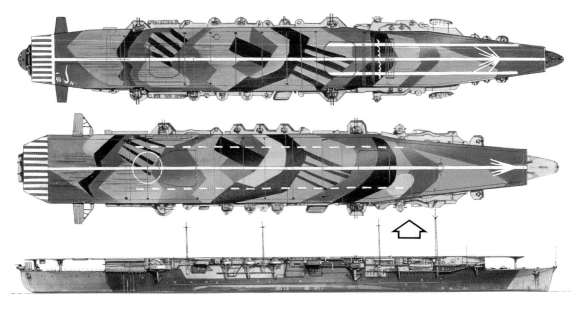

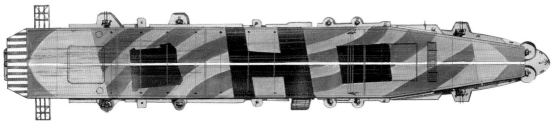

The top view shows *Zuiho* as it appeared in October 1944. For its last battle, *Zuiho* has been painted with a flight deck disruptive camouflage scheme. The extended flight deck compared to sister ship *Shoho* is evident. The middle two views show light carrier *Chitose* also at the Battle of Leyte Gulf. The ship is painted with a flight deck disruptive scheme and the antisubmarine hull scheme. The bottom view shows escort carrier *Chuyo* in 1944. In addition to the camouflage scheme, the ship also shows the late-war changes made to all escort carriers.

FLEET CARRIER WARTIME CONSTRUCTION

Taiho

Design and construction

Construction on the "Great Phoenix" began in 1941. This ship was the first Japanese carrier designed to receive damage and continue fighting. To achieve this, a new design feature was introduced – an armored flight deck designed to withstand 1,000lb bombs. Unlike the only other armored carriers then in service with the RN, *Taiho* had only an armored flight deck of between 2.9in and 3.2in – the sides of the hangar were not armored. A strong armored belt of up to 5.9in was also installed. Another unique design feature was the enclosed bow designed to improve seaworthiness. A large island similar to that on the Hiyo class was built, again using a slanted stack.

Taiho could also act as a support carrier, and for this purpose it carried additional ordnance and 33 percent more than the usual supply of aviation fuel.

Taiho Construction				
Ship	Built at	Laid down	Launched	Completed
Taiho	Kobe by Kawasaki	7/10/41	4/7/43	3/7/44

Taiho was designed on the basis of the Shokaku class. To compensate for the greater upper weight from the armored flight deck, the ship was built with one deck less than *Shokaku* to reduce its center of gravity. Only two elevators were fitted, forward and aft of the armored area of the flight deck, as it was not desired to weaken the integrity of the armored flight deck. Two hangars were provided; on its only combat operation, *Taiho* embarked 75 aircraft.

Taiho had a unique appearance with its large island, slanted stack, and distinctive enclosed bow as is evident in the top view. The middle views show *Amagi* as it appeared in 1945. Note the addition of six 4.7in rocket launchers on the forward flight-deck edge. The ship is in its late-war camouflage scheme, including a disruptive pattern on the flight deck and an antisubmarine scheme on the hull. The bottom view is of *Shinano*. Its lineage from a Yamato-class battleship is evident.

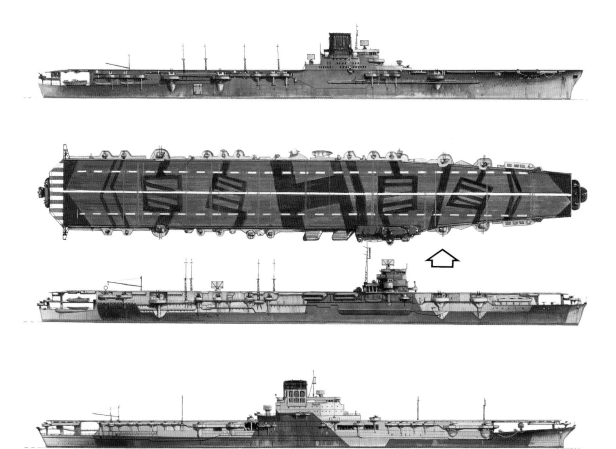

Taiho pictured after its arrival at Tawi Tawi anchorage in May 1944. A number of A6M fighters and B6N attack aircraft can be seen on the flight deck aft. (*Ships of the World* magazine)

Armament and service modifications

Antiaircraft protection was provided by a new weapon that had been introduced earlier on the Akizuki class of antiaircraft destroyer. This was the excellent Type 98 antiaircraft gun, a 100mm weapon with a maximum range of 21,300 yards, longer than the older Type 89 5in gun. *Taiho* was the only carrier to use this weapon and had six dual mounts fitted three on each side of the flight deck. Seventeen triple 25mm guns were placed around the flight deck and on the island. Twenty additional single mounts were also fitted. Two No. 21 radars were also carried, one on the forward top of the island and one on the lower aft section of the island.

Wartime service

Upon completion in March 1944, the ship moved to the Mobile Fleet's anchorage near Singapore for sea trials and aircrew training. *Taiho* was chosen as the flagship of the Mobile Fleet, and much was expected of it during the impending decisive battle. On June 19, while launching strike aircraft against the USN carrier fleet, *Taiho* was hit by one torpedo from submarine *Albacore*. The resulting damage flooded the forward elevator well and resulted in a slight bow trim, but this was not judged to be serious and the ship maintained 26 knots. However, the single torpedo had cracked the aviation fuel tanks in the area of the forward elevator and caused gasoline to mix with water in the elevator well. The crew's response demonstrated the uneven standard of damage-control training in the IJN. All hangar doors and hatches were opened, increasing the spread of vapor fumes. The damage-control officer switched on all fans throughout the ship, turning the ship into a floating bomb. Just over six hours after being torpedoed, a huge explosion took place that buckled the flight deck upwards and blew out the sides of the hangar. The explosion also ruptured the hull and caused a loss of power. Unable to fight the fires, the ship became a raging inferno and sank with a third of its crew.

Taiho Specifications

Displacement: 29,300 tons standard
Dimensions: Length 855ft / beam 91ft / draft 32ft
Maximum speed: 33kt
Range: 10,000nm at 18kt
Crew: 1,751

Unryu Class

Design and construction

With its final fleet-carrier design, the IJN returned to its prewar concept of a fast carrier with little protection and a relatively large air group. With war looming, the Japanese took steps to construct a large number of fleet carriers. In the construction programs for 1941 and 1942, six carriers were ordered. To facilitate their timely completion, the ships were patterned after *Hiryu*, not the larger and more complex Shokaku class or *Taiho*. The first three ships were laid down in 1942 and another three in 1943. Of these, only three, *Unryu*, *Amagi*, and *Katsuragi* were completed. Construction of the other three, *Kasagi*, *Ikoma*, and *Aso*, was suspended in 1945, with the ships only 84 percent, 60 percent, and 60 percent completed, respectively. Another 11 ships of the class were ordered but never laid down.

The basic hull was almost identical to *Hiryu* with the same distribution of armor. The biggest difference from *Hiryu* was the placement of the island forward on the starboard side. Only two elevators were fitted to service the two hangars and a total of 63 aircraft could be carried (57 plus another six in reserve). In line with battle experience, aviation fuel capacity was halved, and the space around the fuel tanks was filled with concrete. Of the three

Katsuragi on trials. The similarity to the Soryu class is obvious. (Naval History and Heritage Command)

B6N

D4Y

This plate shows *Taiho* as it appeared on June 19, 1944 as the ship was participating in the Battle of the Philippine Sea. At 0810hrs, one torpedo from submarine *Albacore* hit *Taiho* on the starboard side in the area of the forward elevator. This single hit started a chain of events that resulted in a fatal internal explosion at 1432hrs. The inset shows a B6N "Jill" torpedo bomber and a D4Y "Judy" dive-bomber of the Naval Air Group 601 assigned to *Taiho*.

ships completed, *Unryu* and *Amagi* carried the same machinery as the Soryu class, providing a top speed of 34 knots. *Katsuragi* was completed with two sets of destroyer turbines, but speed was only slightly reduced at almost 33 knots.

Armament and service modifications

The weapons fit was similar to that on *Hiryu*. Six Type 89 mounts were fitted, three on each side of the flight deck. However, only a single fire-control director was provided for all six positions. Short-range antiaircraft protection was provided by 16 triple and three single 25mm mounts on *Unryu* and *Amagi* when completed. Shortly after completion, another four triple mounts were added along with another 13 single mounts for a total of 76 guns. This was increased during the final months of the war to 22 triple and 23 single mounts for a final total of 89 guns. All three ships also received six 28-barrel 4.7in rocket launchers for short-range antiaircraft defense. Two No. 21 radars were fitted, one on the island and a second along the aft edge

Unryu Class Construction				
Ship	Built at	Laid down	Launched	Completed
Amagi	Nagasaki	10/1/42	10/15/43	8/10/44
Katsuragi	Kure Navy Yard	12/8/42	1/19/44	10/15/44
Unryu	Yokosuka Navy Yard	8/1/42	9/25/43	8/6/44
Aso	Kure Navy Yard	6/8/43	11/1/44	Never
Ikoma	Kobe by Kawasaki	7/5/43	11/17/44	Never
Kasagi	Nagasaki by Mitsubishi	4/14/43	10/19/44	Never

of the flight deck. Two No. 13 radars were also fitted, one on the mainmast and a second on one of the four hinged radio masts.

Wartime service

The three completed ships of the Unryu class were destined never to participate in a fleet action and it is almost certain that none of the ships ever embarked a full air group. Only one saw active service transporting aircraft and high-priority cargo to the Philippines. Late in the war, the two surviving ships were laid up in Japanese ports because of fuel shortages.

> ## Unryu Class Specifications
>
> **Displacement:** 17,150 tons standard
> (*Amagi* 17,460 tons, *Katsuragi* 17,260 tons)
> **Dimensions:** Length 742ft / beam 72ft / draft 26ft
> **Maximum speed:** 34kt (*Katsuragi* 33kt)
> **Range:** 8,000nm at 18kt
> **Crew:** 1,595

Unryu was the first ship to be commissioned in August 1944. It was assigned to the Mobile Fleet, but with the shortage of trained aircrews, the ship did not accompany the IJN's carrier force on its last mission in the Battle of Leyte Gulf. In December, *Unryu* was assigned the mission of taking an emergency cargo of Ohkas to Manila. *Unryu* embarked a small aviation detachment and headed south. On December 19, the ship was attacked by the submarine *Redfish* and hit by two torpedoes. The second hit the forward aviation fuel tanks and the ship exploded and sank in seven minutes, taking with it all but 147 of the crew.

Amagi was completed only five days after *Unryu*. *Katsuragi* was commissioned into service in October. Neither ship would leave home waters because of fuel, aircraft, and aircrew shortages. *Amagi* suffered light damage in March 1945 from a USN carrier aircraft on Kure. On July 24, another raid took place on Kure, followed by another on July 28. Heavily damaged on the July 24 raid, *Amagi* sank in Kure following additional damage suffered in the July 28 raid. It was the last IJN carrier sunk in the war. *Katsuragi* was also damaged in the July 24 attack but survived to be used as a repatriation ship before being scrapped in 1946.

Shinano

Design and construction

Shinano has the distinction of being the largest carrier built during World War II and remained the largest carrier ever built until the introduction of the USN's supercarriers in the late 1950s. *Shinano* was originally laid down as the third ship of the Yamato class of superbattleships in May 1940. After the start of the war construction on the ship slowed; by June 1942, it was complete only up to the main deck. After Midway, even the IJN could see that battleships were no longer needed, and plans were drawn up to convert *Shinano* into a carrier. Following debate within the Naval Staff on how to employ the ship, what emerged was the concept of using *Shinano* as a support carrier. As such, it was envisioned that it would act as a forward floating fortress able to land and refuel/rearm aircraft from less protected carriers operating to the rear. In accordance with this role and because only a single hangar deck was provided during conversion, it would operate only a small air group (47 aircraft), primarily for self-protection.

Shinano Construction				
Ship	Built at	Laid down	Launched	Completed
Shinano	Yokosuka Navy Yard	5/4/40	10/8/44	11/19/44

The design of *Shinano* mirrored that of *Taiho* in many respects. *Shinano* featured an armored flight deck between the elevators, this time with just over 3in of armor. As on *Taiho*, only two elevators were fitted. These served a single hangar level; the hangar area was divided into two hangars, the forward one being open with shutters and the rear area being enclosed like *Taiho*. As on *Taiho*, a large island with a slanted stack was fitted.

In addition to the armored flight deck, protection for the hull was extensive. The belt armor thickness was halved from its battleship origin, but was still over 8in. An antitorpedo bulge was fitted and another 7.5in of armor was fitted in an armored deck over the machinery and magazine spaces. All the armor brought the trial displacement of the ship to within 2,800 tons of a Yamato-class battleship.

Shinano Specifications

Displacement: 64,800 tons standard
Dimensions: Length 873ft / beam 119ft / draft 34ft
Maximum speed: 27kt
Range: 10,000nm at 18kt
Crew: 2,400

Armament and service modifications

Eight Type 89 mounts were carried, two pairs forward on each side of the flight deck, and another two pairs aft in a

similar arrangement. Each pair was provided with its own fire-control director. *Shinano* was well supplied with short-range antiaircraft protection, having 33 triple 25mm mounts. Twelve short-range rocket launchers were also fitted, arranged in sets of three in a similar fashion to the Type 89 guns. Two No. 21 radars were carried, one forward on the island and one on the aft portion of the island, providing 360-degree coverage. Two No. 13 radars were also carried, one on the mainmast and another on the forward port-side radio mast.

Taken in November 11, 1944, this is the only known photograph of *Shinano*. The ship has taken a starboard heel during a rudder test. The hull camouflage is just visible. (*Ships of the World* magazine)

Wartime service

Shinano had the shortest career of any Japanese carrier. The ship was commissioned on November 18, 1944. Ten days later, it departed Yokosuka and headed south to the port of Kure to complete fitting out. The ship was not fully ready for sea, with incomplete waterproofing and missing counter-flooding and damage-control pumps. This, combined with the inexperience of its crew, spelled disaster when it was struck by four submarine-launched torpedoes from *Archerfish* early on November 29. The damage was not considered to be fatal and its captain continued to steam on at 18 knots. Counter-flooding checked the initial flooding, but *Shinano*'s incomplete condition permitted the flooding to spread. All power was lost when the boiler rooms flooded and soon thereafter the unsinkable *Shinano* capsized with over 1,400 of its crew.

THE ESCORT CARRIERS

As discussed above, one component of the IJN's shadow carrier program was the use of passenger liners for conversion into carriers. The largest of these conversions became the Hiyo class and were considered so successful by the Japanese that they were typed as regular, not auxiliary carriers. Before the two largest liners were laid down, another five liners were subsidized by the IJN for possible conversion into carriers. Four of these were eventually converted into escort carriers, with the fifth being lost before it could be converted. In its place, a German liner was requisitioned.

The Japanese intended that these conversions would work with the Combined Fleet. Because these ships had a fairly low top speed (21–23 knots), and lacked catapults, they were never considered satisfactory for fleet work. As such, they were used primarily for aircraft ferrying operations and aircrew training. Later in the war, when the IJN realized it could no longer ignore commerce protection and created the Grand Escort Command, the remaining escort carriers were utilized in a convoy protection role.

Taiyo Class

Design and construction
In 1937, the IJN subsidized the Nitta Maru class of three passenger liners. All were structurally designed to be converted into auxiliary carriers. The last of the three ships, *Kasuga Maru*, was actually the first completed as a carrier. In 1940, *Kasuga Maru* was requisitioned while still under

Taiyo Class Construction				
Ship	Built at	Laid down	Launched	Completed
Taiyo	Nagasaki	1/6/40	9/19/40	9/5/41
Chuyo	Nagasaki	5/9/38	5/20/39	3/23/40
Unyo	Nagasaki	12/14/38	10/31/39	7/31/40

construction, and conversion to a carrier was begun. Work was not completed until September 1941 when the ship, now named *Taiyo*, was commissioned. Conversion of the first two ships, *Nitta Maru* and *Yawata Maru*, was not completed until November and May 1942, respectively, when they emerged as *Chuyo* and *Unyo*.

The conversions were fairly austere and took only six months. When completed, the ships emerged as flush-deck carriers with the navigation bridge placed forward under the flight deck. In typical Japanese fashion, exhaust gases were vented by means of a downward-sloped stack located amidships on the starboard side. To increase speed, the original diesel engines were replaced with turbines but the result was an unsatisfactory 21 knots. Two elevators serviced a single hangar. *Taiyo* had the capacity to operate 23 aircraft (with four more in reserve) and the other two ships could carry 30 aircraft.

Armament and service modifications

When completed, *Taiyo* was equipped with six of the older 4.7in antiaircraft guns in single mounts and four twin 25mm mounts. *Taiyo*'s armament was updated in 1943 with the fitting of additional 25mm guns, and in 1944 when the 4.7in guns were removed and replaced with two Type 89 mounts. By 1944, a total of 64 25mm guns were embarked.

The two sisters commissioned in 1942 were armed with the usual Type 89 mounts. *Chuyo* had 14 25mm guns when sunk in 1943; by 1944, *Unyo* had 64 25mm guns. All three ships were equipped with a No. 21 radar fitted on the forward starboard flight-deck edge.

Taiyo pictured with five A6M fighters on deck. The designed aircraft mix for these ships was 21 fighters and nine attack aircraft. However, when they were assigned to the Grand Escort Command, only B5Ns were carried. (*Ships of the World* magazine)

Kaiyo clearly showing its mercantile origins. Note the raised No. 21 radar on the flight deck and the port-side Type 94 fire-control director. (*Ships of the World* magazine)

Wartime service

All three ships were sunk by submarines. *Taiyo* was the first unit commissioned in September 1941 and actually conducted two aircraft ferry runs before the start of the war. In August 1942, it worked briefly with superbattleship *Yamato* during operations near Guadalcanal; this proved to be *Taiyo*'s only front-line appearance. It was torpedoed twice by submarines between September 1942 and September 1943, but survived. In December 1943, *Taiyo* was transferred from the Combined Fleet to the Grand Escort Command and assumed its new role of convoy escort. In this capacity, *Taiyo* was struck for the final time by one torpedo from submarine *Rasher* in August 1944. The ship's aviation fuel tanks exploded and the ship sank quickly with fewer than 100 survivors.

Chuyo was commissioned in November 1942. It conducted 13 deployments, carrying aircraft, supplies, and passengers. During the course of these missions from December 1942 until December 1943, *Chuyo* was torpedoed on three different occasions by US submarines. The third attack, by USS *Sailfish*, proved fatal. Though the ship's aviation fuel tanks did not

Taiyo Class Specifications

Displacement: 17,830 tons standard
Dimensions: Length 591ft / beam 74ft / draft 26ft
Maximum speed: 21kt
Range: 8,500nm at 18kt
Crew: 850 (*Taiyo* 747)

blow up, the quick sinking of the ship resulted in the death of 1,250 crew and passengers, including 20 US prisoners being transported to Japan.

Unyo was commissioned in May 1942 and followed a similar career pattern to its two sister ships. After many ferry runs, it was assigned to the Grand Escort Command in December 1943. *Unyo* was hit by three submarine torpedoes in January 1944 but survived. Hit again by two torpedoes launched from *Barb* in September 1944, *Unyo* sank.

Kaiyo

Design and construction
Kaiyo was the smallest of the escort carrier conversions. In 1938, construction began on passenger liners *Argentina Maru* and *Brazil Maru*. The *Brazil Maru* was sunk before conversion could be ordered, but in December 1942 the *Argentina Maru* entered the yards to begin conversion into a carrier. Work was completed in November 1943 and was nearly identical to that of the Chuyo class. Again, the original diesels were replaced with turbines, but speed was still only 23 knots. Two elevators serviced a single hangar. *Kaiyo* had the capacity to operate 24 aircraft (nominally 18 fighters and six bombers).

Kaiyo Construction				
Ship	Built at	Laid down	Launched	Completed
Kaiyo	Nagasaki	2/22/38	12/9/38	5/31/39

Armament and service modifications
Kaiyo emerged with four Type 89 mounts. Eight triple 25mm mounts were fitted, and another 20 single mounts were added later for a total of 44 guns. Eight depth charges were also carried for antisubmarine work. A No. 21 radar was added forward on the flight-deck edge.

Wartime service
Kaiyo joined the fleet in November 1943 and was used to ferry aircraft and escort convoys throughout 1944. In 1945, the ship became a training carrier in the Inland Sea and was used as a target for kamikaze pilot training. The ship suffered minor damage at Kure in March 1945. It was later sunk on July 24, 1945 by USN carrier aircraft.

Kaiyo Specifications

Displacement: 13,600 tons standard
Dimensions: Length 546ft / beam 72ft / draft 27ft
Maximum speed: 23kt
Range: 7,000nm at 18kt
Crew: 587

Shinyo

Design and construction

Like all the other IJN escort carrier conversions, *Shinyo* was originally built as a passenger liner. In this case, it was the German liner *Scharnhorst*, which was serving a Pacific route when the war began and was unable to return to Germany. The Japanese purchased the ship with the original intent of using it as a troop transport, but after Midway plans were begun to convert it into a carrier to train new aircrews. Conversion work began in September 1942. As the layout of the *Scharnhorst* was similar to Japanese liners of the Nitta Maru class, *Shinyo*'s conversion was similar to that of the Taiyo class with the primary differences being the addition of external bulges to increase stability and the retention of *Scharnhorst*'s original turbo-electric drive system. Two elevators were fitted to service the flush deck, single-hangar carrier, which could operate 27 aircraft with six more in reserve.

Shinyo in November 1943 during speed trials. Note the No. 21 radar in its raised position forward of the mainmast. (*Ships of the World* magazine)

Shinyo Construction				
Ship	Built at	Laid down	Launched	Completed
Shinyo	Bremen	unknown	1934	1935

Armament and service modifications

Shinyo was commissioned with four Type 89 mounts. A total of ten triple 25mm mounts were originally fitted; in July 1944 additional single mounts were added to bring the final total to 50 25mm guns. A No. 21 radar was added on the forward edge of the flight deck on the starboard side.

Wartime service

After joining the fleet in December 1943, *Shinyo* was assigned to the Grand Escort Command. From July 1944, the ship escorted convoys, providing air cover against submarine attack. In November 1944, while escorting a convoy bound for Singapore, *Shinyo* was struck by as many as four torpedoes from submarine *Spadefish*. The poorly protected aviation fuel tanks exploded causing a large fire that claimed the ship and most of its crew.

Shinyo Specifications

Displacement: 17,500 tons standard
Dimensions: Length 651ft / beam 84ft / draft 26ft
Maximum speed: 22kt
Range: 8,000nm at 18kt
Crew: 948

BATTLESHIPS

At the start of the Pacific War, the IJN included ten battleships, giving it the third largest battle line in the world after the American and British navies. These ships would soon be joined by two "superbattleships" of the Yamato class, easily the largest battleships ever built. Japanese prewar strategy still saw the battleship as the final arbiter of fleet action. Held in reserve for the expected decisive fleet engagement, Japanese battleships saw relatively little service during the early and middle parts of the war. Eventually, all were committed to stopping the USN's advance, and all but one were destroyed by war's end.

JAPANESE BATTLESHIP DEVELOPMENT

The launch of the British *Dreadnought* in 1905 had made all existing battleships obsolete. Not until January 1909 did the IJN begin construction of its first true dreadnought, *Settsu*. Its sister ship *Kawachi* was begun four months later. By 1910, the IJN planned to put its cherished 8-8 fleet plan into reality (the numbers referring to the desired numbers of battleships and battlecruisers required to produce a modern, homogeneous battle line). Given the economic aftermath of the war with Russia, such an immediate expansion was impossible, but approval was given for the construction of a single battleship and four battlecruisers. These four battlecruisers became the Kongo class, and the single battleship was the lead Fuso-class ship. In 1913, the Navy Ministry requested three new battleships, which also received funding in due course. The first to be launched was *Yamashiro*, the

The two ships of the Fuso class, seen here, were the IJN's first attempt to produce a battleship superior to that of any other nation. In the background is *Haruna*. (Naval History and Heritage Command)

sister ship of *Fuso*, and the other two were planned as improved versions of the Fuso class.

Navy Minister Tomosaburo Kato requested funding for four more battleships in 1915, which was refused, but in 1916, funding was granted for one battleship and two battlecruisers. While the IJN was having problems reaching its cherished 8-8 goal, the American Congress passed a navy bill in 1916 which included massive funding for capital ships. In response, the Japanese Diet (parliament) passed an authorization in 1917 for three additional battleships, followed in 1918 by approval for two additional battlecruisers. The IJN finally seemed to be on the verge of realizing its 8-8 fleet.

The battleship approved in 1916 became *Nagato*, which was to carry 16in guns, larger than any gun then in service in any other navy. The 1917 battleship authorizations became *Nagato*'s sister ship *Mutsu*, and the even larger *Kaga* and *Tosa*. These were 38,500-ton ships, mounting ten 16in guns, with more armor and a higher speed than the Nagato class. Laid down in 1920, both would later fall victim to the Washington Naval Treaty.

Kongo's appearance upon completion in 1912. Its World War I origins are clearly shown by its very small bridge and two large tripod masts. When first completed, the ship had three smokestacks and 3in guns fitted atop the main armament. (*Ships of the World* magazine)

Hyuga being launched on January 27, 1917. Despite its best efforts, the IJN remained in a position of numerical battleship inferiority to the US and Royal Navies. (Naval History and Heritage Command)

Kaga gained a reprieve from the scrapyard when it was converted into a carrier in 1923. *Tosa* was turned over to the Gunnery School in June 1924 for use as a target, and was sunk in February 1925, but not before it rendered invaluable data for reconstruction of existing ships and for design of future battleships. The 1916 battlecruisers were named *Amagi* and *Akagi*. These were to be joined by *Atago* and *Takao*; all were 40,000-ton designs carrying ten 16in guns, and possessing a top speed of 30 knots. None were destined to join the battle fleet: *Amagi* was damaged in an earthquake while under construction and was scrapped; *Akagi* survived to be converted into an aircraft carrier; and the final two were canceled.

In 1919 the Americans had announced further plans for capital ship construction. Without a Japanese response, American naval dominance was assured. To keep pace, the IJN planned another four battlecruisers and four battleships, but this was clearly beyond the means of the Japanese economy. Japan's inability to compete successfully with the US in a battleship construction race was the driving force behind the Japanese government's decision in 1922 to participate in the Washington Naval Conference (see

In the first encounter between American carrier airpower and the IJN's superbattleships, the Japanese came off a poor second. Here *Musashi* is shown under intense torpedo and bomb attack on October 24, 1944, during the Battle of Leyte Gulf. By 1944, the US Navy could sink even the most heavily armored ship by air attack, an eventuality totally unforeseen when the Yamato-class superbattleships were designed in the late 1930s. (Naval History and Heritage Command)

Chapter 1). The treaty dashed Japanese hopes of ever achieving the sacred 8-8 fleet, or of maintaining the IJN at the crucial 70 percent of USN strength.

Throughout the interwar period, the Japanese continually looked for ways to compensate for their position of numerical inferiority against the USN. The preferred method was to create a qualitative superiority to swing the balance in its favor. With the collapse of the Washington Naval Treaty, the IJN was given a new chance to create a qualitative edge. The Japanese announced in December 1934 that they would renounce the treaty (technically in force until 31 December 1936) and were already making plans to turn the tables dramatically on the USN. Accordingly, the Naval General Staff had approved secret plans to build four superbattleships. These were equipped with 18in guns and sufficient armor to withstand 18in shellfire. Authorization of the first two ships, *Yamato* and *Musashi*, was given in 1936, and the final two superbattleships, later canceled, were approved in September 1939.

BATTLESHIP WEAPONS

Eight of the 12 Pacific War Japanese battleships carried 14in main guns. This gun was based on a British Vickers design. The 16.1in guns fitted aboard the Nagato class were of Japanese design. The heaviest guns ever fitted aboard a warship were the 18.1in guns used on the Yamato class. This weapon was designed in 1939 and was called the 40cm (or 16in) Type 94 gun by the Japanese for security reasons.

Secondary batteries were intended principally to defeat destroyer attack. The 6in secondary guns for the Kongo and Fuso classes were based on Vickers designs. These 72-ton guns could fire four to five rounds per minute.

Japanese Battleship Weapons	
Type	Maximum range
Main guns	
14in/45 41st Year Type 1908	38,770yd
16.1in/45 3rd Year Type (1914	42,00yd
18.1in/45 Type 94	45,960yd at 45-degree elevation
Secondary guns	
6in/50 41st Year Type (1908)	22,970yd at 45-degree elevation
5.51in/50 3rd Year Type (1914	21,600yd at 35-degree elevation
6.1in/60 3rd Year Type (1914)	29,960yd at 45-degree elevation

These were replaced by the Japanese-designed 5.5in gun on the Ise and Nagato classes with a lesser weight of 36 tons and a rate of fire of six rounds per minute. The Yamato class returned to a 6in-size gun fitted in triple mounts. These were originally mounted on Mogami-class cruisers, but became excess when this class was up-gunned to 8in guns. The turrets weighed 177 tons, and possessed a rate of fire of 5 rounds per minute.

Since both navies used the same British equipment suppliers, Japanese battleship fire control was developed initially in conjunction with the RN.

The rear 16in gun turrets on *Mutsu*. The Japanese were the first to put a 16in gun into service. Each turret weighed just over 1,000 tons. Firing cycle at low elevation was 21.5 seconds. (Naval History and Heritage Command)

An overhead view of the Type 89 5in antiaircraft gun. This twin mount was fitted on all Japanese battleships of the Pacific War, but proved mediocre in service. It was inferior to its US Navy counterpart, the 5in/38 dual purpose gun. (*Ships of the World* magazine)

During World War I, the IJN attempted to develop its own fire-control instruments, but, during the interwar years, it gradually fell behind the US and Royal Navies. In 1926, the Japanese obtained sophisticated fire-control tables for *Kongo* from the British. These provided the basis for the first fire-control tables manufactured in Japan, and by the 1930s, the IJN had developed its own fire-control system that could measure a target out to 43,740 yards. However, this system was heavy, and relied on manual instead of automatic inputs. On the other hand, Japanese fire-control optics were very good and crews were well trained in their use. The desire to get fire-control optics as high as possible, thus extending their range, resulted in larger and taller "pagoda" towers on battleships.

Overall, the quality of Japanese battleship gunnery was mediocre during the war. Japanese battleships were presented with only a handful of opportunities to use their main guns. On March 1, 1942, *Hiei* and *Kirishima* engaged a US destroyer south of Java with 297 rounds of 14in fire, scoring a single hit. During the Guadalcanal campaign Japanese battleships participated in two night surface actions. In the first, *Hiei* and *Kirishima* gained several 14in hits against targets at point-blank range, and in the second *Kirishima* engaged American battleships and scored only a single hit at close range with its 14in guns. During the Battle of Leyte Gulf, Japanese battleship gunnery was worse than undistinguished. At Surigao Strait, *Yamashiro* scored no main battery hits in another night action. Most condemning was the gunnery of four Japanese battleships that surprised a force of six slow American escort carriers off the island of Samar. In an action of over two hours, only one of the escort carriers was sunk. Of the seven American destroyers and destroyer escorts present, only three were sunk. The confused nature of the action precludes a definitive accounting for the number of hits scored by Japanese battleships, but the mere survival of the bulk of the American force speaks volumes. During the war, the state

The standard light antiaircraft weapon used aboard IJN warships during the Pacific War was the Type 96 25mm gun. The most prevalent version aboard battleships was the triple mount, shown here. It was a dismal failure and proved unable to counter growing American airpower. (Naval History and Heritage Command)

of Japanese fire control fell farther behind the USN after the Americans developed radar-controlled gunnery. Throughout the entire war, Japanese battleships never engaged in the type of long-range gunnery duel for which they were designed.

Antiaircraft protection was increasingly important as the war went on. Of the 11 battleships lost during the war, six were sunk solely or primarily by American aircraft. Long-range antiaircraft protection was provided by the 5in Type 89 gun for which the specifications are provided in the previous chapter. The weapon itself was respectable, but its fire control was inadequate and doctrine for its use flawed. Japanese crews were trained to use barrage fire at the estimated height of the attacking aircraft. Against carrier aircraft that did not maintain a constant course and height, this was virtually useless. Additionally, the IJN did not develop a proximity fuse during the war, further reducing the effectiveness of its 5in weapons. In desperation, the Japanese developed incendiary shrapnel rounds for 14, 16, and 18.1in guns to improve long-range antiaircraft protection. These operated with fuses set to explode a number of incendiary tubes at pre-designated altitudes. The effect was spectacular, but proved ineffective in service.

The standard light antiaircraft gun throughout the war was the Type 96 25mm gun, which is also described in the previous chapter. This weapon was ineffective in its envisioned role – despite a growing profusion of these weapons, Japanese battleships proved vulnerable to air attack, while losses of attacking American aircraft were low. The lack of an intermediate-range gun, like the US Navy 40mm Bofors, was to cost the Japanese dearly.

BATTLESHIP RADAR

The IJN lagged far behind the USN in the development and use of radar. While radar was an instrumental part of USN air defense and surface gunnery doctrine, the IJN was slow to realize its potential and was handicapped by inferior equipment. The first set was the No. 21 air- and surface-search radar, of which the large mattress-like antenna was placed on the top of battleship towers. When the dedicated air-search radar, the No. 13, was introduced in 1943, because of its long ladder-like antenna it was mounted in pairs on the mainmast of most Japanese battleships. On some occasions, the performance of this radar was good. At the Battle of Leyte Gulf, the No. 13 radars on *Hyuga* and *Ise* detected groups of aircraft at 105 and 125 miles, respectively.

The final type of radar found aboard IJN ships was the No. 22 Modification 4M radar designed for surface search. This featured a twin-horn antenna design – one for transmitting and one for receiving. On battleships, these instruments were mounted in pairs on both sides of the bridge or on the foremast. In September 1944, a fire-control version of the radar was developed and designated Modification 4S. For surface targets, the No. 22 (4) could theoretically detect a battleship target at 38,276 yards, a cruiser-sized ship at 21,872 yards, and a destroyer-sized target at 18,591 yards. The range error was 820–1,640ft and the bearing error up to three degrees. Though the Japanese heavily practiced the use of radar-controlled gunnery in 1944, in service it proved of little value because the accuracy of the No. 22 was inadequate for gunnery control.

THE BATTLESHIP CLASSES

Kongo Class

Design and construction
After the launching of the world's first class of battlecruiser in 1907, the Royal Navy's *Invincible*, the IJN was determined to build a superior ship. After much work, the Japanese came up with an 18,725-ton design. However, in the meantime, the British had already laid down a larger battlecruiser, the 26,270-ton *Lion*. The Japanese decided to scrap their design and seek British assistance and expertise. Accordingly, in 1910, an order was placed with the Vickers firm for a 27,000-ton improved Lion design to be built at the Vickers shipyard in Barrow-in Furness.

The first ship of the class, *Kongo*, was laid down in 1911 and entered service in 1913. *Kongo* was the last major IJN ship built outside Japan. After completion, it arrived in home waters in November 1913. Three more ships were completed to the same design. *Hiei* was built using a large number of parts imported from Britain and *Haruna* was built from all-Japanese parts.

Kongo Class Construction				
Ship	Built at	Laid down	Launched	Completed
Kongo	Barrow by Vickers Armstrong	1/11/11	5/18/12	8/16/13
Hiei	Yokosuka Navy Yard	11/4/11	11/21/12	8/4/14
Haruna	Kobe by Kawasaki	3/16/12	12/14/13	4/19/15
Kirishima	Nagasaki by Mitsubishi	3/17/12	12/1/13	4/19/15

Kongo as it appeared after its first modernization. The ship's appearance has been altered with the provision of a large tower structure and the deletion of one of the tripod masts. The three smokestacks have been retained; note the large caps on the forward stack. Its primary armament remains unaltered. (*Ships of the World* magazine)

The final ship of the class, *Kirishima*, was also of all-Japanese construction. The Kongo class was built as a battlecruiser class, and as such, possessed relatively light protection. Even after extensive modernization, the weakness of the class remained its inadequate protection. As built, the entire weight of armor on the ship was 6,500 tons, or some 25 percent of the standard displacement. The main belt was 8in at the waterline and 6in above it. The main belt tapered to 3in forward, and aft and below the main waterline belt was another 3in. The barbettes had 10in of Vickers cemented armor, and the turret faces 9in. The turret roofs had a mere 3in; overhead protection for the remainder of the ship was limited to a 2in armored deck.

The Kongo class was the fastest of the IJN's modern dreadnoughts. The maximum speed of 27.5 knots was provided by four shafts powered by Parsons turbines from steam generated by 36 Yarrow boilers. The original 36 boilers were coal-fired with oil sprayers. Three smokestacks were required to service the eight boiler rooms.

Armament

The Kongo class was originally planned to mount the same 12in guns as contemporary British battlecruisers. However, the British had been testing a 13.5in gun that was planned for *Lion*. When the Japanese learned of this, they decided to upgrade *Kongo*'s main armament. In fact, anticipating an American move to a 14in gun, the Japanese worked with the British to develop such a weapon and placed it on *Kongo*.

The four main turrets on *Kongo* were arranged two forward, one amidships, and one astern. All had traverse to both sides, giving *Kongo* a powerful broadside of eight 14in guns. When completed, this arrangement made it the most powerful ship afloat.

Secondary armament was 16 6in guns arranged eight per side in casemates. This was more than the usual number, and reflected the Japanese concern for destroyer torpedo attacks. When completed, the class was fitted with 3in pedestal-mounted single guns – 16 in *Kongo* and eight in the remainder of the class. A peculiar Japanese feature was a heavy armament of torpedo tubes on their capital ships. Eight 21in submerged torpedo tubes were installed, making this the heaviest torpedo armament of any capital ship of its day.

Service modifications

The Kongo class had the longest life of any Japanese dreadnought. They began as battlecruisers, but ended their careers as fast battleships. During the course of their career, each ship was given two major modernizations. The first modernization took place between 1927 and 1932, *Haruna* being the first unit to undergo work and *Hiei* the last. In order to address the ships' principal weakness, another 3,811 tons of armor were added to improve horizontal protection over the magazine and machinery spaces. Antitorpedo defenses were enhanced, with the addition of bulges that increased the beam to over 95ft. The armament was left unaltered except for the removal of four torpedo tubes. However, the maximum elevation of the main armament was increased to 43 degrees, thus increasing its range. The propulsive system was modernized by the removal of the 36 original boilers and the fitting of ten (*Haruna*) or 16 (*Kongo* and *Kirishima*) newer, but still mixed-firing boilers. This allowed the forward stack to be removed. Provisions were made to embark three floatplanes for spotting of gunnery, but no catapult was fitted.

Hiei before 1929, when it began its conversion into a training ship, as required by the London Naval Treaty. (Yamato Museum)

Hiei was a special case. Between 1929 and 1932, *Hiei* was demilitarized to meet the provisions of the London Naval Treaty by having its main armor belt removed and its top speed reduced to 18 knots by the removal of 25 of the original boilers. Its after 14in turret was removed and later all 6in secondary guns were also deleted.

Another, more radical, modernization for the entire class was begun in 1933 with *Haruna*. After this work, the ships were typed as battleships. Protection was further increased to a total of 4.75in of horizontal armor. Torpedo protection for the machinery spaces was also increased. The existing machinery was entirely replaced and 11 oil-fired Kanpon boilers and new turbines increased power to 136,000 shaft horsepower (shp) with the resulting maximum speed of between 29.7 and 30.5 knots. The stern was rebuilt and made 25ft longer, which also helped to increase speed. The appearance of the class was altered, with a heavy pagoda tower being fitted. Armament was adjusted with the deletion of two 6in guns and the final four torpedo tubes. Antiaircraft armament was increased with the addition of four Type 89 twin 5in guns, and by 1936, of ten twin 25mm mounts. A catapult was added abaft the No. 3 turret to launch the three floatplanes.

The top profile shows *Hiei* in December 1941, as it appeared during the Pearl Harbor raid. Its World War I ancestry can clearly be seen from its hull form, the casemate secondary armament, and the amidships 14in turret. The second profile shows *Kongo* as it appeared in October 1944 in its late-war configuration during the Battle of Leyte Gulf. Note the different tower style as opposed to *Hiei* and the addition of radar and numerous triple 25mm gun mounts.

The last of the four ships to be modernized was *Hiei*. Work on it was completed in 1940 to the same configuration mentioned, with the difference that its bridge was built in a configuration similar to the new Yamato class.

During the war, modifications to the class centered on its antiaircraft and radar fit. *Hiei* and *Kirishima* were both lost before any major additions were made. *Kongo* was the first ship in its class to be equipped with radar when it received a No. 21 on its foretop rangefinder in August 1942. In early 1943, after the loss of *Hiei* and *Kirishima*, additional concrete protection was added in the area of the steering gear. Also at this time, two triple 25mm mounts were added, and two 6in guns removed. In January 1944, four more 6in guns and two twin 25mm mounts were removed and the antiaircraft fit further strengthened with the addition of two 5in Type 89 mounts and four triple 25mm mounts. In June 1944, No. 22 and 13 sets were fitted. The total of antiaircraft guns was brought up to over 100 with the addition of 13 triple and 40 single 25mm guns. In August, another 18 single 25mm guns were fitted in Singapore – by this time, only eight of the 6in guns remained.

Haruna's wartime modifications were similar. In October 1942, a No. 21 radar was installed. During a February–March 1943 overhaul, a No. 22 set was installed, six 6in guns removed, and additional 25mm guns fitted. As on *Kongo*, concrete protection was added in the vicinity of the steering gear. In June 1944 a No. 13 radar and more 25mm guns were installed. Before it sortied to participate in the Battle of Leyte Gulf, the total antiaircraft fit was six dual Type 89 5in guns and 122 25mm guns (30 triple, two double, and 28 single).

Hiei, seen after it had been demilitarized. Its after 14in turret has been removed. Also evident is its missing belt armor. The reduced size of the forward stack is due to the reduced number of boilers. At this time it retains its secondary armament, but this was later also removed. (Naval History and Heritage Command)

Kongo Class Specifications (following 1933–34 modernization)

Displacement: 32,056 tons standard; 36,601 full load
Dimensions: Length 739ft / beam 95ft / draft 32ft
Maximum speed: 30kt
Range: 10,000nm at 18kt
Crew: 1,221; approximately 1,500 in 1944

Kongo in 1936, in the configuration in which it would go to war. The tower has been further augmented and the mainmast reduced. The forward stack was removed in its first modernization. Despite two extensive modernizations, it remained comparatively weakly armored. (*Ships of the World* magazine)

Wartime service

At the beginning of the war, *Kongo* and *Haruna* were assigned to cover the invasions of Malaya and the Philippines. The same two ships would later provide distant cover for the Dutch East Indies invasion in January 1942. By March 1942, they joined *Hiei* and *Kirishima*, which had spent the entire war escorting the carrier fleet, to conduct a massive raid into the Indian Ocean with the IJN's carrier force. This was the only time in the entire war that all four Kongos operated together. For the Midway operation, *Kongo* and *Hiei* were assigned to the Midway invasion force, while *Kirishima* and *Haruna* escorted the carriers. In this role, *Haruna* was slightly damaged.

All four Kongo-class ships were active in the struggle for Guadalcanal, beginning in August 1942. *Kirishima* and *Hiei* participated in the carrier Battle of the Eastern Solomons. On October 13, *Kongo* and *Haruna* conducted the most successful Japanese battleship action of the war. Together, they plastered Henderson Field with almost 900 14in rounds, destroying over 40 aircraft. Later in October, all four participated in the Battle of Santa Cruz: *Kongo* and *Kirishima* were both attacked by carrier aircraft but were undamaged.

In November, *Kirishima* and *Hiei* were tasked to repeat the bombardment of Henderson Field as part of an operation to move a major convoy to Guadalcanal. The USN committed a cruiser–destroyer force to prevent the bombardment. Early on November 13, a vicious night battle developed with the intercepting American force. *Kirishima* scored hits on the cruisers *San Francisco* and *Helena* and against a destroyer and in return was hit by a single 8in shell. *Hiei* took the brunt of American attention. It was struck by some 28–38 8in shells from the cruisers *San Francisco* and

Portland, and some 70–75 5in shells. In return, *Hiei* crippled *San Francisco* and damaged the cruiser *Atlanta* and a destroyer. Despite the topside devastation on *Hiei*, it suffered little underwater damage. However, two 8in shells flooded its steering compartment, which prevented it from departing the area. In the morning, *Hiei* became the target of some 70 aircraft sorties from the undamaged airfield on Guadalcanal as it circled at 5 knots. By evening, it was scuttled after being hit by several bombs and as many as four torpedoes.

Kirishima led another Japanese attempt to deliver a battleship bombardment of Henderson Field. Early on November 15, *Kirishima* and its escorts entered Ironbottom Sound, but this time they were intercepted by two modern American battleships, *Washington* and *South Dakota*. In the first battleship clash of the Pacific War, the Japanese came off a distant second. *South Dakota* suffered extensive topside damage from Japanese gunfire, but *Washington* sank *Kirishima* with 16in gunfire.

Wartime photography of Japanese battleships is rare. This shot shows *Hiei* in home waters in July 1942. Note the aerial recognition flags placed atop Nos. 2 and 4 turrets, and that the rangefinder atop its tower has been painted white. (Naval History and Heritage Command)

Kirishima in 1939 in the configuration in which it would go to war. The speed of the Kongo class made them the Japanese battleships best suited to perform carrier escort duties, and they spent much of the war in this capacity. (*Ships of the World* magazine)

The next combat action for the two remaining Kongo-class ships did not occur until June 1944, during the Battle of the Philippine Sea. Both were assigned to the Vanguard Force escorting Carrier Division 3. *Haruna* was hit aft by four bombs; *Kongo* was undamaged. At the Battle of Leyte Gulf in October, *Kongo* was damaged by near misses by dive-bombers. *Haruna* suffered only minor damage from destroyer gunfire.

While returning to Japan after the battle, *Kongo* was attacked by the submarine *Sealion II* on November 21, 1944. The Americans scored two torpedo hits, one forward and one under the second stack on the port side. Within two and a half hours, *Kongo* had capsized due to uncontrolled progressive flooding; 1,250 crewmen were lost and only 237 survived. *Kongo* was the only Japanese battleship lost to submarine attack during the war. *Haruna* returned to Japan in December, where it was repaired and moved to Kure. In carrier raids on March 19 and July 24, 1945, *Haruna* suffered minor damage from single bomb hits. *Haruna*'s end came on July 28, 1945 when it came under concerted attack by carrier aircraft and US Army Air Force bombers. A total of eight more bombs sank it in shallow water. It was scrapped in place between 1946 and 1948.

This scene depicts the clash between *Kirishima* and battleship USS *Washington* during the Second Naval Battle of Guadalcanal. *Washington* targeted *Kirishima* from the point-blank range of 8,400 yards and from that range sent 75 16in projectiles and 107 5in rounds toward *Kirishima*. Of the 75 main rounds fired, nine hit; additionally, over 40 5in rounds scored hits. *Kirishima* tried to fight back, but its nearest shell was 200 yards off *Washington*'s port quarter.

Fuso Class

Design and construction

The same bill that authorized the construction of the four Kongo-class ships also authorized the construction of a new class of battleship designed to work in conjunction with the battlecruisers. As usual, the Japanese tried to better the foreign competition. To do this, *Fuso* mounted 12 14in guns, all in twin gun centerline turrets. This was a heavier broadside than the ten guns of the American New York class, and *Fuso* also possessed a higher speed. When completed, *Fuso* was the largest and most powerfully armed battleship in the world.

The ship's armor accounted for some 29 percent of the ship's design displacement, for a total of 8,588 tons. This was sufficient to provide a 12in waterline main belt, which was tapered down to 6in below the waterline to cover the magazines and machinery. The belt tapered out to 4in at its extreme ends. Horizontal protection was light with a maximum of only 2in. The turrets were more heavily armored than those on *Kongo*, with 12in of face armor – the barbettes were fitted with 8in, and the conning tower was provided with a maximum of 14in.

When first constructed, *Fuso* employed a coal/oil mixed firing system with its 24 boilers. These powered a steam turbine system to drive four main shafts with 40,000shp, which was enough to drive the ship at 23 knots.

Fuso in 1933, with its trademark pagoda tower, single stack, and large after control tower. *Fuso* can most easily be distinguished from its sister ship *Yamashiro* by the forward-pointing position of No. 3 turret. (Yamato Museum)

Fuso Class Construction				
Ship	Built at	Laid down	Launched	Completed
Fuso	Kure Navy Yard	3/11/12	3/28/14	11/8/15
Yamashiro	Yokosuka Navy Yard	11/20/13	11/3/15	3/31/17

Armament

The 14in armament of the Fuso class was increased 50 percent over that of the Kongo class. Though 12 14in guns were included in the design, giving the Fuso class a superior main armament to its American and British contemporaries, the location of the main armament was not ideal. Two of the six dual 14in turrets were mounted amidships on the centerline, and both had restricted arcs of fire. The retention of midship turrets also affected the ship's internal layout.

As with the Kongo class, *Fuso* mounted a strong secondary armament of 16 6in guns, all fitted in casemates, eight per side. Antiaircraft armament was originally limited to four 3in guns. The Japanese practice of fitting torpedoes to their capital ships continued on *Fuso*. It was fitted with six submerged 21in torpedo tubes.

Service modifications

In the 1930s, both ships underwent extensive modernization that would dramatically change their appearance. *Fuso* was the first to enter the yards from April 1930 to May 1933. During this process, armor protection was increased and the total weight of armor was raised to 12,199 tons or some 42 percent of the ship's total displacement. Improvements focused on improving horizontal protection, which was brought up to a maximum of 4in. Attempts were made to increase protection from torpedo attack by providing two blisters covering from the top of the belt down to the bottom of the hull. The lower blister increased the beam to a maximum of 127ft.

A major part of the modernization was the complete replacement of the main machinery. The original 24 boilers were replaced with six Kanpon oil-

Yamashiro, photographed in Chinese waters following its 1930–35 modernization. (Naval History and Heritage Command)

Pictured are the two aft main battery turrets on a Fuso-class battleship. These are Type 41 14in/45cal guns, the standard Japanese battleship main gun. It was based on a Vickers design with a firing cycle of 30–40 seconds at maximum elevation. (*Ships of the World* magazine)

fired boilers, and new Kanpon 75,000shp turbines were fitted. This new machinery, nearly twice as powerful as the original equipment, and the addition of 25ft to the stern part of the hull, resulted in an increased maximum speed of almost 25 knots.

The modernization resulted in changes to the ships' armament. The 12 14in guns were retained, but their maximum elevation was increased to 43 degrees. Two of the 6in casemate guns were removed, and the elevation of the remainder increased to 30 degrees. The antiaircraft armament was heavily reinforced, with the original 3in guns being removed and four twin Type 89 5in guns added. Short-range antiaircraft protection was provided by eight 25mm twin mounts. During the modernization, the torpedo tubes were removed.

At the conclusion of the modernization, both ships emerged with a drastically altered appearance. The salient feature of the class became the tall pagoda tower that replaced the earlier tripod mast. The aft control tower was also increased in height. The reduction in the number of boilers meant one of the stacks was removed. Both ships were fitted with aircraft handling facilities for three aircraft. *Yamashiro*'s modernization was begun in December 1930 and completed in March 1935. The work was similar to that performed on *Fuso*, but with some external differences. Aside from a difference in catapult placement, the pagoda tower on *Yamashiro* was of a heavier appearance and extended farther aft. This required that the stowed position of No. 3 turret was in the aft position, not forward as on *Fuso*.

In August 1942, after Midway, consideration was given to converting the Fuso class into hybrid battleship-carriers. Plans were begun and work was scheduled to begin in June 1943, but the scheme was canceled.

As second-line units, relatively little effort was expended during the war to increase the ships' combat capabilities. In July 1943, *Fuso* received 21 additional 25mm antiaircraft guns (17 single mounts and two twin mounts) to bring its total 25mm fit to 37. Also during this time, it received a No. 21 radar. In August 1944, *Fuso* received its final modifications, when it was fitted with another eight triple, six twin, and 17 single 25mm guns. Added to another five single guns on movable mounts, this brought its total 25mm gun fit to 95. The ship also received ten 13mm machine guns, two No. 13 (located on its stack) and two No. 22 radars. *Yamashiro*'s wartime modifications were similar to Fuso's. In July 1943, it received a No. 21 radar. In July 1944, another 66 25mm guns (eight triple, nine twin, 24 single) were added, together with 16 13.2mm machine guns. *Yamashiro* also received two No. 13 and two No. 22 sets.

Wartime service

At the start of the war, *Fuso* and *Yamashiro* were in home waters with most of the IJN's other battleships, usually at the Combined Fleet's anchorage at Hashirajima in Hiroshima Bay. On May 29, 1942, the two ships departed Hashirajima to take part in the Midway operation. Deployed as part of the distant screen for the invasion, they returned to Japan having seen no action. Not until August 1943 did the ships leave home waters again. *Fuso* was used to carry troops and supplies to Truk in the Central Pacific. It remained attached to the Combined Fleet, and in May 1944 took part in the abortive attempt to reinforce Biak Island. In July 1944, *Fuso* returned to Japan, being attacked by an American submarine en route without being damaged.

Yamashiro was much less active, being designated as a midshipman training ship in September 1943. After refit in Japan, *Fuso* and *Yamashiro* were assigned to active service in September 1944.

In October 1944, both ships arrived at Lingga Anchorage, south of Singapore to participate in Operation *Sho-go* (Victory). Because of their slow speed, *Fuso* and *Yamashiro* were detached from the main body of the First Striking Force and formed into Force "C" to enter Leyte Gulf from the south. The fleet departed Lingga on October 20 and headed to Leyte. On October 24, *Fuso* was attacked by carrier aircraft in the Sulu Sea and suffered damage from a bomb hit on its

Fuso Class Specifications (following 1935 modernization)

Displacement: 34,700 tons standard; 39,154 full load
Dimensions: Length 698ft / beam 100.5ft / draft 31.75ft
Maximum speed: 24.75kt
Range: 8,000nm at 14kt
Crew: 1,400 (1935); this was probably up to 1,800 or 1,900 in 1944

stern that destroyed its aircraft and catapult. To block the entry of Force "C" into Leyte Gulf, the Americans deployed the surface strength of the Seventh Fleet, centered on six battleships. Entering Surigao Strait in the early morning hours of October 25, the two battleships came under torpedo attack by PT boats and destroyers. *Fuso* was hit at 0309hrs by one or two torpedoes. By 0338hrs, the resulting fire had spread to the ship's magazines, and at 0345hrs it blew up and split into two sections; there were no survivors.

The same torpedo attacks that proved deadly to *Fuso* also damaged *Yamashiro* at 0321hrs when a single torpedo hit the ship on its port quarter, which forced two magazines to be flooded, and the subsequent loss of two main gun turrets. At 0331hrs, another torpedo hit amidships and slowed the ship to 5 knots. *Yamashiro* worked back up to 15 knots and continued up the strait, only to come under concentrated cruiser and battleship gunfire. The target of hundreds of shells, *Yamashiro* was hit an untold number of times. It returned fire, but its only success was possibly contributing to the damage of a single American destroyer. After a lull in the American barrage, *Yamashiro* headed south back down the strait. At 0409hrs, it was hit by two more destroyer-launched torpedoes, which finally resulted in the ship capsizing at 0419hrs. Of the crew of approximately 1,400, only three were rescued.

These were iconic Japanese battleships, with their towering pagoda-style bridge structures. The top profile is of *Yamashiro* as it appeared in June 1942 during the Battle of Midway. The ship has six 14in twin turrets, indicative of its design dating from World War I. The second profile is of *Fuso* as it appeared in October 1944 in its late-war configuration. Note the different appearance from its sister ship. *Fuso*'s pagoda is less massive and its No. 3 turret is stowed in the forward position.

Ise Class

Design and construction

The two ships of this class were approved in late 1912, but work was not started on them until 1915. Originally it was planned that these were to be an improved version of the Fuso class. However, when completed, so many improvements had been made that they were considered a separate class. Dimensionally, the Ise class was similar to the Fuso class, with an identical beam and an extra 10ft in length. The main difference was the positioning of the main armament. The Ise class retained a battery of 12 14in guns, but the two center turrets were positioned closer together, allowing a wider arc of fire. This also allowed the 24 coal-fired Kanpon boilers with supplementary oil sprayers to be repositioned for better efficiency – the increased output of the main machinery resulted in 45,000shp and a top speed of 23.5 knots.

Ise Class Construction				
Ship	Built at	Laid down	Launched	Completed
Ise	Kobe by Kawasaki	5/10/15	11/12/16	12/15/17
Hyuga	Nagasaki by Mitsubishi	5/6/15	1/27/17	4/30/18

Protection was generally similar to the Fuso class, but was still somewhat below that of foreign designs. The main belt had a maximum of 12in of armor, as did the conning tower and the face of the main turrets. Turret barbette armor was increased to 12in and deck armor remained at an inadequate 2in. The total weight of armor, 9,680 tons, accounted for 30 percent of the total displacement.

Ise pictured in Chinese waters in May 1939. This is the configuration in which it went to war, and in which it remained until converted to a carrier-battleship in 1943. (Naval History and Heritage Command)

Armament

Ise and *Hyuga* were fitted with 12 14in guns of the same type that *Fuso* had. As on *Fuso*, the main battery was arranged in six turrets, though the arrangement was improved. The secondary armament was increased to 20 guns, 18 arranged in casement and two fitted abreast the forward stack. However, the gun selected was different, the Japanese-designed 5.5in. Provisions were also made for 16 3in guns to be fitted on the top of the main turrets, but it is unclear if these were ever fitted. Antiaircraft protection was limited to four 3in guns, and, as was typical for Japanese capital ships, six 21in submerged torpedo tubes were also fitted.

Service modifications

The Ise class was the most modified of any IJN battleship. They began service during World War I as "superdreadnoughts" and ended their careers in World War II as the world's only battleship-carriers.

Both ships underwent a major reconstruction at Kure before the war. *Hyuga* was the first between November 1934 and September 1936, followed by *Ise* from August 1935 to March 1937. This reconstruction generally paralleled that of the Fuso class. The hull was lengthened by 25ft and completely new machinery was installed. Eight oil-fired boilers replaced the combination coal/oil fired boilers, and with new turbines, power almost doubled to 80,000shp, which resulted in a new top speed of 25.3 knots. The smaller number of boilers allowed the forward stack to be removed, leaving one stack amidships.

Ise in 1943, immediately after conversion into the world's first carrier-battleship. The conversion, while extensive, was comparatively simple. Nos. 5 and 6 turrets were removed, and were replaced by a flight deck that overhung the stern. The starboard catapult can be seen – its interference with the arc of fire of Nos. 3 and 4 turrets is obvious. All of the secondary 5.5in guns have been removed. The four starboard Type 89 5in guns can be seen, but many of the ship's 25mm guns have yet to be fitted. (*Ships of the World* magazine)

The main armament was left unaltered, but the maximum elevation was increased to 33 degrees. This was later increased for Nos. 1–4 turrets to 43 degrees. Four of the 5.5in guns were removed, including the two mounted near the forward stack. The antiaircraft suite was significantly upgraded, the 3in guns were removed and four twin Type 89 guns were fitted, and short-range antiaircraft coverage was provided by ten twin 25mm guns. The torpedo tubes were removed.

Armor enhancements included augmenting horizontal protection over magazine and machinery spaces to 4.7in and fitting a bulge for protection against torpedo attack. This bulge increased the beam by over 17ft. It incorporated separate compartmentation and an inch of steel at the ship's side. Internal arrangements to defeat torpedo attack included two longitudinal bulkheads and the two fuel bunkers placed outboard to absorb shock. Other modifications included the construction of a large pagoda superstructure. A catapult was added on the starboard side of the quarterdeck and up to three floatplanes could be carried.

The most dramatic modification of any Japanese battleship began in 1943. After heavy carrier losses in the first year of the war, the IJN searched for ways to get additional aircraft to sea quickly. One idea was to create hybrid carrier-battleships out of the two Ise-class battleships. This idea was approved and *Hyuga* was converted from May to November 1943 at Sasebo

The top profile shows *Ise* in its June 1942 configuration during the Battle of Midway. Note the placement of the amidships 14in gun turrets which are grouped together, unlike on the previous Fuso class. The lower profile depicts *Hyuga* as it appeared in October 1944 during the Battle of Leyte Gulf as a converted battleship-carrier. A flight deck has replaced the Nos. 5 and 6 turrets, and extends from the aft control station to over the stern. The ship carries a total of 31 triple 25mm mounts.

Navy Yard and *Ise* from February to August 1943 at Kure Navy Yard. The two after 14in turrets were removed and a 230ft-long flight deck was installed from the forward end of the aft control station to the ship's stern. A single T-shaped elevator moved aircraft from the hangar to the flight deck, which was covered with 8in of concrete as a means to restore the ship's balance after removal of Nos. 5 and 6 turrets. This deck was not large enough to allow the launching or recovery of aircraft. Launching of aircraft was performed by two new catapults fitted forward of the new flight deck. These large 82ft catapults restricted the arcs of fire of Nos. 3 and 4 turrets. Once launched, aircraft would recover ashore or on a conventional carrier. By using the flight deck and the 131ft-long hangar, up to 22 aircraft could be carried – nine in the hangar, 11 on the flight deck, and two on the catapults. These were originally intended to be D4Y2 "Judy" dive-bombers, but a shortage of aircraft meant that a mix of 14 E16A1 "Paul" reconnaissance-dive-bombers and eight D4Y2s was eventually settled on. To the Japanese, this awkward arrangement was justified, as it added 44 dive-bombers to their carrier fleet's striking power.

As with other Japanese battleships, antiaircraft weaponry was greatly increased as the war went on. During their conversion, the Ise class received another four twin Type 89 guns for a total of eight. The twin 25mm guns were removed and replaced by 19 triple mounts. To compensate for the extra weight, all casement 5.5in guns were removed. Additional 25mm guns were added in May 1944 until a final total of 104 guns were fitted, 31 triple mounts and 11 single mounts. In September 1944, six 30-barrel 5in rocket launchers were fitted on sponsons located on the aft portion of the flight deck. These rockets were fitted with incendiary shrapnel charges and were

Hyuga, as seen by a British cruiser in Chinese waters in December 1938. *Hyuga* had already undergone its final modernization from November 1934 to September 1936, and this was its final prewar configuration. The ship was destined to play a minor role during the war. (Naval History and Heritage Command)

activated by a time fuse, but proved ineffective in service. Since no aircraft were available late in the war, the catapults were removed in October–November to restore the field of fire for the aft 14in guns.

Ise was one of the first IJN ships to be fitted with radar. In May 1942, it received one of the first experimental No. 21 air-search radars on top of its bridge. Two No. 22 surface-search radars were fitted lower on the pagoda structure during conversion; these were replaced with two improved No. 22 sets in May 1944, in addition to two No. 13 air-search radars. *Hyuga* had an experimental No. 21 briefly installed in May 1942. This was replaced during its carrier conversion and two No. 22 sets fitted. In June 1944, it received improved No. 22s and two No. 13s.

Wartime service

During the early part of the war, *Ise* and *Hyuga* rarely left home waters. During gunnery drills in the Inland Sea in May 1942, *Hyuga*'s No. 5 turret exploded and 51 crewmen were killed. The turret was not repaired, but was later removed and replaced with a circular armored plate, on which four triple 25mm guns were installed. On May 29, both ships departed Japan to take part in the Midway operation, but saw no action.

After their conversion into carrier-battleships, both ships were assigned to Carrier Division 4 in August 1944. In October, as the Americans moved to invade the Philippine Islands, *Ise* and *Hyuga* were finally committed to

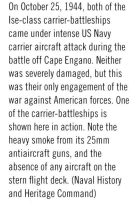

On October 25, 1944, both of the Ise-class carrier-battleships came under intense US Navy carrier aircraft attack during the battle off Cape Engano. Neither was severely damaged, but this was their only engagement of the war against American forces. One of the carrier-battleships is shown here in action. Note the heavy smoke from its 25mm antiaircraft guns, and the absence of any aircraft on the stern flight deck. (Naval History and Heritage Command)

action. However, Air Group 634, Carrier Division 4's assigned air group, was decimated in action off Formosa earlier in the month, so the carrier-battleships entered action with no embarked aircraft. Both ships were assigned to the Northern Force, and departed home waters on October 20, and by October 25, they came under intense American carrier air attack in action off Cape Engano. The Americans threw 527 sorties at the Northern Force, most being directed at the four carriers present, all of which were sunk. In the morning strikes, *Ise* took eight near misses and one hit on No. 2 turret. *Hyuga* was damaged by near misses. In the afternoon, *Ise* was the center of American attention. The lucky ship suffered 34 near misses, which ruptured hull plates, but only a single bomb hit that damaged the port catapult. It escaped with minor damage from leaking. Surviving multiple submarine attacks, both ships arrived in Japan with no further damage.

In November, the sisters departed for Singapore, arriving there on January 1, 1945. Each battleship was loaded with 5,000 drums of oil and other strategic materials for the return trip to Japan. Escaping submarine attack, they arrived at Kure on February 20. Lacking fuel and aircraft, the two ships were not used again operationally. Both were used as floating antiaircraft batteries in the area of Kure. In this capacity, both were subjected to a series of American carrier aircraft attacks that eventually resulted in their destruction. During the first attack on March 19, 1945, *Ise* was hit by two bombs and *Hyuga* was hit by one. On July 24, *Ise* was hit by five bombs and many near misses, but damage-control efforts restored the ship to an even keel. On July 24, south of Kure, *Hyuga* was attacked by 50 aircraft, suffering ten bomb hits and multiple near misses. The subsequent flooding forced its crew to run it aground. *Ise* was finished off on July 28 with 18 bomb hits and many near misses. It sank by the bow in shallow water.

Ise Class Specifications (following 1934–37 modernization)

Displacement: 35,800 tons standard; 40,169 full load; 38,676 after conversion into carrier-battleship
Dimensions: Length 708ft / beam 104ft / draft 30ft
Maximum speed: 25.3kt
Range: 7,870nm at 16kt; 9,500nm at 16kt after conversion
Crew: 1,360; 1,463 after carrier conversion

Nagato Class

Design and construction

This two-ship class was constructed under the 1916 and 1917 programs. The ships were designed by Hiraga Yuzuru, the most famous of Japanese naval architects. He intended to build a ship that incorporated a number of technological and design advances, with the goal of building a battleship qualitatively superior to any other navy's. The original design was finalized

Nagato Class Construction				
Ship	Built at	Laid down	Launched	Completed
Nagato	Kure Navy Yard	8/28/17	11/9/19	11/25/20
Mutsu	Yokosuka Navy Yard	6/1/18	5/31/20	10/24/21

The plate shows the two ships of the Nagato class. The top profile shows *Mutsu* as it appeared in August 1942 during the Battle of the Eastern Solomons. Its appearance has been unaltered since the start of the war, and it would remain essentially unchanged until its loss from a magazine explosion in June 1943. The lower profile is of *Nagato* as it appeared in October 1944 in its late-war configuration during the Battle of Leyte Gulf. Its appearance has been altered by the addition of radar and 96 25mm guns in single, double, and triple mounts.

without the benefit of the lessons from the great dreadnought clash at Jutland in 1916, so Hiraga was forced to recast his design. What emerged was a ship more powerful than the most advanced dreadnought of the day, the Royal Navy's Queen Elizabeth class. *Nagato* was bigger at 32,720 tons, faster, and carried larger guns.

Nagato's engineering system was entirely of Japanese design and manufacture. Originally 15 oil-fired and six mixed-firing Kanpon boilers were installed, which produced the steam to drive Kanpon turbines on four screws. This was sufficient to develop 80,000shp and could drive the ship at 26.5 knots, far superior to the USN's 16in gun dreadnoughts, the 21-knot Colorado class.

For protection, the Nagato class possessed slightly inferior armor protection compared to the Colorado class. *Nagato* and *Mutsu* possessed a main belt of 12in plus another 12in on the barbettes. The conning tower armor was 14.6in, while the main turrets possessed 18in of frontal armor, 11in of side, 7.5in of rear armor, and 9in on the turret roof. Horizontal

protection consisted of an upper deck and two armored decks with a maximum of 5.7in. In total, protection accounted for 31.7 percent of the design standard displacement.

A beam view of the battleship *Mutsu* taken in the late 1930s. This configuration was basically unchanged until its loss in June 1943. (Naval History and Heritage Command)

Armament

Because the *Nagato*'s 16in guns fired a heavier shell, its designers reduced the number of main guns from 12 to eight, producing considerable savings in weight and space. When commissioned in November 1920, *Nagato* was the first battleship in the world to carry 16in guns. The eight guns were arranged in four twin turrets, two forward and two aft, with the Nos. 2 and 3 turrets superfiring. The turrets had 30-degree elevation. Secondary armament was the now-standard 5.5in gun; 20 were fitted, all in casemates. Four 3in guns provided antiaircraft protection. The Japanese continued their custom of fitting torpedo tubes on capital ships, fitting eight 21in tubes on the Nagato class – four above water, and four submerged.

Service modifications

Both ships were reconstructed in the mid-1930s; *Nagato* was the first to enter the yards in April 1934 at Kure, followed by *Mutsu* in September 1934 at Yokosuka. Work was completed on the ships in January 1936 and September 1936, respectively.

The nature of the reconstruction paralleled that of the other Japanese battleships. To enhance underwater protection, a torpedo bulge was added that extended from the bottom of the hull up to above the side armor. The bulge was composed of two sections, with the upper compartments filled with crushing tubes, and the lower one used as a fuel bunker. The new bulges increased the beam to 111ft. Increasing horizontal protection was

another concern, so the machinery and magazine spaces were covered with 1.5in of armor on the upper deck and another inch to the upper armored deck; maximum horizontal armor in some areas was now more than 8.1in. Following reconstruction, the total weight of armor rose to 32.6 percent of displacement.

To compensate for the increased beam, the hull was lengthened by 26ft. All of the original 20 boilers were removed and replaced with four Kanpon oil-fired boilers, in addition to six smaller rebuilt boilers; new turbines were also fitted. The reduction in the number of boilers permitted the forward stack to be removed. The new machinery saved 500 tons of weight, but resulted in no increase of power. Because the displacement increased to over 46,000 tons full load, the top speed dropped from 26.7 knots to 25 knots. Only minor modifications were made to the armament. The elevation of the secondary armament was increased to 35 degrees and antiaircraft protection was enhanced by removing the four 3in guns and replacing them with four twin Type 89 guns. The torpedo tubes were removed.

In 1937, a new catapult was fitted that replaced the original model fitted in 1933. Three floatplanes were carried. In 1939, ten twin 25mm antiaircraft guns were added.

During the war, *Mutsu* was not modified before its loss. *Nagato* received little modification until later in the war. In May 1943, *Nagato* was equipped with a No. 21 radar and two additional 25mm triple antiaircraft guns. When *Nagato* returned to Japan in June 1944, it received extensive modifications to its radar and antiaircraft suites. At this time, two No. 22 and two No. 13 radars were fitted. Two of the 5.5in secondary guns were removed and the total number of 25mm antiaircraft guns brought up to 96 – 16 triple, ten twin, and 28 single mounts. Also at this time, all portholes below the upper deck were plated over. In 1945, *Nagato* was modified for use as a floating antiaircraft battery. Its 5.5in guns were removed, and many additional triple 25mm mounts were added. The stack and mainmast were removed to improve arcs of fire for the antiaircraft guns. By the time the ship was surrendered, only the main battery remained onboard.

Wartime service

Nagato and *Mutsu* began the war assigned to Battleship Division 1. *Nagato* also served as flagship of the Combined Fleet. In this capacity, it was from its decks that orders to start the Pacific War were issued. Both ships remained in home waters until May 29, when they departed to take part in the Battle of Midway. Being deployed some 300 miles behind the Japanese carrier force, they saw no action during the battle. *Nagato* remained in home waters through 1942, but *Mutsu* departed Japan in August, and deployed to Truk to take part in the Guadalcanal campaign. Even in the forward area it was little used, but did participate in the Battle of Eastern Solomons in August, before returning to Japan in January 1943. On June 8, 1943, *Mutsu* was at anchor at Hashirajima. Just after noon, *Mutsu*'s No. 3 turret magazine

Opposite: *Mutsu* in 1941, showing its massive beam and forward 16in main battery. The beam has been increased by the fitting of a torpedo bulge. The Imperial Chrysanthemum is evident on its bow. (Yamato Museum)

exploded, breaking the ship in half. Of the crew of 1,474, only 353 survived, and only 13 of 153 visiting flying cadets and instructors were saved. Initially it was thought that the Type 3 "Sanshiki-dan" incendiary shells for the main battery were to blame, but tests showed this was not the case, and final blame was conveniently assigned to a disgruntled seaman assigned to No. 3 turret who was facing theft charges.

Nagato remained in home waters through mid-August 1943, before deploying to Truk. Following the IJN's evacuation of Truk, *Nagato* and the Mobile Fleet moved to Lingga. During the Battle of the Philippine Sea in June 1944, *Nagato* was assigned to escort Carrier Division 2. It was not damaged during the American air raids on the Mobile Fleet on June 20.

After the Japanese defeat at Philippine Sea, *Nagato* returned to Japan for refit and repair. By July, it had returned to Lingga and was now assigned to Force "A" of the First Striking Force. *Nagato* and six other of the IJN's battleships departed Lingga on October 18 to attack the American invasion force off Leyte. On October 24, *Nagato* suffered two near misses in the morning, and in the afternoon it was hit by two bombs and experienced three near misses. Damage was light, but the ship's speed was impaired temporarily.

On October 25, Force "A" came upon the six escort carriers of "Taffy 3." For the first time in the war, *Nagato* used its main batteries against an enemy, opening fire at 20 miles. Overall, its part in the battle was minor. It only fired 45 rounds from its main gun and 92 5.5in rounds. Its only claim was a damaged cruiser (in fact no cruisers were present, so its actual target was a

Nagato as it appeared immediately before the Battle of Leyte Gulf. All of its radars are noticeable, with the No. 21 atop the tower, the two No. 22s just below the tower rangefinder, and two No. 13s on its mainmast. Much of its increased antiaircraft fit can also be seen. The aircraft crane has been rigged, and an F1M2 "Pete" aircraft can be seen. Behind *Nagato* are *Yamato* and *Musashi*. (*Ships of the World* magazine)

destroyer). While retiring, *Nagato* was hit by another two bombs forward, one of which destroyed its anchor deck. Overall, despite two days of intense air attack, damage to *Nagato* was minimal, with 38 killed and 105 seriously wounded.

After Leyte Gulf, *Nagato* returned to Japan on November 25. With no fuel available, it was modified for use as a floating antiaircraft battery and assigned to the Yokosuka Naval District. In April 1945, *Nagato* was reassigned as a reserve ship. The ship was stripped of its remaining 5.5in guns, and most antiaircraft guns were moved to a nearby mountain. The crew was reduced to 1,000 men. *Nagato* was heavily camouflaged, with its main guns covered with scaffolding, and trees placed on its upper deck. Despite this attempt at concealment, it was subjected to carrier air attack on July 18, 1945. One bomb hit the bridge causing heavy casualties, and another hit aft of the mainmast. This was the only damage, and in this condition *Nagato* was the only Japanese battleship to survive the war. On August 30, *Nagato* was boarded and taken over by the USN. Its end was ignominious. On March 18, 1946, *Nagato* departed Yokosuka at its best speed of 10 knots for Eniwetok. It proved unseaworthy because of unrepaired war damage and later ran out of fuel. After finally arriving by tow at Eniwetok, it was moved to Bikini Atoll in May 1946. There it was subjected to two atomic bomb tests in July 1946. Following the second, it capsized on July 29 in about 160ft of water.

> **Nagato Class Specifications (following 1934–36 modernization)**
>
> **Displacement:** 39,130 tons standard; 46,356 full load
> **Dimensions:** Length 734ft / beam 108ft / draft 31ft
> **Maximum speed:** 25kt
> **Range:** 8,560nm at 16kt
> **Crew:** 1,368; 1,475 in 1942; approximately 1,735 in 1944

Yamato Class

Design and construction

The Yamato class comprised the largest battleships ever built. These ships were the result of the Japanese strategy of countering American numerical superiority with a qualitative overmatch. *Yamato* was commissioned in February 1942, only weeks after Pearl Harbor displayed the emerging importance of the aircraft carrier. Thus, despite all the efforts put into its design, *Yamato* was obsolete by the time it entered service. The Yamato class has been condemned as a failure as neither ship was ever used for its intended role, and both were sunk by aircraft. However, examining the IJN's dilemma in the mid-1930s, the Japanese decision to build an enormously expensive class of superbattleships appears rational, even inspired. The IJN was unable to compete with the USN on a quantitative basis, so it was forced to seek a qualitative edge. The eventual nemesis of the class, carrier airpower, was a

A fine study of *Yamato* as it conducted trials in 1941. Its fine lines and raked stack gave it a graceful appearance. Note the beam 6.1in triple turret. (Yamato Museum)

relatively primitive tool when the ships were designed, and no navy foresaw the rapid technological advances of carrier aircraft, and the subsequent domination of airpower. When completed, *Yamato* became the mythical symbol not only of Japanese sea power, but of the entire nation.

Planning for *Yamato* began in the fall of 1935. Twenty-three various designs were considered before the final plan was accepted in July 1936. The architects were challenged to come up with a design to meet the Naval General Staff requirements that called for a ship with nine 18.1in guns, armor capable of withstanding 18in shellfire, underwater protection capable of defeating torpedoes with a 660lb warhead, a top speed of 27 knots, and a cruising range of 8,000 miles at 18 knots. To accomplish this, the designers determined that the ship needed a displacement of 69,000 tons.

Two superbattleships were authorized in 1936. *Yamato* was built in Kure after the dock there was deepened, and gantry cranes strengthened to handle the enormous armor plates. *Musashi* was built at the Mitsubishi shipyard at Nagasaki after this facility was extended some 50ft into the hillside. Extreme security precautions taken during the ships' construction were successful in denying US Naval Intelligence an accurate assessment of their size and capabilities throughout the war. In 1939, two more were authorized. The first of these was named *Shinano* and the second (No. 111) was never named. *Shinano* was intended to be completed with a different armor scheme, and to be equipped with the new Type 98 4in/65 antiaircraft gun.

After Midway, it was decided to complete it as an aircraft carrier. It was finally completed in late 1944. The fourth Yamato-class ship was only 30 percent complete before work was stopped in November 1941.

The hull had a very broad beam of 127.7ft, with overall length being 863ft. Draft was relatively shallow for a ship with such a large displacement. However, fully loaded the draft was still 34.5ft, which required that several harbors be dredged. A new feature was a giant bulbous bow that was shown during tests to reduce hydrodynamic drag. The enormous beam allowed the four main turbines and their boilers to be placed side-by-side instead of in tandem along the length of the hull. This reduced the area that had to be armored to protect the machinery to a very low 53.3 percent of the ship's length.

As demanded in the design specifications, the armor scheme was of such a scale that it provided the class with an unparalleled degree of protection in surface combat. Armor was laid out in an all-or-nothing principle with almost all armor being placed in the central main citadel to protect vital machinery and magazine spaces. In order to minimize the portions of the ship that were to be protected, the ship was designed with an unprecedented beam instead of a long narrow hull design. *Yamato* was the most massively armored ship ever, with a total weight of armor of 22,534 tons or 33.1 percent of the design displacement. The armored center section featured a main belt of just over 16in inclined at 20 degrees, half of which was below the waterline. The lower armor belt was just under 11in in the area of the magazines, and 8in covering the machinery spaces. The ends of the armored citadel were covered by two transverse 11.8in bulkheads. Deck armor was between 7.9 and 9.1in, which was thought to be capable of withstanding armor-piercing bombs of up to 2,200lb dropped from 3,280ft. The front of the barbettes was covered by 21.5in of armor plate with the sides covered by 16in, both specially hardened. The three main turrets featured some 26in of armor on their face, 10in on the sides, 9.5in in the rear, and almost 11in on the roofs. The conning tower was covered by a maximum of 19.7in of steel. A torpedo bulge was also fitted, which extended 9.25ft from the main belt, from the waterline to the bottom of the ship.

The propulsive system included four Kanpon geared turbines with steam provided by 12 Kanpon boilers. This provided a total of 150,000shp to the four propeller shafts, which met the design speed of 27.5 knots. *Yamato* was reported to have made in excess of 28 knots in June 1942. Maneuverability was excellent. A small heeling angle even at high degrees of rudder at high speed maintained a good platform for gunnery. The class possessed highly developed damage-control features. The ships possessed increased watertight

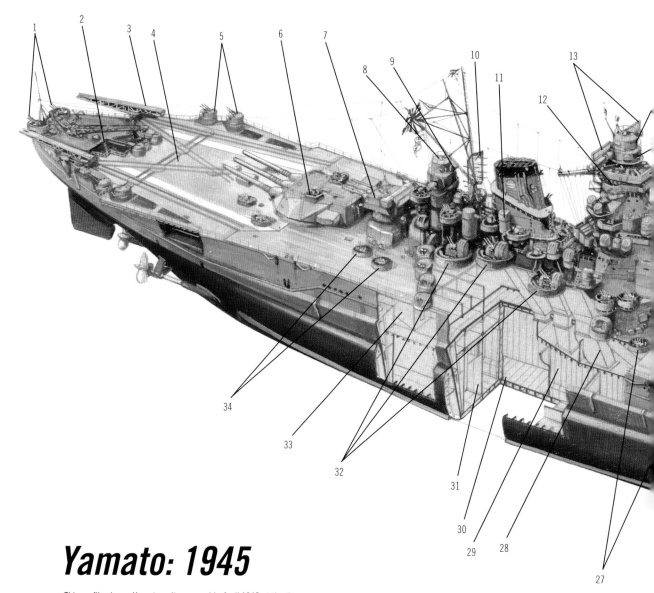

1   2   3   4   5   6   7   8   9   10   11   12   13

34

33

32

31

30   29   28   27

Yamato: 1945

This profile shows *Yamato* as it appeared in April 1945 at the time of its loss. The beam 6.1in turrets have been replaced with three twin Type 89 5in guns. An amazing 50 triple 25mm guns have been fitted, most around the armored citadel. No. 21 and No. 22 radars have been fitted on its tower and No. 13 radars have been placed on its mainmast – also note the large catapults fitted aft and the elevator for servicing the hangar below the main deck.

Key

1 Type 96 triple 25mm antiaircraft gun
2 Aircraft elevator
3 Aircraft catapults
4 Aircraft deck
5 Type 96 triple 25mm antiaircraft gun with shield
6 No. 3 turret
7 6.1in triple gun turret
8 Type 98 low-angle fire control director
9 10m rangefinder
10 No. 13 radar
11 Type 95 machine-gun control director
12 No. 22 radar
13 No. 21 radar
14 Type 98 low-angle fire control director
15 15m main battery rangefinder
16 Air defense combat station
17 Combat bridge

18 Type 95 machine-gun control director
19 Compass bridge (second bridge)
20 Armored conning tower
21 6.1in triple gun turret
22 No. 2 Turret
23 Gyro room
24 No. 1 Turret
25 Officer quarters
26 Crew quarters
27 Type 96 triple 25mm antiaircraft gun
28 Boiler uptakes
29 Boiler rooms
30 Engine rooms
31 Cooling machinery room
32 Type 89 5in/40cal aircraft gun Model A-1-3
33 Galley
34 Type 96 triple 25mm antiaircraft gun

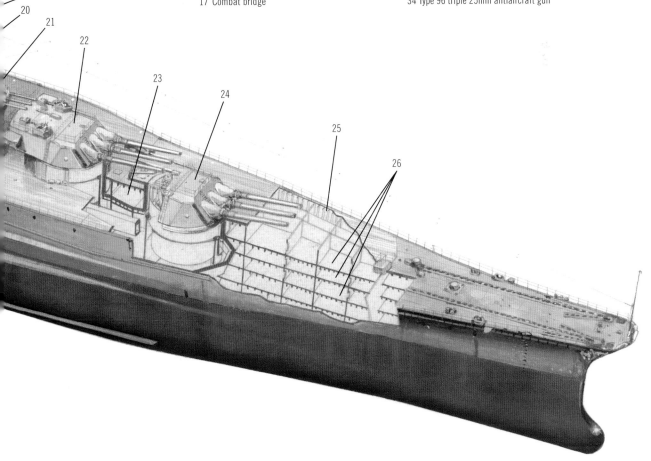

compartmentation and a reserve buoyancy of 57,450 tons. Stability could be maintained with a list of 20 degrees. Any list of up to 18.3 degrees could be corrected by the flooding and pumping system.

However, as formidable as the design appeared on paper, there were problems. The armor distribution scheme proved to be faulty. The entire bow and stern sections were unarmored, depending on compartmentation only. However, compartments in these areas were too large, and this, combined with the lack of armor, meant that damage translated into flooding and a list. The pumping system was unable to cope with excessive flooding in the bow and stern areas. The Achilles heel for the class was a defective joint in the armor at the junction of upper and lower side belts. When this failed, the armored citadel was compromised. Protection above the waterline had priority, which meant there were no voids that could absorb torpedo blasts. Additionally, the maximum width of the antitorpedo bulge around the machinery spaces was only 16.7ft, well below that of foreign battleships designed during the same period. The lack of depth was compounded by the fact that the bulge was tied to the main belt armor. In 1943, the Americans introduced a new explosive, Torpex, with twice the explosive power of TNT. This rendered all the calculations of *Yamato*'s designers obsolete. While *Yamato*'s sheer size and heavy armor made it difficult to destroy, the weakness of its antitorpedo defenses was amply demonstrated during the war.

A port-quarter shot of *Yamato* on trials. Note the catapults fitted aft; just behind these is the aircraft elevator.
(Yamato Museum)

Armament

The centerpiece of the Yamato-class design was the main armament of 18.1in guns – the largest ever placed on a battleship. Each gun weighed 162 tons, and the rotating components of the triple turret totaled 2,774 tons, equivalent in weight to a fleet destroyer. Each gun fired an enormous 3,219lb projectile. The rate of fire was 1.5 rounds per minute. Secondary armament comprised four triple turrets with 6.1in guns. These were placed fore and aft, and one on each beam. The Japanese had hoped that these turrets would also augment the ships' antiaircraft protection, but they proved inadequate in that role, which resulted in the removal of the beam turrets.

Antiaircraft protection was below the standard provided to contemporary USN battleships. Long-range protection was provided by 12 5in guns mounted in six twin mounts. These were grouped amidships, three per side, and placed above the beam 6.1in triple turrets. As designed, the Yamato class was provided with 24 25mm guns in eight triple mounts and four 13mm machine guns on the bridge tower.

The Yamato class featured extensive facilities for handling aircraft. Two 59ft catapults were fitted on the quarterdeck. There was a hangar deck located below the main deck that could handle seven aircraft; however, the normal number was much less, usually three or four.

Service modifications

With the exception of augmenting their radar and antiaircraft fits, neither ship underwent any major modification during the war. While at Kure in July 1943, *Yamato* received two No. 21 radars placed atop the rangefinder on its bridge. Additionally, four triple 25mm guns were fitted on the weather deck, making a total of 36 25mm guns.

Yamato's next modifications took place in February 1944, when the two beam 6.1in turrets were removed and replaced with six twin 5in Type 89 shielded mounts. At this time, another 24 triple 25mm guns and 16 single 25mm guns were added. Nos. 22 and 13 radars were also installed. Later, between June 29 and July 8, 1944, another five 25mm triple mounts were installed. In November 1944, *Yamato* was drydocked to repair battle damage from Leyte. At this time, almost all of the single 25mm mounts were removed, and nine additional triple mounts added. *Yamato*'s final antiaircraft fit was an impressive 152 25mm guns in 50 triple and two single mounts.

During *Musashi*'s final fitting out in Kure, another four triple 25mm guns and two No. 21 radars were added. This was followed in July 1943 by the addition of two No. 22 radars. In April 1944, while in Kure for repairs to torpedo damage, *Musashi*'s two beam 6.1in turrets were removed, and replaced by a total of six 25mm triple mounts. Seven other triple mounts and 25 single mounts were also added at this time. *Musashi*'s final antiaircraft suite was thus 130 25mm guns – 35 triple and 25 single mounts. Also during its final refit, No. 13 radar was added and depth-charge rails were fitted on the stern.

Wartime service

Despite the massive resources put into their design and construction, the two units of the Yamato class saw little action during the war. *Yamato* assumed the role of flagship for the Combined Fleet on February 12, 1942. It was considered combat ready on May 27, 1942 and departed two days later for the Midway operation. In August 1942, it deployed to Truk, where it served as a headquarters ship. It was not committed to action during the six-month battle for Guadalcanal and its prolonged periods of inactivity and comfortable fittings earned it the nickname "Hotel Yamato."

After returning to Japan in May for refit, *Yamato* again deployed to Truk in August 1943. During a transport mission, *Yamato* suffered its first war damage on December 25, 1943 when it was struck by submarine-launched torpedoes northwest of Truk, when USS *Skate* gained contact on the superbattleship and fired four stern tubes; one or two torpedoes hit on the starboard side near No. 3 turret. The damage caused the joints between the upper and lower main armor belts to fail, flooding the upper magazine of No. 3 turret and allowing a total of 3,000 tons of water to enter the ship. Following emergency repairs at Truk, *Yamato* returned to Japan in January 1944.

Musashi was commissioned on August 5, 1942. It departed Japan on January 18, 1943, and arrived at Truk on January 22 to assume duties as the flagship of the Combined Fleet from its sister ship. In May, it returned to Japan with the ashes of Admiral Yamamoto who had been killed in April 1943. While in Japan, the emperor visited *Musashi* on June 24. It returned to Truk in August 1943. Following a sortie in October in response to an expected raid on Wake Island, *Musashi* returned to Yokosuka in February 1944. Departing Japan later in the month, it transported two battalions of troops to Palau, and remained there for a month. While departing Palau on the night of March 29 to avoid an expected air raid, it was hit by one of six torpedoes fired by the submarine *Tunny*. The torpedo struck the bow and created a 19ft-diameter hole, causing the ship to flood with 3,000 tons of water. *Musashi* was forced to return to Kure in April 1944 for repairs. By May, *Musashi* rejoined *Yamato* at Lingga.

Yamato departed Kure in April 1944 and arrived at Lingga on May 1. On June 10, 1944 both *Yamato* and *Musashi* were committed to Operation *Kon*, to relieve the Japanese garrison on Biak Island off the northern coast of New Guinea. However, before the superbattleships could join the operation, the Americans invaded the island of Saipan and Operation *Kon* was canceled. During the Battle of the Philippine Sea, both *Yamato* and *Musashi* were assigned to the Vanguard Force. Neither was damaged and both returned to Lingga in July 1944.

The Battle of Leyte Gulf proved the toughness of the Yamato-class design. During the approach of Force "A" to Leyte, the Japanese came under intense carrier air attack on October 24, 1944. *Musashi* quickly become the focus of the American aviators' attention. The first air strike placed a bomb on top of No. 1 turret that failed to penetrate. However, the first torpedo hit amidships caused a 5.5-degree list due to flooding. The second raid resulted in two more bomb hits and three torpedo hits, all on the port side – the resulting 5-degree list was corrected by more counterflooding, but now *Musashi* was down 6ft by the bow and its speed was reduced to 22 knots. The next attack resulted in six more bomb hits and four torpedo hits, two to port and two to starboard. Counterflooding reduced the starboard list to 1 degree, but now the ship was down 13ft by the bow, with little extra capacity for counterflooding.

After a brief respite, the American attacks continued to focus on *Musashi* which had fallen astern of the rest of the formation. The next attack placed four more bombs on the ship, and hit it with three more torpedoes. The last attack of the day provided the final blows – as many as ten bombs struck the ship, combined with as many as seven torpedoes. The last two torpedoes struck aft on the port side, and the ship developed a 10-degree list to port.

Japanese Battleship Color Schemes

All IJN battleships were painted in a dark navy gray. The basic shade has been described in the previous chapter. The hull below the waterline was painted in a reddish-brown mixture of 65 percent brown, 20 percent red, 10 percent black, and 5 percent white. Black semi-gloss paint covered the upper part of the stack and the fore and mainmasts. The rangefinders atop battleship towers were painted white as a recognition symbol. Canvas was used in all blastbags and to cover reels and searchlights, and as wind screens at various levels of the tower. This was white in peacetime, but in wartime was replaced by light brown or gray canvas.

The deck was unpainted teak. This would weather to a gray-tan over time. Linoleum covered the parts of the weather deck devoted to aircraft operations. This was a dark brown color. The linoleum was laid in 6.6in-wide sheets and was joined by brass strips. On *Yamato* and *Musashi*, the aircraft deck was covered with concrete that was left unpainted, which, as it aged, turned from a medium gray to a darker gray.

Unlike the USN and RN, the IJN did not customarily use camouflage schemes on its battleships. However, as dictated by tactical circumstances, forms of camouflage were occasionally used. *Yamato* and *Musashi* had black camouflage applied to their wooden decks in October 1944 for an expected night action in San Bernardino Strait. Most of the black was soot from the ships' stacks. In 1945, as the IJN's last battleships huddled in home waters under threat of air attack, the Japanese took measures to make them less conspicuous. *Haruna* was painted olive green with light green turrets and gray-color stripes on the turret. *Ise* was camouflaged olive green with dark green, yellow, gray, and red-brown splotches. *Hyuga* maintained its dark gray, with dark green curves on its turrets. *Nagato* had much of its upper superstructure painted olive green with brown splotches.

Yamato under attack by USN carrier planes in the Inland Sea on March 19, 1945. On this occasion, it was not seriously damaged, but it had less than three weeks to live. With the augmentation of its 25mm antiaircraft suite, this was its final configuration prior to its loss. (Naval History and Heritage Command)

At this point, it was clear the ship could not be saved, and *Musashi*'s captain tried to run the ship ashore on the nearest island, but the engines stopped before this could be done. *Musashi* sank at 1930hrs, rolling over to port. Of the ship's crew, 1,376 survivors were rescued, but 1,023 were lost. The punishment absorbed by *Musashi* was a testament to its design and its well-trained damage-control crew. The exact number and location of bomb and torpedo hits is still unclear. Japanese sources suggest 11 torpedoes, ten bombs, and six near misses, but American sources indicate 19 torpedo (ten port, nine starboard), and 17 bomb hits, plus 18 near misses.

As *Musashi* was acting as a sponge for American bombs and torpedoes, the remainder of Force "A" suffered relatively little. *Yamato* took three bomb hits; the first destroyed the port chain locker when it exploded below the waterline and holed the bow. Two more bombs hit No. 1 turret. The damage to its bow resulted in *Yamato* taking 3,000 tons of water and developing a 5-degree list. This was reduced to 1 degree by counterflooding, and the ship was able to continue with the rest of the formation. The following day, when the Japanese surface force came across Taffy 3, *Yamato* used its 18.1in guns against a surface target for the first and only time of the war. It opened fire on a carrier at 20 miles and immediately claimed hits. However, it was forced to execute torpedo evasion maneuvers, and was absent for portions of the battle. On October 26, during the retirement of Force "A," it was hit by another two bombs, one on the forecastle and a second near No. 1 turret.

> ## Yamato Class Specifications
>
> **Displacement:** 62,315 tons standard; 69,998 full load
> **Dimensions:** Length 863ft / beam 127.7ft / draft 34.5ft
> **Maximum speed:** 27.5kt
> **Range:** 7,200nm at 16kt
> **Crew:** 2,300 (design); *Yamato* 3,300 in April 1945

By November 23, 1944, *Yamato* had returned to Kure. On March 19, 1945, it suffered minor damage from a single bomb hit on the bridge while under attack from carrier aircraft in the Inland Sea. The American invasion of Okinawa in April 1945 prompted the IJN to commit its remaining surface units to attack American naval forces supporting the invasion. At 1520hrs on April 6, *Yamato* sortied with a light cruiser and eight destroyers as a Surface Special Attack Unit to conduct the IJN's last major operation of the war. Despite myth, *Yamato* was issued with enough fuel for a round trip to Okinawa, though its return was considered unlikely. The small force was tracked by submarines and aircraft and, on the following day, over 400 carrier aircraft attacked the fleet. In no case did a bomb penetrate *Yamato*'s armored deck, but no ship could withstand the pounding of torpedoes that the Americans concentrated on its port side. Learning from the *Musashi* episode, American torpedo bombers deliberately concentrated their attacks on one side of the ship. Hit by as many as 11 or 13 torpedoes and at least eight bombs, *Yamato* rolled over to port. An explosion of its aft magazines left a huge plume of smoke visible in Kyushu, over 100 miles away, and marked the end of the IJN. Only 269 survivors were rescued while 3,063 were lost. American losses were ten aircraft and 12 aircrew.

HEAVY CRUISERS

The IJN's heavy cruiser force was demonstrably one of its most successful components during the Pacific War. By 1941, the Japanese had fielded 18 heavy cruisers, putting them on numerical parity with the USN. Japanese cruisers entered the war with a reputation for superior size and firepower compared to their American and British counterparts, suspected by many to be the result of breaking treaty limits in place between the wars. The exploits of the IJN's heavy cruisers during the first part of the war confirmed the positive prewar expectations of the Japanese and made them feared opponents by the Allies. While the Japanese retained the bulk of their battleships in home waters during the early and middle part of the war, their heavy cruisers spearheaded Japanese expansion into the Dutch East Indies. When the Japanese were forced onto the defensive in mid-1942, heavy cruisers again provided the backbone for their resistance in the Solomons for the rest of the year. After a comparatively quiet 1943, during which no cruisers were lost, 1944 marked

Classification of Japanese heavy cruisers

Japanese heavy cruisers were known by several terms before the name "heavy cruiser" was finally adopted. The 1898 Warship and Torpedo Boat Classification Criteria called for a ship of greater than 7,000 tons designed displacement to be considered a first-rate cruiser. Officially, they were also called "A Class" cruisers and unofficially they were also called "large-model cruisers." By World War II, however, the Japanese had settled on "heavy cruiser" (*junyokan*), bringing them in line with the rest of the world's navies.

Furutaka in its original configuration, with single 7.9in guns in "semi-turrets." It was later modernized and its appearance changed to resemble that of the Aoba class. To the left of *Furutaka* are *Aoba* and *Kinugasa*. (Naval History and Heritage Command)

the effective end of the IJN's heavy cruiser force. By the end of the war, only two heavy cruisers remained afloat, both in a damaged condition.

JAPANESE HEAVY CRUISER DEVELOPMENT

From the period of 1922 up through the end of 1936, the IJN was restricted in the numbers and types of heavy cruisers it could build by a series of international naval treaties, outlined in Chapter 1. In fact, the entire concept of a "heavy cruiser," as it came to be known, was a construct from the treaty system. The Washington Naval Treaty of 1922 placed a limit on the size of cruisers (10,000 tons maximum) and a restriction of the size of the armament (no larger than 8in guns). However, while the overall tonnage of capital ships and aircraft carriers was restricted, there was no similar limit placed on cruisers. The effect was to start a treaty cruiser building spree, with the 10,000-ton limit becoming the baseline for Japanese cruiser designs.

Myoko on April 16, 1927, during its launch at the Yokosuka Navy Yard. It was the first of eight Washington Treaty cruisers launched by the IJN in the next eight years. (Naval History and Heritage Command)

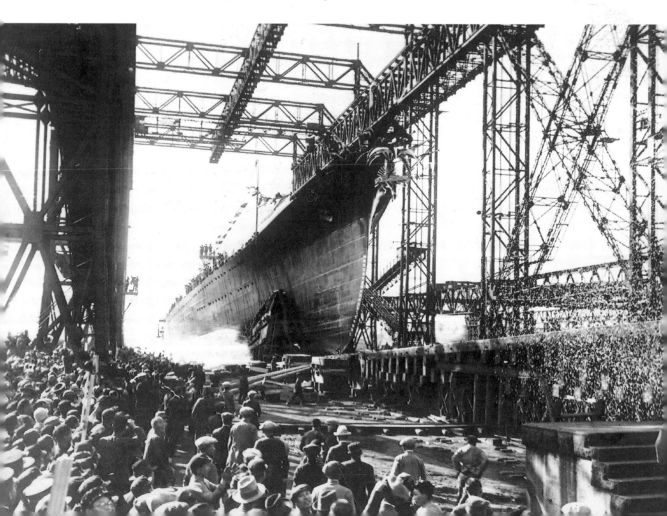

The *Mogami* (lower), *Mikuma* (center), and *Kumano* (upper) in Japanese waters in summer 1938. The Mogami class comprised Sentai 7 and played an important part in Japan's expansion in the initial period of the war. (Naval History and Heritage Command)

The design of the IJN's first heavy cruisers actually pre-dated the Washington Treaty. By July 1922, the Japanese had announced plans for the construction of eight cruisers – four of the pre-treaty 7,500-ton scout cruisers and four 10,000-ton ships. The scout cruisers became the Furutaka and Aoba classes and the first class of 10,000-ton cruisers constituted the Myoko class. The epitome of Japanese treaty cruiser design was the follow-on to the Myoko class, the four-ship Takao class.

After an attempt to implement further overall tonnage restrictions to cruiser construction failed at the Geneva Naval Conference in 1927, the major naval powers tried again in London in 1930. This time it was agreed to place a cap on cruiser tonnage, and existing and future cruisers were broken into two types. Type A (or heavy) cruisers were defined as ships with guns greater than 6.1in and Type B (or light) cruisers were ships with guns smaller than 6.1in. The 10,000-ton maximum and 8in gun restrictions remained in effect. The London Naval Treaty of 1930 set the final course for the IJN's heavy cruiser force. The allotted total tonnage for Japanese Type A cruisers was 108,400 tons standard; this had already been reached by the 12 Type A cruisers in service. For Type B cruisers, the Japanese limit was 100,450 tons standard. Per treaty stipulations, the tonnage of vessels ready for replacement could be used for new construction. For the IJN, this amounted to 50,955 tons. The Japanese decided that this remaining tonnage would be used to build four 8,500-ton units before 1936, followed by another two later. These six ships were later upgraded to become heavy cruisers, thus rounding out the IJN's prewar heavy cruiser force at 18 units.

JAPANESE HEAVY CRUISER WEAPONS

From the start, Japanese heavy cruiser designs emphasized firepower, and it was expected that the IJN's cruisers would out-gun and out-range their foreign contemporaries.

Main Battery

After a brief flirtation with 7.9in guns, the Japanese decided to upgrade existing ships and build all future ships with 8in guns. The 8in gun mounted in a twin turret was adopted in 1931. It was a respectable weapon, but was consistently plagued with a large salvo dispersion – during gunnery trials in

Japanese Heavy Cruiser Main Guns				
Type	Class	Max. elevation (degrees)	Max. range (yards)	Rate of fire (rpm)
Type 3 No. 2 Model C	Aoba	40	31,606	2–3
Type 3 No. 2 Model D	Myoko	40	31,606	2–3
Type 3 No. 2 Model E	Takao (less *Maya*)	45	32,153	2–3
Type 2 No.2 E1	Maya	70*	32,153	2–3
Type 3 No. 2 Model Mogami	Mogami	45	32,153	2–3
Type 3 No. 2 Model E2	Furutaka	45	32,153	2–3
Type 3 No.2 Model E3	Tone	45	32,153	2–3

* Maximum theoretical elevation for antiaircraft firing only; maximum elevation against surface targets 45 degrees.

1933, this was noted to be as much as 528 yards over a range of 21,100 yards. The Japanese attempted to alleviate this problem with the installation of a device in 1938 that produced a very slight delay in the firing of the two guns in a turret, a measure that reduced interference. This served to reduce dispersion to 416 yards at 21,873 yards range for the classes with ten 8in guns. Dispersion problems for the ships with only six guns were consistently less.

As the IJN was expecting to be outnumbered in any major clash with the USN, the Japanese placed great emphasis on out-ranging their likely opponent so as to hit first without the threat of effective response. Due to continual modernization of heavy cruiser fire-control equipment, by 1937 the engagement range for 8in guns was extended to greater than 21,873 yards. The Japanese calculated that even at this maximum battle range, their hit probability was 6 percent. This was a wildly optimistic assessment, and as will be seen later the quality of Japanese cruiser gunnery at extended ranges during the war was mediocre at best.

The IJN's heavy cruisers were designed to maximize their capabilities during night combat. To provide illumination at night, the Japanese used a combination of searchlights and star shells. The most powerful cruiser searchlight had an effective range of 6,562 yards; if two searchlights were trained on the same target, the effective range was increased to 8,749 yards. This constituted the effective range of the cruisers in night combat. The searchlights were controlled by a searchlight control station, which was equipped with powerful binoculars. Several types of binoculars were installed on the bridge, some as large as 7in. Night-fighting prowess was also enhanced by the development of flashless powder adopted in 1938, which concealed the source of gunfire.

Chokai firing a broadside with its 8in gun battery in 1933. Despite constant practice and attention to long-range gunnery, the accuracy of Japanese cruiser gunnery at extended ranges was notable for its lack of wartime success. At closer ranges, however, the IJN's well-drilled cruiser crews were deadly. (Naval History and Heritage Command)

Torpedo Armament

The biggest difference in Japanese cruiser design compared to American heavy cruisers was the inclusion of heavy torpedo armament. A heavy torpedo battery was crucial to allow the cruiser to play its leading role in night combat and gave the vessels a long-range punch not possessed by foreign rivals. There was a clear danger to mounting such weapons – if their unprotected large warheads were hit during combat, the resulting explosion could wreck vital parts of the ship. In fact, there was considerable tension between the Naval General Staff who formulated design requirements and the principal designers of the ships about whether to include torpedoes at all. In the end, the Naval General Staff got its way and a heavy torpedo armament became a staple of Japanese cruiser design.

Heavy cruisers employed triple and quadruple torpedo mounts. In addition to a large number of torpedoes carried in the tubes (up to 16), another set of reloads was carried. Reloading was a key skill that was constantly practiced and could be executed in a matter of minutes. In 1938, the Japanese provided their cruisers with the Type 93 Model 1 Modification 2 torpedo, which had been adopted by the IJN in 1935. This remarkable weapon, later given the nickname "Long Lance" by the Allies, possessed a 1,082lb warhead and was wakeless. It could travel up to 43,746 yards at

The forward two 8in turrets on a Takao-class cruiser. These turrets were adopted in 1931 and weighed 171 tons. One of the shortcomings of Japanese heavy cruiser 8in gun turrets was their relative lack of protection, with only 1in of armor all round. Comparable US Navy treaty cruiser turrets were provided with as much as 8in of frontal armor. (*Ships of the World* magazine)

36 knots, 35,000 yards at 40 knots, or 21,873 yards at 48 knots. Fire control for torpedo combat was provided by a director computing system located on the bridge, which was used for targets between ranges of 10,936 yards and 43,746 yards. A second director was used for ranges under 10,936 yards.

A torpedo mount on a Japanese cruiser. The provision of torpedoes on their cruisers gave the Japanese an important advantage early in the war when they enjoyed the initiative, but when the IJN was forced onto the defensive and its cruisers subjected to increasing air attack, these weapons proved a liability and directly contributed to the loss of several ships. (*Ships of the World* magazine)

Antiaircraft Armament

The standard Japanese heavy cruiser long-range antiaircraft weapon was the 40cal Type 89 5in high-angle dual mount gun. This gun was mounted on all heavy cruiser classes except Furutaka and Aoba because of weight and size issues and the Takao class, which did not receive them before the war because of production shortages. These ships retained the older 4.7in single mounts. The most modern fire director was the Type 94, but only the *Aoba* and both ships of the Tone class received it before the war due to production shortages. *Maya* received it during its conversion to an antiaircraft cruiser during the war. Specifications for the Type 89 gun are provided in Chapter 3.

Japanese Heavy Antiaircraft Gun 45cal Type 10 4.7in

Muzzle velocity: 2,706ft/sec
Rate of fire (rpm): 10–11 max, 6–8 effective
Effective range:
Horizontal: 17,060yd
Vertical: 11,007yd
Effective: 9,241yd
Shell weight: 45.08lb

Japanese Heavy Cruiser Names

Based on 1905 directions from the Navy Minister, first-class cruisers were named after mountains. Second-class (eventually light) cruisers were named after rivers or streams.

Ashigara – a mountain in Kanagawa Prefecture
Atago – a mountain near Kyoto
Chikuma – a stream in Nagano Prefecture
Chokai – a mountain in Yamagata Prefecture
Furutaka – a mountain on the island of Etajima near Hiroshima
Haguro – a mountain in Yamagata Prefecture in northwest Honshu
Kako – a river in Hyogo Prefecture (confusion was caused by the fact that the name had originally been allocated to a 5,500-ton light cruiser)

Kinugasa – Mount Kinugasa near Kyoto
Kumano – a river in Mie Prefecture in Honshu
Maya – a mountain in Hyogo Prefecture
Mikuma – a river in Oita Prefecture in northeast Kyushu
Mogami – stream in Yamagata Prefecture
Myoko – a mountain in Niigata Prefecture
Nachi – a mountain in Wakayama Prefecture
Suzuya – a stream in southern Sakhalin
Takao – a mountain near Kyoto
Tone – a river on the Kanto Plain

Light Antiaircraft Armament

Before the war, the IJN decided to provide all cruisers with a standard light antiaircraft armament of four twin Type 96 25mm mounts grouped amidships and two twin 13mm machine guns fitted forward of the bridge. The inadequacies of the 25mm gun have already been discussed. Despite the growing profusion of 25mm guns on heavy cruisers during the war, these ships grew increasingly vulnerable to air attack.

The 4.7in high-angle gun was the IJN's standard treaty cruiser heavy antiaircraft gun. It dated from 1926 and lingered on into the war on as many as eight cruisers. It weighed 10 tons. (*Ships of the World* magazine)

HEAVY CRUISER RADAR

The Japanese began to equip all their cruisers with radars from mid-1943, doing so when ships returned to Japan for repair and refit. The first set fitted was the No. 21 radar. This instrument was fitted on the top of the foremast. The radar room was located in the foremast. The No. 13 air-search radar was introduced in 1943 and on heavy cruisers was fitted on the aft part of the foremast or the leading edge of the mainmast. The final type of cruiser radar was the No. 22 Modification 4M radar designed for surface search. These were mounted in pairs on both sides of the bridge or on the foremast.

THE HEAVY CRUISER CLASSES

Furutaka and Aoba Classes

Design and construction
The Japanese were developing the 7,500-ton scout cruiser well before the Washington Treaty came into effect, though even once the treaty was ratified, both their maximum displacement and gun caliber fell within treaty limits. The concept of the large scout cruiser was about producing a ship capable of performing scouting duties against the enemy's main fleet, while protecting the Japanese main fleet from enemy scouting forces. It was intended that these ships have superior capabilities to their nearest Allied counterparts of the day, the American Omaha-class cruisers and the RN's Hawkins class. As was to be the pattern for all of their heavy cruisers, the Japanese aimed to put a lot on a relatively small hull. In the case of the 7,500-ton ships, it was planned that they would mount six 7.9in/50cal single mounts and six 21in torpedo tubes. This configuration would give them a considerable firepower advantage over the American Omaha vessels. A high top speed of 35 knots was also required to enable the ships to keep formation with other Japanese scouting forces. To put so much on a relatively small hull would only be possible with the incorporation of many weight-saving measures. These were the responsibility of Constructor Captain (later Rear Admiral) Yuzuru Hiraga.

After construction began on the first two ships, the Naval General Staff pressured the design section to modify the design of the 7,500-ton units to fit the new 8in twin gun turrets. Work on the first two ships, *Furutaka* and *Kako*, was already too far along to accommodate such a change, but it was agreed to fit the new turrets on the next two ships,

Kinugasa and *Aoba*. Another major modification was to fit a catapult on the last two ships, which in turn required the redesign of the aft superstructure. The redesign also incorporated an upgraded antiaircraft fit and correction of some problems found with the smokestack and bridge of *Furutaka* and *Kako*.

Furutaka and Aoba Class Construction				
Ship	Built at	Laid down	Launched	Completed
Furutaka	Nagasaki by Mitsubishi	2/5/22	2/25/25	3/31/26
Kako	Kobe by Kawasaki	11/17/22	4/10/25	7/20/26
Aoba	Nagasaki by Mistubishi	2/4/24	9/25/26	9/20/27
Kinugasa	Kobe by Kawasaki	1/23/24	10/24/26	9/30/27

To achieve their design speed, the 7,500-ton vessels had the highest length-to-beam ratios of any Japanese cruiser. The hull was characterized by a graceful flush upper deck with an undulating sheer line. This design and other weight-saving measures meant that the hull was only 33 percent of trial displacement for the two units of the Furutaka class (32 percent on *Aoba*). Propulsion was provided by four sets of turbines that produced a total of 102,000 shaft horsepower. Twelve boilers located in seven boiler rooms provided the steam. As completed, all four ships either reached or exceeded their 35-knot design speed. Endurance was designed to be 7,000nm at 14 knots.

Protection was not a design emphasis. On both classes, belt and deck armor amounted to just over 12 percent of trial displacement. The main belt on the side was 3in (running for 262ft of the ship's length) and the overhead protection consisted of a maximum of 1.37in of steel armor on the armored deck and another 1.9in of high-tensile steel on the middle deck. The forward and aft magazines were given additional protection, as were the steering gear rooms.

Overall, the protection was inadequate against 8in shells, but was judged to be sufficient to deflect 6in shells at between 13,123 and 16,404 yards' range. Underwater protection was limited to a small bulge located below the waterline at the lower edge of the main belt. This, and the internal subdivision, which featured a centerline bulkhead to limit flooding to one side of the ship, provided minimal protection against torpedoes but was comparable to foreign designs.

Furutaka/Aoba Classes Specifications (after reconstruction)

Displacement: 11,273 standard; 11,660 tons full load
Dimensions: Length 607.5ft / beam 55.5ft /57.67ft / draft 33ft
Maximum speed: 33–34kt
Range: 7,900/8,223nm at 1kt
Crew: Furutaka class: 50 officers and 589 enlisted; *Kinugasa*: 50 officers and 607 enlisted; *Aoba*: 54 officers and 626 enlisted since it was fitted to be squadron flagship

Armament

As designed, the Furutaka class mounted a main armament of six 7.9in Type 3 50cal guns in six "semiturrets." These were of simple construction and provided minimal protection to the crews. All six were mounted on the centerline, allowing a full six-gun broadside. The Naval General Staff's push to mount the twin 7.9in turrets on the Aoba class resulted in a greater elevation (thus a greater maximum range) and a greater rate of fire because of the reduced physical strain on the gun crew. As originally completed, antiaircraft armament was limited to four single 3in guns on the Furutaka class and four upgraded 4.7in guns on the Aoba class. Despite the strong objections of Hiraga, the Furutaka and Aoba classes featured fixed torpedo tubes inside the hull. Six pairs were originally fitted.

Provision of aircraft was key to the ships' role as scouting cruisers. No suitable catapult was available when design work began, so the Furutaka class was provided with a take-off platform for a single floatplane instead. This proved awkward, and it was easier and faster to crane the floatplane into the water and recover it in the same way. In March 1928, *Kinugasa* became the first Japanese ship to carry a catapult, soon joined by *Aoba*.

Service modifications

Being the earliest Japanese heavy cruisers, both these classes were reconstructed before the Pacific War. The first to go in for modernization were *Furutaka* and *Kako*. Their modernization occurred earlier than planned; the ships had to go into repair for engine overhauls and the Japanese used that opportunity for a complete modernization. *Kako* was modernized at Sasebo from July 1936 until December 1937 and *Furutaka* at Kure from April 1937 until April 1939. Principal work included replacing the 7.9in guns with rebored 8in guns. The new turrets were known as E2 Model turrets, arranged as on the Aoba class with two forward and one aft.

The fixed torpedo tubes were replaced by two quadruple torpedo tube mounts, located one on each side. Since eight reloads were carried, each ship carried 16 torpedoes. All ships retained the 4.7in high-angle guns. Four twin Type 96 guns were fitted amidships and two twin Type 93 13mm machine guns fitted forward of the bridge.

The forward superstructure was almost totally rebuilt, which allowed for the modernization of the fire-control systems for the main, torpedo, and antiaircraft batteries. A heavier catapult was also fitted. These improvements added another 562 tons of weight. To compensate, the beam was increased by adding larger antitorpedo bulges filled with watertight steel tubes to increase buoyancy. The fitting of the bulges increased stability and actually

Furutaka in June 1939, after completion of modernization work at Kure. This was the ship's final configuration. Note the three 8in turrets and the reworked bridge. (*Ships of the World* magazine)

reduced draft despite the additional weight from the modernization. Speed was slightly reduced to 33 knots with the increase in weight being compensated for by the replacement of the original 12 boilers with ten oil-fired Kanpon boilers. This increased horsepower to 110,000shp. Effective endurance was increased to 7,900nm at 14 knots by the addition of greater fuel storage.

Modernization of the Aoba class was very similar. Both ships underwent work at Sasebo, *Kinugasa* beginning in October 1938 and Aoba in November 1938; both returned to service in October 1940. When completed, the two classes presented a similar appearance, with the only obvious differences being in the bridge appearance and the arrangement of the crane and catapult.

After the start of the war, three of the four ships of these classes were sunk before further modification. However, *Aoba* was considerably modified during its career. Damage in October 1942 included destruction of its No. 3 turret, which was removed and then plated over. A 25mm triple gun mount was temporarily fitted in its place. In August 1943, *Aoba* returned to Kure for major repairs. The No. 3 turret was replaced, two additional 25mm triple mounts were fitted, and a No. 21 radar was fitted. Damage to the engines, however, meant a permanent speed reduction to 28 knots.

In July 1944, *Aoba* received four triple and 15 single 25mm guns at Singapore; this gave the ship a total of 42 25mm barrels. Before the Battle of Leyte Gulf, the ship carried a No. 13 and No. 22 radar. The ship's final antiaircraft component, following a refit in June 1945, was five triple, ten double, and 15 single 25mm guns.

Wartime service

In November 1941, the four ships of the Furutaka and Aoba classes composed Sentai 6 (literally Division 6 in Japanese, but referring to a cruiser division) under Rear Admiral Aritomo Goto. Their first action was covering the successful invasion of Guam on December 1941. Sentai 6 then proceeded to cover the second Japanese attempt to invade Wake Island. Under cover of two of the Pearl Harbor carriers, Wake was successfully invaded on December 23. Sentai 6 was then dispatched to cover the invasion of Rabaul and Kavieng on January 23, 1942, and remained assigned to the Fourth Fleet (South Sea Force). In March 1942, the ships covered the invasion of Lae and Salamaua on New Guinea.

The next operation, the attempt to seize Port Moresby on New Guinea, did not go as well for the Japanese. Sentai 6 departed Truk on April 30 as part of the Main Body escorting the light carrier *Shoho*. After providing distant cover for the seizure of Tulagi in the Solomons on May 3, they again joined with *Shoho*. On May 7, 93 US carrier aircraft attacked *Shoho*, sinking it under a barrage of torpedoes and bombs. The Port Moresby operation failed and marked the first strategic Japanese setback of the war.

Sentai 6 remained in the South Pacific and was assigned to the newly created Eighth Fleet based at Rabaul. On August 7, the four cruisers departed Rabaul and headed toward Guadalcanal, where the local garrison had reported that the Americans had just landed. Sentai 6, along with fleet flagship *Chokai*, attacked the warships covering the American landing force and put on perhaps the best Japanese display of naval gunnery during the entire war. The Battle of Savo Island on August 9 resulted in the destruction of four Allied heavy cruisers (three American and one Australian). Engaging the surprised Americans at fairly close range – 5,500 yards and less – and assisted by searchlights, star shells, and flares from the Japanese ships' aircraft, gunnery results were very good, in excess of 10 percent hits. In exchange, *Kinugasa* was hit twice and *Aoba* once, but damage was not significant. The Americans extracted a measure of revenge when, on August 10, en route to Kavieng, submarine *S-44* fired four torpedoes at *Kako*; three hit and the cruiser blew up and sank.

The next major surface engagement off Guadalcanal occurred in October 1942. Known as the Battle of Cape Esperance, it was the first Japanese defeat in a night action during the war. The Japanese force was built around the three surviving cruisers of Sentai 6. Against an American cruiser force with the advantage of radar, Admiral Goto was slow to react. His flagship, *Aoba*, was hit by 24 shells and heavily damaged and the admiral killed. *Furutaka* was hit by a large number of shells (up to 90) and a torpedo;

Kako under way in 1940 in the configuration in which it would go to war. It had a very active war before being torpedoed and sunk in August 1942. (Naval History and Heritage Command)

additionally, some of its torpedoes exploded, starting additional fires. It sank on October 12 with 33 killed. Of the 225 missing, 115 were taken prisoner. *Kinugasa* was the only bright spot for the Japanese. It hit the US cruiser *Boise* with eight shells, including one that pierced the ship below the waterline and exploded in the forward magazine. The resulting fire would have destroyed the ship had not the water pouring through the hole made by the shell put out the fire. *Kinugasa* also hit the heavy cruiser *Salt Lake City* twice, but damage was slight.

Now only *Kinugasa* remained operational from Sentai 6. On October 15, *Kinugasa* and *Chokai* bombarded Henderson Field on Guadalcanal with 752 8in shells. On November 14, after covering another cruiser bombardment of Henderson, *Kinugasa* was attacked by dive-bombers from *Enterprise*. A bomb hit on the forward part of the bridge, penetrated below the waterline, and caused heavy flooding. The flooding could not be contained and the ship was eventually abandoned with the loss of 51 crewmen.

After Cape Esperance, *Aoba* was sent to Kure for repairs. The No. 3 turret was destroyed, so it was removed and the deck plated over and the ship sent back into action. On April 3, 1943, the ship was attacked by B-17 bombers at anchorage at Kavieng and was heavily damaged by a bomb and by the explosion of two of its torpedoes. The ship was beached, and later towed to Truk for repairs before returning to Japan.

Aoba was now a second-rate unit and was assigned to the First Southern Expeditionary Fleet. On March 1, 1944, the ship entered the Indian Ocean on a commerce raid with the cruisers *Tone* and *Chikuma*. Results were meager.

As part of the IJN's all-out effort during the battle for Leyte Gulf in October 1944, *Aoba* was tasked with escorting troop reinforcements to Leyte. On October 23, it was torpedoed en route to Manila by the submarine *Bream*, a single torpedo hitting its engine room. *Aoba* nevertheless departed the Philippines in November and reached Japan in December, where the damage was deemed irreparable. On March 19, at Kure, American carrier aircraft raided the base and heavily damaged *Aoba* once more. In June, the ship was moored as a floating battery near Kure, where an additional carrier

The top profile shows *Furutaka* in August 1942 as it appeared during the Battle of Savo Island. The Furutaka class can be distinguished from the Aoba class by the different bridge, the smaller second smokestack, and, most readily, by the different positioning of the crane and catapult. The second profile and overhead view depicts *Aoba* in its October 1944 configuration with a No. 21 radar on its foremast and a profusion of 25mm antiaircraft guns.

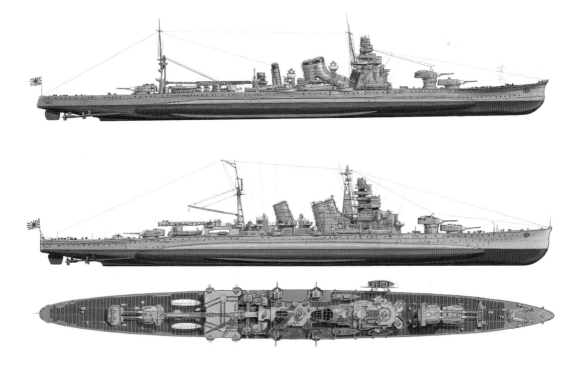

raid on July 24 hit *Aoba* with a bomb, which combined with a near miss caused flooding and a starboard list. The ship settled in 25ft of water. Days later, on July 28, the hulk was hit by another four bombs from B-24s and carrier aircraft, starting fires and breaking off the stern.

Myoko Class

Design and construction

The four units of what became the Myoko class were authorized by the Japanese Diet in March 1923. With the Washington Treaty in effect, these were the first Japanese cruisers designed under the treaty restrictions. The designers of the class, led by Hiraga, had a difficult time achieving the requirements of the Naval General Staff on the allowed 10,000-ton displacement. The original design requirements called for a ship mounting eight 8in guns in four turrets, a torpedo armament of eight 24in torpedo tubes in fixed mounts below the upper deck, protection against 6in shells with vital areas protected against indirect fire by 8in shells, a speed of more than 35 knots, and a radius of 10,000nm at 13.5 knots. Hiraga convinced the Naval General Staff to add another 8in turret, which would enable the ship to out-gun its foreign opponents, and most importantly to eliminate the torpedo armament, since the fixed tubes were actually located over the engine rooms and the detonation of a torpedo warhead could cause crippling damage. Hiraga's modified design, approved in August 1923, adhered to the treaty tonnage limit and did not include torpedo tubes. However, the Naval General Staff was not easily dissuaded, and when Hiraga was sent overseas, his successor was convinced to add 12 fixed mounts.

Myoko in May 1934. It has yet to undergo extensive modernization, but its original 7.9in main battery has been replaced with 8in guns. Note the single 4.7in high-angle guns still embarked and the original configuration of the aircraft-handling facilities. (Naval History and Heritage Command)

Ashigara pictured from a USN ship off the coast of China in 1938. Only minor additional modifications were made before the start of the war. (Naval History and Heritage Command)

In appearance, the ships resembled the previous class of cruisers. The Myokos presented a balanced, powerful appearance, with their profile dominated by a large bridge structure. As with the preceding classes, the Myokos ran into immediate problems with being over their design weight. Despite measures used to reduce the weight of the hull, the designed 2/3 trial displacement (11,850 tons) had reached 13,338 tons. This increase was partly due to the modifications made by the Naval General Staff, but the source of the majority of it remains unknown, according to Japanese sources. Given the fact that this unforeseen extra weight had adversely affected speed, radius, freeboard (thus submerging some of the armor belt), and reserve buoyancy, it is likely that the extra weight was not intentional.

Protection was improved over the previous classes, with armor and protective plates accounting for 16.1 percent of trial displacement. The main belt was 4in and extended just over 404ft, enough to cover the machinery spaces, turret barbettes, and magazines. Deck armor included 1.3–1.4in of steel armor on the middle deck and an upper deck composed of two layers, one with 0.6in and the other of between 0.5in and 1in. Turret barbettes were protected with a maximum of 3in of armor.

Protection against underwater threats was provided by a system of longitudinal bulkheads and submerged bulkheads. The longitudinal bulkheads consisted of two 1.14in plates that covered the side of the ship from the bottom of the main belt to the ship's double hull. The outer bulge ran 305ft and extended to a maximum depth of 8.16in. Altogether, the Japanese calculated that this system would be effective against a contact explosion of some 440lb of high explosive.

Propulsion was provided by four propellers, each driven by a Kanpon turbine. To achieve the design speed of 35.5 knots, 130,000shp was required. Twelve boilers were fitted and placed in nine boiler rooms. When the ships in the class conducted full-power trials, each posted speeds of more than

35 knots. Though the ships each carried 2,470 tons of oil, endurance was reduced from the designed 8,000nm to some 7,000nm due to the weight increase. This radius compared unfavorably with contemporary American and British cruisers.

Myoko Class Construction				
Ship	Built at	Laid down	Launched	Completed
Myoko	Yokosuka Navy Yard	10/25/24	4/16/27	7/31/29
Nachi	Kure Navy Yard	11/26/24	6/15/27	11/26/28
Ashigara	Kobe by Kawasaki	4/11/25	4/22/28	8/20/29
Haguro	Nagasaki by Mitsubishi	3/16/25	3/24/28	4/25/29

Armament

The Myoko class was designed with five dual turrets of 7.9in guns, as intelligence indicated that contemporary Allied cruisers carried only eight main guns. Antiaircraft protection was originally provided by six 4.7in high-angle guns in single mounts. A heavy torpedo armament featured six fixed 24in torpedo launchers on each beam.

Service modifications

Before the war, the class underwent major modernization. The first change occurred between 1931 and 1934, when the original 7.9in guns were replaced by 8in guns. In 1931, the Naval General Staff decided to upgrade the Myoko class further. This was carried out in a series of steps between 1934 and 1936. The first step was implemented in November 1934–June 1935 and was the most extensive. The fixed torpedo tube mounts were removed and replaced by two rotating quadruple mounts. The antiaircraft protection was increased by the removal of the single 4.7in mounts in favor of four twin 5in high-angle guns. Above the new torpedo room, two catapults were fitted with adequate space for three aircraft. Protection was enhanced by the extension of the torpedo bulge. The various additions increased displacement by 680 tons, which reduced the top speed to 34 knots. In the second step, the placement and types of searchlights were improved and a pair of quadruple 13mm Hotchkiss machine guns added. In the third step, the hull was reinforced and modifications made to the tripod mainmast and the foremast.

Plans for a second modernization were completed in June 1938, and executed in 1939. Modifications focused on upgrading the fire control and light antiaircraft armament. Two additional quadruple torpedo mounts

Haguro seen from another Myoko-class cruiser in 1937. In the foreground is a Type 89 dual-purpose twin mount and its Type 91 fire-control director. (Naval History and Heritage Command)

were fitted for a total of 16 tubes with 18 torpedo reloads. A heavier catapult was fitted, which allowed the ships to embark the newest type of reconnaissance seaplane. Despite the fact that the boilers were retubed, operational radius was decreased with the reduction of fuel capacity to 2,214 tons. This equated to an effective radius of 7,463nm at 14 knots. Crew size was increased to 891 (829 men and 62 officers). The weight increase of this modernization totaled 400 tons. As the antitorpedo bulge was replaced with a larger one, this created a larger beam and thus a smaller draft. The larger beam also increased stability.

Myoko in March 1941 after completion of its second modernization. A second set of quadruple torpedo launchers was added in the forward part of the torpedo room, which can be seen in the opening under the forward part of the catapult. *Myoko* possessed a different bridge structure from its sisters with a separate tower for the director and the 8in gun rangefinder. (*Ships of the World* magazine)

Wartime improvements centered on the addition of radar and the provision of larger antiaircraft guns. Between April and July 1943, all four ships returned to Japan for refit and modification. All received a No. 21 air-search radar mounted on top of the foremast and four additional twin 25mm mounts. A second round of modifications was made to the class, beginning in November 1943. Through March 1944, all four ships were fitted with eight single 25mm guns, and *Nachi* and *Ashigara* were fitted with No. 22 radars.

The third and final round of modernization was made after the Battle of the Philippine Sea, when all four ships returned to Kure between June and September 1944. *Myoko* and *Haguro* received No. 22 radars and another four triple and 16 single 25mm guns. *Nachi* and *Ashigara* received two twin and 20 single 25mm mounts. All units also received a No. 13 radar. To save weight, the forward pair of searchlights was removed as well as the aft quadruple torpedo mounts. Only 16 torpedoes were carried – eight in the tubes with eight reloads.

Myoko Class Antiaircraft Fit, October 1944				
Ship	Triple mounts	Twin mounts	Single mounts	Total 25mm guns
Myoko	4	8	24	52
Haguro	4	8	24	52
Nachi	0	10	28	48
Ashigara	0	10	28	48

Wartime service

At the start of the war, the Myoko class comprised Sentai 4. All except *Ashigara* were assigned to cover the invasion of the southern Philippines at the start of war. On January 4, 1942, *Myoko* became the first Japanese heavy cruiser damaged during the war when it was hit by a single bomb from a B-17 while anchored in Davao Gulf; 35 men were killed and repairs took until February 20.

On February 27, 1942, *Nachi* and *Haguro* led a Japanese force against a mixed Dutch–British–American–Australian force. This engagement, known as the Battle of the Java Sea, was the IJN's first opportunity to employ its favored tactic of massed torpedo attack. The results were a mixed bag. A torpedo from *Haguro* sank a Dutch destroyer, and, early on February 28, torpedoes from *Haguro* and *Nachi* sank the Dutch cruisers *De Ruyter* and *Java*. These few hits decided the battle and opened Java to Japanese invasion. Yet the performance of the heavy cruisers was not up to Japanese expectations.

During the height of the battle, 1,271 8in shells were fired from just under 22,000 yards to more than 27,000 yards; only five hit, and four of these were duds. Torpedo accuracy was also dismal, with *Haguro* firing 20 and *Nachi* 16; a total of 153 torpedoes were fired, with only three hits.

The victory at Java Sea was followed on March 1, 1942, with all four Myokos participating in the sinking by gunfire of the British heavy cruiser *Exeter* and a destroyer. Again, the quality of gunnery was an issue, with the four ships expending 1,459 rounds and 24 torpedoes. While *Ashigara* remained in the East Indies, *Myoko* and *Haguro* were then assigned as escorts to the main Japanese carrier force during the Battle of Coral Sea in May 1942. They quickly returned north to participate in the Battle of Midway in June. *Nachi* acted as flagship of the force dedicated to the invasion of the Aleutians.

Despite their formidable night combat capabilities, the Myoko class was not heavily involved in the struggle for Guadalcanal. *Myoko* bombarded Henderson Field during the night of October 15–16. Meanwhile, *Nachi* was assigned as the flagship of the Fifth Fleet responsible for operations in the North Pacific and *Ashigara* was active in the East Indies as flagship of the Second Southern Expeditionary Fleet.

In March 1943, *Nachi*, alongside the Takao-class cruiser *Maya*, took part in the Battle of Komandorski Islands while attempting to move troops and supplies to Japanese-occupied Attu Island in the Aleutians. *Nachi* launched torpedoes at enemy vessels with no result, and a four-hour gun battle was inconclusive. The only American heavy cruiser present, *Salt Lake City*, was damaged, but no American ships were lost and the Japanese operation to supply the island was turned back. *Nachi* was damaged by five 5in shells with the loss of 14 men. Again, Japanese long-range cruiser gunnery had proved ineffective.

A fine overhead view of *Nachi* in 1941, showing its early-war configuration. The large bridge remains after the ship's modernization, but unlike *Myoko*, a single tower on top of the bridge mounts both the fire-control director for the main battery and the rangefinder. Amidships are the four twin Type 89 5in guns and the four twin 25mm twin mounts located near the two smokestacks. Fire-control directors for the antiaircraft weapons are also visible, as are four large searchlights for night combat grouped around the forward smokestack. The aircraft handling area was sufficient to embark three aircraft. (Yamato Museum)

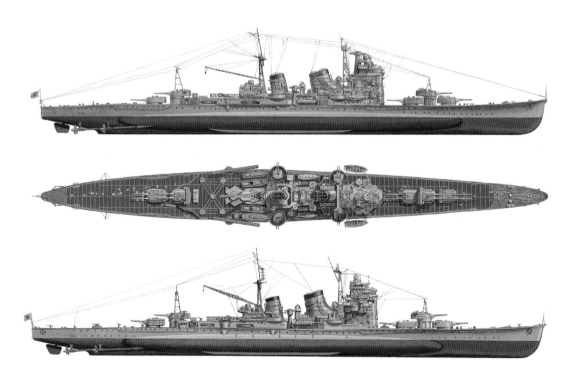

The top profile and overhead view show the February 1942 configuration of *Nachi* as it appeared during the Battle of the Java Sea. At this time, all four ships in the class were basically identical. By 1944, the appearance of the class had changed, as the bottom profile of *Myoko* in its October 1944 configuration indicates. Note the No. 21 radar on the foremast and the No. 13 radar on the mainmast and the addition of many single and triple 25mm mounts.

In late 1943, *Myoko* and *Haguro* were sent to Rabaul. The two cruisers formed the centerpiece of a Japanese surface action group that departed Rabaul on November 1, 1943, in response to the American invasion of Bougainville. The Japanese were unable to cope effectively with American radar-controlled gunnery and the night attack failed. *Myoko* was damaged in a collision with an escorting destroyer and *Haguro* received minor damage from some ten 5in and 6in shells, most of which were duds.

Nachi, later joined by *Ashigara* in April 1944, remained as the nucleus of the Fifth Fleet. Later, in June, *Myoko* and *Haguro* participated in the Battle of the Philippine Sea, but neither was damaged.

All four Myoko-class ships were active in the resulting series of actions, known collectively as the Battle of Leyte Gulf. *Myoko* and *Haguro* were assigned to the principal Japanese force, the First Diversionary Attack Force (also known as the Center Force). In a series of air attacks from American carriers on October 24 in the Sibuyan Sea, *Myoko* was struck by a single Mark 13 torpedo by aircraft from the carrier *Intrepid*. The torpedo struck the starboard side aft and put the starboard screws out of action. Since the ship could now only manage 15 knots, it was ordered to Singapore. After temporary repairs, *Myoko* was ordered to return to Japan. While en route, it was torpedoed again by the submarine *Bergall*; fires ignited and part of the stern broke off. After much effort, *Myoko* was towed back to Singapore, but assessed to be beyond repair. It was later moved to Seletar as a floating antiaircraft battery. *Myoko* was surrendered in September 1945 at Seletar, one of only two cruisers to survive the war afloat. The ship was scuttled by the British in July 1946.

Nachi and *Ashigara* were also engaged at Leyte Gulf as part of the Second Diversionary Attack Force. In the later part of the Battle of Surigao Strait, both cruisers launched eight torpedoes by radar against American units blocking the exit from the strait, then departed the battle area. During the retirement, *Nachi* collided with *Mogami*. *Nachi* proceeded to Manila, where American carrier aircraft sank the cruiser on November 5 off Cavite Naval Base. The cruiser was initially hit by about five bombs and two to three torpedoes and brought to a halt. Another wave of attacks literally tore the cruiser apart, with five torpedoes and 20 bomb strikes breaking it into three pieces. Only 220 crewmen survived the attack.

Ashigara participated in a December 26, 1944, attack on the American beachhead at San José on Mindoro Island in the Philippines. The vessel was hit by a 500lb bomb, but managed to bombard the American beachhead with more than 200 8in shells. In February 1945, *Ashigara* and *Haguro* were transferred to the Tenth Area Fleet and were tasked with transporting troops and supplies around the Dutch East Indies and to islands in the Bay of Bengal. While transiting from Batavia to Singapore on June 8, 1945, *Ashigara* was attacked by the RN submarine HMS *Trenchant*. The submarine delivered a well-planned attack and hit the cruiser with five torpedoes. The ship sank with heavy loss of life among the 1,600 army troops onboard.

Haguro's luck ran out in May 1945 during an operation to run supplies to the Andaman Islands. Early on May 16, four RN destroyers executed a brilliant assault, launching 37 torpedoes at short range. At least three hit the cruiser, which sank with heavy loss of life. This was the last major surface action of World War II.

Takao Class

Design and construction

The Takao class was an improved version of the Myoko class. The chief designer was Constructor Captain Fujimoto, who had succeeded Rear Admiral Hiraga. For the hull, powerplant, protection, and main gun configuration, Fujimoto decided to go with that already used for the Myoko

---

Myoko Class Specifications (after second reconstruction)

Displacement: 13,380 tons standard; 15,933 tons full load
Dimensions: Length 668.5ft / beam 68ft / draft 36ft
Maximum speed: 33kt
Range: 7,463nm at 14kt
Crew: 920 in *Haguro* and *Nachi* (*sentai* flagships); 970 in *Myoko* and *Ashigara* (fitted as fleet flagships)

class. The differences would be in a new type of 8in gun that possessed a greater elevation and was therefore thought to be suitable for antiaircraft work, and in the substitution of rotating torpedo mounts, which were placed on the main deck. Protection was increased and an additional catapult fitted. Aesthetically, the two classes looked dramatically different, as the new class was planned to fit a massive bridge structure.

Since the design of the class predated the trials of the preceding Myoko class, the same issues of excessive weight existed. Despite weight-saving measures, the displacement was 10 percent greater than designed. The total weight of the class devoted to armor and protective plates was 2,368 tons or 16.8 percent of total displacement. This was some 340 tons greater than in the Myoko class. Protection was on the same scale as the Myoko class, but with slight modifications. The area included in the fore and aft armored bulkheads was shorter, as was the side armor belt. However, protection over the fore and aft magazines was heavier. Underwater protection was comparable to the Myoko class, with the antitorpedo bulkheads being calculated to be able to withstand a 440lb high-explosive charge.

Takao Class Construction				
Ship	Built at	Laid down	Launched	Completed
Takao	Yokosuka Navy Yard	4/28/27	5/12/30	5/31/32
Atago	Kure Navy Yard	4/28/27	6/16/30	3/30/32
Maya	Kobe by Kawasaki	12/4/28	11/8/30	6/30/32
Chokai	Nagasaki by Mitsubishi	3/26/28	4/5/31	6/30/32

The salient design feature was the massive new bridge, with three times the volume of Myoko's bridge. Though the weight of such a large structure added to an already overweight design, designers decided the price was worth paying to provide a central location for the increasingly complex equipment needed to conduct gunnery and torpedo combat at greater ranges. Fire control for the main battery and the 4.7in antiaircraft guns, as well as for the torpedo battery, was located in the bridge structure. Also included were spaces for navigation and communication and for command and staff personnel. Some of the vital areas were provided with 0.4in steel plates for protection against aircraft machine guns.

The aircraft facilities on the Takao class were improved over the previous classes. Two catapults were fitted and enough room was provided for three aircraft. The propulsion system was similar to that on *Myoko*. Four shafts developed a total of 130,000shp. All four ships developed speeds of 35 knots

or greater during trials. The design endurance was 8,000nm at 14 knots, but the excess weight meant that this range was reduced by some 1,000nm.

Atago in its original configuration, before its major 1938–39 modernization. During this modernization, the size of its enormous bridge superstructure was reduced and its masts shortened. (Naval History and Heritage Command)

Armament

The armament for the Takao class was identical in layout to that of the Myoko class. The only real difference was the mounting of a new type of 8in gun, which was designed for both antisurface and antiaircraft fire. To accomplish its intended antiaircraft duties, the gun turrets were designed to have a maximum elevation of 70 degrees. In practice, though, it was found that only a 55-degree elevation was possible. Protection of the turrets was provided by 1in of armor all round, sufficient only to give the gun crew splinter protection. The promise of the new 8in gun as an antiaircraft weapon, however, was never realized. The designed firing rate was 5 rounds per minute, but since the gun had to be brought down to 5 degrees to load (taking 8 seconds to depress and elevate), this was never attained. The training speed of such a large turret was also inadequate for antiaircraft work.

The failure of the 8in gun as an antiaircraft weapon meant the burden of air defense fell to single 4.7in guns. The Takao class fitted only four of these weapons, unlike the six on the Myoko class. Close-in air defense was provided by two 40mm Vickers guns and two 7.7mm Vickers machine guns. Both were found to be ineffective and were replaced by 13mm and 25mm Japanese-designed weapons in 1935.

As built, the Takao class featured rotating torpedo mounts in place of the fixed mounts on earlier classes. Measures were taken to reduce the damage to the ship if the torpedoes were hit during combat. The mounts were located outside of the hull and mounted on sponsons to extend beyond the hull surface. In action, the tubes could be trained further away from the ship's hull, and the warheads were protected by a steel casing when not in the tubes. Originally, 12 tubes were planned, but this number was reduced to eight due to weight and space issues. In addition to the eight torpedoes located in the tubes, another 16 were carried as reloads. By means of a system of aerial rails in the torpedo rooms, a second broadside could be fired within three minutes of the first and a third, eight minutes later.

Service modifications

Plans for modernizing the Takao class were complete by April 1938, but the approach of war meant that only two ships in the class were fully modernized: *Takao* at Yokosuka from May 1938 to August 1939 and *Atago* from April 1938 to October 1939. *Chokai* and *Maya* received only limited modernization before the war, including modifications to handle the Type 93 oxygen-propelled torpedo, heavier catapults, and the standard fit of 13mm and 25mm light antiaircraft guns.

During the modernization, the antiaircraft armament was increased, though the projected fit of the Type 89 5in twin guns did not begin until after the start of the war: *Atago* and *Takao* received theirs in May 1942; *Chokai* retained the single 4.7in guns until it was lost in 1944; *Maya* kept hers until reconstruction as an antiaircraft cruiser began in November 1943. The light antiaircraft armament was standardized and in the autumn of 1941 the two twin 13mm mounts were replaced with two 25mm mounts. The torpedo armament was augmented by the substitution of quad mounts for the existing double torpedo mounts.

The largest change was to the bridge structure, which was rebuilt to reduce topweight. When completed, the bridge was much smaller in appearance and was the primary feature for distinguishing *Atago* and *Takao*

Chokai pictured off the Chinese coast in 1938. The massive bridge structure is clearly evident and was retained by *Chokai* until it was sunk in 1944. The *Chokai* was the least modified of its class during the war. (Naval History and Heritage Command)

from their sisters *Maya* and *Chokai*. The bridge accommodated new fire-control equipment and featured the placement of an almost 20ft rangefinder in a separate tower immediately aft of the Type 94 fire-control director.

A fine beam view of *Atago* in August 1939 after modernization. The principal changes during modernization were the reduction in the size of the bridge and the movement of the mainmast further aft. The new bridge structure was topped with the main battery director and a rangefinder measuring almost 20ft. Unlike in the Myoko class, the Takao class placed their torpedo launchers forward, as shown here, and not aft under the aircraft deck. (*Ships of the World* magazine)

Takao Class Antiaircraft Fit, October 1944				
Ship	Triple mounts	Twin mounts	Single mounts	Total 25mm guns
Takao	6	6	30	60
Atago	6	6	30	60
Maya	13	0	27	66
Chokai	0	8	22	38

The other primary change was the alteration of the aircraft-handling facilities and the area of the hangar. To do this, the mainmast was moved 82ft aft. Two heavier catapults were also fitted and moved forward. As on the Myoko class, larger bulges were fitted to increase antitorpedo protection and stability.

During the war, modifications were made to the ships' radar and light antiaircraft fit. In July–August 1943, *Atago* and *Takao* received the foremast-mounted No. 21 radar and two triple 25mm guns, making their total light antiaircraft fit six twin and two triple mounts. *Maya* and *Chokai* received the No. 21 radar and two twin 25mm mounts between August and September, making their total antiaircraft fit eight twin mounts.

In November 1943–January 1944, *Atago* and *Takao* were fitted with No. 22 radars and eight 25mm single guns. *Chokai* could not return to Japan during this period, but was given ten single 25mm guns at Truk. After receiving severe damage in November 1943, *Maya* returned to Yokosuka in December 1943 for repair and conversion into an antiaircraft cruiser. Its No. 3 8in gun turret was removed, as were all its twin 25mm mounts, the single 4.7in mounts, and its old twin torpedo tubes. In their place were fitted six twin Type 89 guns with two Type 94 directors, plus 13 triple and

This is the only close-up photo of *Maya* as an antiaircraft cruiser. The view is from May 1944 and was almost certainly taken at Lingga Roads, where the Mobile Fleet was stationed in preparation for a decisive battle. This view clearly shows how the 8in No. 3 turret was replaced by a pair of twin 5in guns and three triple 25mm guns. (*Ships of the World* magazine)

nine single Type 96 guns. In addition, 36 13mm machine guns on moveable mounts and four quadruple torpedo mounts with no reserve torpedoes were fitted. A No. 22 radar was added, and the No. 21 radar received a larger antenna.

Another round of modernization began after the Battle of the Philippine Sea in June 1944. All four units received a No. 13 radar and *Chokai* finally received a No. 22 set. In June 1944, *Atago* and *Takao* received four triple and 22 single 25mm guns. *Maya* received another 18 single guns, while *Chokai* received 12 more single mounts. Plans were made to convert it as with *Maya*, but since it did not return to Japan until June 1944, these were never carried out.

Wartime service

The four units of the Takao class comprised Sentai 4 at the start of the war. All were initially deployed into the South China Sea to support the Japanese invasion of Malaya. In January and February 1942, Sentai 4 provided distant cover for the invasion of the Dutch East Indies. In late February, the unit moved south of Java to catch fleeing Allied ships – eight were sunk, including the American destroyer *Pillsbury*.

Chokai was assigned to take part in the April 1942 Indian Ocean raid as Vice Admiral Jisaburo Ozawa's flagship. In June 1942, both *Atago* and *Chokai* were assigned to the abortive Midway operation, while *Takao* and *Maya* took part in the Japanese seizure of two Aleutian islands.

Continuing in its role as a fleet flagship, *Chokai* was assigned to the Eighth Fleet in August 1942. As the flagship of Vice Admiral Gunichi Mikawa, it played a central role in the Japanese victory at Savo Island, although it also received the most damage of any Japanese ship present – American cruisers achieved several hits, killing 34 crewmen. Throughout the campaign, *Chokai* was a regular visitor to the waters around Guadalcanal, and on October 14 *Chokai* and *Kinugasa* bombarded Henderson Field. On November 3, the other three ships of Sentai 4 departed Truk to reinforce the

Eighth Fleet. Later, on November 13, *Maya* and *Chokai* left Shortland anchorage to conduct a night bombardment of Henderson Field alongside *Suzuya*. After hitting the airfield with 989 shells, the cruisers were attacked during their withdrawal by aircraft from *Enterprise*. *Kinugasa* was sunk, *Chokai* slightly damaged, and *Maya* more heavily damaged when a dive-bomber struck the ship's mainmast and crashed into its port side, igniting fires. *Maya*'s torpedoes were jettisoned to avoid a disaster and it was sent back to Japan for repairs.

Atago and *Takao* were present at the Second Naval Battle of Guadalcanal. The scenario seemed a favorable one for the IJN, with a large force of destroyers led by two of its finest heavy cruisers working at night against an improvised American force operating in confined waters. *Atago* and *Takao* each launched eight torpedoes at *Washington* from a mere 4,000 yards' range, but all missed. The cruisers did succeed in scoring at least 16 8in hits on *South Dakota*, but caused no critical damage to the heavily armored battleship.

After its repairs, *Maya* was assigned to the Fifth Fleet and took part with *Nachi* in the March 1943 Battle of Komandorski Islands, as already recounted. Later that year, *Takao*, *Atago*, *Maya*, and other heavy cruisers were forward-deployed to Rabaul with the aim of launching a massive cruiser attack on the American invasion forces at Empress Augusta Bay on Bougainville. To forestall such an operation, the Americans hastily mounted a carrier air attack on the cruisers on November 5, while the Japanese vessels were still anchored in Rabaul Harbor. *Takao* was hit by a bomb near No. 2 turret, killing 23 men; it departed the same day with *Atago* for Truk. *Atago* suffered three near misses that caused flooding in the boiler and engine rooms. *Maya* was heavily damaged when a dive-bomber hit the aircraft deck above the No. 3 engine room and started a major fire in the engine room itself that killed 70. *Maya* returned to Japan in December 1943 and underwent major repairs and conversion.

The entire Takao class participated in the Philippine Sea operation. *Maya* was slightly damaged by near misses from carrier air attack. Leyte Gulf, however, was the death knell of the IJN's finest class of cruisers. All four were assigned to the First Diversionary Attack Force. On October 23, the force was ambushed by two American submarines in the Palawan Passage. *Darter* sank *Atago* with four torpedoes and hit *Takao* with two others, setting it afire and stopping it dead in the water. *Dace* sank *Maya* with four torpedoes, killing 470 of 1,105 crewmen. *Takao* was able to get under way and arrived

> ### Takao Class Specifications (*Takao* and *Atago* after reconstruction)
>
> **Displacement:** 13,400 tons standard; 15,186 tons full load (*Takao* and *Atago* 15,641 tons)
> **Dimensions:** Length 668.5ft / beam 67ft (*Takao* and *Atago* 68ft) / draft 36ft
> **Maximum speed:** 35.5kt
> **Range:** 7,000nm at 14kt
> **Crew:** 900–920 by 1941, and if a fleet staff was embarked, this increased further to 970. Wartime modifications brought the crew to approximately 1,100.

Takao

This view depicts *Takao* as it appeared in October 1944 before the
Battle of Leyte Gulf. *Takao* was the lead ship of the IJN's most
powerful class of heavy cruisers. After an eventful wartime career,
Takao was heavily damaged at Leyte Gulf by submarine torpedoes
and sat out the remainder of the war in Singapore. *Takao* is shown
with all wartime modifications, principally an augmented
antiaircraft suite and the addition of radar.

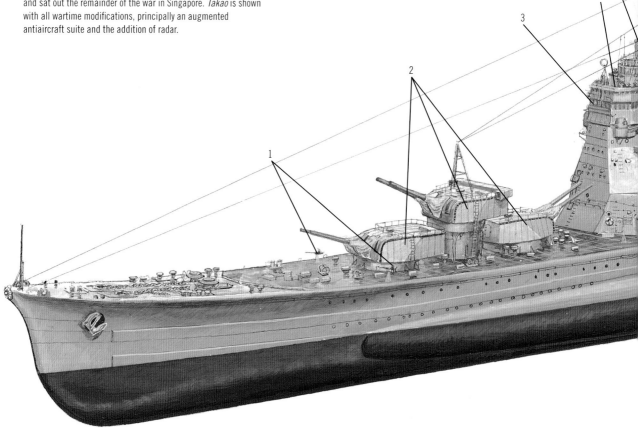

Key

1 Type 96 25mm single machine gun
   (10 shown)
2 7.9in/50cal Model E gun turret (5)
3 Compass bridge
4 Antiaircraft platform
5 Type 94 low-angle director tower
6 6m rangefinder
7 Type 91 high-angle director (for 5in guns)
8 No. 22 radar
9 No. 21 radar
10 Radar room
11 No. 13 radar
12 4.5m high-angle rangefinder

13 60cm signaling searchlight
14 Forward smokestack
15 Type 95 machine-gun control tower
16 Aft smokestack
17 Type 92 110cm searchlight (2 shown)
18 Auxiliary main gun director
19 20m aircraft crane
20 Type 0 long-range reconnaissance floatplane
21 Mainmast
22 Type 96 25mm triple machine gun (4 shown)
23 Kure No. 2, Model 5 catapult
24 Type 89 5in/40cal high-angle gun
   (2 shown)

25 Type 96 25mm double machine gun
   (3 shown)
26 Foremast
27 Generator room
28 Condensers
29 Cruising turbine
30 Low pressure turbine
31 Boiler room 8
32 Boiler room 6
33 Boiler room 4
34 Boiler room 3
35 Type 92 quadruple torpedo mount
   (2 shown)

in Singapore on November 12. The cruiser was deemed irreparable and was moved to join *Myoko* in Seletar Harbor as a floating antiaircraft battery.

Only *Chokai* remained to take part in the October 25, 1944, battle off Samar against American escort carriers and destroyers. *Chokai* was engaged by the destroyer escort *Samuel B. Roberts* with its 5in guns. Minutes after being hit amidships, a secondary explosion, caused by its own torpedoes, knocked out *Chokai*'s propulsion system and rudder. It was then attacked by aircraft from the escort carrier *Kitkun Bay* and hit by 500lb bombs and brought to a stop. Later that morning, the crew was taken off by a destroyer and the cruiser scuttled. All survivors were killed when the destroyer was sunk two days later by American carrier aircraft.

During the night of July 30–31, 1945, the Royal Navy attacked the two surviving damaged heavy cruisers in Seletar Harbor. *Myoko* was undamaged, but the midget submarine *XE3* successfully approached *Takao* and placed six limpet mines under the ship's keel. The blasts of some of the mines blew a 23x10ft hole in the ship's hull and created other serious damage, but it miraculously stayed afloat. It was surrendered in September 1945 and scuttled in October 1946.

Mogami Class

Design and construction

Design of the first class of Japanese light cruiser to be built fully under Washington Treaty restrictions began in 1930. The Naval General Staff gave the design team the same basic requirements used for the 10,000-ton-class cruisers, with the salient exception that these 8,500-ton ships were armed with 15 6.1in guns instead of the usual 8in battery. However, the design had to accommodate the upgrade from 6.1in to 8in as soon as the treaty ceased to apply. Torpedo armament remained heavy – 12 tubes in triple mounts. Design speed was set at 37 knots. As in the earlier heavy cruiser designs, the magazines required protection against 8in shells and the machinery spaces were protected against 6in shells. This set of design requirements was literally impossible to achieve on such a small displacement, even with extensive electric welding to save weight. The design adopted in 1931 was overweight at 9,500 tons. The original Mogami design borrowed much from the Takao class. There were noticeable differences, however. The arrangement of the front three turrets was altered and the Mogamis used a single smokestack instead of two. The ship's heavy antiaircraft armament was increased with the addition of 5in twin mounts.

Predictably, the original design ran into trouble. The launch of the first two ships in the class, *Mogami* and *Mikuma*, came just after the capsizing of the torpedo boat *Tomozuru* on March 12, 1934. This disaster prompted a study of the stability of the IJN's ships, and when the report on the incident was completed in June, several major design changes were decided for the new class of overweight cruisers. To reduce weight and lower the center of gravity, the large bridge structure copied from the Takao design was replaced by a much smaller version. A smaller foremast was also substituted. The seaplane hangar was removed, as were the large structures around the mainmast. When the lead ship commenced trials in March 1935, many problems were also found with the electrically welded hull. After repairs, *Mogami* and *Mikuma* joined the fleet for maneuvers in September 1935, and during a typhoon minor hull damage was incurred. Both units were placed out of service for the second time; trials on the next ship, *Suzuya*, were stopped, as was construction of the final ship in the class, *Kumano*.

A fine port-quarter view of *Mogami* in August 1935. Despite its impressive and compact appearance, the ship was taken in for reconstruction in 1936 to address stability concerns. (*Ships of the World* magazine)

The subsequent reconstruction included the replacement of the welded hull plates with riveted plates and an expanded bulge to enhance stability. These structural improvements added some 1,000 tons in weight, which meant that when *Mogami* was finally completed, it was 1,800 tons over its design displacement. Reconstruction delayed the recommissioning of *Mogami* until February 1938; *Mikuma* and *Suzuya* had their rework completed by October 1937. *Kumano* was completed with the modifications being fitted to the rest of the class, and was commissioned the same day as *Suzuya*.

Mogami Class Construction				
Ship	Built at	Laid down	Launched	Completed
Mogami	Kure Navy Yard	10/27/31	3/14/34	7/28/35
Mikuma	Nagasaki by Mitsubishi	12/24/31	5/31/34	8/29/35
Suzuya	Yokosuka Navy Yard	12/11/33	11/20/34	10/31/37
Kumano	Kobe by Kawasaki	4/5/34	10/15/36	10/31/37

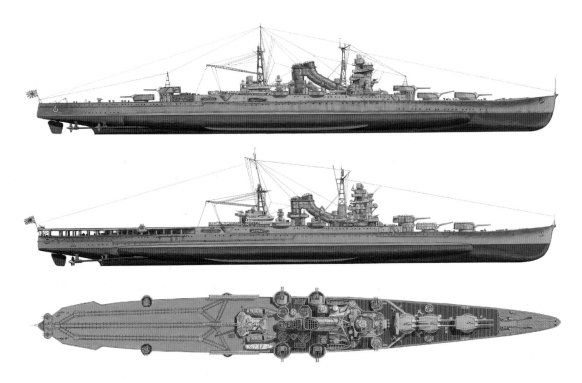

The top profile is of *Mikuma* during the Japanese conquest of the Dutch East Indies and depicts the ship in its early-war configuration. The second profile and overhead view is of *Mogami* in 1944 following its conversion into a hybrid cruiser-carrier. This was by far the most extensive wartime modernization of a Japanese cruiser. The two aft 8in turrets have been removed and the aircraft deck extended to the stern. This permitted as many as 11 floatplanes to be embarked.

Japan's withdrawal from the Washington Treaty on December 29, 1934, and the decision on January 15, 1936 not to sign the Second London Naval Treaty, meant that the Mogami class modernization could proceed without regard to weight or armament restrictions. The Japanese accordingly planned to replace the existing 6.1in guns with 8in guns, mount heavier catapults, and increase the torpedo armament. This work was completed between September 1939 and April 1940.

Protection for the Mogami class was similar to previous classes of heavy cruiser, with a main belt of a maximum 4in of armor and enhanced protection over magazine spaces of up to 5.5in. Overhead protection included an armored deck of 1.4in and an additional 1.6in on the lower deck over the magazines. The propulsion system was more efficient and powerful than that fitted on the Myoko and Takao classes. A total of 152,000shp was generated to meet the design requirement of 37 knots. Since the ships were overweight, however, the design speed was not reached, though all four ships attained 34–35 knots during full-power trials.

Armament

When completed, the Mogami class mounted 15 6.1in guns in five triple turrets. The No. 2 turret was mounted directly behind the No. 1 turret and could only fire broadside. Antiaircraft armament was the standard eight 5in guns in four twin mounts, four twin 25mm mounts amidships, and a pair of 13mm machine guns forward of the bridge. The torpedo armament was 12 tubes in four triple mounts, mounted two per side. In 1939–40, ten 8in guns in five turrets replaced the 6.1in guns.

Service modifications

Mikuma was lost at Midway before any wartime modifications were made. *Mogami* was badly damaged in the same battle and, as will be described below, it was selected for the most extensive modification of any IJN cruiser. For the remainder of the war, modifications focused on improving air defense capability. In fact, plans were made in late 1942/early 1943 for the conversion of *Suzuya* and *Kumano* into antiaircraft cruisers by removing their 8in guns in favor of additional Type 89 5in mounts, but these were not carried out. These units received a No. 21 radar on top of the foremast and four triple 25mm gun mounts, two in front of the bridge in place of the 13mm machine guns and two by the mainmast. In March–April 1944, eight single 25mm guns were added. After the Battle of Philippine Sea in June 1944, further modifications were made with the addition of two No. 22 radars on the foremast and a No. 13 radar mounted on the forward part of the mainmast. Four more triple 25mm mounts were also fitted, two near the bridge and two on the stern. *Suzuya* received ten single mounts and *Kumano* 16.

Mogami Class Antiaircraft Fit, October 1944				
Ship	**Triple mounts**	**Twin mounts**	**Single mounts**	**Total 25mm guns**
Mogami	14	0	18	60
Suzuya	8	4	18	50
Kumano	8	4	24	56

After being damaged at Midway, *Mogami* returned to Japan in August 1942. One of the Japanese lessons from the battle was that the numbers of scouting aircraft operating from the cruisers were inadequate. Accordingly, it was decided to convert *Mogami* into an aircraft cruiser. This entailed the removal of the two aft 8in turrets and the extension of the aircraft deck to the stern of the ship, providing room for 11 seaplanes. During the course of this reconstruction, a No. 21 radar was added on the foremast and the previous light antiaircraft fit was removed and replaced by ten triple 25mm mounts. When *Mogami* was under repair after its November 1943 damage, eight additional single 25mm mounts were added on the aircraft deck. Ten

An overhead shot of a Mogami-class cruiser in February 1943 showing the layout of the five 8in turrets, two of which appear to be painted with air recognition markings. Based on the date, this is probably *Kumano* in the area of Kavieng. (Naval History and Heritage Command)

more single mounts were added in June 1944, together with four 25mm triple mounts.

Wartime service

The four Mogami-class ships formed Sentai 7 at the start of the war. In the initial weeks of the conflict this unit covered invasion convoys destined for Malaya and British Borneo. Not until the landings on Java did the Mogami-class vessels see their first action. In the aftermath of the Battle of the Java Sea, *Mogami* and *Mikuma* engaged the American heavy cruiser *Houston* and the Australian light cruiser *Perth* in the Battle of Sunda Strait on the night of February 28–March 1. The two Allied cruisers were sunk under a hail of torpedoes and searchlight-directed gunfire from the two Japanese cruisers and their escorting destroyers. Unfortunately for the Japanese, in the confusion *Mogami* sank five Japanese units (four army transports and a minesweeper) when its torpedoes missed the intended target (*Houston*) and ran into the anchorage of the invasion fleet. Investigations later in the war confirmed that *Mogami* was the culprit, not the destroyer *Fubuki* as first thought.

Following operations to cover landings in northern Sumatra, the cruisers joined *Chokai* for the Indian Ocean raid. Split into two groups, Sentai 7 accounted for eight Allied merchant ships.

Next up for Sentai 7 was the invasion of Midway. The cruisers made up the Close Support Group with responsibility for shelling the island prior to a Japanese landing. After the battle turned against the IJN, and in an attempt to retrieve the situation, Sentai 7 was ordered to close the island on June 5 and destroy the airfield. When reason finally prevailed, the bombardment was canceled, but by this time the cruisers were only 90 miles from the island. While executing the turn to the east to depart the area, a submarine was spotted and, in the subsequent maneuvers, *Mogami* accidentally rammed *Mikuma*. *Mikuma* was still able to steer, but *Mogami*'s bow was heavily damaged and its speed reduced to 21 knots.

The two undamaged cruisers from Sentai 7 were ordered to depart the area at high speed, but the ordeal of the two damaged ships now began in earnest. On the morning of June 7, American carrier dive-bombers launched three attacks on the two cruisers. The first placed two bombs on *Mogami*. The crew had taken the earlier precaution of jettisoning the torpedoes, so a fire in the area of the torpedo room was put out with no further damage. The second attack was devastating, with two more hits on *Mogami* and at

least five on *Mikuma*. Fires in the engine room brought *Mikuma* to a halt, and when they spread to the torpedo room, its torpedoes exploded and demolished the aft part of the superstructure. The final wave of attackers deposited another bomb on *Mogami*; although it did not sink, its total casualties were 92 dead and 101 wounded. *Mikuma* finally sank on the evening of June 7 with the loss of precisely 700 of its crew. It was the first Japanese cruiser lost in the war.

The remnants of Sentai 7 were moved to the South Pacific after the American invasion of Guadalcanal. Both cruisers were active in the carrier battles of Eastern Solomons and Santa Cruz, and were undamaged. *Suzuya* was ordered to reinforce the Eighth Fleet in early November. On the night of November 13–14, *Suzuya* bombarded Henderson Field with 504 shells.

Sentai 7 remained active in the Solomons into 1943. On July 20, off the island of Kolombangara, aircraft from Guadalcanal attacked *Kumano* and scored a near miss that caused major flooding. *Kumano* was forced to return to Japan for repairs. *Mogami* was caught in Rabaul Harbor in November 1943 and subjected to the same carrier air attack that devastated units of the Takao class. Though it was hit by only a single 500lb bomb, the damage to the forward part of the ship was severe and it was also forced to return to Japan.

The Battle of Leyte Gulf in 1944 marked the end of the Mogami class. All three remaining ships were committed; two were lost during the battle and the third damaged. *Mogami* was assigned to the 3rd Section of the First Diversionary Attack Force. After suffering minor damage due to carrier air attack in the Sulu Sea on October 24, *Mogami* and the rest of its task group tried to force the Surigao Strait the next night. *Mogami* came under heavy fire from American cruisers and was hit by four or five 8in shells, which killed the ship's commanding officer and started a fire amidships. Retreating south down the strait, *Mogami* then collided with *Nachi* and, as the fires

Mikuma shown on fire in the June 7 photo sequence taken by *Enterprise* aircraft. Its forward turrets have their guns askew, the result of bomb damage. The first turret has a *hinomaru* painted on top as an aid to friendly air recognition. The mainmast and aircraft deck are entirely gone, the result of an explosion caused by the ship's torpedoes detonating. (Naval History and Heritage Command)

Mogami Class Specifications (after second reconstruction into heavy cruisers)

Displacement: 15,057 tons full load
Dimensions: Length 668.5ft / beam 68ft / draft 36ft
Maximum speed: 35kt
Range: 7,000–7,500nm at 14kt
Crew: 58 officers and 838 enlisted personnel (1940)

spread, five of its torpedoes exploded, causing additional damage. Its ordeal was far from over, however, as it was hit by another 10–20 6 and 8in rounds from American cruisers. In spite of all this, it appeared as if *Mogami* would actually survive its fearful pounding, but when the remaining engine stopped, the ship went dead in the water. At this point, it was attacked by carrier aircraft and hit by two bombs forward. The acting captain ordered the ship abandoned when attempts to flood one of the forward magazines failed. *Mogami* was scuttled by a destroyer later in the day; 192 of the crew were killed.

Suzuya was also lost on October 25. While engaging American escort carriers off Samar, it suffered a near miss from a bomb that reduced its speed. A second near miss was more serious. This ignited the torpedoes in the forward starboard torpedo tubes, starting a large fire that was fed by the explosion of additional torpedoes. An hour later, the remaining torpedoes exploded as well as the 5in rounds for the Type 89 guns, and the entire ship was set ablaze.

Kumano also came off poorly in the battle off Samar on October 25. Early in the fight it was hit by a single torpedo launched from destroyer *Johnston*. The torpedo struck the bow and reduced its speed to 12 knots. It

Kumano pictured off the Chinese coast in 1938 with its original triple 6.1in turrets. The ship was re-armed with 8in guns by 1940. (Naval History and Heritage Command)

was ordered to return to Singapore. Transiting the Sibuyan Sea the next day, it was attacked by carrier aircraft and suffered three 500lb bomb hits.

Kumano arrived in Manila on October 28 for temporary repairs; it departed November 4 to escort a convoy and return to Japan. On November 6, the cruiser was attacked by four American submarines. *Ray* scored two hits, one of which blew off *Kumano*'s repaired bow. It was towed into a small port on the western coast of Luzon, where more repairs were started to make it seaworthy. Before these were completed, however, the ship was attacked by aircraft from the carrier *Ticonderoga*. These quickly placed four bomb hits and five torpedo strikes on the cruiser, which sank inside Santa Cruz harbor.

Tone Class

Design and construction

The naval program and funding which included the two ships that became the Tone class were approved in March 1934. Naval General Staff requirements for the two 8,450-ton cruisers in the program were almost identical to those for the Mogami class. However, in 1936, while the ships were on the building ways, the requirements were modified. The ships were repurposed as scouting cruisers, which required a larger capacity for seaplanes. Since it was desired that each ship be able to fire its main guns while launching aircraft, the entire main battery was moved forward so as to prevent the possibility of blast damage to the aircraft aft. Once altered, the design called for a ship of 12,500 tons with the ability to carry six to eight seaplanes. Speed was set at 36 knots and range at 8,000nm at 18 knots.

Much of the design for the Tone class was drawn from the Mogami class. The general hull lines were the same as on Mogami and the bridge was very similar. The propulsion system for the new class was identical to that installed in *Suzuya* and *Kumano*. The four sets of turbines created a total of 152,000shp. On full-power trials, both ships reached speeds of more than 35 knots. Endurance was superior, since fuel capacity was expanded to 2,690 tons. In service, this equated to a range of 12,000nm at 14 knots.

This class was the best protected of the IJN's heavy cruisers. The total weight of armor and protective plating was nearly identical to that of the Mogami class, but since all the turrets were grouped forward, a heavier scale of protection could be provided over a more compact magazine area. The main belt was sloped at 20 degrees and over the machinery spaces it reached a maximum of 3.9in thick, tapering to 2.6in. The forward part of the belt

(Overleaf) The saga of *Kumano* during the Battle of Leyte Gulf and after demonstrated the toughness of the IJN's heavy cruisers. After sustaining torpedo and bomb damage during the battle the cruiser attempted to return to Japan. On November 6, 1944, it received another two torpedo hits from USN submarines. Attempts to repair the cruiser were brought to an abrupt halt on November 25 when aircraft from the carrier *Ticonderoga* sank *Kumano* with four 500lb bombs and five torpedoes. This view depicts the cruiser under attack by *Ticonderoga*'s torpedo planes.

that covered the four magazines of the main battery was between 5.7in and 6.1in thick. Overhead protection comprised a middle deck with 1.2in over the machinery spaces, increasing to 2.6in on the outer portions, while another 2.2in of protection was present on the lower deck over the magazines.

Aircraft facilities were designed to carry up to six aircraft, but neither ship ever carried more than five in service. Two catapults were fitted. The aircraft were moved by means of a 79ft crane and a rail system fitted on the ship's deck. No hangar was provided.

Armament

The altered design called for a ship with four triple 6.1in gun turrets, all located forward, five twin 5in guns (the fifth on the centerline aft), four twin 25mm mounts, and two 13mm machine guns in front of the bridge. Unlike *Mogami*, the Tone class was fitted with the more modern Type 94 high-angle director for the 5in guns. A heavy torpedo fit was retained – 12 tubes in triple mounts.

Tone Class Construction				
Ship	Built at	Laid down	Launched	Completed
Tone	Nagasaki by Mitsubishi	12/1/34	11/21/37	11/20/39
Chikuma	Nagasaki by Mitsubishi	10/1/35	3/19/38	5/20/39

Before the construction of the ships had proceeded to the upper deck, existing naval treaties lapsed, so the triple 6.1in turrets were replaced with twin 8in turrets. The placement of the turrets did not change, with all four in a pyramid arrangement forward, which meant Nos. 3 and 4 turrets could only fire broadside. The centerline 5in gun mount was deleted before completion, and the 13mm machine guns were replaced with 25mm guns. A total of 24 torpedoes were carried, 12 in the tubes and another 12 reloads.

Service modifications

After entering service, the Tone class proved very satisfactory. They were considered to be the most comfortable of the IJN's cruisers. No modifications were carried out before the war began. After the onset of war, modifications focused on improvements to the radar suite and the light antiaircraft fit. In February 1943, the ships received a No. 21 radar on the foremast. In June 1944, a No. 13 radar was added to the mainmast and two No. 22 sets were fitted atop the foremast below the No. 21 radar.

Light antiaircraft guns were added in two phases. In February 1943, two additional twin 25mm mounts were added. In the period December 1943 to January 1944, four triple mounts replaced four of the twin mounts and four single 25mm guns were added, and in June 1944, a further four triple mounts were fitted (two in the area of bridge and two aft) as well as numerous single 25mm mounts.

After returning to Japan following the Battle of Leyte Gulf, Tone underwent a final series of modifications. By February 1945, four triple mounts were added on the quarterdeck and the number of single 25mm mounts was reduced from 25 to 18. The final number of 25mm barrels embarked was 62. Also, the No. 21 radar, which was considered obsolete, was removed from the foremast and replaced by a No. 22 Modification 4.

Wartime service

At the start of the war, the two ships of the class formed Sentai 8. The Tone class was ideally suited to operate with the IJN's carrier force, since the ships possessed superior endurance and an increased seaplane capacity. The latter was critical, as Japanese carrier doctrine placed much of the responsibility for scouting on the seaplanes of the escorting battleships and cruisers, thus allowing the maximum number of carrier aircraft to be retained for offensive operations. In November 1941, Sentai 8 was assigned to the Kido Butai, where it remained until after the Battle of Midway.

Both ships accompanied the Japanese carriers on the raids on Pearl Harbor and Wake Island in December 1941; on Rabaul, Kavieng, Lae, and Salamaua in January 1942; and on Port Darwin in February 1942. In late February and early March, the Kido Butai operated south of Java, and *Tone* and *Chikuma* used gunfire to sink a merchant ship and an American destroyer. This was followed by the Indian Ocean raid, in which seaplanes from Sentai 8 performed scouting duties and sighted two British heavy cruisers, which were sunk by air attack. The two ships then returned to Japan in April.

In June 1942, Sentai 8 remained attached to the Kido Butai and played key roles in the Midway operation. It was an aircraft from *Tone* that first spotted the American carrier force, but issued frustratingly vague contact reports. By the time the aircraft reported the actual presence of carriers, a train of events had been set in place that resulted in the destruction of four of the IJN's fleet carriers, the turning point of the Pacific War. During the battle, Sentai 8 was attacked several times by American carrier aircraft, but suffered no damage.

During the Guadalcanal campaign, Sentai 8 still operated with the IJN's reformed carrier force. Both cruisers were active during the carrier battle of the Eastern Solomons in August 1942 and the final carrier battle of 1942 at Santa Cruz. During this battle, *Chikuma* suffered moderate damage on October 26 when it was hit by bombs dropped by dive-bombers from the carrier *Hornet*. Two bombs struck the bridge, then a near miss flooded two

An overhead view of *Tone* in 1941, which clearly shows the layout of the ship's secondary and antiaircraft armament as well as its aircraft-handling facilities. The six 25mm twin mounts can be seen in pairs in front of the bridge, abaft the smokestack, and near the mainmast. This view clearly shows the system of deck-mounted rails and turntables used to move the floatplanes on deck. (*Ships of the World* magazine)

Tone Class Antiaircraft Fit, October 1944				
Ship	Triple mounts	Twin mounts	Single mounts	Total 25mm guns
Tone	8	4	25	57
Chikuma	8	4	13	45

boiler rooms, and finally a bomb hit the starboard forward torpedo room. Fortunately for the Japanese, the ship's torpedoes had been jettisoned only minutes before, so the damage was contained. However, *Chikuma* suffered a heavy loss of life (151 dead and 165 wounded) and repairs were not completed until late February 1943.

Chikuma was part of the ill-fated move of a number of cruisers to Rabaul in November 1943. During the American carrier air attack, it suffered only near misses with no damage. Sentai 8 was then held in readiness for most of 1944, as were the IJN's other heavy cruisers. On March 2, 1944, however, the two ships deployed into the Indian Ocean to conduct commerce raiding. *Tone* sank a British merchant vessel and took 108 crew and passengers on board. Of these, 72 were beheaded on *Tone* during the night of March 8–19.

The next operation for Sentai 8 was the Battle of the Philippine Sea, from which both cruisers emerged undamaged. Before Leyte Gulf, Sentai 8 was disbanded and *Tone* and *Chikuma* were assigned to Sentai 7 with *Suzuya* and *Kumano*. As part of the First Diversionary Attack Force, *Tone* and

This shows *Tone* in June 1942 in its early-war configuration at the Battle of Midway. The unique appearance of the ship is evident, with all 8in turrets placed forward of the bridge and the rear of the ship devoted to aircraft handling. One of the two principal Japanese heavy cruiser floatplanes in service at the start of the war was the Navy Type 94 reconnaissance seaplane (E7N2, perhaps best known by its Allied codename "Alf"). The Type 94 (shown left) was the standard catapult-launched long-range seaplane in service until 1942 when it was replaced by the Navy Type 0 reconnaissance seaplane (E13A1) which was given the Allied codename "Jake" (shown right).

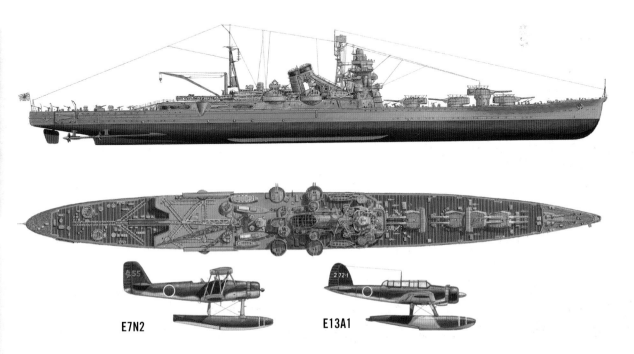

E7N2   E13A1

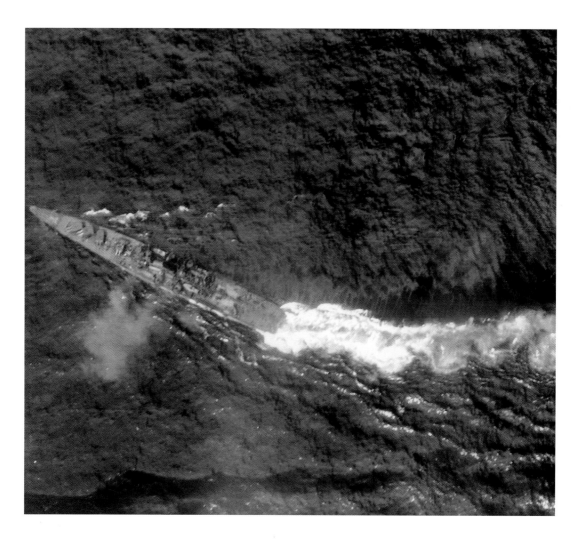

Chikuma under air attack on October 25, 1944, during the battle off Samar. The cruiser has already been torpedoed, and the size of the bow wave indicates that it is slowing down. *Chikuma* later went dead in the water and had to be scuttled by its escorts. (Author's collection)

Chikuma participated in the sinking of the escort carrier *Gambier Bay* off Samar on October 25. The American escort carrier force exacted revenge when an air-launched torpedo hit *Chikuma* amidships, flooding the engine rooms and bringing the ship to a stop. Repairs were unsuccessful, so when the Japanese withdrew, orders were given to scuttle the ship. Its crew was taken off, and it was sunk by torpedo. That night, the destroyer that had rescued *Chikuma*'s crew was sunk; only a single member from *Chikuma*'s crew survived.

Tone emerged from Leyte Gulf with moderate damage. It was hit by three bombs in the Sibuyan Sea on October 24 and, during the battle off Samar, it was struck by a single 5in shell. While withdrawing from the engagement, it was hit by another bomb from an aircraft from the escort carrier *Kitkun Bay*, but was able to retire without further damage.

After returning to Japan and undergoing a refit, *Tone* was moored near Etajima, intended to be used as a training ship at the IJN's Naval Academy. A series of American carrier raids, however, hunted *Tone* to extinction. The first on March 19, 1945, resulted in only light damage. A much larger raid on July 24 placed three bomb hits on *Tone* and delivered at least seven near misses. These caused severe flooding and the ship began to settle by the stern. A further attack on July 28 added a rocket hit. The ship was abandoned for good on August 5 and was scrapped in 1948, the last of the IJN's cruisers to disappear.

Tone Class Specifications

Displacement: 11,215 tons standard; 15,239 tons full load
Dimensions: Length 661.33ft / beam 63.67in / draft 35.75ft
Maximum speed: 35kt
Range: 12,000nm at 14kt
Crew: 59 officers and 815 enlisted personnel as designed

LIGHT CRUISERS

The IJN went to war with 17 light cruisers and another three cruiser-sized training ships. Of these, most were 5,500-ton ships designed to act as destroyer squadron flagships. This made the IJN's light cruisers very different from their American counterparts. During the war, the Japanese built another five cruisers, all but one of which maintained the basic design premise of being able to act as a flagship for the IJN's destroyers.

JAPANESE LIGHT CRUISER DEVELOPMENT

The first cruiser class designed entirely by the Japanese was the four-ship Tone class, of which the lead ship was completed in 1910. These were also the last piston-engine Japanese cruisers. They were followed by the three-ship Chikuma class. These ships were equipped with turbine engines and a larger 6in gun main armament. Both of these classes of protected cruisers (typed as second-class cruisers by the Japanese) were designed to act as scouts for the battle fleet.

Included in the 1916 naval construction program were funds for two light cruisers. These two ships were projected to be only 3,500 tons – smaller than the earlier scout cruisers – and were designed to be flotilla leaders for the IJN's growing number of modern destroyers. Naval construction approved the following year originally included nine cruisers: six improved 3,500-ton ships and three larger 7,200-ton scout cruisers. But by 1917 it

This excellent starboard-quarter view of *Oi* shows it in June 1937 before it was taken into the yards for conversion into a torpedo cruiser. The layout of the main armament is clearly shown. (Naval History and Heritage Command)

was obvious that the 3,500-ton cruisers were inadequate to act as squadron leaders for the current generation of Japanese destroyers and that they did not compare favorably with foreign counterparts. Plans for more of these were scrapped, and a 5,500-ton cruiser design was adopted. Eight of these were funded in 1917 with the ninth ship converted to an experimental ship. In 1918, another three 5,500-ton cruisers were funded.

Four more 5,500-ton ships were approved, though the last unit was quickly canceled. Concurrent with the funding of the series of 5,500-ton cruisers was a series of studies devoted to developing a suitable design for a large scout cruiser. The 5,500-ton design was a dead end as the basis for a larger scout cruiser. The 5,500-ton cruisers featured a main battery of seven 5.5in guns, all in single mounts and only six of which could fire broadside. In comparison, both the American and British navies had also decided to design and build large scout cruisers. In the case of the Americans, this was the 7,500-ton Omaha class with 12 6in guns with a much heavier broadside. The British designed a similar ship, the 9,750-ton Hawkins class with seven 7.5in guns. In response, by 1922 the Japanese settled on a 7,500-ton large cruiser design.

By the time the Washington Naval Treaty was signed, the size and composition of the IJN's light cruiser force was already set. As well as capping construction of capital ships, the Washington Treaty had a dramatic effect on the IJN's cruiser force. Despite the fact that the treaty did not restrict the numbers of cruisers that could be built, it did change the course of Japanese cruiser construction (see also the discussions in Chapters 1 and 5). The only limit placed on cruisers was in maximum tonnage (10,000 tons) and the size of the main battery (8in). Since capital ship construction was capped, all major navies began a cruiser-building spree. For both the Americans and Japanese, the new 10,000-ton limit was the baseline for subsequent designs. The 5,500-ton design was not further developed.

Under the London Naval Treaty of April 1930, which limited cruiser tonnage for all signatories, the Japanese allotments were 108,400 tons (standard) for cruisers with guns bigger than 6.1in, and 100,450 tons for ships with guns up to 6.1in. The Japanese had built up to their limits in the first (heavy cruiser) category, but only had 98,415 tons on the books for light cruisers. Through retirement of old units and allowances to replace aging units, the IJN assembled 50,955 tons to use for construction of new light cruisers. It was decided that this allotment would be used to build four 8,500-ton ships by 1936, followed by two 8,450-ton units. These were heavily armed and well-protected ships, which became the Mogami class and the Tone class, respectively. The four Mogamis were built and armed with 6.1in guns, but were later converted into heavy cruisers after the Japanese withdrew from the London Treaty. The Tone class was completed as heavy cruisers. When the Japanese again planned to build light cruisers, they returned to the destroyer flagship model. Meanwhile, since the London Treaty restricted the number of cruisers that could be built, the 5,500-ton ships underwent modernization in the 1930s. The IJN went to war with 17 light cruisers, 14 of which were the 5,500-ton design.

LIGHT CRUISER WEAPONS

Main Battery

The main battery of Japanese light cruisers did not compare favorably to that of their foreign counterparts. While the Americans and British opted for a 6in main gun for their light cruisers being built in the 1920s, the Japanese settled for a 5.5in weapon. Additionally, Japanese ships carried fewer of these smaller guns compared to the American scout cruisers of the period. The 5.5in gun selected by the Japanese dated from 1914 and was already in service as the secondary gun on two classes of battleships. It was hand-operated, so possessed a relatively low rate of fire, and the range was inferior to the American 6in gun, but it compared favorably to the British gun of the same caliber. In general, Japanese light cruisers were less well armed than their foreign counterparts, and this trend continued when the Japanese designed two new classes of light cruisers in the late 1930s.

Japanese Light Cruiser Main Guns				
Type	Class	Max. elevation (degrees)	Max. range (yards)	Rate of fire (rpm)
Type 3 5.5in/50cal	Tenryu	20	17,220	6–10
Type 3 5.5in/50cal	Kuma, Nagara	25	19,080	6–10
Type 3 5.5in/50cal	Sendai, Yubari	30	20,820	6–10
Type 3 5.5in/50cal	Katori	35	21,600	6–10
Type 41 6in/50cal	Agano	45	22,890	6
Type 3 6.1in/60cal	Oyodo	45	29,865	5

Torpedo Armament

The actual main battery of the IJN's light cruisers was their torpedo armament. Given the primary mission of Japanese light cruisers, a heavy torpedo battery was essential. Light cruisers employed twin and triple mounts when built. It was not until immediately before the war that a select few of the 5,500-ton cruisers received the new Type 92 quadruple torpedo mounts. Even so, the broadside of 15 of the light cruisers was an underwhelming four weapons compared to the eight or nine torpedo broadside of the newest Japanese destroyers. Only a handful of the light cruisers were equipped with the Type 93 Model 1, Modification 2 torpedo before the start of the war.

Japanese Light Cruiser Heavy Antiaircraft Guns				
Type	Class	Max. elevation (degrees)	Max. range (yards)	Rate of fire (rpm)
Type 3 3.15in/40cal	All prewar	75	5,775	13
Type 10 4.7in/45cal	Yubari	75	9,240	6–8
Type 89 5in/40cal	Kuma, Nagara, Sendai, Katori	90	8,090	11–12
Type 98 3.15in/60cal	Agano	90	9,920	25
Type 98 3.9in/65cal	Oyodo	90	15, 260	15

Heavy Antiaircraft Armament

Japanese light cruisers began the Pacific War with no long-range antiaircraft weapon. Most of the 5,500-ton cruisers eventually received a single Type 89 5in twin mount. Aboard light cruisers, the Type 89 was further handicapped by the absence of a dedicated fire-control system. A new 3.15in gun was developed for the Agano class, but each ship received only two of the twin mounts. The best Japanese Navy long-range antiaircraft gun of the war was the Type 98 3.9in twin gun, which was fitted on the Oyodo, as well as the Akizuki class of antiaircraft destroyers and the carrier *Taiho*. It possessed a high muzzle velocity and superb range, and was considered an excellent gun by the Japanese.

Light Antiaircraft Armament

Going into the war, Japanese light cruisers possessed an inadequate light antiaircraft fit. Standard fit at the beginning of the war was a paltry two Type 96 twin 25mm mounts positioned near the forward stack and a quad 13mm machine gun in front of the bridge. No antiaircraft weapon heavier than the 25mm gun was provided. Increasing the vulnerability of the light cruisers to air attack, the 25mm guns were usually not provided with a dedicated fire-control system so the gunners were forced to rely on visual tracking. Despite the growing profusion of 25mm guns on light cruisers during the war, these ships grew increasingly vulnerable to air attack.

LIGHT CRUISER RADAR

As with the heavy cruisers, the Japanese began to equip their light cruisers with radar in mid-1943. This modification occurred when the ships returned to Japan for repair and refit. The most common light cruiser radar was the No. 21 air-search radar. On light cruisers, it was fitted in several places, including on top of the bridge structure, on top of the fire-control station on the foremast, and, on the modern light cruisers, on the face of the rangefinder on top of the rangefinder tower. A few light cruisers also received the No. 13 air-search radar fitted on the mainmast of light cruisers. The No. 22 Modification 4M radar, designed for surface search, was usually mounted in pairs on both sides of the bridge or on the foremast.

THE LIGHT CRUISER CLASSES

Tenryu Class

Design and construction

In May 1916, the IJN began construction of its first class of modern cruisers. The two ships, loosely based on the British C- and D-class light cruisers, were named *Tenryu* and *Tatsuta* and were designed as destroyer squadron leaders. However, at only 3,500 tons, they were soon rendered too small and too slow by the latest Japanese destroyer designs. Newer Japanese destroyers of the period, like the Minekaze class, had a design speed of 39 knots, compared to the *Tenryu*'s 33 knots. The new cruisers were also deficient in firepower, especially when compared to the new class of American scout cruisers of the Omaha class.

High speed was an important design consideration. Several weight-saving measures were used and a high length-to-beam ratio adopted. Three sets of destroyer turbines were fitted and ten boilers installed in three boiler rooms. Two of these were mixed-firing boilers using oil and coal.

Protection of the hull was designed to defeat 4in shellfire from American destroyers. Total armor was only 4.2 percent of displacement. Interior armor in the main belt of 1in was supplemented by outer armor of between 1in

Japanese Light Cruiser Names

Per instructions dating from 1912, cruisers with a displacement of less than 7,000 tons were classified as second-class cruisers. Both the American and British navies had begun calling their smaller cruisers "light cruisers"; unofficially, the Japanese followed suit. In 1930, the London Naval Treaty codified the division of ships into "heavy" and "light" cruiser designations. In 1913 the Navy Minister issued instructions that second-class cruisers were to be named after rivers or streams. First-class, later heavy, cruisers, were named after mountains. However, this distinction became confused because of the fact that six ships designed and built in the aftermath of the London Treaty as light cruisers retained their original river and stream names after they were converted to heavy cruisers before the war. The three training ships of the Katori class were not actually considered cruisers, so were not named after streams. Rather, they were named after famous shrines of Japan.

Abukuma – a river flowing through two prefectures in northeastern Honshu
Agano – a stream in Niigata Prefecture in northern Honshu
Isuzu – a river in Mie Prefecture in southern Honshu
Jintsu – a river flowing through Toyama Prefecture, emptying into the Sea of Japan
Kashii – a Shinto shrine in Fukuoka Prefecture
Kashima – a Shinto shrine in Ibaraki Prefecture
Katori – a Shinto shrine in Chiba Prefecture
Kinu – a river flowing through two prefectures north of Tokyo
Kitakami – a river flowing through northeastern Honshu
Kuma – a river flowing through Kumamoto Prefecture in eastern Kyushu
Nagara – a river flowing through Mie Prefecture in southern Honshu

Naka – a river flowing through two prefectures north of Tokyo
Natori – a river in Miyagi Prefecture in northeastern Honshu
Noshiro – a stream in Akita Prefecture in northern Honshu
Oyodo – a stream in Miyazaki Prefecture on Kyushu
Sakawa – a stream in Kanagawa Prefecture near Mount Fuji
Sendai – a river that originates and flows through Kagoshima Prefecture in the southwestern tip of Kyushu
Tama – a river in southeastern Tokyo
Tatsuta – a stream in Nara Prefecture in central Honshu
Tenryu – a river flowing through three prefectures in central Honshu
Yahagi – a stream in Aichi Prefecture in central Honshu
Yubari – a river on Hokkaido that begins in Mount Yubari
Yura – a river in Kyoto Prefecture in central Honshu

and 1.5in. Deck armor was 0.9–1.4mm thick. The class featured a simple and small bridge with conning tower armor of 2in.

Armament

As completed, the main armament was four Type 3 5.5in guns. All were single mounts and all were situated on the centerline. Fire control for the main battery was provided by a fire-control director located in the foremast. Rangefinding was provided by two 8ft-long rangefinders, one on the bridge and one on the aft superstructure. Antiaircraft armament was a single Type 3 3.15in high-angle gun mounted aft, and two 6.5mm machine guns amidships. The torpedo armament was two triple centerline Type 6 21in triple mounts. These were the first triple mounts fitted in any ship in the IJN. There were no reloads.

Service modifications

Between completion and 1940, neither ship received significant modifications. Consideration was given to converting both ships into antiaircraft cruisers in 1935–36, with each ship mounting four Type 89

Tenryu Class Construction				
Ship	Built at	Laid down	Launched	Completed
Tenryu	Yokosuka Navy Yard	5/17/17	3/11/18	11/20/19
Tatsuta	Sasebo Navy Yard	7/24/17	5/29/18	3/31/19

twin 5in high-angle guns, but lack of space in shipyards made this impossible. In 1938–39, more thought was given to conversion into an antiaircraft cruiser, with the new Type 98 3.15in twin mounts, but this was also dropped. In November 1940, in preparation for war, both ships were lightly modernized. The 3.15in antiaircraft gun was removed, as were the 13mm machine guns fitted in 1937, replaced by two Type 96 twin 25mm guns placed abreast the forward stack. The compass bridge received a permanent cover and the mixed-firing boilers were converted to oil only.

Since both units were considered second-line units by 1939, wartime modifications were minor. Between February 23 and 27, 1942, while at Truk, both cruisers received two twin 25mm mounts aft. No other modifications were made to *Tenryu* before it was lost, but *Tatsuta* received a fifth 25mm twin mount and possibly a No. 21 or 22 radar during an August–September 1943 refit.

This 1934 view shows a Tenryu-class cruiser at high speed with its torpedo tubes trained to starboard. The two aft 5.5in guns are discernable in this blurry image. The dark color of the linoleum deck covering compared to the standard gray color of the rest of the ship can also be seen. (*Ships of the World* magazine)

Wartime service

The two ships of the Tenryu class began the war comprising Sentai 18. Their first combat operation was the seizure of Wake Island in December 1941. Though the Japanese suffered heavy losses in the operation, neither cruiser was damaged. Next, Sentai 18 participated in the invasion of Rabaul and Kavieng in January.

On March 8, the cruisers provided cover for the seizure of Lae and Salamaua on the northeastern coast of New Guinea. In response, the Americans attacked the invasion force on March 10 with carrier aircraft, but neither ship was damaged. Subsequently, both ships covered landings at Bougainville, Shortland, and Manus Island through April 8.

The next major operation for Sentai 18 was the invasion of Port Moresby and Tulagi in early

Tenryu and Tatsuta pictured operating together off Truk in September 1941. The austere design of this class is evident with its small bridge structure and weak four 5.5in gun main armament. (*Ships of the World* magazine)

May. As part of the Cover Force for the operation, they were charged with establishing seaplane bases to support the invasion. Both ships returned to Japan in late May for a brief overhaul, and were back at Truk on June 23.

Sentai 18 escorted construction troops to Guadalcanal on July 6. On August 7, American forces landed on Guadalcanal to seize the airfield there. *Tenryu* was part of the Japanese force scraped together to attack the American beachhead. It acquitted itself well. Two of its torpedoes were credited with hitting heavy cruiser *Quincy*, which later sank. The cruiser engaged two American destroyers at different times in the battle, and hit one. In return, it took a single 5in round from cruiser *Chicago*, which wounded two. In total, *Tenryu* fired 80 5.5in shells and all six of its torpedoes.

Both ships were active in constant convoy duty from Rabaul to various points on New Guinea and Guadalcanal throughout 1942. This included the landing of a Japanese invasion force at Milne Bay on August 25 and their evacuation on September 5–6. *Tatsuta* landed the commander of the 17th Army on Guadalcanal on October 9. *Tenryu* was hit by a bomb from a B-17 while anchored in Rabaul on October 2. Twenty-three men were killed, but the ship was repaired locally.

In December, *Tenryu* was designated as the flagship of the Madang Attack Force to move troops to Madang on northeastern New Guinea. On December 18, after leaving Madang, *Tenryu* was hit by two torpedoes from American submarine *Albacore* and sunk. Casualties included 23 dead and 21 wounded.

Tatsuta departed for Japan to repair rudder damage in January 1943. After completion, it was retained in home waters as the flagship of Destroyer Squadron 11, which was composed of new destroyers conducting shakedown cruises. *Tatsuta* remained on training duties into 1944 with the

Tenryu Class Specifications

Displacement: 3,230 tons standard; 4,621 tons full load (1919)
Dimensions: Length 468ft / beam 40.5ft / draft 24.5ft
Maximum speed: 33kt
Range: 5,000nm at 14kt
Crew: 33 officers and 304 enlisted personnel plus space for staff

exception of one run to Truk in October 1943. In February 1944 *Tatsuta* prepared for an emergency transport mission to the Central Pacific. While bound for Saipan, it was hit by two torpedoes from American submarine *Sand Lance* on March 12 and sunk.

Kuma Class

Design and construction

The first two 5,500-ton cruisers, named *Kuma* and *Tama*, were ordered in 1917, and the class became known after the lead ship *Kuma*. As the first of the 5,500-ton units, the class was also known as the 5,500-Ton Model I. The next three 5,500-Ton Model I ships were ordered in 1918.

Plans for the Kuma class were being drawn up as the Tenryu class was under construction. The move from a 3,500-ton ship up to a 5,500-ton design allowed many improvements to be incorporated. To address one of the weaknesses of the Tenryu class, the Kuma class had a longer hull and more powerful machinery in order to attain its design speed of 36 knots necessary to operate with the newer destroyers. A higher freeboard made the ships more seaworthy and provided more crew living space. The ships of the Kuma class were considered to be good sea boats.

Like the Tenryu class, the Kuma-class ships had a light bridge structure, abaft of which was a tripod mast on which the fire-control platform was located, along with two searchlights. There was also a small aft superstructure abaft the pole mainmast.

The last unit of the Kuma class, *Kiso*, was built with a 30ft flying-off platform forward-mounted above the first two turrets. The platform was removed in 1922, but the superstructure retained the shape of the hangar.

Protection was still limited to that required to defeat a 4in shell. The side belt featured an internal 1in of armor and a 1.5in external plate; the armored deck was 1.1in thick.

Kuma Class Construction				
Ship	Built at	Laid down	Launched	Completed
Kuma	Sasebo Navy Yard	8/29/18	7/14/19	8/31/20
Tama	Nagasaki by Mitsubishi	8/10/18	2/10/20	1/29/21
Kiso	Nagasaki by Mistubishi	6/10/19	7/15/20	5/4/21
Oi	Kobe by Kawasaki	11/24/19	7/15/20	10/3/21
Kitakami	Sasebo Navy Yard	9/1/19	7/3/20	4/15/21

The design speed was 36 knots, which required 90,000shp. Four shafts were used, each driven by a 22,500shp turbine. Twelve boilers were fitted, including a small number of mixed-firing boilers (two in the Kuma and Nagara class, and four in the Sendai class).

Armament

The main battery on the first 5,500-ton cruiser class was increased to seven single 5.5in guns. Two were placed forward, two on each side of the forward superstructure, and three aft, which meant that only six guns could fire broadside. This was the standard layout maintained for the next two classes of 5,500-ton cruisers. Fire control was provided by a director mounted on top of the forward tripod mast and by 8ft rangefinders mounted between the second and third smokestacks. As completed, the antiaircraft armament was limited to two single 3.15in guns placed adjacent to the first stack and two 6.5mm machine guns.

The torpedo armament was increased to a total of eight tubes, mounted in four twin mounts. The first set was placed abaft the forward superstructure and the second abaft the third stack. Since they were not placed on the centerline, only four could be fired to each side. Eight reloads were provided.

Service modifications

The 14 5,500-ton cruisers were unmodified until the ships underwent a series of modification from 1931 to 1941. The changes were basically the same for all three classes and centered on the ships' aircraft handling arrangements, antiaircraft fit, and alterations to the bridge and superstructure.

The flying platform arrangement forward of the bridge never proved successful in service. After a brief experiment on three ships placed a small catapult in place of the flying platform in 1930–31, it was decided to put a 62ft catapult on 11 ships (less *Kitakami*, *Oi*, and *Kiso*, which had been demilitarized as required by the London Treaty). On *Kuma* and *Tama* and the six ships of the Nagara class, the catapult was placed aft between the Nos. 5 and 6 5.5in guns. On the three units of the Sendai class, the catapult was placed between the Nos. 6 and 7 guns. A crane to lift the seaplane from the water was placed on the mainmast, which was converted from a pole to a heavier tripod.

The antiaircraft fit of all 14 ships was improved, and had been largely standardized by 1941 and the start of the war. Compared to foreign light cruisers it remained deficient. The original 3.15in single guns were replaced first by twin 13mm mounts and finally by a Type 96 twin 25mm mount. The original 6.5mm machine guns were replaced by 7.7mm mounts. The Nagara- and Sendaiclass units received a quadruple 13mm mount fitted in front of the bridge.

The bridges on the Kuma class were modified in 1932–34. This included covering the compass bridge and building a rangefinder tower above the bridge with either an 11.5ft or a 13ft rangefinder. After all modifications,

In the same sequence of photographs taken at Tsingtao, China, on July 16, 1935 comes this fine view of *Kuma*'s aft section. The three aft 5.5in guns are clearly shown and the aft twin torpedo tube mount has been swung out. The catapult between gun mounts Nos. 5 and 6 carried a single reconnaissance seaplane, in this case the Type 90-3; this aircraft was obsolete by the start of the war and was replaced by the Kawanishi E7K2 Type 94. (Naval History and Heritage Command)

This prewar view of *Kiso* shows its unique bridge structure. Of the Kuma-class cruisers, only *Kiso* received the aircraft hangar in the front of the bridge, which made its bridge higher than other ships in the class. *Kiso* also has flared stacks on its first two stacks, another unique feature. (Naval History and Heritage Command)

the full-load displacement of the ships exceeded 7,000 tons, which brought maximum speed down to 32–33 knots. To maintain stability, extra ballast was added. *Kiso* had antirain caps fitted on two forward smokestacks, which gave it a unique appearance; it retained these until it was sunk.

On August 25, 1941, *Oi* and *Kitakami* were ordered to Sasebo for urgent conversion into "torpedo cruisers." These ships were to play an important role in the Japanese plan to crush the American battle fleet during a decisive battle. Originally *Oi*, *Kitakami*, and *Kiso* were all to be converted into torpedo cruisers to form a special squadron that had the firepower to deliver a massive torpedo attack. By 1938 it was clear that there were insufficient Type 92 quadruple mounts, so *Kiso* was not modified. The actual conversion was not carried out until definite war preparations were begun so that the Americans would not gain knowledge of the creation of the torpedo cruisers. The conversion was to be very extensive, with all existing armament removed and replaced by four twin Type 89 high-angle mounts, four twin Type 96 twin 25mm mounts, and 11 quadruple torpedo mounts. When the ships arrived in the yards in August 1941, there were insufficient Type 89 mounts and torpedo tubes. The conversion was modified to retain the four forward 5.5in guns and remove the aft three. Only ten quadruple torpedo mounts were fitted per ship; five on each side with a total of 40 torpedoes. No reloads were carried, but provisions were made to transfer torpedoes between mounts if necessary. Two twin 25mm guns were placed abreast of the first stack. The torpedo fire-control station in the foremast was modified to allow torpedo combat at ranges greater than 32,700 yards. Both ships received a 20ft rangefinder above the compass bridge. The displacement increased to

Kuma Class Modifications (final configuration when lost)					
Ship	Kuma	Tama	Kiso	Oi	Kitakami
Torpedo tubes	8 (2x4)	8 (2x4)	8 (2x4)	24 (4x6)	0
5.5in guns	6	5	5	4	0
Type 89 twin 5in guns	0	1	1	0	2
Triple 25mm guns	2	5	4	2	12
Twin 25mm guns	2	4	4	2	0
Single 25mm guns	0	18	18	0	31
13mm guns	0	7	10	0	0
Radar	None	Nos. 21, 22	Nos. 21, 22	None	Nos. 13 (2), 22

5,860 tons standard displacement and speed dropped to 31.67 knots in a December 1941 speed trial on *Kitakami*.

Kuma-class wartime modifications centered on augmenting the antiaircraft armament. To do this, most ships had at least one of their 5.5in single guns and their catapult removed. In 1943 a couple of twin or triple 25mm mounts were added. Later in 1943 and into 1944, *Tama* and *Kiso* received a Type 89 twin 5in gun in addition to as many as 18 single 25mm guns and additional triple mounts. *Kuma* never carried radar, but *Tama* and *Kiso* received a No. 21 set on top of the foremast and a No. 22 farther down.

Oi and *Kitakami* went through several major changes after their conversion into torpedo cruisers. The first occurred in August 1942 when they were modified as fast transports in order to operate in the Solomons area. This entailed the removal of the four aft quadruple torpedo mounts, which were replaced with two 46ft barges. In addition, two triple 25mm mounts were fitted aft, and depth-charge rails provided. A more drastic fast transport conversion was planned in May 1943, but never carried out.

After *Kitakami* was torpedoed in January 1944, it was decided to convert it into a *kaiten* carrier. The *kaiten* was a piloted version of the Type 93 long-range torpedo. Since it had the benefit of human guidance and was expected to be very accurate, it was seen as a potentially devastating weapon.

Kiso in its northern waters' camouflage scheme, which it wore from December 1941. The ship is identifiable by its unique camouflage and its two forward flared stacks. The positions of the white canvas-covered torpedo mounts can also be seen. (*Ships of the World* magazine)

Kuma Class Specifications

Displacement: 5,100 tons standard; 7,094 tons full load (1920)
Dimensions: Length 532ft / beam 46.5ft / draft: 29ft
Maximum speed: 36kt
Range: 6,000nm at 14kt (actual)
Crew: 37 officers and 413 enlisted personnel plus space for staff (5 officers and 22 enlisted)

Work began in August and was based on the unfulfilled plans for a complete conversion into fast transports. The work was extensive and not finished until November. All armament was stripped and replaced with two Type 89 mounts (one forward, one aft) and a total of 67 25mm guns (12 triple and 31 single mounts). Two depth-charge rails and two throwers were also fitted. The ship's main armament now became eight Model 1 *kaiten*s, which were carried and launched on two sets of rails mounted aft on each side of the ship. One could be launched every eight minutes. The removal of the aft turbines reduced the ship's top speed to 23 knots. The bridge was modified, and the torpedo direction equipment removed and replaced by additional antiaircraft fire-control equipment. Two No. 13 air-search radars and a No. 22 set were fitted. Crew size rose to 615.

Wartime service

Kuma participated in the invasion of the Philippines and then remained there as part of the local defense forces. Subsequently it became part of the Southwest Area Fleet, responsible for defending the Dutch East Indies. *Kuma* underwent a refit in October–November 1943 at Singapore. On January 11, while operating out of Penang, it was hit by two torpedoes fired from the British submarine *Tally Ho*. It quickly sank by the stern with a loss of 138 men.

Tama and *Kiso* began the war assigned to Sentai 21 and spent much of their careers serving together. Sentai 21 was assigned to the Fifth Fleet and was responsible for defending the North Pacific. Both cruisers were camouflaged with white bows and sterns, and white patches on their superstructure to blend in with the Northern Pacific environment. Both were assigned to the Kiska Seizure Force in June 1942. During this operation, Kiska was taken on June 7, 1942 followed by Attu Island. These two islands became the focal points of the Aleutians campaign.

In March, the IJN attempted to run a convoy to Attu Island. This resulted in the Battle of Komandorski Islands on March 27, 1943 when the Americans decided to contest the Japanese plan. *Tama* was part of the Japanese force assigned to escort the convoy, and which failed to reach its destination in the face of a smaller American force. During the battle, *Tama* fired 136 5.5in shells and four torpedoes, receiving only two 5in hits in return, both on the catapult, which wounded only one.

After the Americans regained Attu in May 1943, *Tama* and *Kiso* took part in the successful evacuation of the garrison from Kiska on July 29.

Kiso took 1,189 Japanese Army personnel to safety. Next, the cruisers were shifted to the South Pacific to act as fast transports. In October 1943 near Rabaul, *Tama* incurred a near miss from an aircraft bomb and *Kiso* took a direct hit. *Tama* and *Kiso* returned to Japan in late 1943 for major modification. Following completion, they resumed transport duties to the Bonin Islands and homeland defense duties. Both units were committed to the IJN's all-out effort to repel the American invasion of the Philippines in October 1944. *Tama* was assigned to the Northern Force. On October 25, this force came under attack from American carrier aircraft. *Tama* was hit by an aircraft torpedo and eventually limped unescorted to Okinawa at 14 knots. It was detected and attacked by American submarine *Jallao*, which hit it with three torpedoes. *Tama* sank quickly with the loss of all hands.

Kiso was assigned duties to reinforce the Philippines. It departed Japan on October 27 and arrived in Manila on November 10. On November 13, while under way in Manila Bay, it was attacked by American carrier aircraft and hit by three bombs. These resulted in a heavy loss of life (only 104 of 819 crewmen were saved) and the ship gradually sank. The wreck remained eight miles off Manila until it was refloated for scrapping in 1955.

Oi and *Kitakami* began the war assigned to Sentai 9. Both remained in home waters until the Midway operation where they were part of the Main Body and saw no action. In August 1942, both were converted into high-speed transports, which led them to transport missions out of Truk and Rabaul until March 1943. From March 1943, both were assigned to the Southwest Area Fleet where they conducted escort and transport duties. While serving in this capacity, *Oi* was hit by two torpedoes from the American submarine *Flasher* on July 19, 1944, after leaving Manila. The resulting flooding could not be checked and the ship sank that afternoon with the loss of 153 men.

Kitakami also fell victim to submarine torpedoes, in this case to two weapons from the British submarine *Templar* on January 27, 1944. However, the ship survived and returned to Singapore for repairs. After returning to Japan in August 1944, it began a conversion into a *kaiten* carrier. In this capacity, it saw little service due to a lack of fuel. On July 24, 1945 it was attacked by carrier aircraft in the Kure area. *Kitakami* suffered ten near misses from bombs, and these sufficed to disable its engines, rendering it immobile. After the war, the cruiser was towed to Kagoshima where it was used as a repair ship for units involved in repatriation services. The cruiser was finally scrapped in 1946–47.

Nagara Class

Design and construction

The final three 5,500-ton units authorized in 1917 were ordered in the fiscal year 1920. Since these ships were different from the Kuma class, they were known as the modified Kuma class, or more commonly as the Nagara class, after the lead unit in the class. They were also referred to as 5,500-Ton Model II. The second set of three Nagara-class ships were laid down later in 1920.

The Nagara class was similar to the Kuma class, using the same hull shape, the same power plant, and the same layout for the main armament. The principal difference was the construction of the bridge, which was modified to accommodate an aircraft hangar. The Nagara class employed a very short flying-off platform for aircraft, and a hangar placed in the front of the forward superstructure below the bridge. In turn, this made the

This plate shows three ships of the Kuma class at different points of the war. *Tama* is shown in the top profile in its 1942 configuration. Note the camouflage scheme unique to her, the placement of the 5.5in guns, and the catapult aft. The middle profile is *Kiso* in its late-war 1944 configuration. The bottom profile is *Kitakami* in its torpedo-cruiser configuration. While the forward part of the ship remained basically unaltered, the placement of five starboard side Type 92 quadruple torpedo launchers can be readily seen.

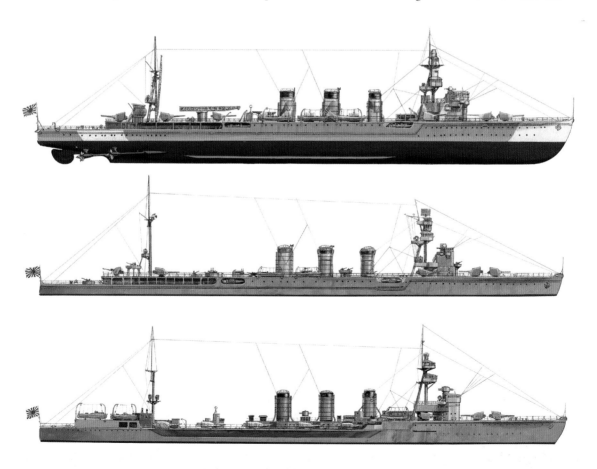

Nagara Class Construction				
Ship	Built at	Laid down	Launched	Completed
Nagara	Sasebo Navy Yard	9/9/20	4/25/21	4/21/22
Isuzu	Nagasaki by Mitsubishi	8/10/20	10/29/21	8/15/23
Natori	Nagasaki by Mitsubishi	12/14/20	2/16/22	9/15/22
Yura	Sasebo Navy Yard	5/21/21	2/15/22	3/20/23
Kinu	Kobe by Kawasaki	1/17/21	5/29/22	11/10/22
Abukuma	Nagasaki by Mitsubishi	12/8/21	3/16/23	5/26/25

bridge level higher. A 33ft platform was fitted above the No. 2 gun. There was no provision made for returning the seaplane to the ship. This arrangement proved impractical and was quickly replaced with a catapult in place of the platform.

Another difference was the incorporation of the new 24in torpedoes, which required larger torpedo tubes. Also, the main deck was extended aft so that it covered the aft set of torpedo tubes. There was no aft superstructure.

Armament

As originally built, the armament of the Nagara class was identical to that of the Kuma class. The only exception was the provision of 24in torpedoes, replacing the 21in weapons of the previous class.

Service modifications

The aircraft-handling arrangement located in front of the bridge proved a failure. This led to a bridge-modification program, which was carried out from 1929 to 1934. Each ship emerged with a different bridge arrangement, but each had its catapult moved aft to a position between 5.5in guns Nos. 5

Yura in December 1923 as completed. The ship is equipped with an aircraft hangar beneath the bridge and a short flying platform. *Yura* was the first 5,500-ton cruiser lost during the war. (Yamato Museum)

A starboard-quarter view of *Kinu* in January 1937. The location of the catapult between 5.5in gun mounts Nos. 5 and 6 and the addition of the aircraft crane to the mainmast can be seen. The aircraft is a Type 94 reconnaissance seaplane, the standard early-war aircraft for the 5,500-ton cruisers equipped with aircraft-handling facilities. (Yamato Museum)

and 6. The superstructure had a rangefinder tower built on top of the bridge, equipped with a main rangefinder. This was a 20ft instrument on *Abukuma*, 15ft on *Nagara* and *Isuzu*, 13ft on *Natori*, and 12ft on *Yura* and *Kinu*. By the start of the war, the 3.15in antiaircraft guns had been replaced with two twin 25mm mounts.

As war neared, *Abukuma* and *Kinu*, as flagships of destroyer squadrons, were earmarked to receive the new Type 93 torpedoes. However, shortages meant that only *Abukuma* received quadruple mounts in place of the aft twin mounts between March and May 1941. Sixteen Type 93 torpedoes were embarked, including eight reloads. The forward twin torpedo mounts were also removed.

Nagara Class Modifications (final configuration when lost)						
Ship	*Nagara*	*Isuzu*	*Natori*	*Yura*	*Kinu*	*Abukuma*
Torpedo tubes	8 (2x4)	8 (2x4)	8 (4x2)	8 (4x2)	8 (4x2)	8 (2x4)
5.5in guns	5	0	5	7	5	5
Type 89 twin 5in guns	1	3	1	0	1	1
Triple 25mm guns	2	11	2	0	2	4
Twin 25mm guns	6	0	2	2	2	2
Single 25mm guns	14	17	4	0	0	24
13mm guns	10	0	4	4	4	10
Radar	No. 21	Nos. 13, 21, 22	No. 21	None	No. 21	Nos. 21, 22

Wartime modifications were similar to those made to the Kuma class. As shown in the chart below, all but one (*Yura*) of the Nagara class underwent several changes and no two units were modified in the exact same way. As with the Kuma class, the focus of wartime modification work was the improvement of the ships' weak antiaircraft armament. To keep topweight within acceptable limits and to provide arcs of fire for the new weapons, this required that some of the existing 5.5in guns and the ships' catapults be removed. On almost all ships, the guns removed were the Nos. 5 and 7 mounts aft. In the place of the No. 7 mount, a Type 89 twin 5in high-angle mount was fitted. Light antiaircraft guns were added in two phases. In the first phase, usually in 1943 into early 1944, additional 25mm twin or triple mounts were added in the area of the aft torpedo tubes abaft the third stack. In the second phase, the Japanese added 25mm mounts wherever there was an adequate firing arc. This included triple 25mm mounts aft and a number of single 25mm guns, up to 24, throughout the ship. The light antiaircraft fit was further augmented by a number of 13mm guns, usually positioned on the bridge (replacing the 13mm quadruple mount in front of the bridge) and on elevated positions between the stacks.

On some ships (*Nagara* and *Isuzu*) the twin torpedo tubes were replaced with quadruple mounts. These replaced the aft mounts and included the removal of the forward mounts. Most ships also received depth-charge racks fitted on the stern.

Radar was also fitted to five of the ships. This was most often the No. 21 air-search radar. Two ships, *Isuzu* and *Nagara*, had the No. 21 set placed on top of the bridge structure. *Abukuma*, *Natori*, and *Kinu* had the same radar placed on top of the fire-control station on the foremast. The first ship to receive radar was *Abukuma* in April–May 1943 and the last was *Natori* in 1944.

Isuzu was the only Japanese light cruiser that underwent a conversion into an antiaircraft cruiser. Work began in May 1944 and lasted until September. All of the single 5.5in mounts were removed and replaced by two additional Type 89 twin mounts for a total of three. A Type 94 high-angle fire-control system was fitted on the foremast. The light antiaircraft armament was increased to 50 (11 triple and 17 single). All four twin torpedo mounts were removed and replaced with two quadruple mounts aft. The catapult was also removed. A complete radar suite was added; the No. 21 radar remained above the bridge, and a No. 13 and a No. 22 were added

Nagara departing Kure in 1938. This view shows the box-like shape of the forward superstructure and the platform fitted in front of the bridge for the quadruple 13mm gun. (*Ships of the World* magazine)

to the mainmast. For antisubmarine duties, a hydrophone and sonar were fitted, and two depth-charge rails added on the stern.

Wartime service

The six Nagara-class ships enjoyed active and diverse careers. Several acted as flagships for submarine or destroyer squadrons during the war, and they were often deployed in transport or local defense missions. Increasingly, as the war went on, they were seen as second-line units and not employed as main fleet forces.

Nagara had a long and active career. It began the war assigned to the forces conducting the Philippines invasion and in January and February 1942 participated in the invasion of the Dutch East Indies. In April 1942, *Nagara* was assigned as the flagship of the Destroyer Squadron 10. This was the destroyer escort for the First Air Fleet, the IJN's carrier force. *Nagara's* first operation as a carrier escort was the disastrous Midway operation. *Nagara* remained with the carrier force for the opening phase of the Guadalcanal campaign, participating in the Battle of the Eastern Solomons in August. In the second carrier battle of the campaign, the Battle of Santa Cruz on October 26, *Nagara* again operated with carrier forces.

In November 1942 *Nagara* and six of its destroyers were committed to the Japanese attempt to reinforce Guadalcanal. It escorted two battleships ordered to bombard the airfield on November 13. In a savage night battle it sustained one hit on mount No. 7, which killed six and wounded seven. In return, it fired 136 rounds, engaging the American cruisers *San Francisco* and *Atlanta*. *Nagara* returned two nights later in another attempt to bombard the airfield. This time, the Japanese encountered an American force led by two modern battleships. *Nagara* sank the destroyer *Preston* with gunfire, then fired a close-range torpedo broadside at one of the battleships which missed.

In November, it was assigned as flagship of Destroyer Squadron 4, with the new cruiser *Agano* taking its place as flagship of Destroyer Squadron 10. It supported the evacuation of Guadalcanal in January 1943. In July 1943, Destroyer Squadron 4 was deactivated and *Nagara* became flagship for Destroyer Squadron 2. This lasted until August when it was relieved by the new cruiser *Noshiro*.

In November *Nagara* moved reinforcements to Kwajalein in response to the American invasion of the Marshalls. In this capacity, it was attacked by American carrier aircraft, but suffered only light hull damage from near misses. In May 1944, following a major refit during the war, it was assigned as flagship of Destroyer Squadron 11. In June it began its new career as a fast transport. In this role it was torpedoed by the American submarine *Croaker* on August 7 off Kyushu by a single torpedo. It sank with the loss of 348 men.

Isuzu began the war assigned to the forces operating off the Chinese coast. It participated in the seizure of Hong Kong in December 1941 and remained there until April 1942. From there, it operated in the Dutch East Indies into September, when it was designated as the flagship of Destroyer Squadron 2 and was immediately committed to the fierce fighting around Guadalcanal. *Isuzu* screened battleships *Kongo* and *Haruna* when they bombarded Guadalcanal's airfield on October 14. *Isuzu* was again present two nights later when two cruisers conducted another bombardment. It participated in the Battle of Santa Cruz on October 26. While covering another cruiser bombardment, *Isuzu* was bombed on November 14 by US Marine Corps dive-bombers and suffered two near misses, which flooded one of its boiler rooms. It returned to

---

Nagara Class Specifications

Displacement: 5,170 tons standard; 7,204 tons full load (1922)
Dimensions: Length 532ft overall / beam 46.5ft / draft 29ft
Maximum speed: 36kt
Range: 6,000nm at 14kt (actual)
Crew: 37 officers and 413 enlisted personnel plus space for staff (5 officers and 22 enlisted)

An excellent view of *Abukuma* on December 7, 1941, taken from one of the oilers of the Pearl Harbor Supply Force. *Abukuma* was the most modified Nagara-class cruiser before the war. It was provided with two quadruple Type 92 torpedo mounts (the port-side mount is visible just aft of the first stack). The former position of the forward twin torpedo mount has been plated over as is evident in this view. The aircraft is a Type 94 reconnaissance seaplane. (*Ships of the World* magazine)

Japan in January for repairs and modification; after its return to service the cruiser was assigned transport duties in the Central Pacific. In December 1943, it was attacked by American carrier aircraft at Roi in Kwajalein Atoll. The December 5 attack resulted in three bomb hits aft and several near misses, which killed 20 of its crew. Again, the cruiser was forced to return to Japan for repairs. After arriving in Japan, conversion to an antiaircraft cruiser began in May 1944.

After completion, *Isuzu* was assigned to Sentai 31, a unit designed to provide antisubmarine protection to fleet units. In this role it took part in the Battle of Leyte Gulf as part of the carrier force. This force suffered heavily losing all four of its carriers, but *Isuzu* suffered only light damage when it was attacked by aircraft and came under fire from American surface units while rescuing carrier survivors. In November *Isuzu* made a transport run from Japan to Brunei and was hit in the stern by a single torpedo from the submarine *Hake*. Repairs were made in Surabaja. *Isuzu* became the last 5,500-ton cruiser sunk when on April 7 it was hit by three torpedoes fired from the submarines *Gabilan* and *Charr* in the Dutch East Indies. The cruiser sank with the loss of 190 crewmen.

This plate depicts units of the Nagara class as they appeared throughout the war. The top profile shows *Abukuma* as it appeared during the Pearl Harbor operation. *Abukuma* differed from the other ships in its class as it had its forward twin torpedo tubes removed and the aft set was replaced by a Type 92 quadruple launcher. *Isuzu* is shown in the middle profile after it was converted to an antiaircraft cruiser. *Nagara* is shown in the bottom profile in its late-war (1944) configuration.

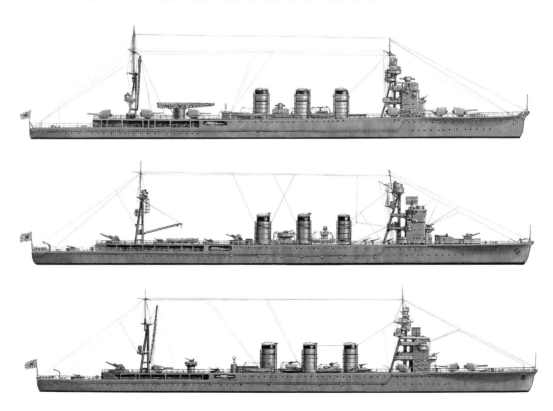

Natori also participated in the invasion of the Philippines at the start of the war as the flagship of Destroyer Squadron 5. It later supported the invasion of the Dutch East Indies in January. With its destroyers, *Natori* participated in the Battle of Sunda Strait against the American heavy cruiser *Houston* and the Australian cruiser *Perth*. *Natori* fired four torpedoes and 29 rounds at *Perth* and later engaged *Houston*. Subsequently, *Natori* remained in East Indies waters through 1942 into January 1943.

On January 9 *Natori* was hit by two torpedoes from the submarine *Tautog*. The stern broke off just aft of No. 7 5.5in mount, but the crew was able to control the flooding and reached Singapore for repairs. It arrived in Japan in June 1943 for permanent repairs and modernization, which were not completed until March 1944. *Natori* was then assigned as flagship of Destroyer Squadron 3 and conducted transport missions in the Central Pacific. On August 17, after exiting San Bernardino Strait en route to Palau, the cruiser was struck by a single torpedo fired from the submarine *Hardhead*. After a second torpedo struck, the ship sank with the loss of 330 men.

Yura had the shortest career of the Nagara class. It began the war assigned as flagship of Submarine Squadron 5, which was tasked to support the invasion of Malaya. By late January 1942, *Yura* was assigned to the forces invading the Dutch East Indies. In February it participated in the interception of Allied ships attempting to leave Singapore.

On April 1, *Yura* entered the Indian Ocean in a major Japanese operation to disrupt Allied shipping in the Bay of Bengal. On April 6 it sank three merchant ships. After a brief stop in Japan for an overhaul, *Yura* was assigned as flagship of Destroyer Squadron 4 and in this role participated in the Battle of Midway. *Yura* was then committed to the struggle for Guadalcanal, during which it participated in the Battle of the Eastern Solomons in August. In September *Yura* moved to Rabaul and suffered slight damage from a B-17 attack while in the Shortland Islands. From here, it escorted supply runs to Guadalcanal. On October 18 *Yura* was hit by a torpedo from submarine *Grampus*, which failed to explode.

One week later *Yura* became the first Japanese light cruiser lost during the war. On October 25 the ship was hit by two bombs from dive-bombers from Henderson Field. The subsequent flooding reduced speed to 14 knots and it was decided to beach the ship. However, before this was done, more dive-bombers and B-17s arrived to place three more bombs on *Yura*. The fires could not be controlled, and the ship was abandoned and scuttled by destroyers.

Kinu also began the war assigned as flagship to a submarine squadron, in this case Submarine Squadron 5, and was first assigned to support the invasion of Malaya. It continued active during the invasion of the Dutch East Indies into March 1942 and on March 1 was slightly damaged by near misses from Australian and New Zealand air attack. After the surrender of the Dutch, it remained in the area until July 1943. On June 23, the cruiser was again lightly damaged by air attack, this time from American B-24 bombers.

Kinu returned to Japan in August for a refit and modernization. After completion it was again assigned to the Southeast Area Defense Forces. In June 1944 the American invasion of Biak Island on the northern coast of New Guinea brought *Kinu* back in the limelight. It was formed into a transport force to carry troops from the Philippines to Biak, but the force was spotted by American aircraft and the operation canceled on June 3. Another attempt involving *Kinu* was canceled on June 13.

When the IJN responded to the American invasion of the Philippines in October, *Kinu* was again assigned to a transport force to move units from Mindanao to Leyte. On October 24 the *Kinu* departed Manila and was immediately attacked by carrier aircraft. The ship sustained only light damage from near misses, but 47 of its crew were killed. After delivering the troops (347), *Kinu* was attacked while returning to Manila by aircraft from escort carriers on October 26. A direct hit on the stern and several near misses caused uncontrolled flooding and the ship sank that afternoon.

Abukuma began the war as flagship of Destroyer Squadron 1, attached to the Pearl Harbor strike force. *Abukuma* stayed with the carriers as they rampaged through the Pacific up until April, participating in the invasion of Rabaul, the raid on Port Darwin, and the Indian Ocean operation.

After a brief refit, it joined the Fifth Fleet and was assigned to the Adak-Attu Seizure Force. The cruiser conducted the invasion of Attu on June 7 and thereafter remained in North Pacific waters, participating in the Battle of the Komandorski Islands in March 1943, where it fired 95 5.5in rounds and four torpedoes. Undamaged in this indecisive clash, it closed out the Aleutian campaign with the evacuation of Kiska in July, when the ship carried 1,202 men to safety.

After the evacuation of Kiska, the North Pacific became decidedly a backwater. However, *Abukuma* remained in the Fifth Fleet still as flagship of Destroyer Squadron 1 through July 1944. In October the Fifth Fleet was given a role in the Japanese response to the Leyte invasion. On October 24, *Abukuma* headed for Surigao Strait. Early the next day it was hit by a torpedo launched from an American PT boat and forced to retire. On October 26, while transiting the Sulu Sea, it was attacked by B-24 bombers. Three hits were scored, which started heavy fires. These spread and soon four torpedoes exploded, forcing the crew to abandon ship; 250 died and 283 were rescued.

Sendai Class

Design and construction

Eight additional 5,500-ton cruisers were planned as part of the 8-8 Fleet Completion Program. The first four were authorized and laid down in 1921. However, the fourth unit was never completed. The final four units, which were scheduled to be built in 1922, were canceled after the signing of the Washington Treaty when the Japanese decided that future cruiser construction would be focused on heavy cruisers. The three remaining units, *Sendai*, *Jintsu*, and *Naka* were named after the lead unit of the class, and were also known as the modified Nagara class. These ships constituted the 5,500-Ton Model III type.

The hull was nearly identical to the two previous 5,500-ton classes, but internally the boiler rooms were laid out differently, which necessitated four stacks instead of the three on the previous classes. The four stacks became the easiest way to distinguish the Sendai class. Another difference was the raked bow given to *Jintsu* and *Sendai*. *Naka* did not possess this modification, but since its construction was delayed by the earthquake that struck Japan in 1923, it had a flared bow based on the heavy cruiser designs then under construction. *Jintsu* received the same bow after it was repaired following a 1927 collision. The bridge was also slightly larger, with the hangar and flying-off platform in the forward superstructure also being retained. As on the Nagara class, there was no aft superstructure and the main deck covered the aft torpedo tubes.

Sendai shown in the 1920s in its early configuration. The 33ft take-off platform over the No. 2 5.5in gun mount and the aircraft hangar below the compass bridge are very evident. This platform could only be used by well-trained pilots and once launched, the aircraft could not recover aboard the cruiser. The entire arrangement was soon determined to be unworkable and the platform was removed and eventually replaced by a catapult mounted aft. (Naval History and Heritage Command)

Sendai Class Construction				
Ship	Built at	Laid down	Launched	Completed
Sendai	Nagasaki by Mitsubishi	2/16/22	10/30/23	4/29/24
Jintsu	Kobe by Kawasaki	10/4/22	12/8/23	7/31/25
Naka	Yokohama Dock Company	5/24/24	3/24/25	11/30/25

Armament

The Sendai class was armed identically to units of the Nagara class.

Service modifications

In 1929, the forward flying platform was replaced with a catapult. This was subsequently removed between 1934 and 1937 and moved aft between

Sendai

Sendai shown in 1943 in its final configuration before being sunk by American surface forces. The mid-war appearance of this Sendai-class unit featured the removal of one 5.5in Type 3 gun in favor of two Type 96 25mm triple mounts, the substitution of quadruple torpedo launchers for the earlier twin mounts and the addition of a No. 21 radar.

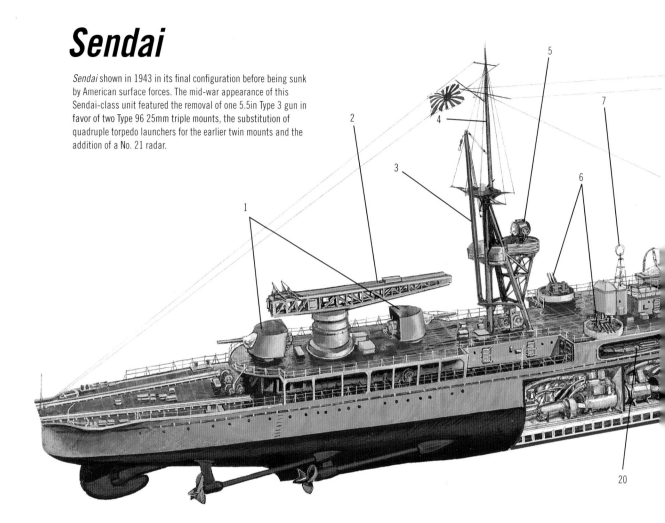

Key

1 5.5in Type 3 gun (6 – 5 shown)
2 Kure Type No.2, Model 3 catapult
3 Aircraft crane
4 Mainmast
5 Type 92 43in (110cm) searchlight (3)
6 Type 96 25mm triple mount (2)
7 Type 90 radio direction finder antenna
8 Secondary rangefinder
9 Type 96 25mm twin mount (2 – 1 shown)
10 30ft cutter (3 shown)
11 Foremast
12 No. 21 air and surface search radar
13 Fire command platform
14 Target survey platform

15 4m rangefinder
16 1.5m navigational rangefinder tower
   (2 – one not shown)
17 Compass bridge
18 13mm quadruple mount
19 Boiler room 1
20 Type 8 24in twin torpedo mount
   (4 total – 2 shown)
21 Boiler room 2
22 36ft motor boat
23 Boiler room 3
24 Boiler room 4
25 Forward engine room
26 Aft engine room

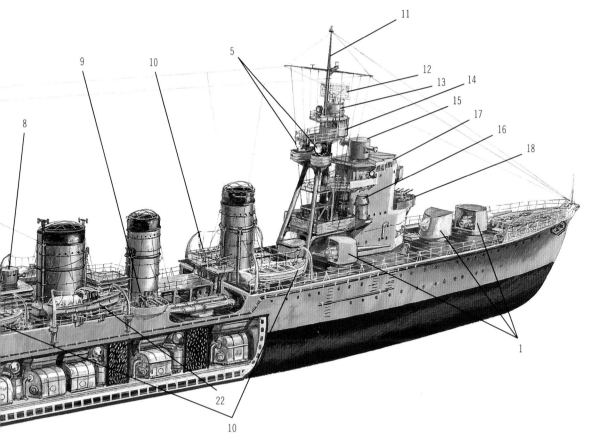

This 1927 photograph provides an overhead view of a Sendai-class cruiser. The seven 5.5in guns are evident as are the twin torpedo mounts located abreast the forward stack; the aft set of torpedo tubes have both been trained out and can be seen abaft the third stack. (*Ships of the World* magazine)

5.5in gun mounts Nos. 6 and 7. When the bridge was modified all three ships were fitted with a 13ft rangefinder above the bridge. Before the start of the war, all three units were earmarked to receive Type 93 oxygen-propelled torpedoes since all three were flagships of destroyer squadrons. This was done March–May 1941 for all except *Sendai*. *Jintsu* and *Naka* received two quadruple Type 92 torpedo mounts aft. The forward twin mounts were removed and the area plated over and converted to crew quarters. Before the start of the war, all received two twin 25mm mounts.

All three ships were lost fairly early in the war during 1943 and early 1944. This limited the amount of modification the class received. In May 1943 *Sendai* had one 5.5in mount removed and two triple 25mm gun mounts installed. A No. 21 radar was added on top of the fire-control position on the foremast. *Sendai* was not further modified before its loss.

Naka received a similar modernization from June 1942 to April 1943. One 5.5in gun was removed and replaced by a Type 89 twin 5in mount. Two triple 25mm guns were also added and the 13mm quadruple mount in front of bridge was replaced with a twin 13mm mount. A No. 21 radar was added atop the foremast. The catapult was retained as on *Sendai*. No other

Sendai Class Modifications (final configuration when lost)			
Ship	*Sendai*	*Naka*	*Jintsu*
Torpedo tubes	8 (4x2)	8 (2x4)	8 (2x4)
5.5in guns	6	6	7
Type 89 twin 5in guns	0	1	0
Triple 25mm guns	2	2	2
Twin 25mm guns	2	2	2
Single 25mm guns	0	0	0
13mm guns	4	2	2
Radar	No. 21	No. 21	None

modifications were made before the ship was lost. The only modifications to *Jintsu* were the additions of two triple 25mm mounts in the area of the torpedo tubes aft.

Wartime service

The prewar career of the Sendai class included the disastrous Special Great Maneuvers of August 1927. During these exercises, *Jintsu* rammed and sank a destroyer at 28 knots at night. *Naka* rammed a second destroyer, cutting off its stern. When war began, the Sendai-class ships were the most modern of the 5,500-ton cruisers. As such, *Jintsu*, *Sendai*, and *Naka* began the war as flagships of Destroyer Squadrons 2, 3, and 4, respectively. In their capacity as destroyer squadron flagships, all saw heavy action during the first part of the war and all were committed to the savage battles in the Solomons. Accordingly, all were lost fairly early in the war.

Sendai began the war as flagship of Destroyer Squadron 3. It escorted Malaya invasion convoys into January 1942. On January 27, *Sendai* saw its first action when two destroyers (one British, one Australian) attempted to intercept the convoy which *Sendai* and its destroyers were escorting. In the ensuing action (the battle off Endau), the British destroyer was sunk for no Japanese losses. After the fall of Singapore in February 1942, *Sendai* participated in the invasion of Sumatra in March.

After a refit, *Sendai* took part in the Battle of Midway as an escort to the Main Body. When the Americans attacked Guadalcanal, Destroyer Squadron 3 was ordered to Truk. *Sendai* was soon active off Guadalcanal, conducting night-time resupply missions and shelling American-held Tulagi (once) and Guadalcanal (twice) during September. On the night of November 14–15, it was part of the Japanese attempt to shell Henderson Field. The mission failed with the loss of the battleship *Kirishima*, but *Sendai* was undamaged. In this night battle, it engaged American destroyers with torpedoes and gunfire.

From January 1943, *Sendai* was involved in constant patrol and escort duties in the Northern Solomons, returning to Japan

This view of *Sendai* in 1937 near Shanghai, China shows the cruiser in its final configuration before going to war. The four stacks are easily discerned; this was the primary difference from the preceding Kuma and Nagara classes. Note the aft catapult fitted between 5.5in gun mounts Nos. 6 and 7. The crane mounted on the mainmast for aircraft handling can also be seen. (Naval History and Heritage Command)

Sendai Class Specifications

Displacement: 5,195 tons standard; 7,609 tons full load (1925)
Dimensions: Length 532ft / beam 46.5ft / draft 29ft
Maximum speed: 35.25kt
Range: 6,000nm at 14kt (actual)
Crew: 37 officers and 413 enlisted personnel plus space for staff (5 officers and 22 enlisted)

May–June 1943 for refit and limited modernization. Upon its return to action, it resumed escort duties in the Solomons. On November 1, American forces landed on Bougainville Island. The Japanese reacted immediately, sending a cruiser-destroyer force against the invasion. *Sendai* was part of the force gathered for this purpose. The action began early the next day. *Sendai* spotted the Americans and launched four torpedoes (all missed). In return it was smothered by 6in gunfire from four American light cruisers. Severe fires and flooding resulted, and the ship was abandoned with the loss of 185 of its crew.

Naka began the war as flagship of Destroyer Squadron 4. This unit was assigned to escort convoys headed for Luzon. In this capacity, *Naka* was lightly damaged by American air attack on December 10. By late December it shifted to support the invasion of the Dutch East Indies. On January 24, the convoy *Naka* was escorting was attacked by four American destroyers. *Naka* had been drawn off by a Dutch submarine, and the four American ships proceeded to savage the convoy for no losses.

In the Battle of the Java Sea on February 27, 1942, both *Naka* and *Jintsu* were present as an Allied cruiser-destroyer force attempted to engage a Japanese invasion convoy. Though the battle was won by Japanese torpedoes, which sank three Dutch ships, all of the torpedoes fired by *Naka* (8) and *Jintsu* (12) missed their targets. However, the aircraft off these cruisers played an important role by tracking the Allied force during the night.

On March 31, while covering the occupation of Christmas Island, *Naka* was attacked by the American submarine *Seawolf*. One torpedo hit aft, which caused extensive damage. *Naka* was repaired at Singapore in May before returning to Japan. From April 1943, *Naka* operated in the Central Pacific in various escort and transport roles. In February 1944 it was caught in the major American carrier raid on Truk and on the 17th of that month it departed Truk to aid the torpedoed cruiser *Agano*. *Naka* came under immediate air attack. One torpedo hit forward and broke the hull in two. Only 210 of its crew were rescued.

Jintsu began the war as flagship of Destroyer Squadron 2, and its first action escorting the Mindanao invasion force. In January 1942 it supported the invasion of the Dutch East Indies and participated in the Battle of the Java Sea as mentioned above. In March *Jintsu* returned to Japan. In June it escorted the Midway Invasion Force and subsequently was committed to the increasingly savage battles around Guadalcanal. On August 25 *Jintsu* was subjected to air attack while escorting a convoy to the island. A 500lb bomb hit forward, killed 24, wounded 27, and forced a return to Japan for repairs.

Jintsu returned to Truk in January 1943 to resume duties as flagship of Destroyer Squadron 2. It departed Rabaul on July 12 to conduct a reinforcement of Kolombangara in the Central Solomons. In the resulting Battle of Kolombangara on July 13, 1943, the Japanese successfully employed their usual torpedo tactics, but this victory proved painful when *Jintsu* was hit by radar-controlled gunfire from three Allied light cruisers. The intense shellfire destroyed the bridge and the boiler rooms and *Jintsu* went dead in water. It was later hit by a destroyer-launched torpedo that broke the ship in half. *Jintsu* sank with heavy loss of life.

Yubari Class

Design and construction

Construction of an experimental cruiser was authorized in the 1917 construction program. However, no funds were immediately available and the design was not approved until October 1921 so the ship was not laid down until June 1922. The intent of the design was to create a ship that possessed a heavy armament and high speed on the smallest possible displacement. The design must be considered a success since it created a ship with the same speed, radius, and broadside armament on a much smaller displacement than the 5,500-ton cruisers.

Yubari Class Construction				
Ship	Built at	Laid down	Launched	Completed
Yubari	Sasebo Navy Yard	6/5/22	3/5/23	7/31/23

The primary recognition feature of *Yubari* was its trunked stack. This was a design feature that would become common on subsequent Japanese cruisers. Other features on *Yubari* also proved successful and were incorporated into future designs. These included a bow curve, no more mixed-firing boilers, and, most importantly, the weight-saving feature of incorporating

Yubari in about 1925 after the stack was raised to address the problem of gases going into the bridge. This view clearly shows its compact appearance and the arrangement of its main battery of six 5.5in guns in four gun houses. The two double torpedo mounts are also discernable amidships. (Naval History and Heritage Command)

Yubari Class Specifications

Displacement: 2,890 tons standard; 4,447 tons full load (August 1923)
Dimensions: Length 457.5ft overall / beam 39.5ft / draft: 23.75ft
Maximum speed: 35.5kt
Range: 3,310nm at 14kt (actual)
Crew: 328 officers and enlisted personnel

side and deck armor to increase the longitudinal strength of the hull. This meant the hull of *Yubari* was only 31 percent of displacement as opposed to 38 percent on the 5,500-ton cruisers. Even with these weight-saving measures and an overall smaller displacement, total armor on *Yubari* was almost twice that of the 5,500-ton ships.

Nevertheless, though the basic design principles were proven successful, the ship was overweight by 419 tons, or 14 percent of displacement. This was beyond what was considered normal by Japanese designers. The ship's design speed was 35.5 knots, achieved by eight boilers generating 57,900shp through three shafts.

Armament

The main battery was the same broadside, six 5.5in guns, as mounted on the 5,500-ton cruisers. The difference was that the six guns on *Yubari* were mounted in a combination of two single mounts and two twin mounts. The twin mounts were actually gun houses protected by only a 0.4in steel front plate. The tighter grouping of the mounts fore and aft also allowed for a higher rate of fire. Fire control was provided by a director on the foremast and two 10ft rangefinders placed on either side of the compass bridge.

The torpedo armament was two twin torpedo mounts with four reserve torpedoes. Antiaircraft protection was provided by a single 3.15in gun amidships and two 7.7mm machine guns.

Service modifications

In 1924, the height of the stack was raised by 6.5ft to avoid the problem of gases going into the bridge. In 1932–33, while in a yard, the 3.15in gun was removed and spray shields placed around the torpedo tubes. In 1935 two twin 13mm machine guns were fitted. These were replaced by twin 25mm mounts in 1940.

The ship received no modification (except the addition of a hydrophone set between August and October 1943) until its first major wartime refit period from December 1943 to March 1944. During this time, the ship's antiaircraft armament was greatly increased. The single 5.5in guns were removed; in the place of the forward mount, a Type 10 4.7in high-angle gun was fitted. The number of 25mm guns was increased to 25 with the addition of a triple mount replacing the aft 5.5in gun, two additional triple mounts fitted on the aft superstructure, two twin 25mm mounts fitted forward of the bridge, and eight single mounts. A No.22 radar replaced the searchlight atop the bridge and two depth-charge rails were added aft. Speed was reduced to 32 knots.

Wartime service

Yubari began the war as flagship of Destroyer Squadron 6 of the Fourth Fleet charged with protection of the Mandate Islands. For the first part of the war, *Yubari* saw action with *Tenryu* and *Tatsuta*, participating in the invasions of Wake, Rabaul and Kavieng, and Lae and Salamaua. When American carrier aircraft attacked the Lae/Salamaua invasion force, *Yubari* took near misses fore and aft that caused hull damage and small fires. These resulted in 14 dead and 30 wounded. It was forced to return to Truk for repairs, which were completed in mid-April. Its next operation was the invasion of Port Moresby when *Yubari* was assigned to the Port Moresby Attack Force (the invasion convoy). *Yubari* returned to Truk after the failure of the operation. Following a short refit in Japan from May 23 to June 15, it returned to Truk on June 23.

The highlight of *Yubari*'s career was its participation in the Battle of Savo Island following the American invasion of Guadalcanal. It took a dud hit early in the action, but one of its torpedoes hit the American heavy cruiser *Vincennes*, which later sank. *Yubari* then proceeded to pound the destroyer *Ralph Talbot*, which escaped by moving into a rain squall. In total, *Yubari* fired 96 5.5in shells and four torpedoes during the battle.

Yubari missed the rest of the Guadalcanal campaign after it was assigned to escort convoys to and from Truk into 1943. On April 1, 1943, it arrived at Rabaul for front-line duties but was promptly damaged by a mine on July 5 that forced it home for repairs. The cruiser returned to Rabaul by November 1943 only to be ordered back to Japan in December to augment its antiaircraft armament.

After completion of this refit, *Yubari* was ordered to escort convoys in the Central Pacific. It embarked 365 army troops and supplies at the Palau Islands and headed to Sonsorol Island to the southwest. After disembarking the troops and their supplies, the cruiser was struck by a single torpedo from the submarine *Bluegill* on April 27, 1944. The single hit flooded two boiler rooms and the flooding could not be stopped. Early on the next day, *Yubari* sank with a loss of 19 crewmen.

Agano Class

Design and construction

The 5,500-ton cruisers were designed specifically with duties as destroyer squadron flagships in mind. However, by the late 1930s these ships were increasingly unsuited for their assigned role. In the view of the IJN, these

Agano Class Construction				
Ship	Built at	Laid down	Launched	Completed
Agano	Sasebo Navy Yard	6/18/40	10/22/41	10/31/42
Noshiro	Yokosuka Navy Yard	9/4/41	7/19/42	6/30/43
Yahagi	Sasebo Navy Yard	11/11/41	10/25/42	12/29/43
Sakawa	Sasebo Navy Yard	11/21/42	4/9/44	11/30/44

shortcomings were significant and included just about everything that was worth mentioning. The 5,500-ton cruisers were now slower than the newest Japanese destroyers, possessed less endurance, and, perhaps most importantly, did not possess any advantage in firepower. The old cruisers could present a broadside of six 5.5in guns and four torpedo tubes. The newer destroyers had a broadside of six 5in guns (which had a greater rate of fire) and up to nine torpedo tubes. The older ships were also viewed as deficient in their scouting capabilities since they carried only a single floatplane – the Japanese thought that two were necessary.

As long as the Japanese were bound by the London Naval Treaty, their cruiser construction was limited. This restriction was lifted when Japan announced its intention to leave the treaty. The Naval General Staff planned to build 13 6,000-ton cruisers, six for destroyer squadrons, and seven for submarine squadrons. These were to be built from 1939 to 1945. The final decision on the program was made in September 1938. Four destroyer squadron flagships were to be ordered (these became the Agano class) and two submarine squadron flagships (these became the Oyodo class). This proposal was approved in March 1939 as part of the Fourth Naval Replenishment Program.

The design of the new class was not finalized until October 1939. The final result was a beautiful ship with a graceful deck line in which the sheer was less pronounced from amidships to the stern than other 1930s Japanese cruiser

Noshiro running trials in June 1943. The view shows the uncluttered design to full effect. Unlike the lead ship in the class, *Agano, Noshiro* was completed with a No. 21 radar on the front of the fire-control tower. (*Ships of the World* magazine)

designs. The design appeared uncluttered, with a small bridge structure, a single stack, and three main turrets. A significant portion of the topside space was devoted to aircraft handling facilities, which included a catapult, a platform for two aircraft, and an aircraft crane mounted on the mainmast aft. Overall, the ship gave an impression of being underarmed, which it was.

Armor was improved compared with previous light cruisers, but was still limited. The design specifications called for protection of the magazine and machinery spaces against 6in and 5in gunfire. The side belt incorporated 2.4in of armor, which extended beyond the machinery spaces. Protection of the forward and aft magazines was supplemented by a 2.2in belt of steel. Deck armor was only 0.8in over machinery and magazine spaces; total armor for the entire ship was just 656 tons. The small beam prevented any antitorpedo protection from being provided, but internal compartmentation was extensive.

The class was designed to attain 35 knots. This required a total of 100,000shp generated by four sets of turbines. Six boilers were placed in five boiler rooms. On trials, both *Agano* and *Yahagi* slightly exceeded their design speed.

Armament

The new cruiser's main battery was six Type 41 6in/50 guns. These dated from 1912 and had been in service as secondary guns on Japanese battleships. In the Agano class, they were mounted in three twin turrets. Antiaircraft armament featured the new 3.15in high-angle gun designed specifically for the Agano class. However, only two twin mounts were fitted. Light antiaircraft armament was limited to two triple 25mm mounts in front of bridge and two twin 13mm mounts near the mainmast.

The Agano class did possess a major increase in torpedo firepower. Two quadruple Type 92 torpedo mounts were fitted below the aircraft platform. These were on the centerline and were rotatable, so could fire in either direction. Eight reserve torpedoes were also carried, which could be reloaded in 20–30 minutes. All four ships were completed with two depth-charge racks on the stern. The ships were also provided with a hydrophone for passive detection and a sonar for active detection of submarines.

This port beam view of *Yahagi* was taken in December 1943 only a few days before commissioning. The clear photograph shows the beauty of the design and the several differences of the third ship of the class upon completion. The catapult is a smaller 64ft version and the Type 94 high-angle directors have been moved forward to the area of the stack. The ship's antiaircraft suite was also heavier upon completion. (*Ships of the World* magazine)

Agano Class 25mm Gun Fit				
Ship	Triple mounts	Twin mounts	Single mounts	Total 25mm guns
Agano	4	2	0	16
Noshiro	10	0	18	48
Yahagi	10	0	28	58
Sakawa	10	0	42	72

Service modifications

Wartime modifications focused on improving the radar and light antiaircraft fit. Since the last two ships were finished late into the war, both incorporated improvements already made on the two ships in service.

Agano was completed without radar, but a No. 21 set was added in June 1943. This was placed on the front of the rangefinder tower, giving the radar a 360-degree rotation. The other ships were completed with a No. 21 radar. In July 1944 *Noshiro* and *Yahagi* were fitted with a No. 22 and a No. 13 radar. The No. 22 set was fitted on both sides of the bridge at the level of the antiaircraft command platform. The large No. 13 set was fitted on the trailing side of the foremast. *Sakawa* was completed with all three radars in place.

Agano received little modification before being sunk. When it received its radar in June 1943, the cruiser also received two triple and two twin 25mm mounts. *Noshiro* received additional 25mm guns to bring its total to 32 (eight triple and eight single) in its early 1944 repair and refit period. *Yahagi* was also augmented to 32 25mm guns before leaving Japan for combat duty. After the Battle of the Philippine Sea both *Noshiro* and *Yahagi* received additional radar (Nos. 22 and 13) and had their light antiaircraft fit increased to 48 25mm guns (10 triple, 18 single with another four relocatable guns). *Yahagi*'s final modifications in November–December 1944 increased the 25mm total to 58 – 10 triple and 28 single.

Wartime service

Agano was the first ship to reach completion but was not assigned to an operational unit until November 1942. At this time it assumed flagship duties for Destroyer Squadron 10, relieving *Nagara*. After arriving at Truk in December, it was in action later in the month, participating in the seizure of Madang and Wewak on New Guinea. In January, it covered the evacuation of Guadalcanal.

Agano's first real action was in the Battle of Empress Augusta Bay on November 2. Though it was undamaged in the battle, the combat debut of the new class of cruiser was not auspicious. It contributed nothing to the battle, which resulted in a Japanese defeat and the sinking of *Sendai* as described earlier. *Noshiro* entered service in August 1943 as flagship of Destroyer Squadron 2, replacing the sunken *Jintsu*. On November 3 it was ordered to depart Truk with seven heavy cruisers to complete the destruction of the American forces off Bougainville. After arriving at Rabaul two days later, the cruiser force was attacked by American carrier aircraft. Both *Agano* and *Noshiro* were caught in port but neither suffered serious damage. However, when the Americans returned on November 11, *Noshiro* again incurred only slight damage but *Agano* was hit by an aircraft torpedo outside Rabaul harbor. The hit sheered the stern section away, but flooding was limited and the ship reached the safety of Rabaul.

> ## Agano Class Specifications
>
> **Displacement:** 7,710 tons design; 8,534 tons full load
> **Dimensions:** Length 572.35ft / beam 49.9ft / draft 18.5ft
> **Maximum speed:** 35kt
> **Range:** 6,000nm at 18kt
> **Crew:** 51 officers and 649 enlisted personnel as designed; *Sakawa* had 55 officers and 750 enlisted when completed.

The next day *Agano* departed Rabaul for Truk. It was attacked by the submarine *Scamp*, which hit the cruiser with one of a six-torpedo broadside. The hit flooded all boiler rooms, and *Noshiro* was forced to take *Agano* in tow. On November 16 *Agano* reached Truk under tow; the cruiser subsequently departed on February 15 for Japan. It was struck by the submarine *Skate* north of Truk the next day with two torpedoes. The damage was severe and resulted in a loss of power and progressive flooding. *Agano* sank early on February 17.

Noshiro continued operations out of Truk. On January 1, 1944, it was attacked by carrier aircraft north of Kavieng. One direct hit destroyed its No. 2 turret and several near misses caused severe hull damage. *Noshiro* was forced to return to Japan for repairs. After the completion of the repairs, *Noshiro* arrived at Lingga in April. *Yahagi* also arrived at Lingga in February as flagship of Destroyer Squadron 10. Both ships took part in the Battle of the Philippine Sea and were undamaged. After a short refit in Japan, they returned to Lingga in July.

Both *Noshiro* and *Yahagi* were assigned to Force "A." In the October 25 Battle of Samar, *Yahagi* led the destroyers of Destroyer Squadron 10 and *Noshiro* led those of Destroyer Squadron 2. In the battle, *Yahagi* launched seven torpedoes at American escort carriers without result. The cruiser was hit by a single 5in destroyer shell. It underwent numerous air attacks during the battle and after, but suffered only near misses. However, losses, primarily to strafing, totaled 80 crewmen killed or wounded.

Noshiro also survived the battle with a single 5in hit, but did take several damaging near misses from escort carrier aircraft. It engaged two escort carriers with gunfire and claimed several hits. The next day, October 26, while withdrawing, it was attacked by carrier aircraft and hit by a single torpedo, which resulted in flooding, loss of power, and a severe list. A second torpedo hit that evening sank the ship with a loss of all but 328 of its crew.

Yahagi returned to Japan in November. When the Americans invaded Okinawa, the cruiser was assigned to the Surface Special Attack Force as part of Operation *Ten-Ichi-Go* (Heaven Number One). The cruiser departed on April 6 en route to Okinawa with the superbattleship *Yamato* and eight destroyers in the IJN's last major operation. The following day this small force came under intensive air attack. Early in the action, an air-launched torpedo hit *Yahagi*. The hit destroyed the engine rooms and brought the ship dead in the water. The cruiser was helpless at this point and was struck by another six torpedoes and at least 12 bombs and sank with the loss of 446 crewmen.

Sakawa was assigned to Destroyer Squadron 11 in December 1944. Due to fuel shortages, it was unable to take part in the *Ten-Ichi-Go* operation. *Sakawa* remained in the Inland Sea on training duties until July 1945. It was surrendered intact and employed as a repatriation transport until February 1946. Subsequently, the cruiser was used as a target in the atomic tests at Bikini Atoll. In the July 1 test, it was badly damaged by an air burst and sank the next day.

Oyodo Class

Design and construction

The IJN also had a requirement for a cruiser designed to act as the flagship for a submarine squadron. This requirement was linked to the Japanese concept of submarine warfare in which long-range cruiser submarines would concentrate to attack enemy fleet units at extended ranges. The flagship cruiser was needed to provide targeting for the submarines and to coordinate their operations. To do this, it needed aircraft for scouting purposes, high speed and great endurance, and sufficient armament to combat enemy light units. Communications and accommodations for the embarked staff were also important. There were never enough cruisers to cover the submarine squadron flagship requirement and the 5,500-ton units occasionally assigned to act in this role were unsatisfactory.

Oyodo Class Construction				
Ship	**Built at**	**Laid down**	**Launched**	**Completed**
Oyodo	Kure Navy Yard	2/14/41	4/2/42	2/28/43

In the 1930s, the IJN had a requirement for seven flagship cruisers for its seven submarine squadrons. Originally it was thought that the new class of cruisers being designed to replace the 5,500-ton units could support both destroyer and submarine flagship duties, but this was soon proven to be wishful thinking. Several different designs were created in 1938 until a definitive design for "Cruisers C" was completed in October. The same appropriations funding that provided for the four new Agano-class units approved in March 1938 also included funding for two new submarine flagship cruisers. Construction of the first ship was delayed, and this meant a subsequent delay in the start of the construction of the second, which ultimately resulted in its cancelation.

The design of the new class, named after the first ship laid down, *Oyodo*, was identical to that of the Agano class in regard to its hull lines and forward superstructure. The armament differed as described below, but the most important difference between the two cruiser designs was the aircraft-handling facilities. The original design for the Oyodo class called for a special 144ft catapult fitted aft on the ship's centerline. Forward of the catapult was a hangar capable of storing four aircraft, with deck stowage for another two. These were of a new design with the high speed and long range required for scouting duties.

The top and middle profiles show *Agano* as it was completed. The ship gives a graceful and speedy appearance, though it also seems to be underarmed and weakly armored. The bottom profile shows *Oyodo*, a one-of-a-kind light cruiser built for fleet command and control. This is the ship's configuration in October 1944. The ship is shown with the smaller catapult fitted earlier in 1944 and a profusion of 25mm gun mounts.

Oyodo Class Specifications

Displacement: 10,417 tons design; 11,433 tons full load (February 1943)
Dimensions: Length 629.75ft / beam 54.5ft / draft 19.5ft
Maximum speed: 35kt
Range: 10,315nm at 18kt
Crew: 53 officers and 723 enlisted personnel

The propulsion system was more powerful than the Agano class. Four sets of turbines generated 110,000shp, which translated to a maximum speed of 35 knots. The radius of action as designed was 8,700nm at 18 knots; however, in service, it proved to be 10,000nm at 18 knots.

Protection was designed to withstand 6in shellfire or a 550lb bomb dropped from 9,900ft. The side belt armor was 2.4in, supplemented by an armored box covering the forward magazines and the machinery spaces amidships with an additional 1.2–3in of armor. The main deck was covered by 1.2in of armor over the machinery spaces and 2in over the magazines. No antitorpedo defenses were provided.

Armament

The main battery was positioned forward since the after part of the ship was devoted solely to aircraft-handling facilities. Two triple 6.1in turrets were used: these were turrets removed from the Mogami-class cruisers when they were converted to heavy cruisers. Long-range antiaircraft protection was provided by four new 3.9in twin high-angle mounts. Short-range antiaircraft protection, as completed, was six triple 25mm mounts. No torpedo mounts were fitted, making this the only Japanese light cruiser not to carry torpedoes when completed.

Service modifications

The ship was completed without radar. In April 1943 a No. 21 radar was installed on the rangefinder tower. In March 1944 *Oyodo* was modified from its role as a submarine squadron flagship to that of Combined Fleet flagship. The hangar was converted into space for an office and living quarters for the staff. The large catapult was replaced with a smaller 62ft model. After this modification, only two seaplanes could be carried. Six additional triple and 11 single 25mm gun mounts were also added, bringing the total to 47.

In early October 1944 six more single 25mm mounts were added. A No. 13 radar was added on the mast above the hangar and two No. 22 radars were placed on the bridge wings. In late October, four more single 25mm guns were added for a final total of 57 – 12 triple and 21 single mounts.

Wartime service

After the ship was commissioned in February 1943, it was immediately apparent that the role it was designed for no longer existed. It was assigned to the IJN's carrier fleet since *Oyodo*'s large cruising radius and decent antiaircraft capability made it suited to act as a carrier escort. Its first mission beyond home waters was a transport mission to Rabaul in July 1943. Following this, it remained at Truk for the next seven months. On January 1, 1944, on a mission to Kavieng, *Oyodo* came under carrier air attack but suffered only light damage. It returned to Japan in March 1944 for conversion. After modification, *Oyodo* moved to Tokyo Bay to assume its new role as Combined Fleet flagship. In late September the Combined Fleet moved ashore so *Oyodo* returned to fleet service and was again assigned to the carrier force.

Oyodo departed with the carrier force on October 20 for the Battle of Leyte Gulf. During the heavy air strikes launched by the Americans against the IJN's last carrier force, *Oyodo* was damaged by two rockets and a near miss from a bomb that killed eight and wounded 12. After Leyte Gulf, *Oyodo* was sent to Lingga. From there it took part in the San Jose intrusion operation against the American beachhead on Mindoro on December 26. This was a totally ineffective undertaking during which *Oyodo* was hit by two bombs (one a dud) and fired 98 main battery rounds. The cruiser was repaired at Singapore.

In February 1945 *Oyodo* was ordered to return to Japan with the battleships *Ise* and *Hyuga*. All three ships, as well as their three escorting destroyers, were loaded with oil, strategic materials, and key personnel for the transit north. Despite the efforts of as many as 25 American submarines, the force arrived safely in Japan on February 20.

During the last months of the war, *Oyodo*, like the rest of the Imperial Fleet, was hunted down in home waters by American carrier strikes. On March 19 at Kure, it was struck by three bombs. By April, it was repaired and made combat-ready. On July 24, *Oyodo* was hit by five bombs but this damage was contained by the crew. The next attack on July 28 was fatal. At least four bomb hits and many near misses to starboard opened the plates to the forward engine room and an aft boiler room, which resulted in flooding and the ship's capsizing in only 25ft of water. The ship was raised in 1947 and scrapped by August 1948.

Katori Class

Design and construction

The three units of the Katori class were not intended to be combatant ships. The Japanese classified them as "training cruisers," although this was not actually a subcategory of cruisers, but a separate class meant for training ships. The genesis of the class began in 1937 when the Naval General Staff

This photograph was captured by American forces on Kwajalein in 1944. It shows a Katori-class training cruiser; based on the absence of a white band on the stack indicating a flagship of a *sentai*, this is probably *Katori*. Because there seems to be no addition of 25mm twin gun mounts forward of the bridge the photo was taken sometime prior to August 1942. (Naval History and Heritage Command)

decided it needed a new class of training ships to conduct long-range training cruises for midshipmen. Originally it was planned to modify three aging Kuma-class units, but after Japan renounced the naval treaties, this plan was dropped.

The new class of ship emphasized accommodations and training facilities. Accordingly, much of the equipment found on other IJN ships was fitted, including an array of different weapons, fire-control and navigational equipment, and both steam turbine and diesel engines. The bridge was designed to accommodate a large number of midshipmen.

Overall, living quarters were generous by IJN standards. Given this, they were well suited to act as fleet flagships during wartime. The first two ships were authorized in 1937 and the third in 1938. A planned fourth ship was canceled in 1941.

The basic design of the class reflected its mission. They gave an austere appearance with a basic forward superstructure, a single stack, and a small aft superstructure. Since speed was not a design requirement, the length-to-beam ratio was only 8:1, which gave the ships a stubby appearance. The combined turbine and diesel propulsion system was sufficient for only 8,000shp, but this met the design speed of 18 knots.

Katori Class Construction				
Ship	Built at	Laid down	Launched	Completed
Katori	Yokohama by Mitsubishi	8/24/38	6/17/39	4/20/40
Kashima	Yokohama by Mitsubishi	10/6/38	9/25/39	5/31/40
Kashii	Yokohama by Mitsubishi	10/4/39	10/15/40	7/15/41

Armament

The original armament of the Katori class included four 5.5in guns in twin gun houses mounted fore and aft, and a Type 89 twin 5in mount aft. Four 2in saluting guns were fitted on *Katori* and *Kashima*, but these were removed in August 1942. Two were fitted on *Kashii* upon its completion. *Katori* and *Kashima* were given two twin 25mm mounts, which were placed abreast the bridge. When the saluting guns were removed, two additional twin 25mm guns were added. *Kashii* was completed with four twin 25mm guns. Two twin torpedo mounts were fitted abreast the funnel. No torpedo reloads were carried. A catapult was also fitted abaft the stack with room for a single floatplane.

Service modifications

Katori received no modifications with the exception of the addition of two twin 25mm mounts already mentioned. Two ships underwent conversion

The Tenryu and Katori classes. The top profile shows *Tenryu*, the first modern Japanese light cruiser. The ship's main armament of four 5.5in guns and two triple torpedo mounts is evident. The middle profile is *Katori* in its prewar training cruiser configuration. The ship presents an austere appearance with a single stack, a catapult amidships, and twin 5.5in gun houses fore and aft. The bottom view is *Kashii* in 1945 just before its loss after it had been converted to an antisubmarine cruiser.

Kashii was escorting a convoy in the South China Sea when it was attacked by carrier aircraft on January 12, 1945. This view is from an aircraft from USS Hancock. Kashii was struck by a torpedo on its starboard side and two bombs, one of which detonated the depth charge magazine. The ship sank in shallow water, which kept the bow above water for some time as shown in this view. (Naval History and Heritage Command)

into antisubmarine sweeping ships. The first to be converted was *Kashii*, between March and April 1944. This work included the removal of the torpedo mounts, which were replaced by two Type 89 twin 5in mounts, and the addition of four triple 25mm mounts for a total of 20 25mm guns (four triple, four twin). A No. 21 radar was fitted on the foremast. To equip it in its new role as a submarine hunter, hydrophones and sonar were installed in addition to two depth-charge racks and four throwers on the quarterdeck, with 300 depth charges that were stowed in a concrete-lined magazine created from the former headquarters spaces. In June–July 1944 *Kashii* received another ten single 25mm guns and eight single 13mm machine guns. Also at this time, a No. 22 radar replaced the No. 21 on the foremast.

Kashima received similar modifications from December 1944 to January 1945. In addition to the works described above, it received ten single 25mm mounts, and a No. 22 radar was fitted on the foremast. Final modifications in February 1945 included adding a No. 13 radar on the foremast and eight more single 25mm guns.

Wartime service

Katori, commissioned in April 1940, conducted only a single training cruise before it was pulled from training duties to be converted to a fleet flagship. It was originally assigned as flagship of Submarine Squadron 1 in November 1940, but then was designated flagship of the Sixth (submarine) Fleet in May 1941. On February 1, 1942, while at Kwajalein, it was attacked by American carrier aircraft but was only slightly damaged. After repairs in Japan, it returned to Truk in April. Aside from two short refit periods in Japan, *Katori* remained in the Central Pacific, mostly at Truk, as Sixth Fleet flagship, until February 1944. At this time it was transferred to the General Escort Command

and was ordered home for conversion into an antisubmarine ship. Unfortunately for *Katori*, its departure from Truk coincided with the arrival of the American carrier force then raiding Truk. On February 17 it was hit by an aircraft torpedo but made emergency repairs and was proceeding slowly until it encountered an American cruiser force making a sweep around the atoll. *Katori* was sunk by gunfire 40nm northwest of Truk.

Kashima was the only training cruiser to survive the war. With *Katori*, it completed its only training cruise in 1940 before being pulled for conversion into a flagship. It was assigned flagship of Sentai 18 on November 15 and later as flagship of the Fourth Fleet on December 1, 1941. In this capacity, it spent most of its time at Truk. It did conduct two refits in Japan, but by November 1943 was ordered to turn over Fourth Fleet flagship duties to *Nagara* and return to Japan to resume training duties.

> ## Katori Class Specifications
>
> **Displacement:** 5,890 tons standard; 6,720 tons full load
> **Dimensions:** Length 437.9ft / beam 54.5ft / draft 3.75ft
> **Maximum speed:** 18kt
> **Range:** 9,900nm at 12kt
> **Crew:** 315 officers and enlisted personnel in ship's company with space for 275 midshipmen

From December 1943 until December 1944, *Kashima* conducted training cruises for midshipmen in the Inland Sea. During this time it was also employed in a series of emergency transport runs. In December 1944 it began conversion into an antisubmarine sweeping ship. This was completed in late January 1945. During its brief tenure as a submarine hunter, *Kashima* operated in the East China Sea and in the Sea of Japan, without success. The ship was surrendered after Japan's defeat and was used as a repatriation transport until November 1946, after which it was scrapped.

Kashii did not enter service until July 1941. It was immediately based in French Indochina from which it provided escort for Malaya invasion convoys at the start of war. *Kashii* transitioned in February to escort invasion forces bound for Sumatra. After the surrender of the Dutch East Indies, it remained in the southwest area operating out of Singapore. As was the case for *Kashima*, *Kashii* returned to Japan in December 1943 to resume training of midshipmen. This was short-lived. In March, *Kashii* was subordinated to the General Escort Command after conversion into an antisubmarine sweeping ship. This conversion was completed in a month in Kure Navy Yard.

In its new career as a submarine hunter, *Kashii* was assigned as flagship of Surface Escort Division 1, responsible for running convoys between Japan and Singapore. On its fifth return trip from Singapore, *Kashii*, now flagship of the Escort Squadron 101, encountered an American carrier task force then rampaging through the South China Sea. The ten-ship convoy *Kashii* was escorting was annihilated and the ship took a torpedo amidships and two bomb hits, one of which penetrated the depth-charge magazine. Only 19 of its crew survived.

DESTROYERS

During the Pacific War, arguably the most successful component of the IJN was its destroyer force. These ships were generally larger than their Allied counterparts and were better armed in most cases. Equipped with a large, long-range torpedo (eventually called "Long Lance" by the Allies), these ships proved themselves as formidable opponents. In the first part of the war, Japanese destroyers were instrumental in an unbroken string of Japanese victories. However, it was not until the Guadalcanal campaign of 1942–43 that they fully demonstrated their power. In a series of night actions, they devastated Allied task forces in a number of daring attacks using their deadly torpedoes. In the campaign in the Central and Northern Solomons through the rest of 1943, Japanese destroyers were essentially left to fend for themselves against the increasing power of the US Navy. These superb offensive platforms performed well in the initial period of the war, but as the American offensive in the South Pacific and later the Central Pacific gained speed, the weaknesses of Japanese destroyers were ruthlessly exposed.

JAPANESE DESTROYER DEVELOPMENT

The growing IJN took an early interest in torpedo boats. As early as 1879, the Japanese began ordering torpedo boats from British, French, and German yards. Increasingly, many of these boats were built in Japan using foreign parts and foreign designs. By 1898, construction of larger British destroyer designs was begun. These boats played important roles in the war against Imperial Russia in 1904–05 and reinforced the Japanese belief that torpedo boats were an important component of the fleet. Coming out of the war with Russia, the

Fumizuki under attack from the light carrier *Monterey*'s aircraft on January 4, 1944, off Kavieng. The ship was only lightly damaged in this attack, but was sunk the next month at Truk by a single torpedo, with the loss of 29 crewmen. (Naval History and Heritage Command)

A Group I Special Type destroyer with its three triple-torpedo mounts trained to port. The torpedo broadside of the Special Type destroyers made them formidable offensive platforms. (*Ships of the World* magazine)

Japanese concentrated on building destroyers of British design in Japan.

By the onset of World War I, the Japanese were short of modern destroyers. In response, construction began on a class of ships based on a British design, but fitted with a heavier armament than comparable British and German ships. By the end of the war, Japanese destroyer construction had diverged into two paths, a first-class destroyer of around 1,300 tons with three or four 4.7in guns and six 21in torpedo tubes, and a second-class destroyer of some 850 tons with three 4.7in guns and six torpedo tubes.

Throughout this design evolution, the Japanese placed emphasis on the destroyer as a platform to bring a heavy torpedo load against the enemy battle line. This meant the Japanese favored larger ships with a heavy torpedo armament. This translated into a ship maximized for surface engagements at the expense of other missions. Such an approach was epitomized by the introduction of the "Special Type" destroyers, which carried an impressive torpedo armament. The basic design precept was carried forward to the next five classes of Japanese destroyers. This also marked the Japanese destroyer as primarily an offensive weapon, maximized for its role as a night-combat torpedo platform.

The Asashio, Kagero, and Yugumo classes (the last two classes referred to by the Japanese as Type A units) were essentially a return to the Special Type ships from the late 1920s, since all were designed for maximum firepower and speed and were built without reference to treaty restrictions. These ships continued the Japanese emphasis on a heavy torpedo armament. A heavy gun armament was also an important design criterion, but these weapons were not dual purpose, which proved a major weakness later in the war. When combined with inferior antisubmarine sensors and weapons, the result was an unbalanced design. Type A units were superb torpedo boats, but lacked the attributes required for a truly successful fleet destroyer.

The large Type B, or Akizuki class, was a better-balanced design. These ships featured a reduced torpedo armament, but included a true dual-purpose gun battery. However, these large ships were too complex for mass production and, of the 12 units produced, most entered service too late to make a difference.

DESTROYER WEAPONS

Torpedo Armament

The key weapon aboard Japanese destroyers was the torpedo. The Minekaze and Kamikaze classes carried six torpedoes in three Type 6 twin launchers. These ships used the 6th Year Type 21in torpedo developed in 1917. The Mutsuki class introduced the 24in torpedo and the Type 12 triple launcher. The Special Type destroyer also used the Type 12 launcher. The Mutsuki and Special Type ships used the 8th Year Type torpedo developed in 1919, and then the Type 90, which was introduced in 1930. This was the weapon in use at the start of the war. By the end of 1942, the use of the Type 90 was discontinued.

The signature Japanese destroyer weapon of the Pacific War was the Type 93 torpedo. This was a revolutionary weapon, which used oxygen as the torpedo propellant. This was a much more powerful source of energy that enabled much greater ranges. The use of compressed oxygen also created space for a much larger warhead and offered nearly wakeless running. After

Japanese Destroyer-launched Torpedoes				
	6th Year Type	**8th Year Type**	**Type 90**	**Type 93**
Length	22.41ft	27.58ft	27.83ft	29.5ft
Diameter	21in	24in	24in	24in
Weight	3,157lb	5,207lb	5,734lb	5,940lb
Warhead	441lb	761lb	825lb	1,078lb
Propulsion	Steam	Steam	Steam	Oxygen
Speed/Range	36kt / 7,650yd	38kt / 10,900yd	46kt / 7650yd	48kt / 21,900yd
	32kt / 10,900yd	32kt / 16,400yd	43kt / 10,900yd	40kt / 35,000yd
	26kt / 16,400yd	28kt / 21,900yd	35kt / 16,400yd	36kt / 43,700yd

a long development period, the torpedo entered service in 1935. The range and power of this weapon was far in excess of the standard American destroyer torpedo, and thus its potential was not understood by the Americans until 1943. Eventually it was named "Long Lance" by the Americans, after it had sunk or crippled numerous American and Allied ships. The Hatsuharu class used the Type 90 triple launcher to employ the Type 93 and subsequent classes used the Type 92 quad launcher.

Main Battery

Older Japanese destroyers carried four hand-worked single 4.7in guns. These were exposed mounts provided with only a small shield. Beginning with the Special Type units, the size of the main battery was increased to a 5in gun. For the first time ever on any destroyer, the gun was provided with an enclosed shield. This was only 0.1in thick, but it provided protection from the weather. The first ten Special Type units were fitted with the Type A twin mount, with a maximum 40-degree elevation. The later Special Type ships introduced the Type B mount, which had a 75-degree elevation in an attempt to make the mounts capable of antiaircraft fire. However, training and elevation were so slow that these mounts were useless in this role. The Shiratsuyu class introduced the Type C mount with a 55-degree elevation. The failure of the Japanese to develop a true dual-purpose 5in gun for destroyer use became a critical weakness later in the war as Japanese destroyers were increasingly exposed to American air attack. The twin mount also had a dispersion problem when employed against surface targets.

Japanese Destroyer Main Guns		
	4.7in/45cal 3rd Year (1914)	5in/50cal 3rd Year
Shell weight	45lb	50.7lb
Muzzle velocity	2,707ft/sec	2,986–3,002ft/sec
Firing cycle	12sec	6–12sec
Maximum range	17,500yd	20,100yd

Antiaircraft Armament

Going into the war, Japanese destroyers possessed totally inadequate antiaircraft protection. Only light weapons were in use, and the only intermediate size weapon, the Vickers 40mm single mount introduced in

1927, proved a failure in service. Older ships carried single 7.7mm Lewis guns at the start of the war. Special Type units carried paltry one or two twin 13mm mounts. Later in the war, single 13mm mounts were introduced to increase the number of guns available for antiaircraft protection.

The standard Japanese antiaircraft gun of the war was the Type 96 25mm weapon introduced in 1936 and first fitted aboard the Asashio class in 1937. Later in the war, the twin mount was replaced by a triple mount and, in a desperate bid to further increase the numbers of antiaircraft weapons in 1944, single mounts were placed on destroyers wherever a clear arc of fire was possible. Despite the growing profusion of 25mm guns, Japanese destroyers grew increasingly vulnerable to air attack throughout the war.

This is a close-up view of the aft 4.7in gun on destroyer *Mikatsuki* after it was beached and destroyed in July 1943. The breechblock of the gun has been removed, but this view shows the later type of shield mounted on Mutsuki-class units. (Naval History and Heritage Command)

DESTROYER RADAR

Japanese destroyers did not begin the war equipped with radar. Not until mid-1943 did select destroyers finally receive the No. 22 radar. Destroyer foremasts were modified to allow the placement of the No. 22 radar above the bridge structure, and a radar room was built further down the foremast. Early Japanese radars were unreliable and their operators often poorly trained. Even after the introduction of radar, and certainly in the first part of the war, the first indication that a Japanese destroyer captain received of an approaching enemy, even at night, was from one of his lookouts using high-quality optics. Reliance on optics instead of electronics became increasingly problematic as the Americans introduced better radars and became increasingly adept at their use. During the night battles off the Solomon Islands between August and November 1943, the lack of modern radar was the single most important factor, leading to heavy losses by the Japanese destroyer force.

THE DESTROYER CLASSES

Minekaze Class

Design and construction

Following World War I, the Japanese began development of a new first-class destroyer design. Fifteen of these ships were ordered in the 1917–20 programs and units began to enter the fleet in 1920. These ships were originally only given numbers, as were all destroyers up through the Special Type, until 1928, when they were assigned names.

The new class was a hybrid of traditional British and German destroyer designs, as the IJN had been exposed to German design techniques after receiving five German destroyers after World War I as reparations. Design requirements for the new class called for a larger ship with a higher speed. Another important design consideration was seaworthiness, which was an important factor since the waters of the Western and North Pacific could be very rough. To meet the requirements for seaworthiness, Japanese designers employed a design component from German destroyers by moving the bridge back and placing a well in front of the bridge. This well area was meant to reduce the impact of heavy seas on the bridge. The forecastle was lengthened and a turtleback aspect given to the forward part of the ship.

To increase the utility of the main guns in heavy seas, the main battery was positioned as high up on the ship as possible, and all guns were sited on

Minekaze shown in August 1932. This view shows the raised forecastle and the well in front of the bridge structure. The four 4.7in guns are also visible, as is the forward torpedo mount under canvas. This configuration was maintained up until the start of the Pacific War. (*Ships of the World* magazine)

the centerline. The last three ships of the class (*Nokaze*, *Namikaze*, and *Numakaze*) were built to a slightly different design and are referred to as the Nokaze class. Instead of placing two 4.7in guns amidships, the arrangement was modified so that only one gun remained between the stacks and two were mounted together on the aft deckhouse. This allowed for better ammunition-handling arrangements.

To meet the requirement for high speeds, the ships were fitted with geared turbines, replacing the direct drive turbines on earlier destroyer classes. These were capable of 38,500shp, which translated to a maximum speed of 39 knots.

This basic design was used for the next three classes of Japanese destroyers, a total of 36 ships. Until the advent of the Special Type destroyers in 1929, these 36 ships constituted the core of the Japanese destroyer force.

Minekaze Class Construction				
Ship	Built at	Laid down	Launched	Completed
Akikaze	Nagasaki by Mitsubishi	6/7/20	12/14/20	4/1/21
Hakaze	Nagasaki by Mitsubishi	11/11/18	6/21/20	9/16/20
Hokaze	Maizuru Navy Yard	11/30/20	7/12/21	12/22/21
Minekaze	Maizuru Navy Yard	4/20/18	2/8/19	3/29/20
Namikaze	Maizuru Navy Yard	11/7/21	6/24/22	11/11/22
Nokaze	Maizuru Navy Yard	4/16/21	10/1/21	3/31/22
Numakaze	Maizuru Navy Yard	8/10/21	2/25/22	7/24/22
Okikaze	Maizuru Navy Yard	2/22/19	10/3/19	8/17/20
Sawakaze	Nagasaki by Mitsubishi	1/7/18	1/7/19	3/16/20
Shiokaze	Maizuru Navy Yard	5/15/20	10/22/20	7/29/21
Tachikaze	Maizuru Navy Yard	8/18/20	3/31/21	12/5/21
Yakaze	Nagasaki by Mitsubishi	8/15/18	4/10/20	7/19/20
Yukaze	Nagasaki by Mitsubishi	12/24/40	5/28/21	8/24/21

Armament

Minekaze-class units were launched with an armament of three twin 21in torpedo mounts. One mount was positioned in the well in front of the bridge structure and the other two abaft the second stack. The main gun battery comprised four 4.7in single guns. These were positioned one forward and one aft, with the other two amidships. These were open mounts exposed to the weather except for a small shield. Two 6.5mm machine guns were also fitted upon completion.

This overhead view of a Minekaze-class destroyer clearly shows the layout of the ship with its four 4.7in guns and torpedo battery of three twin mounts. (*Ships of the World* magazine)

Service modifications

As war approached, the Minekaze-class ships were considered second-line units. Before the war, *Nadakaze* and *Shimakaze* were converted into destroyer transports and renumbered Patrol Boats 1 and 2. In 1941, *Sawakaze* had most of its armament removed for conversion into an aircraft rescue ship. The remaining 12 units in the class received modifications in keeping with their new role as escorts. The two amidships 4.7in guns were removed, as were the two aft torpedo mounts. The antiaircraft armament was increased to as many as ten 25mm guns. The minesweeping gear on the fantail was removed and replaced by four depth-charge launchers and 36 depth charges. The increased displacement reduced speed to 35 knots.

By September 1942, *Yakaze* was largely disarmed and converted into a target ship. In 1944, the surviving ships were further modified to augment their antiaircraft fit. The number of 25mm guns was increased to between 13 and 20, with a combination of twin and single mounts. Most ships also received 13mm machine guns.

Two ships surviving into 1945 underwent conversion into *kaiten* (manned torpedo) carriers. *Namikaze* and *Shiokaze* had their sterns modified so that *kaiten*s could be launched astern. *Shiokaze* could carry as many as four *kaiten*s; *Namikaze* only two. Both had all their torpedo tubes removed and retained only their forward 4.7in gun. Antiaircraft armament was six twin 25mm mounts and a number of single 25mm mounts. *Namikaze* was fitted with a No. 22 radar on its foremast, while *Shiokaze* received a No. 13 radar on its mainmast. Other ships to receive radar included *Yukaze*, which received a No. 13 set, and *Sawakaze*, which was fitted with a No. 22 radar. *Sawakaze* was fitted with an experimental 5.9in antisubmarine rocket launcher in place of the forward 4.7in gun. Its speed was reduced to 16 knots.

Wartime service

Akikaze began the war assigned to Destroyer Division 34, subordinate to the Eleventh Air Fleet, and supported the invasion of the Philippines and later the Dutch East Indies and Malaya during the initial period of the war. By June 1942, it had moved to Rabaul, where it supported operations in the Solomons and New Guinea. In August, it suffered heavy damage in an air attack south of Rabaul. It was again damaged by air attack in December 1943, but repaired at Truk. In 1944, it was assigned to duties in the Central Pacific. It participated in the Battle of Leyte Gulf and was sunk off Luzon on November 3, 1944 by the American submarine *Pintado*.

Hakaze began the war assigned to Destroyer Division 34. During the first months of the war, it was active in the South China Sea area moving airbase materials from Indochina to Borneo and Malaya. In April 1942, it moved to Rabaul to support the upcoming invasion of Port Moresby. It conducted several transport runs to Munda on New Georgia Island in support of airfield construction there. On January 23, 1943, it was torpedoed off Kavieng by the American submarine *Guardfish*.

Hokaze was assigned to Destroyer Division 3 at the start of the war. In April 1942, it was reassigned to conduct operations in northern waters and participated in the invasion of Kiska in June. It was torpedoed and damaged by the American submarine *Thresher* in Makassar Strait on June 27, 1943, and was sunk by the American submarine *Paddle* in the Celebes Sea on July 6, 1944.

Minekaze was assigned to the Sasebo Naval District in April 1942 and was active escorting convoys to Saipan, Truk, and Rabaul. Later it shifted to escort duties in the East China Sea. On February 10, 1944, it was torpedoed and sunk by the American submarine *Pogy* 85 miles north-northeast of Formosa.

Namikaze began the war assigned to Destroyer Division 1 subordinate to the Ominato Guard District. It conducted escort operations in mostly northern waters until being torpedoed on September 8, 1944 in the Kuril Islands. It was moved to Maizuru Navy Yard for conversion into a *kaiten* carrier but saw no action after conversion. It survived the war to be used as a repatriation ship and was given to China in 1947.

Nokaze began the war assigned to Destroyer Division 1. It conducted patrol duties in northern waters, including participation in the Aleutians operation in June 1942. It was moved into the South China Sea in January 1945, where it was torpedoed and sunk by the American submarine *Pargo* on February 20, 1945. *Nokaze* was the last destroyer sunk by submarine attack during the war.

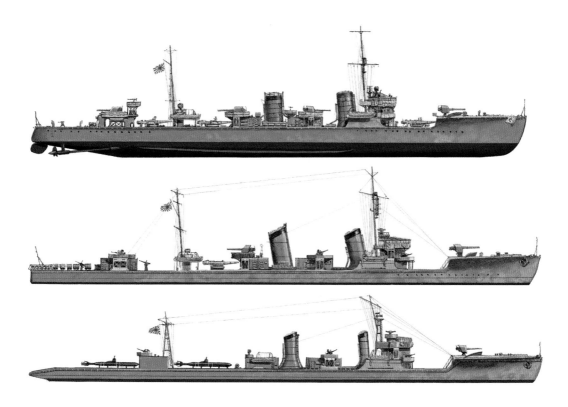

Numakaze was assigned to Destroyer Division 1 at the beginning of the war. It remained in northern waters until September 1943, conducting general escort duties until transferred for duties in the East China Sea. On December 18, 1943, it was torpedoed and sunk by the American submarine *Grayback*.

Okikaze began the war assigned to Ominato Guard District but was reassigned to Yokosuka Naval District in April 1942. It performed escort duties primarily in and near Tokyo Bay. In the course of these duties, it was sunk by the American submarine *Trigger* on January 10, 1943, off Tokyo Bay.

Sawakaze began the war assigned to Yokosuka Naval District and was used as an aircraft rescue ship during flight training from carriers. In May 1945 *Sawakaze* was used as a target ship for *kamikaze* training. It survived the war.

Shiokaze was assigned to Destroyer Division 3 at the start of the war and participated in the invasion of the southern Philippines. It supported operations in the Dutch East Indies and into the Indian Ocean, escorting the carrier *Ryujo*. It participated in the Aleutian operation in June 1942. It was subsequently transferred to convoy escort duties in August and assigned to southern routes. It surrendered at Kure at the end of the war.

Tachikaze was assigned to Destroyer Division 34 at the start of the war. It supported the invasion of the Philippines and later the Dutch East Indies. By July 1942, it had moved to the southwestern Pacific to support operations, primarily in the Solomons. It was heavily damaged by an air attack on Rabaul in December 1942, but was repaired in Japan and returned to Rabaul, where it was twice more damaged by air attack. It was caught at Truk during the massive American carrier air attack on February 17, 1944, and sunk by a torpedo hit aft.

Yakaze was assigned to the Kure Naval District at the beginning of the war as a target ship. It surrendered at Yokosuka in a damaged condition in August 1945.

Yukaze began the war assigned to Carrier Division 3 and escorted the carrier *Hosho* during the Battle of Midway. It continued to act as plane guard for *Hosho* for pilot training in the Inland Sea until the end of the war. It was used as a repatriation ship after the war, and then handed over to Great Britain and scrapped in 1947.

> **Minekaze Class Specifications (as completed)**
>
> **Displacement:** 1,345 tons standard; 1,650 full load
> **Dimensions:** Length 336.5ft / beam 30ft / draft 9.5ft
> **Maximum speed:** 39kt
> **Range:** 3,600nm at 14kt
> **Crew:** 148

Kamikaze Class

Design and construction

The second group of Minekaze-class ships was ordered in 1921–22. Because of the differences in design, these were designated as a new class, although these ships were virtually identical to the last three ships of the Minekaze class. Displacement was slightly increased and the greater beam and draft improved stability. This compensated for the increased weight of the

Kamikaze Class Construction				
Ship	Built at	Laid down	Launched	Completed
Kamikaze	Nagasaki by Mitsubishi	12/15/21	9/25/22	12/28/22
Asakaze	Nagasaki by Mitsubishi	2/16/22	12/8/22	6/16/23
Harukaze	Maizuru Navy Yard	5/16/22	12/18/22	5/31/23
Matsukaze	Maizuru Navy Yard	12/2/22	10/30/23	4/5/24
Hatakaze	Maizuru Navy Yard	7/3/23	3/15/24	8/30/24
Oite	Uraga (Tokyo)	3/16/23	11/27/24	10/30/25
Hayate	Ishikawajima (Tokyo)	11/11/22	3/23/25	12/21/25
Asanagi	Fujinagata (Osaka)	3/5/23	4/21/24	12/29/24
Yunagi	Sasebo Navy Yard	9/17/23	4/23/24	4/24/25

The Kamikaze class was a virtual repeat of the last three units of the preceding Minekaze class, as shown by this 1936 view of *Kamikaze*. Like the Minekaze class, the Kamikaze class was obsolescent by the start of the war and was assigned secondary duties. (Yamato Museum)

modified bridge structure, which now featured a fixed steel covering overhead in place of the previous canvas. The engineering plant was the same, but the increased weight decreased top speed by 2 knots.

Armament

In terms of the numbers and placement of armament, the Kamikaze-class ships were essentially repeats of the last three ships of the Minekaze class. Torpedo armament was unchanged, but the mounts were now power-operated. The main gun battery was also unchanged and used the same arrangement as the late Minekazes. The antiaircraft fit was changed to two single 7.7mm machine guns, mounted on each side of the bridge. The last three ships of the class were the first to be equipped with depth charges. These were deployed by two rails on the stern and two single-sided Type 81 depth-charge projectors.

Service modifications

Typical wartime modifications entailed a loss of surface warfare capabilities in exchange for increased antiaircraft weaponry. This most often included the removal of the aft 4.7in gun and the aft bank of torpedoes, and the increase of 25mm guns to 10–13 in twin and single mounts. As an example, by 1944 *Yunagi* had lost one torpedo mount and two 4.7in guns, but received four twin and five single 25mm guns. It also received a No. 13 radar on the mainmast. *Kamikaze* and *Harukaze* survived until 1945, and by then each had lost one torpedo mount and their aft 4.7in gun. In their place, four twin and two single 25mm guns were added. These modifications increased displacement to some 1,523 tons, which brought top speed down to 35 knots.

Wartime service

Asakaze was assigned to Destroyer Division 5 at the start of the war and supported the invasions of the Philippines, Malaya, and the Dutch East Indies. It participated in the Battle of Sunda Strait on March 1, 1942, during which the Australian light cruiser *Perth* and American heavy cruiser *Houston* were sunk. It remained active in the southwest area into 1944. While escorting a convoy to Manila, it was torpedoed and sunk by the American submarine *Haddo* west of Lingayen Gulf on August 23, 1944.

Asanagi was assigned to Destroyer Division 29 and participated in the capture of the Gilbert Islands in December 1941 and then the second Japanese attempt to take Wake Island on December 23 the same year. It assisted in the invasion of Rabaul in January 1942. After escorting the Lae/Salamaua invasion force, it was damaged by an American carrier attack in March. It escorted the Port Moresby invasion convoy during the Battle of the Coral Sea. It subsequently moved to Truk and was sunk by the submarine *Pollack* on May 22, 1944, near the Bonin Islands.

Harukaze was assigned to Destroyer Division 5 and supported the advance into the Dutch East Indies. On March 1, 1942, it participated in the Battle of Sunda Strait, where it suffered minor damage. In November 1942, it suffered heavy mine damage off Surabaya. After repairs, it resumed escort duties in the Central Pacific. In November 1944, it was torpedoed and damaged by the submarine *Sailfish* in the Luzon Strait. It was later damaged by a carrier air attack in January 1945, which forced a return to Japan where it was surrendered, unrepaired, at the end of the war.

Hatakaze began the war assigned to Destroyer Division 5, and was active in this division into March 1942. In May 1942, it was assigned to the Yokosuka Naval District and assumed escort duties from there. In December 1944, it was reassigned to duties in the East China Sea. On January 15, 1945, it was sunk by an American air attack in Takao, Formosa.

Hayate became the first Japanese destroyer lost in the war when, while it was part of Destroyer Division 29, on December 11, 1941, 5in shore batteries on Wake Island probably hit its torpedo tubes, creating a large explosion that quickly sank the ship, with no survivors.

Kamikaze was assigned to Destroyer Division 1, which was subordinate to the Ominato Guard District, with the three late units of the Minekaze class. It spent almost the entire war active in northern waters. In January 1945, it moved to the South China Sea. In May 1945, it escorted the heavy cruiser *Haguro* on a mission to the Andaman Islands. British destroyers sank the *Haguro* and damaged the *Kamikaze*. In June, it escorted the heavy cruiser *Ashigara*, which was sunk by a British submarine attack. It survived the war and was surrendered in Singapore in August 1945, and then used as a repatriation ship.

Matsukaze began the war assigned to Destroyer Division 5 and acted as other ships of that division during the first period of the war. In June 1943, it was assigned to duties operating from Rabaul and was active conducting

(**Overleaf**) *Yunagi* was the only Kamikaze-class ship to engage in surface combat with Allied forces during the war. Compared to the earlier Minekaze class, the bridge structure has been modified and the placement of the two aft 4.7in guns altered. During the battle, *Yunagi* engaged American destroyer *Jarvis* in a private duel, as shown in this scene.

Kamikaze Class Specifications (as completed)

Displacement: 1,400 tons standard; 1,720 full load
Dimensions: Length 336.5ft / beam 30ft / draft 10ft
Maximum speed: 37kt
Range: 3,600nm at 14kt
Crew: 148

multiple transport runs to islands in the Central and Northern Solomons area. It was caught in Truk in February 1944 during an American carrier air attack and suffered moderate damage. On June 9, 1944, it was sunk by the American submarine *Swordfish* near the Bonin Islands.

Oite was assigned to Destroyer Division 29 at the start of the war. It participated in the initial unsuccessful Japanese invasion of Wake Island on December 11, 1941, where it was damaged by gunfire from Marine coastal batteries. It took part in the successful attempt to seize the island on December 23. It also assisted in invasion of Rabaul in January and Lae/Salamaua in March 1942. During the Battle of Coral Sea, it escorted the Port Moresby invasion convoy. Operating out of Rabaul, it made several transport runs, including to Guadalcanal. Later it moved to Truk to assume escort duties. During the American carrier air attack on Truk on February 18, it was hit and sunk by an air-launched torpedo.

Yunagi was assigned to Destroyer Division 29 at the start of the war and participated in the December 1941 invasion of the Gilbert Islands and then the second attempt to capture Wake Island on December 23. It participated in the invasion of Rabaul in January 1942. In March, it was assigned to the Lae/Salamaua invasion force, but suffered moderate damage as a result of American carrier air attacks on March 10, which forced a return to Japan for repairs. It returned to Rabaul in time to participate in the Battle of Savo Island on August 9, 1942. From Rabaul, it engaged in multiple transport runs. On July 5, 1943, one of these resulted in an engagement off New Georgia Island. A Japanese torpedo barrage, including weapons from *Yunagi*, sank an American destroyer, with no Japanese losses. Days later, on July 13, *Yunagi* participated in the Battle of Kolombangara. After Japanese units withdrew from the Solomons, it assumed escort duties in the Central Pacific. It participated in the Battle of the Philippine Sea. On August 25, while escorting a convoy to Manila, it was torpedoed and sunk by the American submarine *Picuda*.

Mutsuki Class

Design and construction

The 12 ships of the Mutsuki class were ordered in 1923. As was standard with the previous two classes of first-class destroyers, the new ships were completed with numbers only; names were not given until 1928.

In most respects, the Mutsuki class was identical to the Kamikaze class. However, the Mutsuki class did introduce several new features and clearly demonstrated the Japanese predilection for a heavy torpedo armament. These were the first destroyers built under the Washington Naval Treaty. While this treaty did not restrict destroyer numbers or design directly, it did force the IJN to accept inferiority in capital ships. In an effort to compensate for this weakness, the Japanese attempted to arm other types of ships as heavily as possible. This trend was immediately observable with the new Mutsuki design, which was given a heavier torpedo armament in order to threaten capital ships.

In addition to the difference in the torpedo armament, the principal difference in appearance was the adoption of an S-shaped bow, which had a more prominent flare and provided improved seaworthiness. This also resulted in a slightly greater length, which slightly increased displacement. Machinery was the same as on the Kamikaze class, with the exception of two ships that received foreign-made turbines. Full-load speed for the class was disappointing and barely exceeded 33 knots.

Armament

The biggest difference in the Mutsuki class was the alteration of the torpedo armament. For the first time on a Japanese destroyer, 24in tubes were fitted. The Mutsuki-class ships carried six 24in tubes in two triple launchers. Though unworkable in heavy seas, a mount was still placed in the well position forward of the bridge. Use of triple mounts instead of the previous twin torpedo mounts provided more deck space and a more attractive overall design. For the first time, spare torpedoes were provided, with each tube having a reload. Gun armament remained unaltered at four 4.7in single mounts arranged in a similar fashion to the Kamikaze class. Two 7.7mm machine guns were placed abreast the bridge for antiaircraft protection. Antisubmarine armament included two stern depth-charge racks and two Type 81 projectors. A total of 18 depth charges were carried.

Service modifications

Before the war, units in the class received shields for the torpedo mounts, and the two stacks were raked. Wartime modifications commenced soon after the war began, and centered on augmenting the ships' antiaircraft fit. Some ships immediately received additional twin 13mm machine guns forward of the bridge and abaft the aft stack. In 1942, *Mikazuki* had a boiler removed and its aft stack was reduced in size – it was the only ship of the class so modified. *Yayoi* had a similar reduction to its forward funnel; again,

Mutsuki Class Construction				
Ship	Built at	Laid down	Launched	Completed
Mutsuki	Sasebo Navy Yard	5/21/24	7/23/25	3/25/26
Kisaragi	Maizuru Navy Yard	6/3/24	6/5/25	12/25/25
Yayoi	Uraga (Tokyo)	1/11/24	7/11/25	8/28/26
Uzuki	Ishikawajima (Tokyo)	1/11/24	10/15/25	9/14/26
Satsuki	Fujinagata (Osaka)	12/1/23	3/25/25	11/15/25
Minazuki	Uraga (Tokyo)	3/24/25	5/25/26	3/22/27
Fumizuki	Fujinagata (Osaka)	10/20/24	2/16/26	7/3/26
Nagatsuki	Ishikawajima (Tokyo)	4/16/25	10/6/26	4/30/27
Kikuzuki	Maizuru Navy Yard	6/15/25	5/15/26	11/20/26
Mikazuki	Sasebo Navy Yard	8/21/25	7/12/26	5/7/27
Mochizuki	Uraga (Tokyo)	3/23/26	4/28/27	10/31/27
Yuzuki	Fujinagata (Osaka)	11/27/26	3/4/27	7/25/27

it was the only ship of the class so adapted. Between September 1942 and December 1943, *Uzuki* had its stern modified to facilitate the launching and recovery of landing barges. It was the only ship of the class to be modified as a destroyer transport.

There was no standard modification for the class, as exhibited in the table below. Those ships surviving into 1943 began to lose one or two of their 4.7in guns, and four units had their aft bank of torpedo tubes removed. This provided more deck space for cargo and reduced top weight. The three ships that survived into the second half of 1944, *Uzuki*, *Satsuki*, and *Yuzuki*, were further modified and received between 16 and 22 25mm guns.

Satsuki was the first unit to get radar, which did not occur until February–March 1944. Only two other units received radar and these were the No. 13 set fitted on the mainmast.

Wartime service

Fumizuki began the war assigned to Destroyer Division 22 and supported the invasion of the Philippines and the Dutch East Indies during the first phase of the war. In January 1943 it moved to Rabaul and supported three evacuation runs from Guadalcanal in February. It remained based at Rabaul and conducted several transport runs to points on New Britain and in the Solomons. It suffered minor damage from air attack on Rabaul on November 2, 1943, and again on January 4, 1944. It was caught in Truk on February 17, 1944. A single torpedo hit caused gradual flooding, which sank the ship the next day.

Kikuzuki began the war assigned to Destroyer Division 23 and participated in the invasion of Guam in December 1941, followed by the invasion of Rabaul in January 1942. It supported the Lae/Salamaua operation in March. In May, it was assigned to the Tulagi invasion force. An American carrier air attack caught *Kikuzuki* in Tulagi Harbor on May 4, 1942, and hit it with one torpedo. The ship was beached, but sank the next day.

Kisaragi was assigned to Destroyer Division 30 at the commencement of war. In the first attempt to seize Wake Island on December 11, 1941, it was hit by bombs from aircraft. The crew was unable to put out the fires, and the ship suddenly blew up and sank with the loss of all aboard.

Mikazuki began the war assigned to Carrier Division 3 to perform plane guard duties for carriers *Hosho* and *Zuiho* in home waters. In June 1942 it escorted *Zuiho* during the Battle of Midway. After modification between March and June 1943, it was assigned to operate from Rabaul. It was present at the battles of Kula Gulf and Kolombangara in July 1943. It grounded on a reef near Cape Gloucester on July 27, and was sunk the next day by B-25 bombers.

Minazuki began the war assigned to Destroyer Division 22 and supported the invasions of the Philippines and the Dutch East Indies, remaining in the southern areas until early 1943. After moving to Rabaul, it conducted a series of transport runs, mostly in the Central and Northern Solomons. It was damaged in July by air attack. It escorted the final convoy into Rabaul in February 1944. On June 6, 1944, it was sunk by the American submarine *Harder* off Tawi-Tawi.

Mochizuki was assigned to Destroyer Division 30 at the start of the war, and took part in the two operations against Wake Island in December 1941. It participated in the January 1942 capture of Rabaul, the March 1942 landings at Lae/Salamaua, and the Battle of the Coral Sea in May. Operating from Rabaul, it participated in the October 15 bombardment of Henderson Field on Guadalcanal, followed by three troop transport runs to the island. It escorted the important mid-November 1942 troop convoy to Guadalcanal, and participated in the Battle of Kula Gulf on July 5–6, 1943. On a transport run on October 24, 1943, it was attacked by American aircraft and sunk by a bomb hit in the engineering space, 90 miles south-southwest of Rabaul.

Several Mutsuki-class destroyers in a prewar review. At the start of the war, the Mutsuki class comprised three destroyer divisions. Massed destroyer attack was an integral part of Japanese naval doctrine. (*Ships of the World* magazine)

Final Fit for Mutsuki-class Units						
Ship	Torpedo launchers	4.7in mounts	25mm mounts	13mm mounts	7.7mm mounts	No.13 Radar
Mutsuki	2	4	0	2 twin	2 single	No
Kisaragi	2	4	0	0	2 single	No
Yayoi	2	4	3 triple	1 single	1 single	No
Uzuki	1	2	3 triple 2 twin 6 single	2 single	0	Yes
Satsuki	2	3	2 triple 2 twin 9 single	5 single	0	Yes
Minazuki	2	3	2 triple 2 twin	2 twin	0	No
Fumizuki	1	2	2 triple 2 twin	2 twin	0	No
Nagatsuki	2	4	0	1 twin	2 single	No
Kikuzuki	2	4	0	1 twin	2 single	No
Mikazuki	1	2	2 triple 4 twin	0	0	No
Mochizuki	2	3	2 triple 2 twin	0	0	No
Yuzuki	1	2	2 triple 2 twin 6 single	2 single	0	Yes

Mutsuki began the war assigned to Destroyer Division 30 and participated in the two December 1941 Wake Island operations, followed by the invasion of Rabaul in January 1942 and the invasion of Lae/Salamaua in March. It took part in the Battle of the Coral Sea as an escort to the main invasion convoy. Between June 25 and July 1, it escorted the lead echelon of airfield construction crews to Guadalcanal. After the American seizure of the airfield, it conducted a bombardment of Henderson Field on August 24. On the next day, it was hit by a B-17 bomber 40 miles northeast of Santa Isabel Island during the Battle of the Eastern Solomons and sunk.

Nagatsuki began the war assigned to Destroyer Division 22 and participated in the landings on the Philippines and later in Malaya and the Dutch East Indies. It moved to the Rabaul area in January 1943 and participated in the evacuation of Guadalcanal in February. Operating from

Rabaul, it made transport runs throughout the Solomons. In a battle off New Georgia Island on July 4–5, it participated in the sinking of American destroyer *Strong*. It was subsequently sunk on July 6, 1943, after running aground on Kolombangara Island during the Battle of Kula Gulf, and was finished off the same day by American aircraft.

Satsuki began the war assigned to Destroyer Division 22 and participated in the landings on the Philippines, Malaya, and the Dutch East Indies. It moved to the Rabaul area in January 1943 and participated in the evacuation of Guadalcanal on February 1, 4, and 7. It remained active out of Rabaul and participated in the battles of Kula Gulf and Kolombangara in July. In 1944, it conducted escort missions in the Central Pacific and the South China Sea. On September 21, it was caught by an American carrier aircraft in Manila Harbor and sunk by three bomb hits.

Uzuki began the war assigned to Carrier Division 2. Its first action was the seizure of Guam in December 1941; this was followed by the occupation of Kavieng in January 1942, the Lae/Salamaua operation in March, and the Coral Sea operation in May. In late June and early July, it escorted a convoy with construction troops to Guadalcanal. It participated in the Battle of the Eastern Solomons and was lightly damaged by a B-17 bomber attack. Following alteration in Japan into a destroyer-transport, it returned to Rabaul by December 1942 and was heavily damaged that month in a collision with a transport. It returned to action to conduct several transport runs in the Northern Solomons. On November 24–25, 1943, it was involved in the Battle of Cape St George, where three of the five Japanese destroyers were sunk. It participated in the Battle of the Philippine Sea in June 1944. As part of the large-scale Japanese efforts to reinforce the island of Leyte in the Philippines, it was torpedoed and sunk by two American PT boats on December 12, 1944, 50 miles northeast of Cebu.

Yayoi was assigned to Destroyer Division 30 at the start of the war and participated in the failed invasion of Wake Island on December 11, 1941, where it suffered minor damage from an American shore battery. It was present at the successful invasion of Wake Island on December 23, the invasion of Rabaul in January 1942, the Lae/Salamaua invasion in March, and the Battle of the Coral Sea in May. It was active in support of operations off Guadalcanal, including the Battle of the Eastern Solomons. It was sunk by air attack on September 11 northwest of Vakuta Island.

Yuzuki began the war assigned to Destroyer Division 23. It participated in invasions of Guam, Kavieng, and Lae/Salamaua. It was damaged by air

> **Mutsuki Class Specifications (as completed)**
>
> **Displacement:** 1,315 tons standard; 1,772 tons full load
> **Dimensions:** Length 336ft / beam 30ft / draft 10ft
> **Maximum speed:** 37kt (design), 33.5kt in service
> **Range:** 4,000nm at 14kt
> **Crew:** 150

The top and middle views in this plate show Mutsuki-class *Satsuki* as it appeared in 1944, with its augmented antiaircraft and radar fit. Several differences from the earlier Minekaze and Kamikaze classes are evident, including the S-shaped bow, the larger bridge structure, and the shielded 24in torpedo mounts. The bottom view depicts Special Type destroyer *Fubuki* as it was built in 1928.

attack following the May 3, 1942 invasion of Tulagi, but remained active from Rabaul until February 1944. Following the Battle of Leyte Gulf, it was assigned to escort convoys from Manila to Leyte. It was sunk by American aircraft 65 miles north-northeast of Cebu on December 12, 1944.

Fubuki Class

Design and construction

The Fubuki class was the most important and influential Japanese destroyer class. Commissioning began in 1928, and they were at the time the most powerful destroyers in the world, being some ten years ahead of their time in their design. Several new features were introduced, which became standard on future destroyers. They surpassed the firepower of the IJN's light cruisers and remained valuable units throughout the Pacific War.

The effect of the 1922 Washington Naval Treaty on Japanese destroyer design was fully realized in the Fubuki class. Locked into a position of inferiority regarding capital ships, the Japanese sought other ways to redress the balance. The obvious answer was to build other types of ships not restricted by naval treaties and arm them as powerfully as possible. Design work for the new class of destroyer began as early as October 1922 with a proposal for a large 2,000-ton design, which would provide the endurance necessary for long-range Pacific operations, the space for a heavy armament, and machinery for high speeds. Eventually, it was decided to approve a smaller 1,750-ton design, but this was only on the condition that no loss of firepower occurred.

Several modifications took place over the course of production, and the 24 units of the Special Type (as they were also known) broke down into three groups. The 20 ships of the first two groups remained known as the Fubuki class; the final four ships were so different they were given a new class name, becoming the Akatsuki class.

The power of the machinery was increased to 50,000shp, developed by four boilers driving two geared turbines. This translated into a top speed of 35 knots. Increased bunkerage also increased the type's range to 5,000nm. The ventilation ducts to the boiler rooms were of different designs and provided another way to distinguish Group I units from Group II. The first nine ships had massive air ducts abreast the two stacks. The last ship of Group I, *Uranami*, dispensed with the large air ducts and adopted the new design of integrating the ventilation ducts into the platforms built around the stacks. The stacks of Group I ships were circular, while ships from Group II had rectangular-shaped stacks. All ships of Group II adopted the modified ventilation system introduced on *Uranami* and the new type of stacks.

The design of the hull also increased seaworthiness. The removal of the well deck in front of the bridge made it possible to extend the forecastle further aft. The forecastle was raised one deck in an effort to reduce the effect of heavy seas on the forward gun mount and the bridge. The S-shaped curved bow introduced on the Mutsuki class was retained. The flare of the

Uranami was a transition unit between Group I and Group II Special Type destroyers. As the last of the Group I units, it still has Type A 5in mounts, but has the stacks and modified air intakes found on Group II units. (Yamato Museum)

Fubuki Class (Special Type Groups I and II) Construction				
Ship	Built at	Laid down	Launched	Completed
*Fubuki**	Maizuru Navy Yard	6/16/26	11/15/27	8/10/28
*Shirayuki**	Yokohama	3/19/27	3/20/28	12/18/28
*Hatsuyuki**	Maizuru Navy Yard	4/12/27	9/29/28	3/30/29
*Miyuki**	Uraga	4/30/27	6/26/28	6/29/29
*Murakamo**	Fujinagata (Osaka)	4/25/27	9/27/28	5/10/29
*Shinonome**	Sasebo Navy Yard	8/12/26	11/26/27	5/27/28
*Usugumo**	Ishikawajima (Tokyo)	10/21/26	12/26/27	7/26/28
*Shirakumo**	Fujinagata (Osaka)	10/27/26	12/27/27	7/28/28
*Isonami**	Uraga	10/18/26	11/24/27	6/30/28
*Uranami**	Sasebo Navy Yard	4/28/27	11/29/28	6/30/29
Ayanami	Fujinagata (Osaka)	1/20/28	10/5/29	4/30/30
Shikinami	Maizuru Navy Yard	7/6/28	6/22/29	12/24/29
Asagiri	Sasebo Navy Yard	12/12/28	11/18/29	6/30/30
Yugiri	Maizuru Navy Yard	4/1/29	5/12/30	12/03/30
Amagiri	Ishikawajima (Tokyo)	11/28/28	2/27/30	11/10/30
Sagiri	Uraga	3/28/29	12/23/29	1/31/31
Oboro	Sasebo Navy Yard	11/29/29	11/8/30	10/31/31
Akebono	Fujinagata (Osaka)	10/25/29	11/7/30	7/31/31
Sazanami	Maizuru Navy Yard	2/21/30	6/6/31	5/19/32
Ushio	Uraga	12/24/29	11/17/30	11/14/31

* Indicates Group I, all others are Group II

bow was increased, and the hull back to the first stack was flared to some degree to enhance seaworthiness.

The bridge was much larger than on previous classes, since greater height was required to clear the large 5in mount placed forward. The bridge was completely covered and given glass windows. On Group II ships, the bridge was given another level.

What emerged in 1928 with the commissioning of *Fubuki* was a very impressive ship. However, despite the extensive design features employed to reduce weight, including use of welding on the hull and lighter alloys above the main deck, the ships were some 200 tons over their design weight. The overweight issue was even more of a problem with the Group II ships, which had the larger bridge and the heavier Type B gun mounts. Soon after entering service, the ships received shields for the three torpedo mounts, further increasing top weight.

Ayanami pictured on April 30, 1930, the day the ship was commissioned. The size of the bridge structure was later reduced as part of the reconstruction to reduce top weight. *Ayanami* was one of the first Group II Special Type destroyers, and was also one of the first Special Type units lost during the war. (Yamato Museum)

The result of this was a serious stability problem. The first sign of trouble occurred in March 1934, when a torpedo boat employing some of the same design principles as the Special Type destroyers capsized in heavy weather. An investigation revealed the problem to be excessive top weight, but before any modifications could be considered for the Special Type destroyers, disaster struck. On September 26, 1935, while on exercises east of Japan, the fleet ran into a typhoon. Two Special Type destroyers lost their bows in the storm, another three received severe structural damage, and another six experienced some hull damage. As a result, the entire class returned to the yards in November 1935–38 for hull strengthening and top weight reduction. A ballast keel and 40 extra tons of ballast were added. The large bridge structure was reduced in size and the height of the stacks decreased. Magazine stowage was lessened and the number of torpedo reloads was reduced from nine to three (for the center torpedo mount only). Eight of the Group II units received the lighter Type C 5in mount. Bunkerage was increased to create more weight down in the hull. The net result was to increase overall displacement to 2,090 tons, which in turn reduced maximum speed to 34 knots.

Armament

The armament of the Special Type destroyers was their most important feature. The ships gained a 50 percent increase over the previous Mutsuki class in both gunnery and torpedo power. The new 24in torpedoes had proved entirely satisfactory on the Mutsuki class, and these were again used on the Special Type ships. Each had three triple-torpedo mounts and each tube was given a reload for an impressive total of 18 torpedoes.

The main gun armament was increased to a 5in weapon. Six of these were carried in three twin mounts. For the first time on a destroyer these were provided with a weatherproof gun house with a 0.1in thick shield. These gun houses provided no protection against shells or even bullets, and only a bare degree of protection from shrapnel (making them mounts, not turrets). Group I units had the Type A 5in mount with a 40-degree elevation, making them suitable for low-angle targets only. Group II ships were given the Type B mount. The original antiaircraft fit was a pair of 7.7mm machine guns fitted in front of the second stack.

Service modifications

After their reconstruction, the ships were little modified until the start of the war. By then, the antiaircraft armament was a meager one or two 13mm twin mounts located in front of the second funnel.

Wartime modifications focused on the augmentation of the antiaircraft fit. The first step was to fit selected units with a twin 13mm mount in front of the bridge. These 13mm mounts were eventually exchanged for twin 25mm mounts on most units. With the increasing American air threat, the Japanese began to take protection from air attack more seriously. By late 1943 and into 1944, this meant removal of one of the aft 5in mounts and replacement with two triple 25mm mounts on surviving Special Type units. Another raised gun position was built between the two aft torpedo mounts, which provided room for another two triple 25mm mounts. In the later part of 1944, the few units still afloat received additional 25mm guns in the form of single mounts usually positioned on the forecastle and near the stern. As many as 15 were carried in this manner. Some units also received single 13mm mounts.

The first unit to receive radar was *Yugiri*, which received a No. 22 set by November 1943. A total of seven ships received the No. 22 set, which was

Shirayuki in May 1929. It was a Group I Special Type destroyer. Prominent recognition features for Group I units include the Type A 5in guns, round stacks, and the large air intakes for the boiler rooms, all clearly seen in this view. (Yamato Museum)

Ship	Torpedo launchers	5in mounts	25mm mounts	13mm mounts	No. 22 Radar	No.13 Radar
Fubuki	3	3	0	1 twin	No	No
Shirayuki	3	3	0	2 twin 2 single	No	No
Hatsuyuki	3	3	0	3 twin	No	No
Murakamo	3	3	0	2 single	No	No
Shinonome	3	3	0	2 single	No	No
Usugumo	3	2	4 triple 1 twin 10 single	0	Yes	Yes
Shirakumo	3	2	4 triple 1 twin	0	Yes	No
Isonami	3	3	0	3 twin	No	No
Uranami	3	2	4 triple 1 twin 10 single	2 twin	Yes	Yes
Ayanami	3	3	0	2 twin	No	No
Shikinami	3	3	3 triple 10 single	0	No	No
Asagiri	3	3	0	2 twin	No	No
Yugiri	3	3	2 triple	0	Yes	No
Amagiri	3	2	4 triple 1 twin	0	Yes	No
Sagiri	3	3	0	2 twin	No	No
Oboro	3	3	0	2 twin	No	No
Akebono	3	2	4 triple 1 twin 15 single	2 twin 4 single	Yes	Yes
Sazanami	3	3	1 twin	2 twin	No	No
Ushio	3	1	4 triple 1 twin 15 single	4 single	Yes	Yes

positioned on a rebuilt tripod mast above the bridge. Those few units surviving late into 1944 also received the No. 13 radar, which was added to the mainmast aft. The table below describes the modifications made to Special Type units at the time of their loss.

Wartime service

Akebono began the war assigned to Destroyer Division 7 and participated in the invasions of the southern Philippines and the Dutch East Indies. It engaged in the March 1, 1942 action, in which the British heavy cruiser *Exeter* and an American and British destroyer were sunk by torpedoes and gunfire. In May 1942, it participated in the Battle of the Coral Sea as an escort to the Japanese carrier force. In June, it was involved in the Aleutians operation. It conducted escort operations in the Central Pacific throughout 1943 and into 1944. During the Battle of Leyte Gulf in October 1944, it was assigned as part of the Second Diversion Attack Force and participated in the later stages of the Battle of Surigao Strait. On November 5, it was heavily damaged by an American air raid on Manila Harbor, and was sunk in a subsequent raid on November 13.

Amagiri was one of the most active Special Type units and arguably the most famous, as it destroyed the PT boat commanded by future American president John F. Kennedy. It began the war assigned to Destroyer Division 20 and participated in the invasions of Malaya, Sumatra, and the Andaman Islands in the Indian Ocean. It also participated in the April 1942 raid into the Indian Ocean, assisting in the sinking of three Allied merchant ships. It participated in the Midway operation as part of the Aleutians Guard Force. It moved into the South Pacific in August in response to the American seizure of Guadalcanal in the Solomon Islands. Operating out of Rabaul, it conducted five transport missions and three sweep missions in the waters off Guadalcanal, as well as some 20 other missions to points in the Solomons before returning to Japan for refit. In 1943, it participated in the Battle of Kula Gulf on July 5–6 and survived the Battle of Cape St George in November, where American destroyers sank three of five Japanese destroyers present. While conducting missions in the Central Solomons, it rammed and sank PT-109 on August 2, 1943. In March 1944, it was assigned to the Southwest Area Fleet and was sunk by a mine in the Makassar Strait on April 23, 1944.

Asagiri began the war assigned to Destroyer Division 20. It participated in the invasion of Malaya and, on January 27, 1942, assisted in the sinking of the British destroyer *Thanet* off Endau. Later it covered the invasion of Sumatra and the Andaman Islands. In April, it moved into the Indian Ocean and assisted in the sinking of six merchant ships. It participated in the Midway operation as part of the Aleutians Guard Force. On its first transport run to Guadalcanal, it was sunk by air attack on August 28, 1942, 60 miles north-northeast of Savo Island.

Ayanami began the war assigned to Destroyer Division 19 and participated in the invasions of Malaya, Sumatra, and the Andaman Islands. It was involved in the Midway operation as part of the main body. It began the first of seven transport runs to Guadalcanal in October 1942. It was sunk during the Second Naval Battle of Guadalcanal on November 14–15 by 5in guns from the American battleship *Washington* southeast of Savo Island.

Fubuki began the war assigned to Destroyer Division 11 and supported the invasions of Malaya, British Borneo, and the Anambas Islands during the first two months of the war. It was subsequently assigned to support the invasion of the Dutch East Indies in February 1942, and participated in the Battle of Sunda Strait. It moved into the Indian Ocean in March to cover the invasion of the Andaman Islands. It participated in the Battle of Midway in June. It moved to the South Pacific, arriving at Rabaul in late August 1942, and conducted 11 transport or sweep missions to waters off Guadalcanal. It was sunk on October 11, 1942 in the Battle of Cape Esperance by American cruiser gunfire. Unusually, 109 of its crew were saved by American ships.

Hatsuyuki began the war assigned to Destroyer Division 11 and mirrored the activity of *Fubuki* (with the exception of suffering minor damage at Sunda Strait) through August 1942. Activity off Guadalcanal included five transport missions (during one, two American destroyer transports were sunk on September 5) and four sweep missions, including the Battle of Cape Esperance and the Second Naval Battle of Guadalcanal. It returned to Rabaul in June 1943 and conducted four missions in the Solomons before participating in the Battle of Kula Gulf on July 6, where it was damaged by three dud shells. It was sunk by air attack in Shortlands Harbor on July 17, 1943.

Isonami was assigned to Destroyer Division 19 and escorted Malaya invasion convoys, later participating in the invasion of the Dutch East Indies in February 1942. In March, it formed part of the Andaman Islands invasion force. It was part of the main body during the Midway operations in June. It did not reach Rabaul until November 1942. It conducted four transport runs to points on New Guinea into December, then two transport operations in the Solomons, including one to Guadalcanal. It was sunk by the American submarine *Tautog* on April 9, 1943 after departing from Surabaya.

Murakumo was assigned to Destroyer Division 12 with *Shirakumo* and *Shinonome*. During the first period of the war, it escorted invasion convoys to Malaya, British Borneo, and then the Dutch East Indies. It participated in the Battle of Sunda Strait on March 1, 1942. In March, it covered the invasion of Sumatra and the Andaman Islands in the Indian Ocean. It was assigned to the main body for the June 1942 Midway operation. It arrived in Rabaul in late August and conducted ten transport missions (eight to

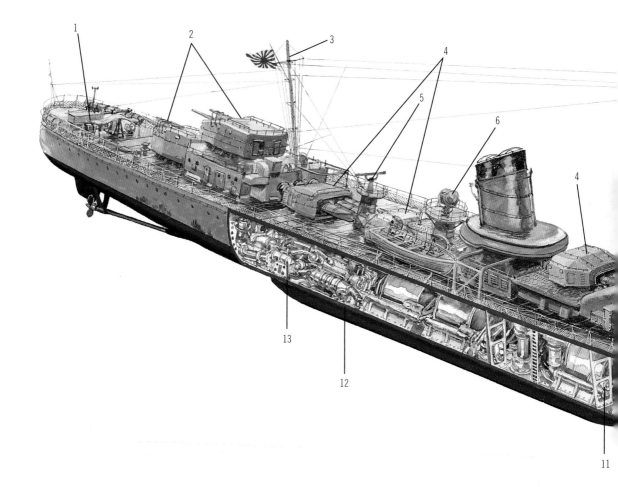

Hatsuyuki

Hatsuyuki as it appeared during the Battle of Cape Esperance in
October 1942. This plate shows the Group II Special Type destroyer
in its early-war configuration. The Group II ship can be
distinguished from the Group I units by its Type B 5in gun mounts
and the lack of large air intakes. Aside from the addition of a twin
13mm mount in front of the bridge, *Hatsuyuki* remained in this
configuration until sunk in July 1943.

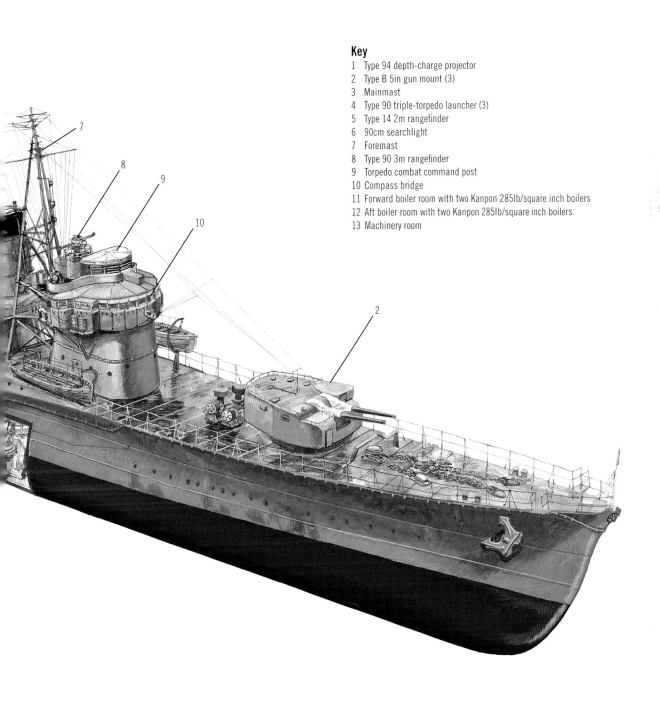

Key

1 Type 94 depth-charge projector
2 Type B 5in gun mount (3)
3 Mainmast
4 Type 90 triple-torpedo launcher (3)
5 Type 14 2m rangefinder
6 90cm searchlight
7 Foremast
8 Type 90 3m rangefinder
9 Torpedo combat command post
10 Compass bridge
11 Forward boiler room with two Kanpon 285lb/square inch boilers
12 Aft boiler room with two Kanpon 285lb/square inch boilers
13 Machinery room

Guadalcanal) and two sweep missions. On its last transport run on October 12, 1942, it was sunk by air attack 90 miles northwest of Savo Island.

Oboro began the war assigned to Carrier Division 5 and participated in the Japanese seizure of Guam in December 1941. While conducting a transport run to Kiska Island in the Aleutians, it was sunk by B-26 air attack on October 16, 1942.

Sagiri was assigned to Destroyer Division 20 at the start of the war. While providing escort for the invasion of British Borneo, it was sunk by the Dutch submarine *K-XVI* off Sarawak on December 24, 1941.

Sazanami began the war assigned to Destroyer Division 7. It was assigned with *Ushio* to bombard Midway Atoll on December 7, 1941. Later it assisted in the invasion of the Dutch East Indies and saw action in the Battle of the Java Sea on February 27, 1942. It participated in the Coral Sea operation in May and the Midway operation in June 1942. In September, it began operations off Guadalcanal, conducting three transport runs and one sweep mission. In August 1943, it was made flagship of Destroyer Squadron 3 and saw action in the battle off Horaniu that month. After departing Rabaul, it was sunk by the American submarine *Albacore* on January 14, 1944.

Shikinami began the war assigned to Destroyer Division 19 and participated in the invasion of Malaya. During the Battle of Sunda Strait of February 28–March 1, it finished off the American heavy cruiser *Houston* with a Type 90 torpedo. It was involved in the Midway operation as part of the main body. It moved to the South Pacific and participated in the Battle of the Eastern Solomons in August 1942, later moving to Rabaul. From there, it conducted 11 transport missions and three sweep mission to waters off Guadalcanal, participating in the Second Naval Battle of Guadalcanal on November 14–15. In March 1943, it was assigned as part of an escort for a troop convoy from Rabaul to New Guinea, and survived Allied air attacks during the Battle of the Bismarck Sea. Subsequently it was assigned to the Southwest Area Fleet. It participated in the abortive troop reinforcement operation at Biak on June 1944 and incurred slight damage due to air attack. It was sunk on September 12 by the American submarine *Growler* south of Hong Kong.

Shinonome was assigned to Destroyer Division 12, and was sunk by two bombs from a Dutch flying boat on December 18, 1941, off Borneo.

Shirakumo was assigned to Destroyer Division 12 and escorted invasion convoys to Malaya, British Borneo, and then the Dutch East Indies. It participated in the Battle of Sunda Strait on March 1, 1942, in which it and *Murakumo* destroyed a Dutch destroyer. In March, it escorted the invasions of Sumatra and the Andaman Islands. It participated in the April Indian Ocean raid and assisted in the destruction of five Allied merchant ships. It

was assigned to the Aleutians Guard Force for the Midway operation. In late August, it was hit by American dive-bombers on its first transport run to Guadalcanal and forced to return to Japan for repairs. In April 1943, it began operations in northern waters until it was sunk on March 16, 1944, by the American submarine *Tautog*.

Shirayuki was assigned to Destroyer Division 11 with *Fubuki* and *Hatsuyuki*, and mirrored their activity through August 1942. It was very active off Guadalcanal, conducting a total of five sweep missions (including the Second Naval Battle of Guadalcanal on November 15) and 13 transport missions. It participated in the three evacuation missions from Guadalcanal in February 1943. It was sunk by skip-bombing on March 3, 1943, during the Battle of the Bismarck Sea.

Uranami began the war assigned to Destroyer Division 19. While escorting a Malaya invasion convoy, it sank Dutch submarine *O-20* on December 19, 1941. Beginning in late February 1942, it participated in the invasion of the Dutch East Indies and in March covered the invasion of the Andaman Islands in the Indian Ocean. It was involved in the Midway operation as part of the main body. It moved to the South Pacific and participated in the Battle of the Eastern Solomons in August, later moving to Rabaul. Operating out of Rabaul, it conducted 12 transport missions and five sweep missions to waters off Guadalcanal; it participated in the Second Naval Battle of Guadalcanal on November 14–15. In March 1943, it was assigned as part of the escort for a troop convoy from Rabaul to New Guinea, and survived Allied air attacks during the Battle of the Bismarck Sea. Subsequently it was assigned to the Southwest Area Fleet. It participated in the abortive troop reinforcement operation at Biak in June 1944. During the Battle of Leyte Gulf, it was sunk by American escort carrier attack on October 26 north-northeast of Panay Island.

Ushio was the only Special Type unit to survive the war. It began the war assigned to Destroyer Division 7 and bombarded Midway on December 7, 1941. It participated in the invasion of the Dutch East Indies and the Battle of the Java Sea on February 27, 1942. With *Sazanami*, it depth-charged and sank the American submarine *Perch* on March 3, 1942. It was involved in the Battle of the Coral Sea as part of the Carrier Striking Force and in the Midway operation as part of the carrier force tasked to cover the Aleutians invasion. It

Shinonome was a Group I Special Type unit. It was the first Special Type destroyer lost in the war, being bombed by Dutch aircraft in December 1941. A magazine explosion resulted in the loss of its entire crew. (Naval History and Heritage Command)

Group II units *Akebono* and *Ushio* pictured before their reconstruction. Both ships still have their large bridge structures. The ships had long war careers, with *Ushio* being the only Fubuki-class ship to survive the war. (Naval History and Heritage Command)

participated in the Battle of the Eastern Solomons in August 1942. Later it conducted three transport runs and one sweep mission to Guadalcanal. It was tasked with Central Pacific escort operations in 1943 and into 1944. For the Battle of Leyte Gulf, it was assigned to the Second Diversion Attack Force and saw action at the Battle of Surigao Strait in October. Later it escorted several troop convoys from Manila to Ormoc on Leyte. It was damaged in an air attack on Manila in November 1944 and eventually returned to Japan. It surrendered, unrepaired, at the end of the war.

Usugumo was the only destroyer not ready for combat operations at the start of the war, since it had struck a mine off China in August 1940. Repairs were completed in July 1942 and it was assigned duties in northern waters. It was present at the Battle of the Komandorski Islands in March 1943, but not involved. It participated in the evacuation of Kiska in July–August 1943. It remained in northern waters until July 7, 1944 when it was sunk by the American submarine *Skate* in the Sea of Okhotsk.

Yugiri began the war assigned to Destroyer Division 20. It participated in the invasions of Malaya and the sinking of the British destroyer *Thanet* off Endau on January 27, 1942. In March, it covered invasions of Sumatra and the Andaman Islands and participated in the Indian Ocean raid in April. It was involved in the Midway operation as part of the Aleutians Guard Force. In its first transport operation to Guadalcanal, it was hit by an American bomb on August 28 and forced to return to Japan for repairs. It returned to Rabaul in January 1943. On its fifth mission out of Rabaul, it was torpedoed by the American submarine *Grayback* northwest of Kavieng and heavily damaged, and was again forced to return to Japan for repairs. It returned to Rabaul in November 1943, and was sunk at the Battle of Cape St George on November 25 by American destroyer gunfire.

Fubuki Class Specifications (as completed)

Displacement: 1,750 tons standard
Dimensions: Length 388.5ft / beam 34ft / draft 10.5ft
Maximum speed: 35kt
Range: 5,000nm at 14kt
Crew: 197

Akatsuki Class

Design and construction

The last four Special Type destroyers incorporated enough differences that they were given a new class name. The primary difference was that these ships only had three boilers, which meant that the forward stack was thinner than for Group I and II units. This was due to a new, larger type of boiler, which operated at a higher pressure and which produced the same 50,000shp with three boilers as earlier ships did with four. The smaller forward funnel became the primary recognition feature for the Akatsuki class (or Group III) compared to earlier units.

In addition to the smaller funnel, the Akatsuki class had a larger bridge structure, because of the addition of another level to provide improved fire-control facilities. These four ships incorporated many weight-saving measures, and *Hibiki* was the first all-welded Japanese ship. This meant that displacement was less than earlier Special Type destroyers, but the Akatsuki class still displayed the same stability problems as earlier Special Type units, and had to be rebuilt in the same manner described above.

Armament and service modifications

The Group III destroyers were armed like the other Special Type units. They were completed with shields to their torpedo mounts, unlike ships in earlier groups. In 1936, these ships underwent the same reconstruction as the earlier

The top and middle profiles in this plate show *Akebono*, a Group II Special Type, in its 1944 late-war configuration. Note that one of the aft 5in twin gun mounts has been replaced by two triple 25mm mounts. The bottom profile is *Akatsuki*, a Group III Special Type. The ship is in its 1942 configuration; note the thin forward funnel which was the main distinguishing feature of Group III units.

Akatsuki Class Construction				
Ship	Built at	Laid down	Launched	Completed
Akatsuki	Sasebo Navy Yard	2/17/30	5/7/32	11/30/32
Hibiki	Maizuru Navy Yard	2/15/30	12/22/32	3/30/33
Ikazuchi	Uraga	3/7/30	10/22/31	8/15/32
Inazuma	Fujinagata (Osaka)	3/7/30	2/25/32	11/15/32

Group I and II units to correct the stability problems. When complete, tonnage was raised to 1,980 tons, which reduced speed to 34 knots.

The class began the war with two 13mm twin mounts positioned in front of the second stack. By late 1943, another twin 13mm mount was added in front of the bridge to the three surviving units. This was replaced by a twin 25mm gun on *Hibiki* and *Ikazuchi* by January 1944. These ships had one of their aft 5in mounts removed and replaced by two triple 25mm mounts by April 1944, and another two triple 25mm mounts were added between the aft torpedo mounts. The last surviving unit, *Hibiki*, had another 20 single 25mm guns added, as well as a No. 22 and 13 radar, before the end of the war. The table below gives the final configuration for each ship in the class.

Wartime service

Akatsuki participated in the invasions of Malaya, the Dutch East Indies, and later the Philippines during the first months of the war. It was assigned to the Kiska invasion force for the Aleutians operation in June 1942. It arrived in the Rabaul area in October 1942 and participated in three transport runs and one sweep mission to Guadalcanal. It was involved in the First Naval Battle of Guadalcanal on November 13, 1942, during which it was sunk by American cruiser and destroyer gunfire.

Hibiki, like its sister ship *Akatsuki*, participated in the invasions of Malaya, the Dutch East Indies, and later the Philippines during the first months of the war. It was assigned to the Kiska invasion force for the Aleutians operation in June 1942. It was damaged off Kiska by air attack on June 12 and forced to return to Japan. It

Group III Special Type unit *Hibiki* seen off the Chinese coast in the late 1930s. The view is taken after the ship had undergone reconstruction, as is seen by the reduced size of the bridge. *Hibiki* survived the war and was handed over to the Soviet Union as reparations. After being re-armed with Russian weapons, it served until 1953 in the Pacific Ocean Fleet. (Naval History and Heritage Command)

Final Fit for Akatsuki-class Units						
Ship	Torpedo launchers	5in mounts	25mm mounts	13mm mounts	No. 22 Radar	No.13 Radar
Akatsuki	3	3	0	2 twin	No	No
Inazuma	3	2	4 triple 1 twin 2 single	0	Yes	No
Ikazuchi	3	3	1 twin	2 twin	No	No
Hibiki	3	2	4 triple 1 twin 20 single	0	Yes	Yes

subsequently performed escort operations in the Central Pacific, and later participated in the evacuation of Kiska in July 1943. In June 1944, it was involved in the Battle of the Philippine Sea. It suffered heavy damage, probably by a mine, on September 6, 1944. It returned to service in January 1945 and was damaged again by a mine in March. It survived the war and was then used as a repatriation ship. In April 1947, it was turned over to the Soviets as reparations and renamed *Pritky*.

Ikazuchi's first combat operation was supporting the invasion of Hong Kong in December 1941, during which it participated in the sinking of two British gunboats. It subsequently supported the invasion of the Dutch East Indies in February 1942 and mop-up actions in the Philippines in March. It was assigned to the Northern Force Main Body for the Aleutians operation in June. It arrived at Rabaul in October 1942 and participated in three transport runs and one sweep mission to Guadalcanal. It was part of the First Naval Battle of Guadalcanal on November 13. It claimed to have sunk the American cruiser *Atlanta* with torpedoes; either *Ikazuchi* or *Inazuma* was responsible. It suffered medium damage from gunfire and was forced to return to Japan for repairs. In February 1943, it was assigned to northern waters and participated in the March 26 Battle of the Komandorski Islands. It returned to the Central Pacific to conduct escort duties, and was sunk by the American submarine *Harder* 200 miles south-southeast of Guam on April 14, 1944.

Inazuma's first combat operation was, with *Ikazuchi*, to support the invasion of Hong Kong in December 1941, and it participated in the sinking of two British gunboats. It was damaged by a collision on January 20, 1942. On March 1, it participated in the action that saw the sinking of the British heavy cruiser *Exeter* and an American and a British destroyer.

Akatsuki Class Specifications (as completed)

Displacement: 1,680 tons standard
Dimensions: Length 389ft / beam 34ft / draft 11ft
Maximum speed: 38kt
Range: 5,000nm at 14kt
Crew: 197

Inazuma claimed two torpedo hits on *Exeter*. It was assigned to the Northern Force Main Body for the Aleutians operation in June. It arrived at Truk in October and participated in the First Naval Battle of Guadalcanal. On November 14–15, it was involved in the Second Naval Battle of Guadalcanal and assisted in the sinking of three American destroyers. Later that month, operating out of Rabaul, it conducted several transport missions to points in the Solomons and New Guinea. In February 1943, it was assigned to northern waters and was present at the Battle of the Komandorski Islands but saw no action. It returned to the Central Pacific to conduct escort duties, and was sunk by the American submarine *Bonefish* near Tawi-Tawi on May 14, 1944.

Hatsuharu Class

Design and construction

Whereas the Special Type destroyers were designed and built without any restrictions, the next class was the first designed under the London Naval Treaty. Unlike the Washington Naval Treaty, which put no restrictions on the size or numbers of destroyers, the London Naval Treaty signed in 1930 capped the IJN's overall destroyer tonnage (105,500 tons) and the maximum tonnage per ship. The largest permissible destroyer was 1,850 tons, but only 16 percent of the overall tonnage figure could be of this size. The remainder could not exceed 1,500 tons. This meant that the continued construction of the Special Type destroyers was no longer an option.

As usual, when faced by treaty restrictions, the Japanese endeavored to place the greatest possible firepower on a design publically compliant with treaty restrictions. For the Hatsuharu class laid down beginning in 1931, the original requirement was to mount the same armament as on the Special Type destroyers on a design lighter by some 260 tons. Twelve of these ships were envisioned, but eventually only six were built.

To pull this off, great scrutiny was placed on weight-saving measures. Electric welding was used extensively and less-powerful machinery was fitted. As on the Akatsuki class, only three boilers were fitted, and these could produce only 42,000shp. This translated to a top speed of 36.5 knots, which was judged to be adequate.

The weight-saving efforts were negated by the adoption of a large bridge structure, similar to the Group III Special Type units, and a heavy armament. The first two ships, *Hatsuharu* and *Nenohi*, were completed in September 1933. During trials, it was soon apparent that these ships had stability problems, since they would list badly while turning. A bulge was immediately installed but, in March 1934, when the torpedo boat *Tomodzuru* capsized because of stability problems caused by an excessive armament on a ship of limited tonnage, it became imperative that the Hatsuharu class be redesigned. The first two ships were sent to Kure for extensive modification. This included moving the superimposed single 5in mount to a position aft on the main deck, followed by a rebuilding of the bridge structure, making it smaller and more compact. The aft torpedo mount on the deckhouse was removed and the length of the deckhouse shortened to make room for the single 5in mount. To further lower the center of gravity, 84 tons of ballast were added. This increased the displacement to 1,715 tons (2,099 tons full load) and the draft to over 11ft, which reduced speed to 33.5 knots.

The second pair of ships was finished to this new design, and the final pair, *Ariake* and *Yugure*, was started to the updated design with further minor modifications (these are often referred to as the Ariake class). The other six units of the class were canceled.

Hatsuharu Class Construction				
Ship	Built at	Laid down	Launched	Completed
Ariake	Kobe by Kawasaki	1/14/33	9/23/34	3/25/35
Hatsuharu	Sasebo Navy Yard	5/14/31	2/27/33	9/30/33
Hatsushimo	Uraga	1/31/33	11/4/33	9/27/34
Nenohi	Uraga	12/15/31	12/22/32	9/30/33
Wakaba	Sasebo Navy Yard	12/12/31	3/18/34	10/31/34
Yugure	Maizuru Navy Yard	4/9/33	5/6/34	3/30/35

Armament

Japanese designers almost matched the armament of the Special Type units on the new class. The main gun battery totaled five 5in guns arranged in a twin mount forward and a single 5in superimposed mount. This was the first time the Japanese used this design feature on a destroyer. A second twin 5in mount was fitted aft. Torpedo armament matched the Fubuki class, with three triple mounts. The difference was that one of the two mounts fitted aft on the Hatsuharu class was placed on top of the aft deckhouse. This was the first class designed to carry the new Type 93 oxygen torpedo. Each of the mounts was provided with reloads. The aft stack was fitted off the centerline because of the placement of the torpedo reloads.

Antiaircraft armament was limited to two single 40mm guns fitted just forward of the second stack. For antisubmarine work, a single Type 94 projector and a stern depth-charge rack were fitted.

Service modifications

After the extensive modifications already described were completed by 1937, the ships received no further alterations before the start of the war. Modifications during the war revolved around augmentation of the antiaircraft armament. Beginning in 1942, the ships received a twin 25mm mount in front of the bridge, and the 40mm guns were replaced by twin 25mm mounts. In 1943, the surviving ships had the single 5in gun mount removed and replaced with a triple 25mm mount. The reload torpedoes for the aft torpedo mounts were also removed. Into 1944, ships began to receive single 25mm guns arranged along the length of the ship and augmented by four 13mm single mounts fitted amidships. The depth-charge load was increased to 36. Half of the class received a No. 22 radar on the foremast and later a No. 13 on the mainmast. The table below gives the final configuration of each ship in the class.

Wartime service

Ariake was assigned to Destroyer Division 27 at the start of the war, with its sister ship *Yugure*. In February 1942, it went to escort the Carrier Striking Force during operations supporting the invasion of the Dutch East Indies, and also escorted the Striking Force during the Battle of the Coral Sea. It was assigned to the Aleutians Guard Force during the Midway operation. By September 1942, it was active conducting missions in the waters off Guadalcanal, with a total of eight transport missions and one sweep mission being recorded, until it was damaged by air attack in December. It was forced to return to Japan for repairs, but was back at Rabaul by July 1943. It was sunk by B-25 air attack on July 28, 1943, while assisting the grounded destroyer *Mikazuki* near Cape Gloucester.

Hatsuharu began the war assigned to Destroyer Division 21 with *Hatsushimo*, *Nenohi*, and *Wakaba*. Its first combat operation was in January 1942 during the invasion of the Dutch East Indies. It participated in the occupation of Attu in the Aleutians in June 1942 and remained in northern waters until October, when it was damaged by B-26 air attack near Kiska.

Hatsushimo (Hatsuharu class) as it appeared in April 1945, accompanying superbattleship *Yamato* on its final sortie. This plate, in profile and overhead, shows the ship in its late-war configuration. The second ship is *Yudachi* (Shiratsuyu class) as it appeared in 1942 before it was sunk in the Second Naval Battle of Guadalcanal in November that year.

Final Fit for Hatsuharu-class Units						
Ship	Torpedo launchers	5in mounts	40mm mounts	25mm mounts	13mm mounts	Radar
Ariake	2	2 twin 1 single	0	3 twin	0	None
Hatsuharu	2	2 twin	0	3 triple 1 twin 15 single	4 single	No.13 No. 22
Hatsushimo	2	2 twin	0	3 triple 1 twin 15 single	4 single	No. 13 No. 22
Nenohi	2	2 twin 1 single	2	0	0	None
Wakaba	2	2 twin	0	3 triple 1 twin 15 single	4 single	No.13 No. 22
Yugure	2	2 twin 1 single	0	3 twin	0	None

After repairs and modifications, it performed general escort duties, primarily in the Central Pacific, until October 1944, when it was assigned to the Second Diversion Attack Force before the Battle of Leyte Gulf. It survived and returned to Manila to be assigned to escort duties for convoys to Ormoc, Leyte. It was sunk by air attack on Manila on November 13, 1944.

Hatsushimo's first combat operation was in January 1942, during the invasion of the Dutch East Indies. It participated in the occupation of Attu in the Aleutians in June 1942 and remained in northern waters until August 1943. It was involved in the Battle of the Komandorski Islands in March 1943 and the successful evacuation of the garrison from Kiska in the Aleutians in July 1943. It was present at the Battle of the Philippine Sea in June 1944, and in October 1944 was assigned to the Second Diversion Attack Force. It survived and returned to Manila to be assigned escort duties for convoys to Ormoc, Leyte. It returned to Japan in February 1945 and was assigned as escort to the superbattleship *Yamato* during its sortie to Okinawa in April. It survived that operation but was sunk by a mine while under American carrier air attack near Maizuru on July 30, 1945. *Hatsushimo* was the last Japanese destroyer sunk in the war.

Nenohi's first combat operation was in January 1942 in support of the invasion of the Dutch East Indies. It participated in the occupation of Attu in June 1942 and remained in northern waters until July 4, 1942, when it was torpedoed by the American submarine *Triton* southeast of Attu.

Wakaba's first combat operation was in January 1942 during the invasion of the Dutch East Indies. It participated in the occupation of Attu and remained in northern waters until May 1944. It was involved in the Battle of the Komandorski Islands in March 1943 and the successful evacuation of the garrison from Kiska in July 1943. It was present at the Battle of the Philippine Sea in June 1944, and in October 1944 it was assigned to the Second Diversion Attack Force. It was sunk on October 24, 1944 by an American carrier air attack west of Panay.

Yugure was assigned to Destroyer Division 27 at the start of the war. In February 1942, it was assigned to escort Carrier Striking Force during operations supporting the invasion of the Dutch East Indies and later escorted the force during the Battle of the Coral Sea in May. It was part of the Aleutians Guard Force during the Midway operation. By September, it was active conducting missions to the waters off Guadalcanal, with a total of six transport missions and one sweep mission in addition to other missions elsewhere in the Solomons. In July 1943, it was active in the Central Solomons and involved in the Battle of Kolombangara, in which Japanese destroyers sank an American destroyer and damaged two light cruisers. On July 20, 1943, it was sunk by aircraft north-northwest of Kolombangara Island, with no survivors.

> **Hatsuharu Class**
> **Specifications (as completed)**
>
> **Displacement:** 1,490 tons standard; 1,802 full load
> **Dimensions:** Length 359ft / beam 33ft / draft 10ft
> **Maximum speed:** 36.5kt
> **Range:** 6,000nm at 15kt
> **Crew:** 228

Yugure in October 1935. It was finished to the modified design earlier in the year, and is often referred to as part of the two-ship *Ariake* class. This beam view shows the modified design created to eliminate the stability problem. The single 5in gun has been moved to the position abaft the aft deckhouse and the bridge has been significantly reduced in size. The number of torpedo mounts was also reduced from three to two. (*Ships of the World* magazine)

Shiratsuyu Class

Design and construction

The stability problems that necessitated the redesign of the Hatsuharu class forced the final six units to be canceled. After the problem had been rectified, these six ships re-emerged as a new class, named the Shiratsuyu class. The redesign caused the new class to be over the tonnage restrictions set by the London Naval Treaty, but this did not concern the Japanese. Another four ships were authorized in 1934, so the class total reached ten units.

Overall, the appearance of the Shiratsuyu class resembled that of the preceding Hatsuharu class, particularly with regard to the layout of the armament. The hull was similar to that class, but the forecastle was shorter and the stern longer. The Shiratsuyu class had a greater displacement; to compensate, the bridge was redesigned and made more compact and the height of the bridge structure reduced. The same propulsion system from the Hatsuharu class was fitted and, with the greater weight and deeper draft, maximum speed was reduced to 34 knots. The asymmetrical arrangement of the stacks on the Hatsuharu class was not repeated.

Shiratsuyu Class Construction				
Ship	**Built at**	**Laid down**	**Launched**	**Completed**
Shiratsuyu	Sasebo Navy Yard	11/14/33	4/5/35	8/20/36
Shigure	Uraga	12/9/33	5/18/35	9/7/36
Murasame	Fujinagata (Osaka)	2/1/34	6/20/35	1/7/37
Yudachi	Sasebo Navy Yard	10/16/34	6/21/36	1/7/37
Samidare	Uraga	12/19/34	7/6/35	1/29/37
Harusame	Maizuru Navy Yard	2/3/35	9/21/35	8/26/37
Yamakaze	Uraga	5/25/35	2/21/36	1/30/37
Kawakaze	Fujinagata (Osaka)	4/25/35	11/1/36	4/30/37
Umikaze	Maizuru Navy Yard	5/4/35	11/27/36	5/31/37
Suzukaze	Uraga	7/9/35	3/11/37	8/31/37

Armament

The Shiratsuyu class featured an advancement in the torpedo armament of Japanese destroyers. Two new Type 92 quad mounts were fitted and eight reloads provided for a total of 16 torpedoes. These ships were the first to be fitted with telephone communications to the torpedo stations.

The main gun battery was identical to that on the Hatsuharu-class ships. *Yudachi* had the Type B gun house fitted, but all others were equipped with the Type C 5in gun house. Originally, the antiaircraft weapons fit was two single 40mm guns on the first six units and the Type 93 twin 13mm machine-gun mount on the last four ships.

The antisubmarine fit on the Shiratsuyu ships was reinforced. Two Type 94 projectors were fitted on the stern, with two stern depth-charge racks. A total of 36 depth charges were carried.

Service modifications

Wartime modifications focused on augmentation of the ships' antiaircraft fit. The first modification was the addition of a twin 25mm mount forward of the bridge. Beginning in late 1942, the single aft 5in gun mount was removed and replaced by a triple 25mm mount. With two triple mounts amidships, the normal light antiaircraft gun configuration going into 1943 was three triple and one twin 25mm mounts.

In 1944, the antiaircraft fit of surviving ships was reinforced further. At least *Samidare*, *Shigure*, and *Umikaze* received an additional ten single mounts located along the length of the ship. In December 1944, *Shigure* received another five single 25mm mounts and four single 13mm machine guns. By 1944, the surviving ships had their spare torpedoes removed to reduce top weight. Ships still in service by 1944 also received radar, with both a No. 22 and a No. 13 set being fitted on the foremast.

Wartime service

Harusame began the war as part of Destroyer Division 4 and was assigned to support the invasion of the Philippines and later the Dutch East Indies. It participated in the Battle of the Java Sea on February 27, 1942. It was

Umikaze running trials in April 1937 before being commissioned the next month. The similarity to the preceding Hatsuharu class is obvious. (Yamato Museum)

assigned to the invasion force for the Midway operation. In August, it was dispatched to the South Pacific, where it participated in the Battle of the Eastern Solomons. It conducted seven transport missions to Guadalcanal. On November 13, it participated in the First Naval Battle of Guadalcanal, but was not heavily engaged. On January 24, 1943, at Wewak, New Guinea, it was torpedoed and heavily damaged by the American submarine *Wahoo*. It returned to service in November 1943 and, in February 1944, was damaged by a carrier air attack on Truk. On June 8, while on a transport run to Biak Island off northern New Guinea, it was bombed and sunk by American B-25s.

Kawakaze was assigned to Destroyer Division 24 at the start of the war and participated in the invasions of the Philippines and the Dutch East Indies. In February 1942, it took part in the Battle of the Java Sea and the sinking of the British heavy cruiser *Exeter* and an American and British destroyer on March 1, 1942. It was part of the Aleutians Guard Force during the Midway operation in June. In August 1942, it moved to the South Pacific. On the night of August 22, it engaged two American destroyers off Guadalcanal and torpedoed one, which was later scuttled. It participated in the Battle of the Eastern Solomons in late August 1942. It conducted several transport and sweep missions to Guadalcanal, including as escort for the October 13–14 battleship bombardment of Henderson Field. It participated in the Battle of the Santa Cruz Islands in late October. In mid-November, it escorted a troop convoy to Guadalcanal. On November 30, it took part in the Battle of Tassafaronga, in which Japanese torpedoes sank one American heavy cruiser and damaged three more. It continued to make supply runs to the island and participated in the evacuation of the Japanese garrison in February 1943. It was sunk by American destroyer torpedoes and gunfire at the Battle of Vella Gulf on August 6, 1943.

Murasame began the war assigned to Destroyer Division 4 and supported the invasion of the Philippines and later the Dutch East Indies. It participated in the Battle of the Java Sea and was assigned to the invasion force for the Midway operation. In August 1942, it was dispatched to the South Pacific. It conducted seven transport missions to Guadalcanal. On November 13, it was part of the First Naval Battle of Guadalcanal. In the van of the Japanese force, *Murasame* was heavily engaged; it torpedoed the American light cruiser *Juneau* and later probably finished off an American destroyer, also using torpedoes. It emerged with only minor damage. It was sunk on a transport run to Kolombangara in the Central Solomons on March 6, 1943, after being disabled by American gunfire and then struck by an American torpedo.

Samidare was assigned to Destroyer Division 2 and saw service like the other ships in this squadron in the initial phase of the war. In August 1942, it was committed to the Solomons campaign and participated in the Battle of the Eastern Solomons. It was involved in the First Naval Battle of Guadalcanal on November 13, and returned two nights later to take part in the Second Naval Battle of Guadalcanal, where it assisted in the sinking of three American destroyers and the damaging of a fourth. In February 1943, it covered the evacuation of Guadalcanal, and in April it conducted several transport runs to other points in the Solomons. In July–August 1943, it shifted to the North Pacific to take part in the evacuation of Kiska. It participated in the Battle of Vella Lavella on the night of October 6, 1943, where either *Samidare* or *Shigure* torpedoed an American destroyer. In November, it participated in the Battle of Empress Augusta Bay and was damaged in a collision with *Shiratsuyu*. It was also probably responsible for torpedoing and damaging an American destroyer. In June 1944, it

Yamakaze sinking, as seen through the periscope of submarine *Nautilus*. The ship was torpedoed off the Japanese coast on June 25, 1942. Its entire crew of 227 was killed in the attack. (Naval History and Heritage Command)

**Shiratsuyu Class
Specifications (as completed)**

Displacement: 1,685 tons standard; 1,980 full load
Dimensions: Length 353ft / beam 32.5ft / draft 11.5ft
Maximum speed: 34kt
Range: 6,000nm at 15kt
Crew: 180

participated in the unsuccessful Biak operation and later in the month was involved in the Battle of the Philippine Sea. It was sunk on August 25 near Palau by the American submarine *Batfish*.

Shiratsuyu was assigned to Destroyer Division 27 at the start of the war, and remained in home waters until May 1942, when it was assigned to escort the Carrier Striking Force at the Battle of the Coral Sea. During the Midway operation, it was part of the Aleutians Guard Force. It moved to the South Pacific and escorted a mid-October convoy to Guadalcanal; after this it conducted another four transport runs and one sweep mission to Guadalcanal. In November 1942, it was damaged by a B-17 attack and forced to return to Japan. It came back to the Solomons and participated in the Battle of Empress Augusta Bay in November 1943, where it was damaged in a collision with the destroyer *Samidare*. It was involved in the unsuccessful Biak operation in June 1944 and was damaged by air attack. On June 15, 1944, it was sunk in a collision with the tanker *Seiyo Maru* southeast of Surigao Strait.

Shigure was the most famous ship of the Shiratsuyu class, becoming known as the Indestructible Destroyer as a result of its service in the Solomons, during which it sustained no casualties during heavy operations. Its early-war service was similar to the other ships of Destroyer Division 27. By October 1942, it was operating out of Rabaul and conducted nine transport missions to Guadalcanal, including escort of the mid-October convoy. It returned to Rabaul in July 1943 and began a period of constant operations, which included the Battle of Vella Gulf in August, when it was the only Japanese destroyer to survive, the battle off Horaniu, in which it again engaged American destroyers, the Battle of Vella Lavella in October, in which its torpedoes contributed to the sinking of an American destroyer, and the Battle of Empress Augusta Bay in November. It was damaged by an American carrier air attack on February 17, 1944, at Truk. It participated in the unsuccessful Biak operation in June 1944, during which it was damaged by an Allied cruiser-destroyer task force. It was involved in the Battle of the Philippine Sea in June 1944, and at the Battle of Leyte Gulf. It saw action at the Battle of Surigao Strait and was the only ship to survive from the Japanese Southern Force. On January 24, 1945, it was torpedoed and sunk by the American submarine *Blackfin*, east of Malaya.

Suzukaze was assigned to Destroyer Division 24 at the start of the war and participated in the invasions of the Philippines and the Dutch East Indies. On February 4, 1942, it was torpedoed by the American submarine

Sculpin and heavily damaged. It returned to service in July and was sent to the South Pacific, where it participated in the Battle of the Eastern Solomons in August. From August 1942 until February 1943, it took part in over ten transport runs to Guadalcanal and five combat missions to the island, including participation in the Battle of Tassafaronga in November 1942. It was also involved in the carrier Battle of the Santa Cruz Islands in October 1942. It covered the evacuation of Guadalcanal in February 1943, and then participated in the Battle of Kula Gulf in July, where it was damaged by American cruiser gunfire. It was sunk on January 26, 1944 by the American submarine *Skipjack* near Ponape Island.

Umikaze began the war assigned to Destroyer Division 24 and participated in the invasion of the Philippines and the Dutch East Indies. It was present at the Battle of the Java Sea in February 1942, but saw no action. It was assigned to the Aleutians Guard Force as part of the Midway operation. It was moved to the South Pacific in August 1942, where it conducted ten transport missions to Guadalcanal and three combat missions. It participated in the Battle of the Santa Cruz Islands in October, and on November 18 incurred heavy bomb damage from a B-17 attack. It was back in service in February 1943 and returned to Rabaul to conduct transport missions to various points in the Solomons. While on escort duties in the Central Pacific, it was torpedoed and sunk by the American submarine *Guardfish* on February 1, 1944, near Truk.

Yamakaze began the war assigned to Destroyer Division 24 and participated in the invasion of the Philippines and the Dutch East Indies. On February 11, 1942, it attacked and sank the American submarine *Shark* with 5in gunfire east of Manado. It participated in the Battle of the Java Sea and the March 1, 1942 action against American and British ships. It was assigned to the Aleutians Guard Force as part of the Midway operation. On June 25, 1942, it was sunk by the American submarine *Nautilus* near Yokosuka, with no survivors.

Yudachi was assigned to Destroyer Division 4 and conducted operations as other ships in this unit during the initial period of the war. By August 1942, it was committed to operations in the Solomons. It participated in 13 transport missions and five sweep missions to Guadalcanal. On a mission on September 5, 1942, it played the primary role in the sinking of two American destroyer transports. On November 13, 1942, it engaged in the First Naval Battle of Guadalcanal. In the van of the Japanese force with *Murasame*, it torpedoed the American heavy cruiser *Portland*, but was heavily damaged by American cruiser and destroyer gunfire; it was abandoned, and later sank.

Asashio Class

Design and construction

The Asashio class, ordered in 1934, became the prototype for the next two classes of IJN destroyers. Laid down beginning in 1935, the entire class of ten ships was completed between 1937 and 1939. The overall layout of the class proved successful in service and created a powerful ship that also presented a graceful and balanced appearance.

By this time, the Japanese had decided to ignore treaty limitations and build the new class of destroyer to meet requirements set by the Naval General Staff. The London Naval Treaty, which restricted the maximum size of destroyers and the IJN's overall destroyer tonnage, did not expire until December 31, 1936, but this inconvenience did not trouble the Japanese. Compared to the preceding Shiratsuyu class, the length of the hull was increased by almost 30ft and displacement was increased by almost 300 tons. The primary difference compared to the previous class, aside from a generally less cramped appearance, was the adoption of a heavier gun armament. The third twin Type C 5in mount was fitted in a superfiring position on the aft deckhouse, as on the Special Type destroyers.

The Asashio class featured improved boilers that operated at higher temperatures. The three boilers drove two turbines and two shafts and generated 50,000shp. This meant that in spite of the greater displacement, the top speed was 35 knots, one knot faster than the preceding Shiratsuyu class. Though the Japanese were happy with the design, there were problems. The sea trials of the lead ship, *Asashio*, produced unsatisfactory steering results. Subsequent ships in the class were provided with a modified stern and improved rudder, which gave a much more compact turning radius. The entire class had problems with the turbines, and it took until the start of the war to modify all ships.

Armament and service modifications

The Asashio class was fitted with a heavy armament, greater than almost all foreign contemporaries. The main gun battery was six 5in guns in three Type C twin mounts. The ships' primary offensive punch was the two Type 92 quad torpedo mounts. Each was provided with four reloads, making a total of 16 embarked torpedoes. The only antiaircraft weaponry was two Type 96 twin 25mm mounts fitted amidships, forward of the second stack. These were the first destroyers to receive the new Type 96 guns.

As the war progressed, the Japanese were forced to augment the antiaircraft fit of their destroyers. This was carried out in several stages. The

Asashio Class Construction				
Ship	Built at	Laid down	Launched	Completed
Arare	Maizuru Navy Yard	3/5/37	11/16/37	4/15/39
Arashio	Kobe by Kawasaki	10/1/35	5/26/37	12/20/37
Asagumo	Kobe by Kawasaki	12/23/36	11/5/37	3/31/38
Asashio	Sasebo Navy Yard	9/7/35	12/16/36	8/31/37
Kasumi	Uraga	12/1/36	11/18/37	6/28/39
Michishio	Osaka by Fujinagata	11/5/35	3/15/37	10/31/37
Minegumo	Osaka by Fujinagata	3/22/36	11/4/37	4/30/38
Natsugumo	Sasebo Navy Yard	7/1/36	5/26/37	2/10/38
Ooshio	Maizuru Navy Yard	8/5/36	4/19/37	10/31/37
Yamagumo	Osaka by Fujinagata	11/4/36	7/24/37	1/15/38

first augmentation, carried out in 1942–43, was to swap the twin mounts amidships with triple mounts and to place a twin 25mm mount on a bandstand forward of the bridge. The second phase, during 1943–44, entailed the removal of the superfiring 5in mount in favor of two 25mm triple mounts. This confirmed the failure of the Japanese 5in guns as antiaircraft weapons. The third stage, conducted in 1944, was to fit between eight and 12 single 25mm guns on the main and forecastle decks. In addition, *Kasumi* received four single 13mm guns. Only four ships, *Asagumo*, *Kasumi*, *Michishio*, and *Yamagumo*, survived into 1944 to receive the full antiaircraft augmentation and radar.

Other important changes included the addition of a No. 22 radar on the modified foremast above the bridge and a No. 13 radar on the leading edge of the mainmast aft. The ships began the war with paravanes on the stern for sweeping moored mines and 16 depth charges deployed by either a Type 94 double-sided projector or stern drop stands. Later in the war, the paravanes

Asashio, shown here in July 1937, probably on sea trials. The ship projects a fine balance of power and speed. *Asashio* had an active wartime career until it was one of the four destroyers sunk at the Battle of the Bismarck Sea in March 1943. (Yamato Museum)

Asagumo in September 1939. Before the war, all Japanese destroyers displayed their name amidships on the hull and the number of their parent destroyer division forward on the hull. Asagumo was the easily the most active and successful Asashio-class unit. (*Ships of the World* magazine)

were removed and the number of depth charges carried was increased. To compensate for this extra topweight, one of the spare sets of reload torpedoes was removed. Nevertheless, total displacement increased to 2,000 tons.

Wartime service

The ten Asashio-class units began the war assigned to Destroyer Divisions 8 (*Asashio, Arashio, Michishio, Ooshio*), 9 (*Asagumo, Minegumo, Natsugumo, Yamagumo*), and 18 (*Arare, Kasumi* and two Kagero-class units). By 1944, only four ships survived, and three of these were moved into Division 4. The class saw heavy action during the war, and none survived.

Arare began the war assigned to the Pearl Harbor Attack Force and remained with the carriers through the Indian Ocean raid in April. It was assigned to escort the invasion convoy for the Midway operation. In June 1942, it conducted escort operations to Kiska Island in the Aleutians. It was hit by a single torpedo from the submarine USS *Growler* on July 5 that year off Kiska and sunk.

Arashio was assigned to support the invasion of Malaya and Dutch East Indies at the start of the war. It escorted the Support Group at the Battle of Midway in 1942, came under air attack, and suffered one bomb hit with 37 dead on June 6. It returned to service in December, conducted transport runs to New Guinea, and then participated in the evacuation from Guadalcanal. It was lost to air attack on March 4, 1943 in the Battle of the Bismarck Sea.

Asagumo was assigned to support the Philippines and Dutch East Indies invasion at the start of the war. During the Battle of the Java Sea, it sank the British destroyer *Electra* on February 27, but was damaged by cruiser gunfire. It was involved in the Midway operation. During the Guadalcanal campaign, it participated in the carrier battles of the Eastern Solomons and Santa Cruz, nine transport runs, and the First Naval Battle of Guadalcanal, where its torpedoes finished off the American destroyer *Laffey*; it was also present at the Second Naval Battle of Guadalcanal. It survived the Battle of Bismarck Sea in March 1943. In May 1943, it moved to northern waters and participated in the evacuation of the Japanese garrison from Kiska. It was involved in the Battle of the Philippine Sea in June 1944. During the Battle of Leyte Gulf, it was assigned to Force "C." During the Battle of Surigao Strait on October 25, 1944, the American destroyer *McDermut* fired a single torpedo salvo that sank or crippled three Asashio-class ships, including *Asagumo*. *Asagumo* had its bow blown off and was later sunk by gunfire, with only 39 survivors.

Asashio was assigned to support the invasion of Malaya and the Dutch East Indies at the start of the war. On February 19–20, 1942, in the Battle of Badung Strait, it sank the Dutch destroyer *Piet Hein* and later damaged a Dutch cruiser and an American destroyer with gunfire, but was hit and damaged in return. It was assigned to escort the Support Group at the Battle of Midway and came under air attack; it suffered one bomb hit with 22 dead. In October, it was sent to Guadalcanal. It participated in the naval battles of Guadalcanal in November, but was not engaged. It was sent to Japan in January 1943 for a quick refit, and returned to Rabaul in time to escort a large convoy from Rabaul to Lae. During the Battle of the Bismarck Sea on March 4, 1943, it was pounded by multiple bomb hits; it quickly sank with all hands.

Kasumi began the war assigned to the Pearl Harbor Attack Force and remained with the carriers through the Indian Ocean raid in April 1942. It was part of the escort for the invasion convoy in the Midway operation. On

The Asashio class was the basis for the next two classes of Type A destroyers. The top view is of the lead ship of the class, *Asashio*, as it appeared in 1941. The second ship shown in both profile and overhead views is the famous Kagero-class ship *Yukikaze*. This view is its configuration in April 1945 which shows the addition of radar and the profusion of 25mm gun mounts.

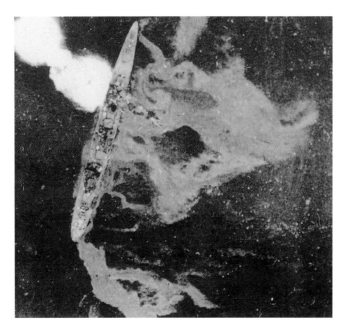

Arashio leaking oil and drifting after being crippled by air attack during the Battle of the Bismarck Sea. The destroyer was initially disabled on March 3, and finally sank the following day with the loss of 72 crewmen. (Naval History and Heritage Command)

July 5, it was hit and damaged by a torpedo from the submarine USS *Growler* off Kiska. It returned to service in June 1943. It survived the Battle of Surigao Strait on October 25, 1944, and then conducted operations in the Philippines area, including two convoys to Leyte. It returned to Japan in February 1945 and was assigned to escort superbattleship *Yamato* on its mission to Okinawa. It was sunk on April 7, 1945 by air attack.

Michishio was assigned to support the Philippines and Dutch East Indies invasion at the start of the war. During the Battle of Badung Strait on February 19, 1942, it was surprised by two old American destroyers and heavily damaged by gunfire, being left dead in the water with 64 casualties. After repairs, it arrived in Rabaul in October 1942. After three transport operations, it was heavily damaged by American air attacks on November 14 and eventually towed back to Japan. It participated in the Battle of the Philippine Sea in June 1944. At the Battle of Surigao Strait, on October 25 it was hit by a torpedo from the destroyer *McDermut*; it sank, leaving only four survivors.

Minegumo was assigned to support the Philippines and Dutch East Indies invasion at the start of the war. During the Battle of the Java Sea, *Minegumo* and *Asagumo* dueled with British destroyers, sinking one. It participated in the Midway operation. During the Guadalcanal campaign, it was involved in the carrier battle of the Eastern Solomons, but was then damaged by air attack on October 5 and forced to return to Japan. It went back to Rabaul in March 1943, but on its first transport mission to Kolombangara Island in the Central Solomons it was engaged and sunk by radar-controlled gunfire from American cruisers and destroyers in Kula Gulf on March 6.

Natsugumo was assigned to support the Philippines and Dutch East Indies invasion at the start of the war. It was involved in the Midway operation. During the Guadalcanal campaign, it participated in the Battle of the Eastern Solomons and three transport runs, but was caught by American aircraft on October 12, 1942 near Savo Island and sunk.

Ooshio was assigned to support the invasion of Malaya and the Dutch East Indies at the start of the war. On February 19–20, 1942, in the Battle of Badung Strait, it assisted *Asashio* in sinking the Dutch destroyer *Piet Hein*; later it was heavily damaged by gunfire and did not return to action until January 1943, when it participated in the evacuation from Guadalcanal. On February 20, it was torpedoed and sunk by the submarine *Albacore* off New Guinea.

Yamagumo participated in the invasion of the Philippines, but struck a mine in Lingayen Gulf on December 31, 1941 and suffered heavy damage. Following repairs, it was assigned to convoy escort duties through early 1944 and sank the American submarine *Sculpin* on November 19, 1943. It participated in the Battle of the Philippine Sea in June 1944. At the Battle of Surigao Strait on October 25, it was struck by three torpedoes from the destroyer USS *McDermut;* it sank in two minutes, leaving two survivors.

> ### Asashio Class Specifications
>
> **Displacement:** 1,961 tons standard
> **Dimensions:** Length 388ft / beam 34ft / draft 12ft
> **Maximum speed:** 35kt
> **Range:** 5,000nm at 18kt
> **Crew:** 200 (230 by 1944)

Kagero Class

Design and construction

The Kagero class was the first class known as Type A by the Japanese. Building on the success of the preceding Asashio class, the Japanese were very content with the design and capabilities of this new destroyer class. The Kagero class compared favorably to other foreign designs built at the same time. For example, compared to contemporary American destroyers, the Kagero ships had a heavier gun armament (but were not dual-purpose like the American 5in guns) and had a much heavier torpedo armament when their reloads were factored in.

The first 15 ships of this class were ordered in the 1937 program. The final four units, sometimes referred to as the Arashi group, were ordered as part of the 1939 program. This brings up an interesting point. Most published histories have only 18 ships in the Kagero class. Recent research in Japan indicates that *Akigumo* was actually one of the last Kagero-class ships built, not one of the first Yugumo-class units. This can be traced to postwar officials trying to make sense out of prewar building plans, which included a number of fictitious destroyers inserted into the plans in an attempt to conceal the extent of the resources devoted to the Yamato-class battleships. The result was the mislabeling of *Akigumo* as a Yugumo-class unit. In fact, it had Type C 5in mounts (not the Type D mounts on the

Kagero Class Construction				
Ship	Built at	Laid down	Launched	Completed
Akigumo	Uraga	7/20/40	4/11/41	9/27/41
Amatsukaze	Maizuru Navy Yard	12/14/38	10/19/39	10/26/40
Arashi	Maizuru Navy Yard	5/4/39	4/22/40	1/27/41
Hagikaze	Uraga	5/23/39	6/18/40	3/31/41
Hamakaze	Uraga	11/20/39	11/25/40	6/30/41
Hatsukaze	Kobe by Kawasaki	12/3/37	1/24/39	2/15/40
Hayashio	Uraga	6/30/38	4/19/39	8/31/40
Isokaze	Sasebo Navy Yard	11/25/38	6/19/39	11/30/40
Kagero	Maizuru Navy Yard	9/3/37	9/27/38	11/6/39
Kuroshio	Osaka by Fujinagata	8/31/37	10/25/38	1/27/40
Maikaze	Osaka by Fujinagata	4/22/40	3/15/41	7/15/41
Natsushio	Osaka by Fujinagata	12/9/37	2/23/39	8/31/39
Nowaki	Maizuru Navy Yard	11/8/39	9/17/40	4/28/41
Oyashio	Maizuru Navy Yard	3/29/38	11/29/38	8/20/40
Shiranui	Uraga	8/30/37	6/28/38	12/20/39
Tanikaze	Osaka by Fujinagata	10/18/39	11/1/40	4/25/41
Tokitsukaze	Uraga	2/20/39	11/10/39	12/15/40
Urakaze	Osaka by Fujinagata	4/11/39	4/19/40	12/15/40
Yukikaze	Sasebo Navy Yard	8/2/38	3/24/39	1/20/40

Yugumo class) and had one of these later replaced by 25mm triple mounts (like other Kagero-class units).

As built, the Kagero ships were virtually identical to the preceding Asashio class. The hull was nearly identical, as was the bridge structure. The only major discernable visual difference was the movement of the reload torpedoes for the forward torpedo mount from an abaft position to forward of the launcher.

The Kagero ships possessed a slightly greater displacement and increased beam to improve stability. They demonstrated some increase in boiler efficiency, which produced 52,000shp, but this did not result in any increase in speed. *Amatsukaze* received a new type of experimental boiler that developed higher pressure, but there was no real increase in performance.

Armament and service modifications

As completed, the arrangement of the armament was identical to the Asashio class. Alterations to the Kagero class were again similar to the Asashio ships,

Kagero-class unit *Isokaze* pictured at Sasebo on November 22, 1940, just before its completion. The ship compiled a fine war record and was not sunk until April 1945. (Naval History and Heritage Command)

and focused on the augmentation of the antiaircraft fit and the addition of radar. In 1942–43, the twin 25mm mounts amidships were replaced by triple mounts and a twin 25mm mount placed forward of the bridge. On all surviving units during 1943–44, the superfiring 5in mount aft was removed and replaced with two 25mm triple mounts. Finally, during the second half of 1944, the seven surviving ships received a number of single 25mm and 13mm guns. This varied from the seven single 25mm guns on *Isokaze* and *Hamakaze* in June 1944 to the 14 25mm and four 13mm guns on *Yukikaze*.

Also during the war, many of the scuttles were welded over to prevent flooding and surviving ships received armor plating around the bridge.

Hamakaze was the first Japanese destroyer to have radar fitted in late 1942 when it returned to Japan for a refit. Since the Kagero ships were front-line units and heavily engaged in the Solomons campaign, they were given priority for receiving radar. Other ships got their radars when they rotated home for repair or refit. At least one ship (*Nowaki*) had the No. 22 radar attached to the foremast without creating a platform, but most had their foremast modified to fit the No. 22. All seven ships still afloat past mid-1944 also received No. 13 radar on the leading edge of the mainmast aft. The Kagero ships began the war with paravanes on the stern and 16 depth charges deployed by either a Type 94 double-sided projector or stern drop stands. With the removal of the paravanes, depth-charge stowage was increased to 36 and two rails placed on the stern.

Wartime service

These ships were at the heart of the IJN's destroyer force. They constituted several Destroyer Divisions – 4, 15, 16, 17, and half of 18.

Akigumo began war assigned to the Kido Butai; it stayed with the carriers through the Battle of Santa Cruz in October 1942. It scuttled the American carrier *Hornet* with torpedoes at Santa Cruz. It participated in the evacuation from Guadalcanal in February 1943. It was active in the Solomons in early 1943 before participating in the successful evacuation from Kiska in July.

Amatsukaze in October 1940, on sea trials before being turned over to the IJN. This views shows the similarity of the Kagero class to the preceding Asashio class, with the best recognition feature being the torpedo reloads abreast the forward stack. Amatsukaze went on to have a distinguished war career. (*Ships of the World* magazine)

It returned to the Solomons and participated in the Battle of Vella Lavella in October. It was sunk by the submarine USS *Redfin* on April 11, 1944 off the Philippines.

Amatsukaze participated in the invasion of the southern Philippines at the start of the war. It was assigned to support the invasion of the Dutch East Indies and participated in the Battle of the Java Sea on February 27, 1942. It was involved in the Midway operation as escort to the invasion convoy. During the Guadalcanal campaign, it participated in the battles of Eastern Solomons and Santa Cruz; during the First Naval Battle of Guadalcanal on November 13, it sank the American destroyer *Barton* with torpedoes, but then was damaged by cruiser gunfire and forced to return to Japan for repairs. It was assigned to general escort duties and torpedoed by the submarine *Redfish* on January 16, 1944 in the South China Sea; it lost its bow and suffered 80 dead. It was repaired at Singapore and was sunk on April 6, 1945 by B-25s near Amoy, China.

Arashi began the war as part of the Malaya and Dutch East Indies invasion forces. In March 1942, it assisted in sinking several Allied ships fleeing Java, including a British destroyer and an American gunboat. It participated in the Midway operation as part of the Kido Butai. It moved to the South Pacific and engaged in several transport missions to Guadalcanal and points on New Guinea. It participated in the Battle of Santa Cruz and later the Battle of Vella Gulf on August 7, 1943, and was one of three Japanese destroyers surprised by American destroyers and sunk by torpedoes and gunfire.

Hagikaze was assigned to support the invasion of Malaya at the start of the war, then assigned to escort the Kido Butai and participated in the Midway operation. It began operations off Guadalcanal in August 1942 and was heavily damaged by a B-17 on August 19. It re-entered service in February 1943 and was assigned to support operations in the Solomons. After several supply missions beginning in April, it participated in the Battle of Vella Gulf on August 7 and was sunk by torpedoes and gunfire.

Hamakaze was assigned to escort the Kido Butai at the start of the war and remained with carriers throughout the Midway operation. It participated in the Battle of Santa Cruz, four missions to Guadalcanal, and the evacuation from the island in February 1943. It was heavily engaged during the remainder of the Solomons campaign, being present at the battles of Kula Gulf and Kolombangara in July 1943 and the indecisive battle off Horaniu against four American destroyers in the Central Solomons in August. It was damaged by air attack on August 26 and forced to return to Japan. It participated in the Battle of the Philippine Sea. It was assigned to Force "A" for the Leyte operation and was slightly damaged by air attack. In April 1945, it was assigned to escort *Yamato*. It was sunk by air attack on April 7.

Hatsukaze was assigned to support the invasion of the southern Philippines at the start of the war. It participated in the invasion of the Dutch East Indies and also in the Battle of the Java Sea on February 27, 1942. It was involved in the Midway operation as escort to the invasion convoy. It participated in the battles of the Eastern Solomons and Santa Cruz. It was hit by a PT-launched torpedo off Guadalcanal on January 10, 1943 and forced to return to Japan. It was sunk with all hands during the Battle of Empress Augusta Bay on November 2, 1943 after a collision with the heavy cruiser *Myoko* and was then destroyed by American destroyer gunfire.

Hayashio began the war assigned to the Philippine and Dutch East Indies invasion forces. It was involved in the Midway operation as part of the invasion force. During the Guadalcanal campaign, it participated in the battles of the Eastern Solomons and Santa Cruz, three transport missions to the island, the mid-October bombardment of Henderson Field, and the unsuccessful mid-November convoy to that island. It was sunk by air attack on November 24, 1943 off Lae, New Guinea.

Isokaze was assigned to escort the Kido Butai at the start of the war and remained with carriers through the Midway operation. During the Guadalcanal campaign, it participated in the battles of the Eastern Solomons and Santa Cruz and the February 1943 evacuation. On August 18, it was involved in the battle off Horaniu. On October 6, 1943, it participated in the Battle of Vella Lavella. It was damaged by a mine on November 4 off Kavieng and forced to return to Japan for repairs. It participated in the Battle of the Philippine Sea. It was assigned to Force "A" for the Leyte operation; it returned to Japan in November and was assigned to escort *Yamato*. It was damaged by air attack on April 7, 1944 and later scuttled.

Kagero was assigned to escort the Kido Butai at the start of the war and remained with carriers through the Indian Ocean raid in April 1942. It

This view shows *Kagero*, lead ship of its class, steaming through heavy seas on December 7, 1941. *Kagero* was assigned as part of the Pearl Harbor striking force. Seven of the nine destroyers assigned to the raid were Kagero-class units, since at the beginning of the war these were the most modern destroyers in the IJN.

participated in the Midway operation as part of the invasion convoy. It moved to the South Pacific and was involved in the Battle of the Eastern Solomons, ten transport/attack missions to Guadalcanal, and the Battle of Santa Cruz. It was present at the Second Naval Battle of Guadalcanal in mid-November and the Battle of Tassafaronga on November 30, 1942. It conducted another four supply runs to Guadalcanal and supported the February 1943 evacuation. After a brief refit in Japan, it returned to the Solomons, was damaged by a mine on May 8 off Kolombangara and then finished off by air attack.

Kuroshio began the war supporting the invasion of the southern Philippines and then participated in the invasion of the Dutch East Indies. It was involved in the Midway operation as part of the invasion convoy. It moved to the South Pacific and participated in the Battle of the Eastern Solomons, three transport missions to Guadalcanal, the mid-October bombardment of Henderson Field, and the Battle of Santa Cruz. At Tassafaronga, its torpedoes may have been among those that crippled the heavy cruiser USS *Pensacola*. From December until February 1943, it participated in seven supply runs and all three evacuation runs to Guadalcanal. After a brief refit in Japan, it returned to the Solomons and was sunk by a mine on May 8 off Kolombangara.

Maikaze began the war as part of the Malaya and Dutch East Indies invasion forces. In February 1942, it was assigned to escort the Kido Butai and stayed with the carriers throughout the Midway operation, the Eastern Solomons, and Santa Cruz. It participated in the evacuation from Guadalcanal and was damaged by air attack. After repairs, it was assigned to general escort duties. It was caught at Truk during an American carrier attack in February 1944 and sunk by cruiser gunfire northwest of Truk with all hands.

Natsushio was assigned to the southern Philippine invasion force at the start of the war. It became the first of 39 Japanese destroyers to be sunk by submarine attack when it was torpedoed off Makassar in the Dutch East Indies on February 8 by the American submarine USS *S-37*; it sank the next day.

Nowaki began the war as part of the Malaya and Dutch East Indies invasion forces. In March 1942, it assisted in the sinking of several Allied ships departing Java. It participated in the Midway operation as part of the Kido Butai; it stayed with the carriers for the Eastern Solomons and later was present at Santa Cruz. It was involved in at least four supply missions to Guadalcanal; during the last, on December 7, 1942, it suffered moderate damage from air attack and was forced to return to Japan for repairs. It was caught at Truk during an American carrier attack in February 1944, but was the only Japanese ship to escape from an American surface task group that included the battleships *Iowa* and *New Jersey*. It participated in the Philippine Sea operation. It was assigned to Force "A" for the Leyte operation and sunk by cruiser and destroyer gunfire off San Bernardino Strait on October 26, 1944 with the loss of approximately 1,000 men – the entire crew of the destroyer and the rescued survivors from the heavy cruiser *Chikuma*.

Oyashio was assigned to the southern Philippine invasion force at the start of the war, and then was active in the invasion of the Dutch East Indies. It participated in the Midway operation as escort to the invasion convoy. It was involved in the Battle of the Eastern Solomons, led three transport missions to Guadalcanal, and then participated in the battleship bombardment of Henderson Field in mid-October 1942. It participated in the Battle of Santa Cruz in October. In November, it engaged in the Second Naval Battle of Guadalcanal. On November 30, it played a key role in the Battle of Tassafaronga, when it possibly torpedoed the heavy cruiser *Pensacola* and more likely torpedoed the heavy cruiser *Northampton*, which later sank. It conducted several more supply missions to Guadalcanal before arriving in Japan for refit. Upon its return to the Solomons, it struck a mine off Kolombangara, and was then sunk by air attack on May 8, 1943.

Shiranui was assigned to escort the Kido Butai at the start of the war and remained with the carriers through the Indian Ocean raid in April 1942. It participated in the Midway operation as escort to the invasion convoy. It was heavily damaged by the submarine USS *Growler* on July 5 off Kiska. Repairs were not completed until November 1943, after which it was assigned to general escort duties. It participated in the Battle of Surigao Strait. It was sunk by American escort carrier aircraft on October 27, 1944 with all hands.

Tanikaze was assigned to escort the Kido Butai at the start of the war; it stayed with carriers through the Midway operation, during which it was slightly damaged. It participated in the Battle of Santa Cruz and then undertook supply missions in December–February 1943, including the evacuation of Guadalcanal. In July 1943, it participated in the Battle of Kula Gulf and contributed to the torpedo barrage that sank the light cruiser USS *Helena*. It was assigned to general escort duties until sunk by the submarine USS *Harder* near Tawi Tawi on June 9, 1944.

Tokitsukaze participated in the invasion of the southern Philippines at the start of the war. It was assigned to support the invasion of the Dutch East Indies, participated in the Battle of the Java Sea on February 27, 1942, and in the Midway operation as escort to the invasion convoy. During the Guadalcanal campaign, it was involved in the battles of the Eastern Solomons and Santa Cruz. In January–February 1943, it was active in several supply and then evacuation missions to Guadalcanal. It was sunk by air attack on March 4 during the Battle of the Bismarck Sea.

Nowaki in August 1943, probably at Yokosuka. The condition of its external paint speaks of its active and near-continual service up to this point in the war. The cable running along the side of its hull is a degaussing cable designed to reduce its vulnerability to magnetic mines. The ship has already received its mid-war modifications as evidenced by the twin 25mm gun in front of the bridge and the triple 25mm mount amidships. (Yamato Museum)

Urakaze was assigned to escort the Kido Butai at the start of the war and remained with carriers throughout the Midway operation. It participated in the Battle of Santa Cruz and six missions to Guadalcanal and New Guinea through 1942. In 1943, it was involved in the evacuation from Guadalcanal and later undertook general escort duties, including several convoys to New Guinea. It participated in the Battle of the Philippine Sea. It was assigned to Force "A" for the Leyte operation and was slightly damaged by air attack. It was sunk by the submarine USS *Sealion* on November 21, 1944 off Formosa with all hands.

Yukikaze was the most famous ship of the Kagero-class destroyers and perhaps of all Japanese Pacific War destroyers. It began the war attached to the southern Philippines invasion force. It participated in the invasion of the Dutch East Indies, including the Battle of the Java Sea. It was involved in the Midway operation as part of the invasion convoy. It arrived in the South Pacific in time for the Battle of Santa Cruz and then was heavily engaged during the First Naval Battle of Guadalcanal, during which it was only lightly damaged. It participated in all three evacuation runs from Guadalcanal in February 1943, and survived the Battle of Bismarck Sea in March. It was engaged in the Battle of Kolombangara in July and assisted in the torpedoing of three American ships. It was present at the Battle of the Philippine Sea. It was assigned to Force "A" for the Leyte operation and emerged unscathed. It escorted *Yamato* in April 1945 and suffered only light damage on April 7 when *Yamato* was sunk. It survived the war to be turned over to the Nationalist Chinese in 1947, and remained in service until 1966. It was finally scrapped in 1970 after a campaign to return it to Japan failed.

> **Kagero Class Specifications**
>
> **Displacement:** 2,033 tons standard
> **Dimensions:** Length 388.5ft / beam 35.5ft / draft 12.33in
> **Maximum speed:** 35kt
> **Range:** 5,000nm at 18kt
> **Crew:** 240

Yugumo Class

Design and construction

The Yugumo class was the ultimate refinement of the Special Type destroyer dating back to 1928. Essentially, the class was a repeat of the Kagero ships with a few minor improvements. The basic layout was unchanged, but displacement rose by some 45 tons and the hull was extended by a few feet.

The first 11 ships of the class were ordered as part of the 1939 program. Another 16 ships (referred to by the Japanese as the *Hamanami* group) were ordered as part of the 1941 program, but of these eight were canceled

Yugumo

The 19-unit Yugumo class was essentially a repeat of the Kagero class. The only major difference was the shape of the bridge structure. *Yugumo* has received some mid-war modifications. The amidships 25mm twin guns have been replaced by triple mounts, and a bandstand has been constructed forward of the bridge for a twin 25mm mount.

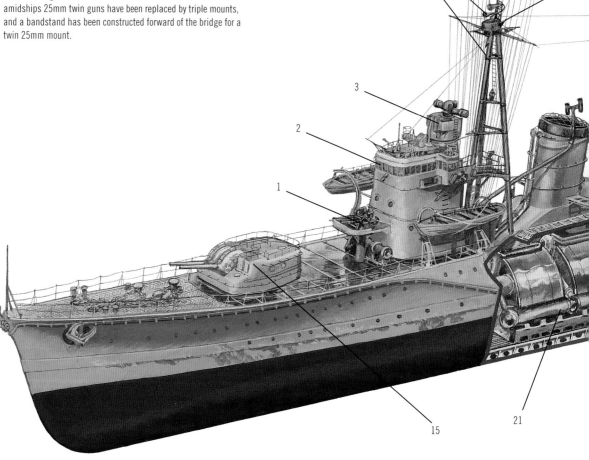

Key
1   Type 96 twin mount
2   Compass bridge
3   Main battery fire-control director and rangefinder
4   Foremast
5   No. 22 radar
6   Lookout post
7   Reloads for forward torpedo mount
8   Type 92 quadruple torpedo launcher (2)
9   Type 96 triple mount (2)
10 90cm searchlight
11 Radio direction finder
12 Type 14 2m range finder
13 Reloads for aft torpedo mount
14 Mainmast
15 Type D 5in gun mount (3)
16 Type 94 depth-charge projector
17 Paravane (2)
18 Drop stands for depth charges
19 Machinery room
20 Aft boiler room
21 Forward boiler room

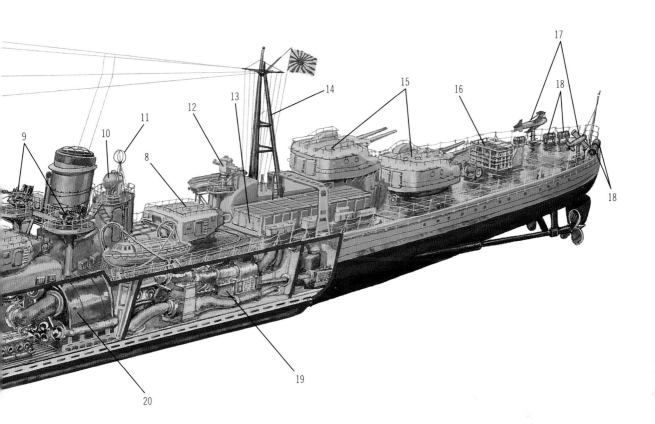

Yugumo Class Construction				
Ship	Built at	Laid down	Launched	Completed
Akishimo	Osaka by Fujinagata	5/3/43	12/5/43	3/11/44
Asashimo	Osaka by Fujinagata	1/21/43	7/18/43	11/27/43
Fujinami	Osaka by Fujinagata	8/25/42	4/20/43	7/31/43
Hamanami	Maizuru Navy Yard	4/28/42	4/18/43	10/15/43
Hayanami	Maizuru Navy Yard	1/15/42	12/19/42	7/31/43
Hayashimo	Maizuru Navy Yard	–	10/20/43	2/20/44
Kazegumo	Uraga	12/23/40	9/26/41	3/28/42
Kishinami	Uraga	8/29/42	8/19/43	12/3/43
Kiyonami	Uraga	10/15/41	8/17/42	1/25/43
Kiyoshimo	Uraga	3/16/43	2/29/44	5/16/44
Makigumo	Osaka by Fujinagata	12/23/40	11/5/41	3/14/42
Makinami	Maizuru Navy Yard	4/11/41	12/17/41	8/18/42
Naganami	Osaka by Fujinagata	4/5/41	3/5/42	6/30/42
Okinami	Maizuru Navy Yard	8/15/42	7/18/43	12/10/43
Onami	Osaka by Fujinagata	11/15/41	8/31/42	12/29/42
Suzunami	Uraga	3/27/42	3/12/43	7/27/43
Takanami	Uraga	5/29/41	3/16/42	8/31/42
Tamanami	Osaka by Fujinagata	3/16/42	12/20/42	3/30/43
Yugumo	Maizuru Navy Yard	6/12/40	3/16/41	12/5/41

before being started. Another eight ships were planned for the modified 1942 program, but these were also canceled.

The primary difference in appearance from the Kagero class was the shape of the bridge structure. On the Yugumo class, there was a forward slope on the front of the bridge structure, which was meant to reduce wind resistance and improve stability. Unlike the Kagero class, which was built in a standard fashion, the Yugumo class was built in three different yards and there were several minor differences between ships. There were actually three variants of the bridge structure (early, mid, and late production), two variants to the mainmast, and placement of the degaussing cable was evident in five different patterns depending on where the ship was built.

Armament and service modifications

The major difference in armament was the adoption of a new 5in twin mount known as Type D. This mount was capable of a maximum elevation of 75 degrees, making it more suitable for antiaircraft work. This is why units of the Yugumo class never had one of their aft 5in mounts removed in favor of additional 25mm mounts to increase antiaircraft protection. Though the increased elevation did make the Yugumo ships' 5in battery nominally capable of antiaircraft work, in fact the Type D was a poor dual-purpose mount, since it possessed slow elevation and tracking speeds and was unable to sustain high rates of fire.

As with the Asashio- and Kagero-class ships, as the war progressed, the antiaircraft fit of the Yugumo units was increased. Early units carried only two twin 25mm mounts forward of the aft stack. Surviving units and those completed later in the war had these replaced by two triple mounts and had a twin mount added forward of the bridge structure. Units surviving into 1944 had a second set of 25mm triple mounts added on a platform abaft the forward stack. Additionally, the six units surviving into 1944 received up to 12 single 25mm guns. *Kiyoshimo* also received a small number of single 13mm guns.

Other important changes included the addition in 1943 of No. 22 radar on the modified foremast. *Naganami* had its foremast modified to provide a platform for the radar. By 1944, surviving ships also received No. 13 radar usually mounted on the mainmast. However, *Kiyoshimo* had its No. 13 placed on the foremast above the No. 22 set. These ships began the war with paravanes on the stern, and a Type 94 double-sided projector and drop stands to deploy depth charges. Later in the war, the paravanes were removed and the number of depth charges carried was increased.

Wartime service

Yugumo-class ships were assigned to Destroyer Divisions 2, 10, 31, and 32. These were considered elite units and were always assigned to escort primary fleet units.

Akishimo joined the fleet in May 1944. It participated in the Battle of the Philippine Sea. In October, it was involved in the Battle of Leyte Gulf as part of Force "A," but played no role since it was assigned responsibility for picking up survivors and escorting cripples. It was sent to Manila in November to escort convoys to Leyte. During these operations, it suffered heavy damage from air attack on November 10 and was forced to return to Manila, where it was hit again by bombs on November 13 and sank the following day.

Asashimo joined the fleet in February 1944 and participated in the sinking of the American submarine *Trout* on February 29. It was involved in the Battle of the Philippine Sea. It participated in the Battle of Leyte Gulf as part of Force "A," but played no role as it was assigned to escort the heavy

cruiser *Takao* back to Singapore. It undertook two convoys to Leyte in November, surviving heavy air attack. It participated in the San Jose bombardment operation in December. It returned to Japan and was assigned to escort *Yamato* to Okinawa in April. It was sunk by an air attack with no survivors on April 7, 1945.

Fujinami began fleet operations in October 1943. It was struck by a dud torpedo on November 5 in Rabaul in an American carrier air attack. It conducted general escort operations in the Central Pacific until March 1944. It participated in the Battle of the Philippine Sea and was assigned to Force "A" for the Leyte operation. It suffered minor damage on October 24 in the Sibuyan Sea and the following day in the action off Samar. It scuttled the heavy cruiser *Chokai* during this action and rescued survivors. It was sunk by carrier air attack on October 27 and lost with all hands.

Hamanami began fleet service in December 1943. It participated in the Battle of the Philippine Sea. It was assigned to Force "A" for the Leyte operation but played no significant role in the October 25 action off Samar. It escorted troop convoys from Manila to Leyte and was sunk by American carrier aircraft in Ormoc Bay on November 11.

Hayanami commenced fleet operations in October 1943 and ventured as far south as Bougainville. It conducted general escort operations through June 1944 before being torpedoed and sunk by American submarine USS *Harder* on June 7 east of Borneo, with no survivors.

Hayashimo joined the fleet in May 1944. It participated in the Battle of the Philippine Sea. In October, it was involved in the Battle of Leyte Gulf as part of Force "A" and was struck by a carrier aircraft-launched torpedo on

October 26, settling in shallow water southeast of Mindoro. It was ultimately abandoned on November 12 after salvage efforts failed.

Kazegumo's first action was the Midway operation, during which it was assigned to the Kido Butai. It remained with the carriers for the battles of the Eastern Solomons and Santa Cruz during the Guadalcanal campaign. It conducted several missions to Guadalcanal, including the unsuccessful bombardment of Henderson Field on November 14. In February 1943, it participated in two of three evacuation missions to Guadalcanal. It was active in operations in the Central Solomons and forced to return to Japan in April after mine damage. It participated in the July evacuation of Kiska. It returned to the Solomons in September and took part in the Battle of Vella Lavella on the night of October 6–7 against American destroyers. In June 1944, it was assigned to take part in an abortive operation to move troops to Biak. It was sunk by the submarine USS *Hake* off Davao on June 8.

Kishinami was fully operational in February 1944. On February 29, it assisted in the sinking of the American submarine USS *Trout*. It participated in the Battle of the Philippine Sea. It was assigned to Force "A" for the Leyte operation and was damaged by air attack. It docked in Singapore in early November to repair damage from grounding. It was sunk by the American submarine USS *Flasher* on December 4, 1944, west of Palawan Island in the Philippines.

Kiyonami began operations in February 1943, performing general escort duties through June. On July 13, it participated in the Battle of Kolombangara, during which Japanese destroyer torpedoes crippled three Allied light cruisers and sank a destroyer. On July 20, while on a transport

Kiyoshimo on the day before its formal completion on May 15, 1944. The ship shows a late-war configuration, with a No. 22 radar on the foremast and one twin and four triple 25mm mounts. However, the No. 13 radar has not yet been fitted nor have any 25mm single guns. Note the paravanes on the fantail. (*Ships of the World* magazine)

Makigumo in March 1942 after completion. The Yugumo-class unit can be distinguished from early classes by the forward slope of the bridge structure, which is evident in this view. The ship had a brief career, being sunk in February 1943 by mines, but 237 of its crew were saved before the ship was scuttled by torpedoes from *Yugumo*. (Yamato Museum)

mission to Kolombangara, it was sunk by US Army Air Force B-25s with only a single crewman surviving.

Kiyoshimo joined the fleet in June 1944 and participated in the Battle of Leyte Gulf as part of Force "A." It was damaged in the Sibuyan Sea by air attack on October 24 and forced to return to Singapore for repairs. It was assigned to take part in the bombardment of the Allied beachhead at San Jose, where it was hit by two bombs from aircraft and finished off by PT boats on December 26, 1944.

Makigumo was assigned to escort the Kido Butai during the Midway operation and remained with the carriers during the Battle of the Eastern Solomons in August 1942. It conducted three transport runs to Guadalcanal in October and then participated in the Battle of Santa Cruz; during the battle it scuttled the crippled American carrier USS *Hornet*. It was involved in the unsuccessful bombardment of Henderson Field on November 14. Following a brief period in Japan for repairs, it participated in the first evacuation mission from Guadalcanal on February 1, 1943. It was sunk by a mine while trying to avoid an American PT boat attack, but almost all of the crew were saved.

Makinami was operational in September 1942 and immediately sent to support operations off Guadalcanal. It participated in two bombardments of Henderson Field in October and later took part in the Battle of Santa Cruz. In November, it escorted the unsuccessful troop convoy bound for Guadalcanal. On November 30, it participated in the Battle of Tassafaronga but did not launch any torpedoes because its decks were loaded with supply drums. It conducted three more supply runs to Guadalcanal and then led the first evacuation run to the island on February 1, 1943, during which it was damaged by air attack. In November 1943, it conducted a troop transport mission to Bougainville. It was sunk by American destroyer torpedoes and gunfire on November 25 during the Battle of Cape St George.

Naganami began fleet operations in September 1942 and was immediately sent to support operations off Guadalcanal. It participated in two bombardments of Henderson Field in October and later took part in the Battle of Santa Cruz. In November, it conducted a transport run to the island, during which it was damaged by air attack, and later it escorted an ill-fated troop convoy to the island in mid-November. On November 30, it participated in the Battle of Tassafaronga and was undamaged. It conducted three more supply runs to Guadalcanal into January 1943. Following a refit in Japan, it participated in the successful July 1943 evacuation from Kiska. It was involved in the Battle of Empress Augusta Bay on November 2, 1943; on November 11, it was heavily damaged by aircraft torpedo in Rabaul harbor and forced to return to Japan for repairs. Upon its return to service, it was assigned to Force "A" for the Leyte operation, but missed most of the battle after being assigned to escort the damaged heavy cruiser *Takao* to Singapore. In November, it was assigned to escort a convoy from Manila to Leyte, and was sunk by carrier air attack on November 11 in Ormoc Bay with heavy loss of life.

Okinami was fully operational in February 1944. It was temporarily assigned to the Biak transport operation in June before participating in the Battle of the Philippine Sea. It was part of Force "A" for the Leyte operation and suffered minor damage from air attack. It escorted a convoy from Manila to Leyte in early November, and then was damaged by air attack at Manila on November 5. It was sunk on November 13 by air attack in Manila Harbor.

Onami entered service in January 1943. It provided cover for the Guadalcanal evacuation in February. It was deployed to Rabaul in October and conducted reinforcement missions to Bougainville and Buka in the Northern Solomons. On November 25, it was sunk with all hands by at least two American destroyer-launched torpedoes at the Battle of Cape St George on another transport mission to Buka.

Suzunami began fleet operations in October 1943. It was sunk on November 11 in Rabaul harbor by a bomb hit from American carrier aircraft with heavy loss of life.

Takanami was assigned to support operations off Guadalcanal. In October 1942, it participated in two bombardments of Henderson Field and in the Battle of Santa Cruz. It escorted an unsuccessful troop convoy to Guadalcanal

Yugumo Class Specifications

Displacement: 2,077 tons standard
Dimensions: Length 391ft / beam 35.5ft / draft 12.33ft
Maximum speed: 35kt
Range: 5,000nm at 18kt
Crew: 228

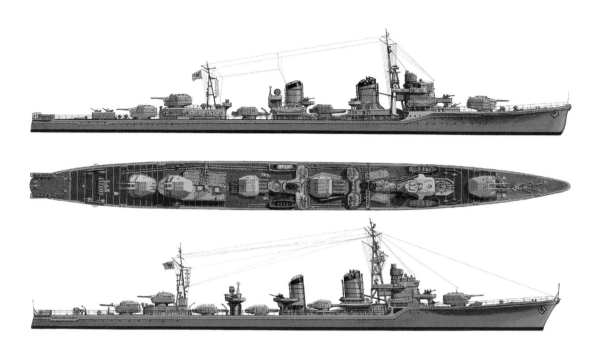

The top and middle plates show the Yugumo-class ship *Kishinami* as it appeared in October 1944. The forward slope of the bridge structure is evident, identifying it as a Yugumo-class unit. The bottom view is *Shimakaze* as it appeared in October 1944. Its configuration is similar to a Yugumo-class unit, but with additional length to allow the addition of a third torpedo launcher. All three of the mounts are quintuple, making it the only Japanese destroyer so equipped.

in mid-November. It played a key role in the Battle of Tassafaronga on November 30. Acting as a scout in advance of the Japanese destroyer force, it drew the bulk of American attention and gunfire, allowing other destroyers to launch torpedo attacks. Before it was sunk by American cruiser gunfire, *Takanami* was able to launch its torpedoes, which severely damaged the heavy cruisers *Minneapolis* and *New Orleans*.

Tamanami was fully operational in July 1943. It operated as far south as Rabaul in November. It conducted general escort duties in the Central Pacific until June 1944, when it participated in the Battle of the Philippine Sea. It was torpedoed on July 7, 1944 by the American submarine USS *Mingo* southwest of Manila, and sank with all hands.

Yugumo was the lead ship of the class. It was completed a couple of days before the attack on Pearl Harbor, but its first operation was not until the Battle of Midway in June 1942, when it was assigned to escort the Striking Force. It remained with the carriers in August at the Battle of the Eastern Solomons and in October at the Battle of Santa Cruz. It conducted several missions to Guadalcanal in November, including the unsuccessful bombardment on November 14. In February 1943, it participated in two of three evacuation missions from Guadalcanal. It was active in operations in the Central Solomons before returning to Japan in May. It participated in the July evacuation of Kiska in the Aleutians. It returned to the Solomons in

September and played a central role in the Battle of Vella Lavella on the night of October 6–7 against American destroyers. *Yugumo* aggressively engaged the American force, but in return was crippled by gunfire. However, its torpedo attack hit the destroyer USS *Chevalier*, which eventually sank. *Yugumo* was finished off by American destroyer gunfire and at least one torpedo.

Shimakaze

Design and construction

The ultimate expression of the heavy fleet destroyer in the mold of a large torpedo boat was the experimental *Shimakaze*. This ship was a prototype that carried an extraordinary torpedo fit and possessed a very high maximum speed. The design was known as the Type C destroyer and was part of the 1939 program.

This view shows *Shimakaze* under air attack on November 11, 1944. The destroyer was assigned to escort convoy TA No. 3 from Manila to Ormoc on Leyte. Approaching the port, the ship was crippled by near misses and drifted throughout the afternoon on fire until exploding. Clearly visible are the three torpedo launchers and the four triple 25mm mounts amidships. (*Ships of the World* magazine)

Shimakaze Construction				
Ship	**Built at**	**Laid down**	**Launched**	**Completed**
Shimakaze	Maizuru Navy Yard	8/8/41	7/18/42	4/30/43

Shimakaze Specifications

Displacement: 2,567 tons standard
Dimensions: Length 415ft / beam 36.75ft /
draft 13.5ft
Maximum speed: 39kt
Range: 5,800nm at 18kt
Crew: 267

The new Type C design was based on the Yugumo-class design, but to accommodate the addition of a third quintuple torpedo mount another 25ft of length was added. The cost in topweight for providing torpedo reloads was too great, so none were carried. To develop the very high speeds necessary to gain a tactical advantage in combat, new boilers and machinery were needed. The new boilers developed very high temperatures and pressure, which in turn developed 76,010shp. The ship received a new type of turbine, which generated 50 percent more power than typical turbines used in destroyers. On trials, it developed an impressive 79,240shp and a speed of 40.9 knots.

Such a complex design was impractical in the face of wartime losses, where expediency and simplicity were essential. Therefore, 16 additional Type C units under the 1942 program were canceled.

Armament and service modifications

Since its three quintuple mounts could be trained to either beam, *Shimakaze* had the largest torpedo broadside of any World War II destroyer. The main gun battery consisted of the usual six 5in guns in three Type D twin mounts, one forward and two aft. *Shimakaze* was launched in May 1943 with a No. 22 radar on the foremast, two triple 25mm mounts amidships, and a twin 13mm in front of the bridge.

In June 1944, it returned to Japan and received a typical mid-war modification. Another set of triple 25mm mounts, seven single 25mm, and one single 13mm gun were added. Also, a No. 13 radar was added to the leading edge of the mainmast.

Wartime service

For such a potentially extraordinary ship, *Shimakaze* had a very ordinary career. In an indication of how it was viewed by the Japanese, it was never directly assigned to a destroyer division but always to its squadron directly. It was one of the first destroyers to receive radar.

After joining the fleet in July 1943, its first action was during the second and successful evacuation mission to Kiska on July 29, during which it acted as flagship for the screening force. In June 1944, it was assigned as part of the abortive Biak transport operation, and then participated in the Battle of the Philippine Sea. Following refit in Japan, it was assigned to Force "A" and participated in the Battle of Leyte Gulf. In the action off Samar, it was unable to use its impressive torpedo battery since it was loaded with survivors from Japanese cruisers sunk earlier. Subsequently, it was assigned to escort convoys from Manila to Leyte. *Shimakaze* was sunk by carrier aircraft on November 11 in Ormoc Bay.

Akizuki Class

Design and construction

To complement the Type A destroyers, the Japanese envisioned another design built to act as antiaircraft screening units for carriers. As originally conceived, these destroyers (called Type B by the Japanese) were large enough to carry four twin mounts of the new Type 98 3.9in guns. To do so without creating topweight problems, the ships were some 700 tons larger and 50ft longer than the preceding Type A units. Not surprisingly, the Japanese decided to increase the Type B's offensive potential before the design was finalized by adding a single quadruple torpedo mount with four reloads. The final result was a fine multipurpose destroyer that the Japanese considered their most successful destroyer design.

The ship presented a very balanced and powerful appearance, making it the most handsome of Japanese destroyers. The four 3.9in mounts were placed in pairs fore and aft, with the Nos. 2 and 3 mounts in a superfiring position. The bridge structure was compact but tall enough to give a field of vision over the No. 2 mount. There was a

Type 98 3.9in Gun

Muzzle velocity: 3,378ft/sec
Rate of fire: 15 rounds per minute
Maximum range: 21,255yd (effective range 15,260yd)
Maximum elevation: 90 degrees
Shell weight: 28.6lb

Akizuki Class Construction				
Ship	Built at	Laid down	Launched	Completed
Akizuki	Maizuru Navy Yard	7/30/40	7/2/41	6/13/42
Fuyuzuki	Maizuru Navy Yard	5/8/43	1/20/44	5/25/44
Hanazuki	Maizuru Navy Yard	2/10/44	10/10/44	1/31/45
Harutsuki	Sasebo Navy Yard	12/23/43	8/3/44	12/28/44
Hatsuzuki	Maizuru Navy Yard	7/25/41	4/3/42	12/29/42
Natsuzuki	Sasebo Navy Yard	5/1/44	12/2/44	4/8/45
Niizuki	Nagasaki by Mitsubishi	12/8/41	6/29/42	3/31/43
Shimotsuki	Nagasaki by Mitsubishi	7/6/42	4/7/43	3/31/44
Suzutsuki	Nagasaki by Mitsubishi	3/15/41	3/4/42	12/20/42
Teruzuki	Nagasaki by Mitsubishi	11/13/40	11/21/41	8/31/42
Wakatsuki	Nagasaki by Mitsubishi	3/9/42	11/24/42	5/31/43
Yoizuki	Uraga	8/25/43	9/25/44	12/26/44

single-trunked stack for the three Kanpon boilers that drove the two turbines and produced 52,000shp, enough to propel the ship at a maximum speed of 33 knots. The layout of the machinery was changed so that there were two separate engine and boiler rooms in an effort to increase resistance to battle damage.

Six of this class were authorized in 1939 and another ten in 1941. Only one of the last four was even laid down before all were canceled. Later units in the class were completed to a simplified hull shape to decrease production time.

Since this class met all expectations, another slightly larger improved group of 16 ships was authorized in the 1942 program with another 22 ships to follow. All of these were canceled before construction started.

Armament and service modifications

The design centered on the Type 98 3.9in gun. Unlike previous 5in guns mounted on Japanese destroyers, this was a true dual-purpose gun. The gun proved excellent in service, combining reliability and a high rate of fire. Its range was actually superior to the standard American 5in destroyer gun. Specifications for the gun are provided below:

In order to engage aircraft effectively, the ships were fitted with the Type 94 fire-control director capable of tracking high-angle targets. As designed,

Arguably the best Japanese destroyer design was the Akizuki class. The top and middle plates are of *Teruzuki* as it appeared in 1942. The bottom view is of *Shimotsuki* as it appeared in October 1944. Among the many changes evident in this late-war configuration is the addition of two types of radars and an augmented antiaircraft fit.

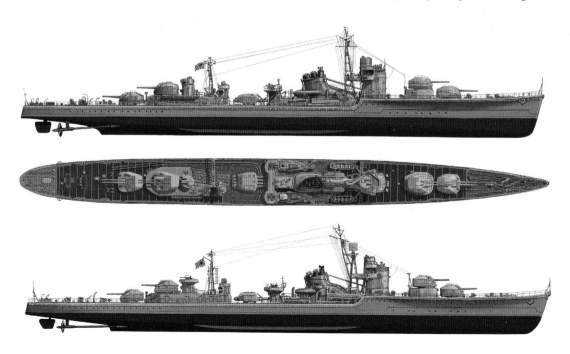

one director was envisioned for each set of forward and aft mounts. The forward fire-control director was placed above the bridge and the second aft on a small deckhouse. Production shortages of the Type 94 meant that the last five ships never received their second director aft, and eventually these were removed on all ships in favor of an additional triple 25mm mount.

The ship's primary offensive punch against surface targets was the standard Type 92 quadruple torpedo mounts capable of firing the Type 93 oxygen-propelled torpedo. Four reloads were also carried. For antisubmarine work, two Type 94 depth-charge projectors and 54 depth charges were originally fitted. Ships built later in the war were completed with stern rails and storage was increased to 72 depth charges.

In spite of the ship's mission to act as an antiaircraft ship, initial light antiaircraft weaponry was limited to an inadequate two twin 25mm mounts placed amidships. *Teruzuki* was the only ship not modified from this configuration, since it was lost in December 1942. As was the case for all other surviving Japanese destroyers, the antiaircraft fit of the Akizuki class was greatly strengthened as the war progressed. The twin mounts were replaced by triple 25mm mounts, and another pair of triple mounts was placed abreast the stack. As already mentioned, a fifth triple mount was added in place of the aft Type 94 director. The final upgrade, which took place in late 1944 or early 1945, added another set of 25mm triple mounts abreast the bridge for a total of seven triple mounts. In this configuration, 20 additional single 25mm guns were added for a total of 41 25mm barrels.

This view shows an Akizuki-class destroyer in an early-war configuration. Only six of the 12 units in the class were completed in time to play any role in operations before the final battles of 1944–45. (Naval History and Heritage Command)

At least five ships, *Fuyuzuki*, *Hanazuki*, *Natsuzuki*, *Suzutsuki*, and *Yoizuki*, were so configured. The four ships sunk in late 1944, *Akizuki*, *Hatsuzuki*, *Shimotsuki*, and *Wakatsuki*, were lost with five triple mounts and a varying number of single mounts (as high as 24 on *Hatsuzuki*). *Niizuki* was lost in 1943 with a total of four 25mm triple mounts.

All except *Akizuki* and *Teruzuki* were completed with a radar platform on the foremast. *Akizuki* and all ships completed mid-war received the No. 21 air-search radar. In addition to the No. 21 radar, destroyers completed in or surviving to 1944 received the No. 13 radar, which was fitted on the leading edge of the mainmast. The last five ships completed during the war replaced the outdated No. 21 radar on the radar platform with a later version of the No. 22 radar, which was maximized for surface search. These ships also received a second No. 13 radar on the foremast above the radar platform.

Wartime service

The Akizuki class made up Destroyer Divisions 41 and 61 and, as intended, were often assigned to carrier screening duty. Their large size also made them ideal flagships, and they were employed in several surface actions in this capacity.

Akizuki joined the fleet in June 1942 and participated in the Battle of the Eastern Solomons in August. In October, it was assigned to escort a

Harutsuki pictured in January 1945 after completion. The ship did not conduct any major operations before being surrendered to the Soviet Union. This beam view shows all the features of a late-war Akizuki-class configuration. Note the No. 22 radar on the foremast and a No. 13 radar on both the fore and mainmast. The ship carried seven triple 25mm mounts and at least 22 single 25mm guns. (Naval History and Heritage Command)

large convoy to Guadalcanal and suffered moderate damage on October 25. It was forced to return to Japan for repairs, but returned to Solomons operations by mid-January 1943. It was torpedoed by the submarine USS *Nautilus* on January 19 and again forced to return to Japan. It was heavily damaged on March 14 when its keel buckled upon departure from Saipan. It was towed ashore and beached, but was returned to service in October. It participated in the Battle of the Philippine Sea. It was assigned to the Northern Force for the Battle of Leyte Gulf and sunk by probable aircraft torpedo on October 25, with heavy loss of life.

Akizuki Class Specifications

Displacement: 2,701 tons standard; 3,700 tons full load
Dimensions: Length 440.33ft / beam 38ft / draft 13.5ft
Maximum speed: 33kt
Range: 5,000nm at 18kt
Crew: 290 (later rising to *c.*330)

Fuyuzuki was operational by June 1944. It was torpedoed by an American submarine on October 12 and suffered medium damage. It escorted the carrier *Junyo* to Manila in November; it then returned to Japan and escorted *Yamato* on its April 1945 mission to Okinawa. It survived the operation with only light damage. It suffered heavy damage from a mine after the war and was not repaired.

Hanazuki was operational by March 1945, but did not leave home waters. It was surrendered and turned over to the United States.

Harutsuki was operational by March 1945 but did not leave home waters. It was surrendered and turned over to the Soviet Union.

Hatsuzuki began fleet operations in March 1943 and was active as far south as Rabaul. It participated in the Battle of Philippine Sea in June 1944. It was assigned to the Northern Force during the Battle of Leyte Gulf. It was sunk by gunfire from four cruisers and several destroyers on October 25.

Natsuzuki hit a mine on June 16, 1945 after entering service. It was surrendered and turned over to Great Britain.

Niizuki began fleet operations in May 1943. On July 5, it led a destroyer transport run to Kolombangara in the Central Solomons. It launched part of an 11-mile torpedo strike (the longest of the war), which sank an American destroyer. The next day, it was sunk at the Battle of Kula Gulf by gunfire from three American cruisers, but by absorbing their attention it allowed other Japanese destroyers to launch torpedoes and sink a light cruiser.

Shimotsuki joined the fleet in June 1944 and participated in the Battle of the Philippine Sea. In October, it participated in the Battle of Leyte Gulf and suffered moderate damage from bomb near misses. It was sunk by three torpedoes from the submarine *Cavalla* after departing Singapore on November 25, with only 46 survivors.

Suzutsuki began fleet operations in March 1943 and conducted several missions to Rabaul through August. On January 16, 1944, it was hit by two submarine-launched torpedoes that blew off its bow and stern, killing 135 crewmen. It returned to service in October, but on October 16 it was again hit by a submarine torpedo and lost part of its bow. It was assigned to escort the superbattleship *Yamato* in April 1945. It was heavily damaged by air attack on April 7 and not fully repaired by the war's end.

Teruzuki's first action was at the carrier battle of Santa Cruz in October 1942, where it was slightly damaged by a bomb. It participated in the First Naval Battle of Guadalcanal on November 13, where it engaged several American ships; it damaged destroyer *Sterett*. It returned two nights later in the Second Naval Battle of Guadalcanal and engaged battleship *South Dakota*; *Teruzuki* was undamaged in both actions. It was sunk by an American PT boat torpedo off Guadalcanal on the night of December 11–12 after fires reached the ship's depth charges and created massive explosions.

Wakatsuki departed Japan in August 1943 for Truk, and participated in the Battle of Empress Augusta Bay off Bougainville Island on November 2. It was involved in the Battle of the Philippine Sea in June 1944 and later as part of the Northern Force during the Battle of Leyte Gulf in October. It was sunk by air attack near Ormoc, Leyte on November 11 with heavy loss of life.

Yoizuki was operational by May 1945, but did not leave home waters. It suffered light mine damage on June 5. It was surrendered and turned over to the Nationalist Chinese, and was scrapped in 1963.

Matsu/Tachibana Class

Design and construction

By 1942, the Japanese realized that heavy destroyer losses could not be made up by continuing the construction of large fleet units. The result was a design that was suitable for quick and massed production. This new class would be able to perform front-line transport duties, which would save the larger destroyers to operate with the fleet. Because these ships were envisioned as general escorts, their armament was on a reduced scale, as was their speed. Nevertheless, the Japanese still saw these units as capable of working with the main fleet if required. These ships have been called destroyer escorts and compared to their American counterparts, but in fact they were larger than American destroyer escorts and better armed.

The design of the new class, which came to be known as the Matsu class, stressed simplicity. This included the equipment on board, which was meant to be operated by crew members without the prewar level of training.

Matsu Class Construction				
Ship	Built at	Laid down	Launched	Completed
Hinoki	Yokosuka Navy Yard	3/4/44	7/4/44	9/30/44
Kaede	Yokosuka Navy Yard	3/4/44	7/25/44	10/30/44
Kashi	Osaka by Fujinagata	5/5/44	8/13/44	9/30/44
Kaya	Maizuru Navy Yard	4/10/44	7/30/44	9/30/44
Keyaki	Yokosuka Navy Yard	6/22/44	9/30/44	12/15/44
Kiri	Yokosuka Navy Yard	2/1/44	5/27/44	8/14/44
Kuwa	Osaka by Fujinagata	12/20/43	5/25/44	7/25/44
Maki	Maizuru Navy Yard	2/19/44	6/10/44	8/10/44
Matsu	Maizuru Navy Yard	8/8/43	2/3/44	4/28/44
Momi	Yokosuka Navy Yard	2/1/44	6/16/44	9/7/44
Momo	Maizuru Navy Yard	11/5/43	3/25/44	6/10/44
Nara	Osaka by Fujinagata	6/10/44	10/12/44	11/26/44
Sakura	Yokosuka Navy Yard	6/2/44	9/6/44	11/25/44
Sugi	Osaka by Fujinagata	2/25/44	7/3/44	8/25/44
Take	Yokosuka Navy Yard	10/25/43	3/28/44	6/16/44
Tsubaki	Maizuru Navy Yard	6/20/44	9/30/44	11/30/44
Ume	Osaka by Fujinagata	12/1/43	4/24/44	6/28/44
Yanagi	Osaka by Fujinagata	8/20/44	11/25/44	1/18/45

Whereas a Yugumo-class ship would take about a year to build, a Matsu-class destroyer could be completed in about six months.

Another area of simplicity was the machinery that could only develop 19,000shp, which translated to a top speed of just under 28 knots. It was thought that this would be sufficient for almost all required duties, but it was much less than previous destroyers, where speed was an area of design emphasis. The reduced length meant that only two boilers were fitted, and these were of a simpler design that did not operate at high temperatures and which drove less powerful turbines. One notable design feature was the separation of the boiler and the machinery rooms, so that a single hit could not knock out all propulsive power.

Twenty-eight units of the original design were ordered and work began in August 1943. In mid-1944, the last ten were canceled and replaced with a further simplified design known as the Tachibana class. The Japanese planned to build another 100 of the Tachibana units, but only another 13 were laid down until all construction was canceled in favor of special-attack units.

Tachibana Class Construction				
Ship *	Built at	Laid down	Launched	Completed
Enoki	Maizuru Navy Yard	10/14/44	1/27/45	3/31/45
Hagi	Yokosuka Navy Yard	9/11/44	11/27/44	3/1/45
Hatsuume	Maizuru Navy Yard	12/8/44	4/25/45	6/18/45
Hatsuzakura	Yokosuka Navy Yard	12/4/44	2/10/45	5/28/45
Kaba	Osaka by Fujinagata	10/15/44	2/27/45	5/29/45
Kaki	Yokosuka Navy Yard	10/5/44	12/11/44	3/5/45
Kusunoki	Yokosuka Navy Yard	11/9/44	1/18/45	4/28/45
Nashi	Kobe by Kawasaki	9/1/44	1/17/45	3/15/45
Nire	Maizuru Navy Yard	8/14/44	11/25/44	1/31/45
Odake	Maizuru Navy Yard	11/5/44	3/10/45	5/15/45
Shii	Maizuru Navy Yard	6/18/44	1/13/45	3/13/45
Sumire	Yokosuka Navy Yard	10/21/44	12/27/44	3/26/45
Tachibana	Yokosuka Navy Yard	7/8/44	10/14/44	1/20/45
Tsuta	Yokosuka Navy Yard	7/31/44	11/2/44	2/8/45

Azusa, Hishi, Katsura, Kuzu, Sakaki, Tochi, Wakazakura, Yadake, and *Yaezakura* were scrapped in various stages of construction.

The Tachibana class was even simpler, to facilitate quick production. The hull form was reduced to straight lines to avoid complex steel work and the bridge structure modified. Since the armament remained the same, the modified foremast (which combined the mast and separate radar tower on the Matsu class) became the primary distinguishing feature of the new class. Mild steel was used, which increased displacement by 50 tons.

Armament and service modifications

The Matsu class was well armed for a ship of its size. The primary offensive weapon was the quadruple torpedo launcher, but no reloads were carried. The main gun battery was changed from the 5in gun mounted on every destroyer since the Fubuki class to the Type 89 high-angle 5in gun that was the primary antiaircraft gun on larger ships. A single mount was fitted forward and provided with only a partial antispray shield, and a dual mount aft was provided with no protection at all. However, the effectiveness of the Type 89 in an antiaircraft role was reduced by the fact that there was no high-angle fire-control director provided in the design.

Antiaircraft weaponry was heavy, with early production units having four triple mounts and usually eight single 25mm guns. All units carried a No. 22 radar abaft of the bridge, and all except very early production ships were fitted with a No. 13 radar on the mainmast aft. Since the class was

designed to act as antisubmarine screening ships, the units carried a large depth-charge load that could be deployed by two Type 94 projectors, two stern racks, and four Type 3 depth-charge loading stands.

Since the class did not even start to reach the fleet until mid-1944, few modifications were conducted for the remainder of the war. By late 1944, the number of single 25mm guns was increased to 13, including one on centerline abaft the second stack. A No. 13 radar was added on the mainmast of those units not previously fitted with it. The Tachibana class, entering service in 1945, was launched with both radars and 13 single 25mm guns.

Later, as many as 19 single guns were fitted. One ship, *Take*, had provisions added on its stern to launch a single *kaiten*, or manned torpedo.

Several Matsu- and Tachibana-class destroyers shown after the war. In the foreground is the Tachibana-class ship *Kaba*, and behind it is an unidentified Matsu-class unit. An examination of *Kaba*'s hull lines shows them to be simplified compared to the adjacent Matsu-class unit in an effort to speed construction times. Note the different arrangements for mounting the No. 22 radar. (*Ships of the World* magazine)

Wartime service

Matsu class
Matsu-class ships made up Destroyer Divisions 43, 52, and 53. Given the time of their completion, few units saw extensive service beyond home waters.

Hinoki began a series of escort missions in October 1944, mostly in Philippine waters. On January 5, 1945, it departed Manila for Indochina, but was intercepted by an Allied force led by the American destroyer

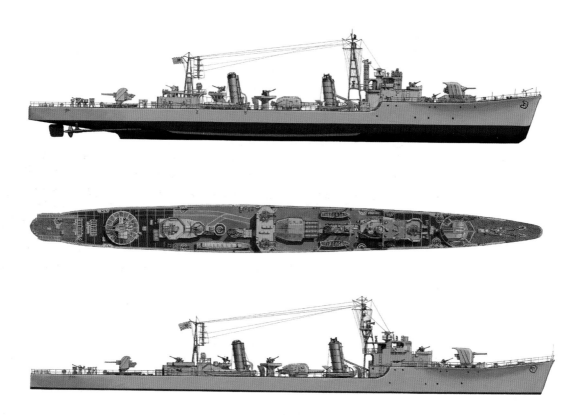

The subject of the top and middle plates is *Hinoki*. It is a Matsu-class unit and represents a late-war (October 1944) configuration. The bottom view is *Tachibana* as it appeared in January 1945 when completed. The primary visible difference between the two classes is the modified foremast; note the absence of a dedicated radar tower for the No. 22 radar on *Tachibana*.

Bennion. It was forced to turn back, and was damaged by air attack from American escort carriers. It attempted to depart Manila again on January 7, but was intercepted by four American destroyers, and sunk by gunfire with all hands.

Kaede began operations in January 1945 by escorting a convoy to Hong Kong. On January 31, it was damaged by air attack south of Formosa and forced to return to Japan. It was surrendered and turned over to China, but did not enter service.

Kashi was sent to southern waters in November 1944. It participated in the San Jose bombardment operation in December. It was damaged by carrier air attack in Formosa in January 1945 and again later in Kure on July 28. It was surrendered and handed over to the United States.

Kaya began a series of escort operations in November 1944; it participated in the San Jose bombardment in December. It returned to Japan and surrendered; it was handed over to the Soviet Union.

Keyaki did not leave home waters after entering service in March 1945. It surrendered, and was turned over to the United States and later expended as a target.

Kiri participated in the Battle of Leyte Gulf in October 1944, assigned to the Northern Force. Later it was active in the southern area on escort duty. It escorted a convoy to Leyte and suffered damage in an air attack on December 12. It returned to Japan and surrendered; it was turned over to the Soviet Union.

Kuwa participated in the Battle of Leyte Gulf as part of the Northern Force. It was sunk by American destroyer gunfire in Ormoc Bay off Leyte on December 3, 1944.

Maki participated in the Battle of Leyte Gulf as part of the Northern Force and was damaged by carrier air attack. It was damaged again by a submarine-launched torpedo in December. It spent the reminder of the war in home waters; it surrendered and was handed over to Great Britain.

Matsu was fully operational in July 1944. On a convoy escort mission to Chichi-jima, it was damaged by carrier aircraft and then sunk by destroyer gunfire on August 4, 1944.

Momi began a series of escort missions in October 1944, mostly in Philippine waters. On January 5, 1945, it departed Manila for Indochina, but was intercepted by an Allied force led by the American destroyer *Bennion*. It was forced to turn back, and was sunk by air attack from American escort carriers.

Momo entered service in July 1944. It operated primarily in Philippine waters from November until it was torpedoed and sunk off Luzon by the submarine *Hawkbill* on December 15.

Maki pictured in July 1944. It was completed with eight single 25mm guns but has not yet received its No. 13 radar. The ship was completed in time to participate in the Battle of Leyte Gulf, where it was damaged by a bomb hit and several near misses. In December 1944, it was struck by a torpedo and again survived, proving the toughness of its design. (*Ships of the World* magazine)

Matsu/Tachibana Class Specifications (as completed)

Displacement: 1,262 tons standard (*Tachibana* 1,289 tons)
Dimensions: Length 328ft / beam 30.5ft / draft 10.75ft
Maximum speed: 27.75kt
Range: 4,680nm at 16kt
Crew: 210

Nara was operational in March 1945; it was heavily damaged by a mine near Shimonoseki Strait on June 30 and not repaired by the war's end. It was surrendered and scrapped.

Sakura commenced operations in February 1945 by escorting a convoy to Formosa. It returned to Japan in March and was sunk in Osaka harbor on July 11 by a mine explosion that killed 130 of its crew.

Sugi participated in the Leyte operation assigned to the Northern Force. It escorted a convoy to Leyte and suffered damage in an air attack on December 7; it was part of the San Jose bombardment operation in late December. It returned to Japan and surrendered; it was turned over to China and served until 1957.

Take was the most successful ship of its class. It was active off Okinawa, Palau, and then the Philippines from mid-1944. On October 24, it assisted in the sinking of the American submarine *Shark II*. It escorted three convoys from Manila to Leyte in November–December 1944. It torpedoed and sank an American destroyer on its third mission. It returned to Japan, surrendered, and was turned over to Great Britain.

Tsubaki escorted a convoy to Shanghai in February 1945. It was damaged by a mine in Chinese waters on April 10. It returned to Japan and was damaged by a carrier air attack on July 24. It surrendered and was scrapped.

Ume was active, from October 1944, primarily in Philippine waters including the escort of one convoy from Manila to Leyte in December. It was sunk by air attack on January 31, 1945 off Luzon, with 77 killed.

Yunagi was operational in March 1945 and assigned patrol duties in northern Japanese waters. It was heavily damaged by air attack near Tsugaru Strait on July 14 and again by air attack on August 9. It surrendered and was scrapped.

Tachibana class

The Tachibana class was completed too late to see any service beyond home waters.

Enoki was sunk by a mine in shallow water on June 26, 1945.

Hagi was damaged by American carrier aircraft at Kure on July 24, 1945. It surrendered at the end of the war and was handed over to Great Britain.

Hatsuume was damaged by mine and air attack in home waters, but surrendered at the end of the war and was handed over to China, re-armed twice, and continued in service until the 1960s.

Hatsuzakura was the most "famous" Tachibana-class ship, since it met units of the US Third Fleet in Tokyo Bay on August 27, 1945 to make arrangements for the surrender ceremony on September 2. It surrendered and was handed over to the Soviet Union.

Kaba was damaged by air attack on Kure on July 24 and August 31. It surrendered at the end of the war and was handed over to the United States.

Kaki was damaged by air attack on Osaka on March 19. It surrendered at the end of the war and was handed over to the United States.

Kusunoki surrendered at the end of the war and was handed over to Great Britain.

Nashi was sunk by air attack near Kure on July 28, 1945. In 1955 the ship was refloated, and it was recommissioned into the Maritime Self Defense Force on May 31, 1956, the only IJN ship to see service in Japan's postwar navy. It remained in service until 1972 as a radar trials ship.

Nire was damaged by B-29 air attack at Kure on June 22. It surrendered at the end of the war and was scrapped in 1948.

Odake surrendered at the end of the war, was turned over the United States, and scrapped.

Shii was damaged by a mine in June 1945. It surrendered and was handed over to the Soviet Union.

Sumire surrendered and was handed over to Great Britain and expended as a target off Hong Kong in 1947.

Tachibana was sunk by American carrier aircraft off Hokkaido on July 14, 1945.

Tsuta surrendered and was handed over to China, but not put into service.

Tachibana-class destroyer *Hatsuzakura* pictured in August 27, 1945 when it met an American destroyer in Tokyo Bay to discuss the entry of the Third Fleet for the surrender ceremony. The austere design of the Tachibana class is evident. Note the distance between the two small stacks, which demonstrates the similar distance between the boiler rooms, in an attempt to reduce the possibility that a single hit could cripple all propulsive power. (Naval History and Heritage Command)

SUBMARINES

At the start of the Pacific War, the Imperial Japanese Navy had an impressive submarine force of 64 units. During the war, it commissioned another 126 large submarines. Nevertheless, the return on this investment for the Japanese was meager.

DEVELOPMENT OF THE JAPANESE SUBMARINE FORCE

The IJN's interest in submarines dates back to 1904. The first Japanese undersea craft were five Holland-class submarines built by the American Electric Boat Company. Soon thereafter, two additional boats were built to the same design in Japan. The Japanese submarine force continued to expand through the direct purchase of a number of units from Great Britain and France, complemented by licensed production of British and Italian designs.

As part of Japan's involvement in World War I, it received seven ex-German U-boats as reparations. In the area of submarine technology, the Germans were the standard-bearers of the day. The seven boats were studied intensely and provided the basis for the subsequent growth of the IJN's submarine force. In addition to the seven boats, several hundred German submarine designers, technicians, and former U-boat officers were brought to Japan under contract. However, by 1928, the German presence had dwindled, and the Japanese had become fully proficient in the design and construction of submarines.

World War I had shown the Japanese that the submarine was a key component of sea power. In particular, the Germans had demonstrated that

KD2 Type *I-52*, together with the KD1 Type boat *I-51*, was one of the prototypes for the IJN's long-range submarines. The large size and hull design gave excellent seakeeping characteristics. *I-52* served briefly during the war before being removed from service. (*Ships of the World* magazine)

the submarine was an ideal weapon as a commerce raider. Nevertheless, the Naval General Staff was more drawn to its potential use as an adjunct to the main battle fleet. Initially the IJN's submarine force was used as a defensive weapon focusing against the USN after it entered the western Pacific. In 1920 the first Submarine School was established in Kure, which greatly increased the level of training force-wide. Another important event was the arrival of Rear Admiral Nobumasa Suetsugu to command the First Submarine Division. He greatly improved the rigor and realism of training and began to devise tactics which would fold the submarine force into the IJN's overall attrition strategy against the USN. Construction of new submarines was molded to support his vision of far-ranging offensive submarines.

Following World War I, Japanese submarine construction emphasized large boats with great speed and range. The first large fleet type (*kaigun-dai*, abbreviated as *kaidai*) was based on a British design and could make 20 knots on the surface with a remarkable range of 20,000 nautical miles. However, this design was less than satisfactory due to engine problems and the Japanese turned to German submarine technology. Based on the German U-139, the Kaidai Type 2 (KD2) was launched in 1922. This design was successful, and served as the prototype for the IJN's concept of a series of fleet submarines built up until World War II.

Under a system established in 1924, Japanese submarines were placed into three classes. This was denoted by the first three Romanized letters in traditional Japanese syllabary – I, RO, and HA. I-boats were first-class or fleet submarines, RO-boats were second-class, somewhat smaller submarines, and HA boats were coastal units or midget submarines possessing limited range and displacement. Submarines were no longer numbered sequentially, but within the various types. After the outbreak of war, on May 20, 1942 a "1" was added in front of each boat's number. Later, new boats took the original numbers created by this measure.

The Japanese developed several types of I-boats. Generally, all fleet boats required a high surface speed and a large torpedo armament. Deck guns were also carried. Their large size was crucial to produce excellent seakeeping characteristics and, above all, range. In addition to the *kaidai*, there were several other types of I-boats. First was the *junsen* type or ocean-cruising submarine. These were designed for independent operations across the Pacific and Indian Oceans. Operational trials of the early I-boats demonstrated that it was not possible to combine the functions of squadron leader, scouting, and raiding into a single hull, as required to support the doctrine of the submarine force. This led to the design of three different

types to specialize in each role. A Types were designed as command submarines to coordinate the operations of a squadron of submarines and possessed long-range radio equipment; B Types were maximized as scouting submarines and equipped with floatplanes; C Types were designed for attack and had additional torpedo tubes. Later, during the war, D Type submarines were introduced as specially designed transport submarines.

The development of RO boats was largely ignored between the wars and never received much attention from the Naval General Staff. In 1924, the variety of small units then in service were designated RO. Thereafter, aside from a prototype designed in 1933 (see K5 Type, p.361), little was done to build RO boats until war appeared imminent. RO boats were designed for coastal operations and did not possess the range to operate across the distances of the Pacific.

The K6 was the standard Japanese medium submarine of the Pacific War. Though well designed, they suffered heavy losses for meager successes. *RO-46* was completed on February 11, 1944, and was sunk by USS *Sea Owl* (*SS-405*) off Wake Island on April 18, 1945. *RO-46* never even reported attacking the enemy. (*Ships of the World* magazine)

SUBMARINE WEAPONS

The IJN's torpedoes were renowned for their range and killing power. Contemporary Japanese torpedoes used pure oxygen instead of air, which gave them excellent range and speed and all but eliminated the conspicuous bubble track that made the torpedo easily visible. Another hallmark was their reliability. Unlike the USN, between the wars the IJN had thoroughly tested its torpedoes in a number of test shots against target ships. This paid off handsomely during the Pacific War.

21in Type 95 (1935) Torpedo Specifications

Weight: 3,671lb
Length: 23.5ft
Explosive charge: 891lb
Ranges: 9,850yd at 49–51kt; 13,100yd at 45–47kt

21in Type 89 (1929) Torpedo Specifications

Weight: 3,677lb
Length: 23.5ft
Explosive charge: 661lb
Ranges: 6,000yd at 45kt; 6,550yd at 43kt; 10,900yd at 35kt

The best Japanese submarine torpedo was the 21in Type 95, which was designed in 1935 and entered production in 1938, with 2,200 being produced. An updated version (Model 2), introduced in 1943, utilized a shorter oxygen vessel, reducing its maximum range to 8,200 yards but possessed a longer warhead with a larger explosive charge of 1,210lb.

Not all submarine torpedoes were oxygen propelled. A number of other torpedoes were used including the Type 96 enriched air and the Type 92 electric, and also, during the first part of the war, a number of older torpedoes, which were propelled by a mix of kerosene fuel and compressed air. The most important older torpedo was the Type 89.

In addition to their torpedo armament, almost all I and RO boat classes were equipped with deck guns. These were intended for use against merchant ships in situations where it

was not necessary or worth expending a torpedo and for self-defense against escorts. During the war, four different types of deck gun were carried by Japanese submarines. The standard deck gun for larger I-boats was the 5.5in gun, which dated from 1922. The Type 88 3.9in gun, introduced in 1928, was fitted on board the KD5 boats but did not see widespread service. Most of the KD Type boats carried the larger 4.7in gun introduced in 1922. The smallest deck gun entering service was the 3in, which was fitted on some units of the KD6 class and all RO boats.

Above: A 3.9in gun fitted forward on the KD5 Type submarine *I-69*. It could be employed against surface targets or as an antiaircraft weapon, and could fire up to 12 rounds per minute. (*Ships of the World* magazine)

Opposite: Introduced in 1922, the 5.5in gun was the standard deck gun on larger I-boats. The gun weighed almost 8.5 tons. It was hand-operated and could fire 5 rounds per minute. (Naval History and Heritage Command)

Submarine Deck Gun Specifications		
Weapon	Maximum range	Shell weight
11th Year Type 5.5in/40cal	17,500yd	83.8lb
11th Year Type 4.7in/45cal	17,500yd	45lb
Type 88 3.9in/50cal	17,700yd	28.7lb
Type 88 3in/40cal	11,800yd	13.2lb

SUBMARINE AIRCRAFT

A peculiar aspect of the IJN's submarine force was its heavy use of aircraft launched from submarines. Other navies experimented with this, but only the Japanese pursued it with such energy. This expanded the scouting range of the submarine and, in theory, permitted the submarine to reconnoiter enemy ships, even in port. Experiments with operating aircraft from submarines began in 1923, and in 1925 the first aircraft was flown off a KRS Type submarine. The first wholly Japanese-designed seaplane to operate from submarines was the E9W1 Submarine Reconnaissance Seaplane, which entered service in 1935.

The most used submarine-launched aircraft in naval history was the E14Y1 (codenamed "Glen" by the Allies). The E14Y1 was a low-wing monoplane with two small floats, and possessed a range of 560 miles and a top speed of 153mph. The aircraft remained in production until 1943; 138 were built. Space was provided for two crewmen, a pilot, and an observer. Two 66lb bombs could be carried.

The components for the E14Y1 could be stored in the submarine's small hangar and could be assembled within 15 minutes from the time the submarine surfaced. With experience, the crew could cut this time to just over 6 minutes. Launching was accomplished by a pneumatic catapult. Recovery was performed by landing in the water near the submarine and having a collapsible crane bring the aircraft aboard for it to be dismantled and stowed in the watertight hangar.

The follow-on to the E14Y1 was the M6A1 Seiran floatplane. Built to operate off AM and STo Type boats, the Seiran was intended to be used not in a reconnaissance role, but as an attack aircraft. The project was undertaken in the utmost secrecy as the success of the entire concept depended on surprise. The aircraft would possess sufficient speed to evade interception and sufficient range to strike targets well inland without giving away the location of the launching submarine.

The Seiran was stowed as a whole aircraft. Provisions were made to warm the engine in its hangar while the submarine was submerged. When the host submarine surfaced, the aircraft could be prepared for launch without its floats in 4.5 minutes, with another 2.5 minutes to fit the floats. Weapons load was one 1,874lb aircraft torpedo, one 1,764lb bomb, or two 550lb bombs.

Series production began in 1944, but was hampered by earthquakes and American bombing. By March 1945, production was stopped and only 14 Seirans were delivered. These Seirans were en route to their first target when the war ended.

SUBMARINE RADAR

One of the IJN's foremost shortcomings during the Pacific War was its failure to develop radar. This had a crippling effect operationally on its submarine force. The lack of an air warning radar on Japanese submarines increased their vulnerability to air attack, especially at night. This was crucial given the already excessive diving times of Japanese submarines. The No. 13 radar was the standard Japanese air-search radar for submarines; however, it was not until April 1944 that this bulky radar was adapted to submarine use. To detect Allied radar, Japanese submarines also employed passive measures. The E27/Type 3 radar detector was introduced well before the Japanese fitted radar to submarines; however, its reliability was suspect. Additionally, late-war Japanese submarines had their hulls and conning towers covered by an antiradar hull coating designated "LI."

The standard surface-search radar was the No. 22. On most submarines, the No. 22 was mounted in front of the conning tower. Theoretical performance of the radar was reduced when placed on a submarine where the set was mounted fairly low to the water.

I SERIES SUBMARINES

KD2 Type

This unit, along with the KD1 Type (*I-51*, scrapped in 1941), was the prototype for the large I-boat designs, which were to become standard for the IJN's submarine force. The design was based on the German *U-139*. After completion in May 1925, it was used in a series of exercises to judge the suitability of the *kaidai*-type large submarines. Five more planned units were canceled following the Washington Naval Treaty.

Armament

Eight 21in torpedo tubes, six bow and two stern; 16 torpedoes; one 4.7in and one 3in deck gun.

Wartime service

I-52 began the war assigned to training duties, until removed from service in July 1942. The hulk was scrapped after the war.

KD2 Type Specifications

Units in class: 1 (*I-52*, changed to *I-152* on May 20, 1942)
Displacement: 1,500 tons surfaced; 2,500 tons submerged
Dimensions: Length 330.75ft / beam 25ft / draft 16.75ft
Machinery: Two diesels with 6,800shp driving two shafts; electric motors with 2,000shp
Maximum speed: 22kt surfaced; 10kt submerged
Range: 10,000nm at 10kt surfaced; 100nm at 4kt submerged
Operating depth: 75ft
Crew: 60

KRS Type Specifications

Units in class: 4 (*I-21* to *I-24* [later *I-121* to *I-124*])
Displacement: 1,383 tons surfaced; 1,768 tons submerged
Dimensions: Length 279.5ft / beam 24.5ft / draft 14.5ft
Machinery: Two diesels with 2,400shp driving two shafts; motors with 1,100shp
Maximum speed: 14.5kt surfaced; 7kt submerged
Range: 10,500nm at 8kt surfaced; 40nm at 4.5kt submerged
Operating depth: 200ft
Crew: 75

KRS Type

These boats were designated large submarine-minelayers and were based on the German U-125/UE II class. They were completed in 1927–28 and were the only dedicated submarine-minelayers put into service by the IJN. Up to 42 mines could be carried in the two mine shafts fitted aft of the conning tower. In 1940, all four were fitted with aviation fuel tanks to refuel flying boats. They maintained their minelaying capabilities.

Armament

Four 21in bow torpedo tubes; 12 torpedoes; one 5.5in deck gun.

Wartime service

During the initial phase of the war all four units were active as minelayers in the East Indies, off the Philippines, and off Australia. The mines laid by *I-124* sank two merchants; *I-124* also scored the only other success of the class when it torpedoed a third freighter. An attempt to use their aviation supply capabilities in May 1942 before the Battle of Midway to refuel H8K flying boats from the French Frigate Shoals came to naught. *I-123* and *I-124* were sunk by Allied surface ships, and the surviving two units were assigned to the training squadron in 1943. *I-122* was later sunk in the Sea of Japan by a US submarine.

J1 Type Specifications

Units in class: 4 (*I-1* to *I-4*)
Displacement: 2,135 tons surfaced; 2,791 tons submerged
Dimensions: Length 320ft / beam 30.25ft / draft 16.5ft
Machinery: Two diesels with 6,000shp driving two shafts; electric motors with 2,600shp
Maximum speed: 18kt surfaced; 8kt submerged
Range: 24,000nm at 10kt surfaced; 60nm at 3kt submerged
Operating depth: 265ft
Crew: 68

J1 Type

These were the first boats of the *junsen* (cruiser) type. As such, they were designed for independent raiding operations or long-range reconnaissance ahead of the battle fleet. To accomplish this they possessed an endurance of 60 days, combined with a high surface speed and a very long range. *I-1* conducted a test cruise of 25,000 miles, thus validating the class concept, at least from a design standpoint. Three were completed in 1926 and the last in 1929. Overall, the *junsen* type proved to be a limited success. The large hull required for long range gave them excellent seakeeping qualities on the surface, but made for limited maneuverability when submerged,

and greatly increased their diving time. In practice during the war, the boats were used not in their intended independent long-range cruiser role, but as normal attack boats. In late 1942, two ships of the class were modified into transports. This entailed the removal of the after 5.5in gun, a reduction in the number of torpedo reloads, and provisions for carrying a 46ft (14m) landing craft or cargo rafts.

I-2 was one of the four boats of the J1 Type. These units were obsolescent at the start of the war, but still saw extensive service. *I-2* was lost on April 7, 1944 off New Ireland to the destroyer USS *Saufley* (*DD-465*). (*Ships of the World* magazine)

Armament
Six 21in torpedo tubes, four bow and two stern; 20 torpedoes; two 5.5in deck guns.

Wartime service
During the initial phase of the war all four units were deployed off Hawaii, where the Japanese hoped the Pearl Harbor raid would force US naval units to sea to be picked off by submarines. The class was also active in the Indian Ocean during early 1942 and later in the Aleutians. At least two of the boats (*I-1* and *I-3*) were modified into transports. All four were turned to supply duties by late 1942 and all were sunk in this capacity. *I-3* was destroyed in December 1942 by US PT boats off Guadalcanal; *I-4* followed later that same month, destroyed by a US submarine; *I-1* was sunk off Guadalcanal in January 1943 by New Zealand surface forces; *I-2* survived until April 1944 when it was destroyed by US destroyers. The four submarines accounted for five confirmed merchant ships.

J1M Type

This single-boat class was nearly identical to the J1 Type, but with provision for an aircraft. When completed in 1932, it was the first Japanese submarine designed to handle an aircraft, but these facilities proved unsuccessful in service. The aircraft components were stored in two watertight cylinders fitted port and starboard aft of the conning tower. Sources conflict on whether a catapult was fitted, but photographic evidence suggests that one was provided. However, the hangar arrangement required excessive time to assemble the aircraft and by 1940 the aircraft-handling equipment was replaced by a second 5.5in deck gun.

J1M Type Specifications

Units in class: 1 (*I-5*)
Displacement: 2,243 tons surfaced; 2,921 tons submerged
Dimensions: Length 320ft / beam 30.25ft / draft 16.5ftin
Machinery: Two diesels with 6,000shp driving two shafts; electric motors with ,600shp
Maximum speed: 18kt surfaced; 8kt submerged
Range: 24,000nm at 10kt surfaced; 60nm at 3kt submerged
Operating depth: 260ft
Crew: 80

Armament

Six 21in bow torpedo tubes and 20 torpedoes; one (later two) 5.5in deck guns; one floatplane (until 1940).

Wartime service

I-5 was deployed off Hawaii during the initial stages of the war, but, like almost all of its sister ships, never engaged a target. It was then sent to the Indian Ocean during early 1942, again with no success. Highlights of its 1943 service included supply missions in the Solomons and assisting in the evacuation of the Japanese garrison from Kiska Island in the Aleutians. The boat failed to score a single success before it was sunk off Saipan in the Marianas in July 1944 by US surface ships.

J2 Type Specifications

Units in class: 1 (*I-6*)
Displacement: 2,243 tons surfaced; 3,061 tons submerged
Dimensions: Length 323ft / beam 29ft 9in / draft 17ft 6in
Machinery: Two diesels with 8,000shp driving two shafts; electric motors with 2,600shp
Maximum speed: 20kt surfaced; 7.5kt submerged
Range: 20,000nm at 10kt surfaced; 60nm at 3kt submerged
Operating depth: 265ft
Crew: 80

J2 Type

This single-boat class was generally completed to the same pattern as *I-5*. This included the awkward aircraft-handling arrangement that launched the aircraft against the boat's forward movement. *I-6* was completed in 1935 with more powerful diesel engines that translated into a higher surface speed at the expense of range.

Armament

Six 21in torpedo tubes, four bow and two stern, and 17 torpedoes; one 5in deck gun, one 13mm machine gun; one floatplane.

Wartime service

I-6 was the most successful of the *junsen* type submarines. On January 11, 1942, 500 miles southwest of Oahu, it sighted and hit carrier *Saratoga* with a Type 89 torpedo. The resulting damage put the carrier out of the war for six months. When deployed to the Indian Ocean in April 1942, it sank two British merchants. After laying German acoustic mines off Brisbane, Australia, it joined its sister ships in running supplies to New Guinea, making nine runs to Lae. Subsequently, it participated in the evacuation of Kiska and then resumed supply duties in the New Guinea and New Britain area. *I-6* was sunk when rammed by a Japanese merchant ship as it surfaced near a Japanese convoy on July 16, 1944.

Below: *I-6* was one of the first Japanese submarines equipped to handle aircraft. The two cylinders aft of the conning tower provided stowage. Assembly and recovery of the aircraft were assisted by the crane. *I-6* was lost with its crew on June 16, 1944, in a collision with a Japanese merchant ship. (*Ships of the World* magazine)

J3 Type

These two boats were the largest Japanese submarines built prior to the Pacific War. Though typed as *junsen*, they were developed from the KD3 and KD4 types, as shown by the design of their conning tower. Their great size made them suitable for squadron commander units. In many respects, these were the ultimate development of the cruiser type boat, with a high surface speed, great endurance, and the retention of a floatplane and aircraft facilities. The two units were completed in 1937 and 1938.

Armament

Six 21in bow torpedo tubes and 20 torpedoes; one 5.5in deck gun, two twin and one single 13mm machine gun; one floatplane.

J3 Type Specifications

Units in class: 2 (*I-7, I-8*)
Displacement: 2,525 tons surfaced; 3,583 tons submerged
Dimensions: Length 358.5ft / beam 29.75ft / draft 17.25ft
Machinery: Two diesels with 11,200shp driving two shafts; electric motors with 2,800shp
Maximum speed: 23kt surfaced; 8kt submerged
Range: 14,000nm at 16kt surfaced; 60nm at 3kt submerged
Operating depth: 330ft
Crew: 80

In early 1943, both boats had their twin 13mm mounts replaced by a twin 25mm gun. Also in 1943, *I-8* had its single 5.5in gun replaced by a twin 5.5in mount, the only time a Japanese submarine was fitted with this weapon. In 1944, *I-8* had its catapult and hangar removed and was fitted with mountings for four *kaiten*s.

Wartime service

Both units were deployed off Hawaii at the start of the war. *I-7* launched its E9W1 floatplane to reconnoiter Pearl Harbor on December 17. Later, *I-7* was moved into the Indian Ocean where it sank a merchant ship. After sinking another merchant in the Aleutians, *I-7* participated in the evacuation of Kiska. It was sunk in July 1943 off Kiska by US destroyers following its last visit. *I-8* had a long and varied career. After operating off Hawaii, it was engaged in making supply runs to Guadalcanal. In June 1943, it commenced

The *junsen* (cruiser) boats were designed for long-range independent operations, with emphasis on range and sea keeping. The top profile shows the J1 Type boat *I-1*. The ultimate development of the *junsen* boats was the J3 Type. *I-8*, shown in the middle profile, retained a heavy armament and added the capability to handle aircraft. A derivative of the J3 Type was the larger A1 Type. Shown in the bottom profile is *I-9*.

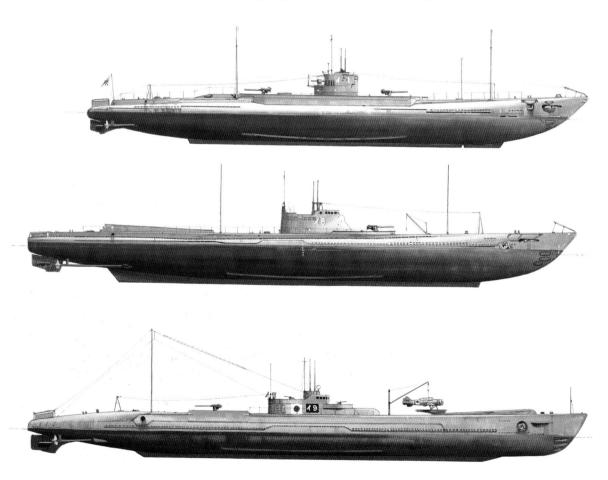

the second trip by an IJN submarine to Europe, arriving in Brest, occupied France, on August 31, 1943. It departed on October 5 with a load of German war technology. Its return to Kure on December 21, 1943 completed a voyage of 30,000 miles. This was the only successful round-trip voyage by a Japanese submarine during the war. In 1944, its sinking of a Dutch freighter in the Indian Ocean was followed by an atrocity in which 98 crew and passengers were killed on the submarine's deck. Two more British merchants were sunk, and in July 1944, when *I-8* sank a US Liberty ship, the massacre of the crew was repeated. *I-8* was sunk off Okinawa by US destroyers in March 1945.

I-8, mid-war, with its dual 5.5in deck gun mounted forward of its conning tower. This was apparently fitted for its trip to Europe. *I-8* was lost on March 31, 1945 off Okinawa to destroyer USS *Morrison* (*DD-560*), with the loss of all hands. (*Ships of the World* magazine)

KD3A/B Types

These ships were derived from the KD2 design with a continued emphasis on surface speed and long range. The four KD3A units differed from the five KD3B variants by the shape of their bow and the configuration of their conning sail. These boats were completed between 1927 and 1930 and were reaching the end of their service lives by the onset of war.

Armament

Eight 21in bow torpedo tubes and 16 torpedoes; one 4.7in deck gun. No aircraft facilities were fitted. In 1945, four boats (*I-156*, *I-157*, *I-158*, and *I-159*) were fitted to carry two *kaiten*s.

Wartime service

I-63 was sunk by collision with *I-60* in 1939. The remaining units were very active early in the war, but from March 1942 all surviving boats were assigned as training assets and removed from active duty. The boats were assigned to support the invasion of the Dutch East Indies where they were fairly

KD3A/B Type Specifications

Units in class: 9 (*I-53* to *I-59* [later *I-153* to *I-159*], *I-60*, *I-63*)
Displacement: 1,800 tons surfaced; 2,300 tons submerged
Dimensions: Length 330ft (*I-56*, *I-57*, *I-59*, *I-60*, *I-63*: 331.33ft) / beam 26ft / draft 15.75ft (*I-56*, *I-57*, *I-59*, *I-60*, *I-63*16ft)
Machinery: Two diesels with 6,800shp driving two shafts; electric motors with 1,800shp
Maximum speed: 20kt surfaced; 8kt submerged
Range: 10,000nm at 10kt surfaced; 90nm at 3kt submerged
Operating depth: 200ft
Crew: 60

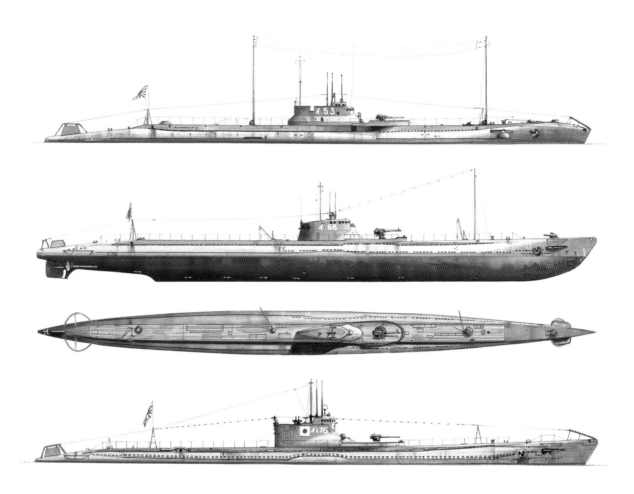

The Kaidai (KD) Type submarines were designed as long-range fleet submarines to operate in squadrons in support of the IJN's surface forces. The top profile shows the lead unit of the KD3A Type, *I-153*. The middle profile shows the next large class of KD boats, the eight-unit KD6 class. These boats were longer and fitted with more powerful machinery than their predecessors, making them the ultimate development of the KD design philosophy, which emphasized range and speed. The bottom profile depicts *I-176*, a member of the KD7 class.

successful, sinking 18 confirmed ships. One ship, *I-58*, sighted the RN's Force Z on December 10 in the South China Sea and launched an unsuccessful torpedo attack. *I-60* was sunk in January 1942 by a British destroyer. The remaining units were involved in the Midway operation and later in the Aleutians. After being assigned to training duties, *I-153* and *I-154* were laid up in January 1944. The other boats continued training duties until the war's end.

KD4 Type

These boats were slightly smaller than the KD3A/B, but otherwise were very similar. The number of torpedo tubes was reduced. One boat was completed in 1929 and the other two in 1930.

Armament

Six 21in torpedo tubes (four bow and two stern) and 14 torpedoes; one 4.7in deck gun. No aircraft facilities were fitted. In 1945, *I-162* had its deck gun removed and was fitted for five *kaiten*s.

Wartime service

I-61 was lost before the war by collision in October 1941. *I-162* spent most of its career in the Dutch East Indies and the Indian Ocean and had success sinking five ships and damaging five more. It returned to home waters in early 1944 where it remained until the war's end. *I-164* also experienced success in the Indian Ocean, sinking five ships early in the war. It was sunk by a US submarine off Japan in May 1942.

> ### KD4 Type Specifications
>
> **Units in class:** 3 (*I-61*, *I-62* [later *I-162*], *I-64* [later *I-164*])
> **Displacement:** 1,720 tons surfaced; 2,300 tons submerged
> **Dimensions:** Length 320.5ft / beam 25.5ft / draft 15.75ft
> **Machinery:** Two diesels with 6,000shp driving two shafts; electric motors with 1,800shp
> **Maximum speed:** 20kt surfaced; 8.5kt submerged
> **Range:** 10,800nm at 10kt surfaced; 60nm at 3kt submerged
> **Operating depth:** 200ft
> **Crew:** 60

KD5 Type

These boats had essentially the same dimensions as the KD4 class, but were slightly heavier due to greater structural strength, which translated into a greater diving depth. All were completed in 1932.

Armament

Six 21in bow torpedo tubes and 14 torpedoes; this class introduced the 3.9in antiaircraft gun, and a 13mm machine gun was added to the aft end of the sail. No aircraft facilities were fitted. In 1945, *I-165* had its deck gun removed and it was fitted to carry two *kaiten*s.

> ### KD5 Type Specifications
>
> **Units in class:** 3 (*I-65* [later *I-165*], *I-66* [later *I-166*], *I-67*)
> **Displacement:** 1,705 tons surfaced; 2,330 tons submerged
> **Dimensions:** Length 320.5ft / beam 26.75ft / draft 15.5ft
> **Machinery:** Two diesels with 6,000shp driving two shafts; electric motors with 1,800shp
> **Maximum speed:** 20.5kt surfaced; 8.25kt submerged
> **Range:** 10,000nm at 10kt surfaced; 60nm at 3kt submerged
> **Operating depth:** 230ft
> **Crew:** 75

Wartime service

I-67 was lost before the war. On its second war cruise in the Indian Ocean, *I-165* sank two ships, followed by three more on its next cruise. After participating in the Midway operation, it returned to the Indian Ocean to sink another five ships, massacring the survivors of one by machine-gun fire. After being converted to carry *kaitens*, it was sunk in 1945 off the Marianas by air attack. *I-166* had a similar career, operating primarily in the Indian Ocean, where it sank six merchants. It was the first Japanese submarine to sink another submarine, when in December 1941 it sank a Dutch boat off Borneo. It survived until July 1944 when a British submarine torpedoed it in the Strait of Malacca.

KD6A/B Types

Longer and fitted with more powerful diesels, these boats could achieve 23 knots surfaced, the highest surface speed of any submarine in the mid-1930s. The KD6B variant was slightly longer and weighed some 25 extra tons which provided an increased diving depth to 278ft. All eight boats were completed between 1934 and 1938. In 1942–43, *I-172* and apparently *I-171* and *I-174* were converted into cargo carriers by removing the deck gun and a number of torpedo reloads. At least *I-172* could carry a 46ft *daihatsu* landing craft in addition to internal and deck cargo.

Armament

Six 21in bow torpedo tubes and 14 torpedoes. The first three boats carried the 3in gun; the last five mounted a 4.7in deck gun. All boats were also equipped with a 13mm machine gun (except *I-174* and *I-175*, which mounted two).

Wartime service

This class scored some major successes, but the loss of all eight boats showed the futility of using large submarines to attack heavily defended US fleet targets. All eight units were deployed to support the Pearl Harbor operation, where *I-70* became the first Japanese submarine lost during the war, on December 10, when it was bombed by carrier aircraft. The class was also active during the Midway operation, when *I-168* scored the biggest Japanese submarine success of the war when it

KD6A/B Type Specifications

Units in class: 8 (KDB6A: *I-68* [later *I-168*], *I-69* [later *I-169*], *I-70*, *I-71* [later *I-171*], *I-72* [later *I-172*], *I-73*; KD6B: *I-74* [later *I-174*], *I-75* [later *I-175*])

Displacement: 1,785 tons surfaced; 2,440 tons submerged

Dimensions: Length 343.5ft (KD6B 344.5ft) / beam 27ft / draft 15ft

Machinery: Two diesels with 9,000shp driving two shafts; electric motors with 1,800shp

Maximum speed: 23kt surfaced; 8.25kt submerged

Range: 14,000nm at 10kt surfaced (KD6B 10,000nm at 16kt); 65nm at 3kt submerged

Operating depth: 245ft

Crew: 70

torpedoed and sank the already damaged fleet carrier *Yorktown*, and a destroyer off Midway on June 6. Later, the KD6 boats participated in the evacuation of Kiska and supply missions in the Solomons. *I-175* scored the other major KD6 success when it responded to the US invasion of the Gilbert Islands in November 1943 and sank the escort carrier *Liscome Bay*. Other ships sunk by this class included a fleet oiler and five merchants. *I-172* and *I-173* were 1942 losses to unknown causes and a US submarine, respectively. *I-168* was lost to US submarine attack in 1943. The final four boats were lost in 1944, two to surface forces and one to air attack, while *I-169* was lost in a diving accident at Truk.

Below: The final development of the KD Type was the KD7. Unlike their KD sisters, the KD7s were only medium-range submarines. After serving unsuccessfully as an attack submarine, *I-176*, shown here, was converted to the transport role by the removal of its 4.7in gun and the addition of fittings for a landing craft. (Kure Maritime Museum)

KD7 Type

This class was the ultimate development of the *kaidai* type and was the largest single class of its type. They were essentially repeats of the KD6 Type with less surface range. Ordered in 1939, the first boat did not enter service until August 1942 and the last was not completed until September 1943. Ten additional boats requested in the 1942 building program were canceled. In 1942–43, *I-176*, *I-177*, and *I-181* were converted for cargo duty with the removal of the forward deck gun and the addition of fittings for a 46ft *daihatsu*.

Armament
Six 21in bow torpedo tubes and 12 torpedoes. Originally, the class was to carry two dual 25mm antiaircraft mounts, but a 4.7in deck gun replaced one of these mounts fitted forward of the conning tower.

KD7 Type Specifications

Units in class: 10 (*I-76* to *I-85* [later *I-176* to *I-185*])
Displacement: 1,833 tons surfaced; 2,602 tons submerged
Dimensions: Length 346ft / beam 27ft / draft 15ft
Machinery: Two diesels with 8,000shp driving two shafts; electric motors with 1,800shp
Maximum speed: 23kt surfaced; 8kt submerged
Range: 8,000nm at 16kt surfaced; 50nm at 5kt submerged
Operating depth: 265ft
Crew: 86

Wartime service

The fate of this class clearly demonstrated the misuse of the IJN's submarine force and its difficulty in mounting successful attacks during the late-war period in the face of increasingly effective US antisubmarine defenses. Seven of the ten boats were sunk within a year of being commissioned and when *I-177* was destroyed in October 1944, the entire class was removed from the IJN's order of battle. In return, the class sank only five merchants, a hospital ship, and one US submarine (the only time during the war that a Japanese submarine sank a US submarine). The most successful boat was *I-176*, which damaged the heavy cruiser *Chester* in October 1942 and sank the submarine *Corvina* in November 1943. *I-180* sank three merchant ships. However, six of the boats scored no successes and several never even launched an attack. Of the ten boats lost, six were sunk by destroyers, two by air attack, one by US submarines, and the unfortunate *I-179* was sunk in a training accident after being in service for less than one month. Many boats of this class spent much of their operational lives performing supply missions.

A1/2 Type Specifications

Units in class: 4 (A1: *I-9* to *I-11*; A2: *I-12*)
Displacement: 2,919 tons surfaced (A2 2,934 tons); 4,149 tons submerged (A2 4,172 tons)
Dimensions: Length 372.75ft / beam 31.33ft / draft 17.5ft
Machinery: Two diesels with 12,400shp (A2 4,700shp) driving two shafts; electric motors with 2,400shp (A2 1,200shp)
Maximum speed: 23.5kt surfaced (A2 18kt); 8kt submerged (A2 6.25kt)
Range: 16,000nm at 16kt surfaced (A2 22,000nm); 90nm at 3kt submerged (A2 70nm)
Operating depth: 330ft
Crew: 100

A1/2 Type

The first boat in this class was laid down in January 1939. A Type submarines were intended to act as headquarters boats to coordinate the operations of submarine squadrons. This was the embodiment of the IJN's doctrine to operate its submarine forces in conjunction with the main fleet. The class was based on the J3 Type, but was provided with additional personnel accommodations and spaces for the command staff and special communications equipment. As in the J3 class, aircraft-handling facilities were provided, but the A1 class moved the catapult forward of the conning tower and faired the hangar into the sail. This much reduced the time required to prepare the aircraft for launch, and for recovery and stowage. Extra fuel and storage capacity provided this class with a patrol duration of up to 90 days. The first two boats in the class were completed before the start of the war; *I-11* was not completed until May 1942. Two additional boats were ordered in the 1942 program but were canceled before construction began. The A2 Type differed from the A1 by the installation of a much less powerful diesel. This resulted in a lower surface speed but, with the additional fuel carried, a longer range. The single A2 boat was laid down in November 1942, but not completed until May 1944.

Armament

Six 21in bow torpedo tubes and 18 torpedoes; one 5.5in deck gun mounted aft; two twin 25mm antiaircraft guns fitted on the sail. The hangar had room for one floatplane.

Wartime service

The A1 boats were used extensively in their intended role as submarine squadron command ships. Both *I-9* and *I-10* were deployed off the Hawaiian Islands at the start of the war, but the only success was *I-10*'s sinking of a freighter. *I-9*'s E14Y1 floatplane was used to reconnoiter Pearl Harbor on February 24, 1942 and later the aircraft also surveyed Kiska Island in the Aleutians. *I-9* was lost off Kiska in June 1943 to US destroyers without sinking a single ship. *I-10* went on from its Pearl Harbor deployment to have a long service life. It sank another 15 merchant ships, mainly in the Indian Ocean, where it also made extensive use of its floatplane, which flew missions over four ports in South Africa in May 1942 and over Diego Suarez in Madagascar. The latter mission set up an attack by Japanese midget submarines on a British battleship in the port. By July 1944, *I-10* was committed in the Japanese effort to defend the

I-9 photographed during the war in what appears to be an overall black or dark gray color scheme. Note the two white bands forward for aerial recognition and the additional symbol aft of a red triangle on a white square. *I-9* was lost with all hands on June 13, 1943 off Kiska Island to destroyer USS *Frazier* (*DD-607*). (*Ships of the World* magazine)

Marianas, where it was sunk by US destroyers. *I-11*'s first war patrol was off Australia, where it sank three freighters. In July 1943, it torpedoed and damaged the Australian light cruiser *Hobart* in the Solomons. In March 1944, it was lost to unknown causes in the area of Ellice Island. *I-12* had a short, unproductive career. Its only patrol was directed against US shipping between the US West Coast and Hawaii. It sank one freighter, machine-gunning the survivors, before being lost to unknown causes in January 1945 north of the Marshall Islands.

AM Type Specifications

Units in class: 2 (*I-13*, *I-14*)
Displacement: 3,603 tons surfaced; 4,792 tons submerged
Dimensions: Length 372.75ft / beam 38.5ft / draft 19.3 ft
Machinery: Two diesels with 4,400shp driving two shafts; electric motors with 600shp
Maximum speed: 16.75kt surfaced; 5.5kt submerged
Range: 21,000nm at 16kt surfaced; 60nm at 3kt submerged
Operating depth: 330ft
Crew: 108

AM Type

This type was originally to be a repeat of the A2 command submarine, but during construction it was modified to serve as an aircraft-carrying submarine. Unlike previous classes, which had aircraft-handling facilities for scouting, these boats could handle two submarine-launched bomber aircraft. In this role, it was intended that they would supplement the even larger STo class. Four units were laid down; two were completed between December 1944 and March 1945, while the two others were almost complete by 1945, when construction was stopped in favor of smaller submarines for defense of the homeland. Three additional units were canceled. The AM ships were the same length as the A2 units, but with a much wider beam. This permitted the aircraft hangar to be enlarged to accommodate two of the larger Seiran aircraft. The catapult remained forward of the conning tower, but the hangar was offset to starboard and the top of the conning tower was offset to port to compensate. Both boats were fitted with a primitive form of snorkel upon completion, which proved unsatisfactory in service. The range of the class was extraordinary, as required by its intended mission of striking targets in the US.

Armament
Six 21in bow torpedo tubes and 12 torpedoes; one 5.5in deck gun mounted aft; two triple and one single 25mm antiaircraft guns fitted on the conning tower. The hangar had room for two floatplanes.

Wartime service
Having expended considerable resources on this class and the I-400 class, the Naval General Staff was indecisive in finding a target for them. Originally,

proposals for San Francisco, Panama, and even New York and Washington were considered, but by March 1945 it was decided to use the aircraft-carrying submarine force against the Gatun Locks of the Panama Canal. This would, it was hoped, stem the flow of reinforcements from the now inactive European theater into the Pacific. By June 1945, however, the target was changed to the USN's fleet anchorage at Ulithi. The new plan, Operation *Arashi* (Mountain Storm), called for *I-13* and *I-14* to carry crated C6N2 "Myrt" long-range reconnaissance aircraft to Truk in order to reconnoiter Ulithi. Target information could then be relayed to the Seiran strike aircraft on the I-400 boats. *I-13* left Japan for Truk on July 11, 1945 and was sunk en route by a US aircraft and destroyer attack. *I-14* departed for Truk on July 14, arriving on August 4, where it unloaded its two C6N2 aircraft. After the Japanese surrender on August 15, *I-14* surrendered at sea to the USN. The boat was later taken to Pearl Harbor, where it was sunk as a target in May 1946.

I-14 after the war in USN hands. This class can be distinguished from the larger but similar I-400 class by the two 25mm triple mounts on the conning tower (I-400 boats had three). The top of the conning tower is offset to port, creating enough space in the hangar for two floatplane bomber aircraft. (*Ships of the World* magazine)

Opposite: *I-29* in March–April 1944 in Lorient, France, prior to its return to Japan. It bears its new armament of a German 20mm Flakvierling mount in the conning tower, and a German 37mm antiaircraft gun aft. *I-29* was sunk by USS *Sawfish* (*SS-276*) on July 26, 1944 in the Luzon Strait before completing the round trip to Japan. (*Ships of the World* magazine)

B1 Type

The B Type units were conceived as long-range scouting units. The actual B1 design was developed from the KD6 Type. The B Type units retained the same aircraft-handling facilities as found on the A1 Type. On the B1, the aircraft hangar was again streamlined into the conning tower and a catapult fitted forward (one unit, *I-17*, had the hangar and catapult fitted aft of the conning tower). The improved streamlining resulted in a better underwater performance.

In total, 20 B1 boats were ordered in the 1939 program. The first was completed in September 1940 and the last in April 1943. This was the largest single class of fleet boats built for the IJN. This class combined the features of the *kaidai* and *junsen* types into a single hull.

Armament

Six 21in bow torpedo tubes and 17 torpedoes; one 5.5in deck gun mounted aft; one twin 25mm antiaircraft gun fitted on the conning tower. This was increased on some units to two and even three twin mounts. Units that arrived in France (*I-29* and *I-30*) were fitted with German 37mm and 20mm quad mounts for their return voyage. The hangar had room for one floatplane. Later in the war, as floatplane operations became too dangerous, several B1 units had their hangar and catapult removed and a second 5.5in gun was fitted forward of the conning tower. In late 1944, *I-36* and *I-37* had their aircraft-handling equipment and their aft deck gun removed in order to carry four *kaiten*s. Later, *I-36* was again modified to carry six *kaiten*s. Units fitted with *kaiten*s also had a second twin 25mm gun added forward of the conning tower.

Below: B1 Type *I-26* was completed in November 1941. Note the streamlined hangar forward of the conning tower. Mounted atop the conning tower is a 25mm dual antiaircraft gun. The 5.5in gun was fitted aft under the radio antennae. *I-26* accounted for a USN light cruiser before being lost to an unknown operational cause off Leyte Island in October 1944. (*Ships of the World* magazine)

Wartime service

This class saw extensive service during the war, being active off the US West Coast (shelling targets and launching the only air attack of the war on the continental US), in the Aleutians, in the South Pacific (often on supply missions), and in the Indian Ocean where it was successful against shipping. Losses were heavy – only *I-36* survived; three were sunk in 1942, nine in 1943, and seven in 1944. Eleven of the class were lost to surface attack; three were lost to Allied submarines, two to air attack, one to mines, one for operational reasons, and one for unknown reasons.

In return, B1 Type boats did enjoy some success, sinking 50 merchant or auxiliary ships and damaging another 13. As was usually the case, most ships sunk were claimed in the Indian Ocean where defenses were less intense. The star B1 performers included *I-26*, which damaged *Saratoga* in August 1942, putting it out of action for several crucial months during the Guadalcanal campaign; *I-26* followed this up by sinking light cruiser *Juneau* in October. The most amazing performance was recorded by *I-19* on September 15, 1942, when a single salvo of six torpedoes sank the carrier *Wasp*, damaged the battleship *North Carolina*, and sank a destroyer. *I-25* sank a Soviet submarine and *I-21* destroyed 11 merchant ships. Three boats of the class, *I-26*, *I-27*, and *I-37*, were involved in incidents against surviving crew members of sunken merchant ships. Three of the boats were sent on missions to carry high-priority cargo to Europe. Two of the boats, *I-36* and *I-37*, survived late enough into the war to be fitted with *kaiten*s, and used them operationally.

B1 Type Specifications

Units in class: 20 (*I-15*, *I-17*, *I-19*, *I-21*, *I-23*, *I-25* to *I-39*)
Displacement: 2,584 tons surfaced; 3,654 tons submerged
Dimensions: Length 356.5ft / beam 30.5ft / draft 16.75ft
Machinery: Two diesels with 12,400shp driving two shafts; electric motors with 2,000shp
Maximum speed: 23.5kt surfaced; 8kt submerged
Range: 14,000nm at 16kt surfaced; 96nm at 3kt submerged
Operating depth: 330ft
Crew: 94

B2 Type Specifications

Units in class: 6 (*I-40* to *I-45*)
Displacement: 2,624 tons surfaced; 3,700 tons submerged
Dimensions: Length 356.5ft / beam 30.5ft / draft 17ft
Machinery: Two diesels with 11,000shp driving two shafts; electric motors with 2,000shp
Maximum speed: 23.5kt surfaced; 8kt submerged
Range: 14,000nm at 16kt surfaced; 96nm at 3kt submerged
Operating depth: 330ft
Crew: 100

B2 Type

The B2 Type units were essentially a repeat of the B1 class, but were slightly larger. The diesels fitted were marginally less powerful, but this resulted in no degradation of performance. Five of the six units in the class entered service during the second half of 1943. Another eight units planned for the 1942 program were canceled.

Armament

Six 21in bow torpedo tubes and 17 torpedoes; one 5.5in deck gun mounted aft; one twin 25mm antiaircraft gun fitted on the conning tower. The hangar had room for one floatplane. As on B1 units, some B2 boats had their hangar and catapult removed and a second 5.5in gun fitted forward of the conning tower. In late 1944, *I-44* had its aircraft-handling equipment and aft deck gun removed in order to carry six *kaiten*s.

Wartime service

Entering the war in the face of well-developed US antisubmarine defenses and sent against fleet targets, this class achieved very little. *I-41* achieved the only success, damaging the light cruiser *Reno* in November 1944. Three units were sunk by US destroyers (*I-41*, *I-45*, and possibly *I-40*) and two units by US submarines (*I-42* and *I-43*), while the last unit (*I-44*) was sunk by acoustic torpedoes from US aircraft during a *kaiten* mission in April 1945.

B3/4 Type Specifications

Units in class: 3 (*I-54*, *I-56*, *I-58*)
Displacement: 2,607 tons surfaced; 3,688 tons submerged
Dimensions: Length 356.5ft / beam 30.5ft / draft 17ft
Machinery: Two diesels with 4,700shp driving two shafts; electric motors with 1,200shp
Maximum speed: 17.75kt surfaced; 6.5kt submerged
Range: 21,000nm at 16kt surfaced; 105nm at 3kt submerged
Operating depth: 330ft
Crew: 94

B3/4 Types

The three units of this class were not completed until March, June, and September 1944. Four other planned units were canceled in 1943. The B3 Type was dimensionally identical to the B2 class. The primary difference was the less powerful machinery fitted in the B3 Type, resulting in decreased surface speed. However, the B3's range was increased due to a greater fuel bunkerage. These boats were fitted from completion with a No. 22 radar fitted on top of the seaplane hangar, as well as snorkels. The B4 variant was planned but never laid down. These eight boats would have been larger, with a surface speed of 22.5 knots, carrying eight torpedo tubes with 23 torpedoes.

Armament

Six 21in bow torpedo tubes and 19 torpedoes; one 5.5in deck gun mounted aft; one twin 25mm antiaircraft gun fitted on the conning tower. The hangar had room for one floatplane. As on B1 and B2 boats, *I-56* and *I-58* had their hangar, catapult, and 5.5in gun removed in 1945 to provide for the fitting of four *kaitens*. Later I-58 was modified to carry six *kaitens*.

Wartime service

Two of the B3 units were lost without inflicting any damage on the enemy. *I-54* responded to the US invasion of Leyte and was sunk by US destroyers on October 28, 1944. *I-56* survived to be converted into a *kaiten* carrier and was lost in April 1945 off Okinawa. *I-58* was a prime player in one of the most controversial episodes in US naval history. On July 30, 1945, it sank heavy cruiser *Indianapolis* with three Type 95 torpedoes. Because the cruiser was not zig-zagging, its captain was held culpable for the ship's loss. With the help of *I-58*'s skipper, his name was finally cleared in 2000. *I-58* survived the war to be scuttled in April 1946.

C1 Type

The units of the C class were intended as attack boats to operate with A Type command boats and B Type scout submarines. Their design was based on the KD6 with the increase of two torpedo tubes to provide maximum firepower. The eight forward tubes were arranged in two forward torpedo rooms, one above the other. The C1 boats were also more maneuverable under water than the KD6. The first ship was laid down in September 1937 and the boats entered service between March 1940 and October 1941.

Armament

Eight 21in bow torpedo tubes and 20 torpedoes; one 5.5in deck gun mounted aft; one twin 25mm antiaircraft gun fitted on the conning tower. No aircraft were carried. Each boat was provided with fittings aft of the conning tower to carry one Type A midget submarine. In early 1943, *I-16* was modified for duties as a supply submarine. The forward 5.5in gun was removed, the number of torpedo reloads was reduced, and fittings were provided aft for a *daihatsu*.

(Overleaf) On September 9, 1942, B1 Type boat *I-25* surfaced off the Oregon coast. On board was a single E14Y1 floatplane with the mission to start forest fires spreading panic among the population. In fact, of the four bombs dropped (two on September 9 and two more in a repeat attack on September 29), only one exploded and this did little damage. This scene depicts the E14Y1 as it is being catapulted from its mother submarine.

C1 Type Specifications

Units in class: 5 (*I-16, I-18, I-20, I-22, I-24*)
Displacement: 2,554 tons surfaced; 3,561 tons submerged
Dimensions: Length 358.5ft / beam 30ft / draft 17.5ft
Machinery: Two diesels with 12,400shp driving two shafts; electric motors with 2,000shp
Maximum speed: 23.5kt surfaced; 8kt submerged
Range: 14,000nm at 16kt surfaced; 60nm at 3kt submerged
Operating depth: 330ft
Crew: 95

The C1 Type was developed from the KD6. *I-16* is pictured here in March 1940. The space aft of the conning tower was reserved for the fitting of a 46-ton Type A midget submarine. (*Ships of the World* magazine)

Opposite: *I-47* at Kure after its surrender. This C2 Type submarine was the only boat of its class to survive the war. *I-47* spent most of its operational life, unsuccessfully, as a *kaiten* carrier. Beyond *I-47* is the B1 Type boat *I-36*; and beyond it the Special Type submarine *I-402*. (Naval History and Heritage Command)

Wartime service

This class was very active during the war and made extensive use of its ability to carry midget submarines. All five units were engaged in the attack on Pearl Harbor, with each carrying a midget submarine. *I-16*, *I-18*, and *I-20* were deployed in the Indian Ocean, where they used their midget submarines to attack British shipping in Diego Suarez. The attack heavily damaged battleship HMS *Ramillies* and sank a tanker. The boats later sank 14 freighters in the Indian Ocean as commerce raiders. Later, *I-16* and *I-20* each launched three more midget attacks off Guadalcanal; only a single USN transport was damaged. While being used as supply submarines, *I-18* was sunk in February 1943 and *I-16* in June 1944, both by US destroyers. *I-20* was also sunk in the Solomons by US destroyers in September 1943. *I-22* and *I-24* were used to ferry midget submarines to attack Sydney, Australia in May 1942. The attack was a failure, sinking only an old accommodation ferry. *I-22* was reported missing in the Eastern Solomons in October 1942. After the attack on Sydney, *I-24* sank a freighter. *I-24* was also used to launch two midget attacks on Guadalcanal and was later used for supply missions in the Solomons. In June 1943, the 2,500-ton submarine was rammed and sunk off the Aleutians by a 675-ton sub-chaser.

C2 Type

The three units of the C2 class were identical to the C1 class with the exception that they had no provisions for carrying midget submarines. The first boat was laid down in November 1942 but the boats were not completed until February–September 1944. Another seven units were canceled before being laid down.

Armament

Eight 21in bow torpedo tubes and 20 torpedoes; one 5.5in deck gun mounted aft; one twin 25mm antiaircraft gun was fitted on the conning tower. In late 1944, *I-47* and *I-48* were converted into *kaiten* carriers by removing their forward 5.5in deck gun and adding fittings for four *kaiten*s. *I-47* was further modified in early 1945 to carry a total of six *kaiten*s.

Wartime service

The three units of this class enjoyed no success during the war and two were sunk for their efforts. *I-46* was sunk by US destroyers in October 1944 off Leyte. After conversion into a *kaiten* carrier, *I-47* made extensive use of this weapon but postwar analysis indicated that its *kaiten*s did no damage. *I-47* survived the war, to be scuttled in April 1946. In its first war patrol as a *kaiten* carrier, *I-48* was sunk in January 1945 west of Ulithi.

> ### C2 Type Specifications
>
> **Units in class:** 3 (*I-46* to *I-48*)
> **Displacement:** 2,557 tons surfaced; 3,564 tons submerged
> **Dimensions:** Length 358.5ft / beam 29.75ft / draft 17.5ft
> **Machinery:** Two diesels with 12,400shp driving two shafts; electric motors with 2,000shp
> **Maximum speed:** 23.5kt surfaced; 8kt submerged
> **Range:** 14,000nm at 16kt surfaced; 60nm at 3kt submerged
> **Operating depth:** 330ft
> **Crew:** 95

C3/4 Types

Due to wartime shortages, the C3 boats were fitted with inferior machinery, which resulted in a much-reduced surface speed. However, additional fuel storage gave a greater range. The number of torpedo tubes was also reduced. The first boat was laid down in March 1942 but the class was not completed until December 1943–April 1944. Fifteen boats were programmed for the C4 Type, which was to be larger, fitted with diesels capable of 20.5 knots on the surface and equipped with eight torpedo tubes. These were all canceled in 1943.

C3/4 Type Specifications

Units in class: 3 (*I-52, I-53, I-55*)
Displacement: 2,564 tons surfaced; 3,644 tons submerged
Dimensions: Length 356.5ft / beam 30.5ft / draft 16.75ft
Machinery: Two diesels with 4,700shp driving two shafts; electric motors with 1,200shp
Maximum speed: 17.75kt surfaced; 6.5kt submerged
Range: 21,000nm at 16kt surfaced; 105nm at 3kt submerged
Operating depth: 330ft
Crew: 94

Armament

Six 21in bow torpedo tubes and 19 torpedoes; two 5.5in deck guns; one twin 25mm antiaircraft gun fitted on the conning tower. In February 1944, *I-52* had its antiaircraft suite increased to three twin 25mm mounts. In 1945, *I-53* was converted into a *kaiten* carrier by removing both 5.5in deck guns. Initially, four *kaiten*s could be carried; this was later increased to six.

Wartime service

Like the B2 units, the B3 boats enjoyed little success and only one survived the war. *I-52* attempted the fifth and final transit by an IJN submarine to Europe, departing Japan in March 1944. On June 23, 1944, west of the Cape Verde Islands, it was sunk by an American air-launched acoustic torpedo. *I-53* scored a noteworthy success when one of its *kaiten*s sank a US Navy destroyer escort in the Philippine Sea on July 24, 1945. This was the only warship sunk by this ineffective weapon. *I-53* survived the war, to be scuttled in April 1946. *I-55* was sunk on its first patrol in July 1944 by US destroyers off Tainan Island in the Marianas.

SH Type Specifications

Units in class: 1 (*I-351*)
Displacement: 3,512 tons surfaced; 4,290 tons submerged
Dimensions: Length 363.75in / beam 33.5ft / draft 20ft
Machinery: Two diesels with 3,700shp driving two shafts; electric motors with 1,200shp
Maximum speed: 15.75kt surfaced; 6.3kt submerged
Range: 13,000nm at 14kt surfaced; 100nm at 3kt submerged
Operating depth: 300ft
Crew: 77 (plus 13 aircrew)

SH Type

The Japanese penchant for developing specialized submarines was displayed once again in the design of the SH Type. This class was intended to support the operations of flying boats in forward areas. The boat was able to carry 365 tons of aviation gas, 11 tons of fresh water, 60 550lb bombs and 15 aircraft torpedoes. Design began before the war, but the first unit was not laid down until May 1943. When completed in January 1945, it was useless in its intended role, and was commissioned as a submarine oil tanker. A second boat, *I-352*, was destroyed at Kure by bombing before completion. Four additional units were canceled.

Armament

Four 21in bow torpedo tubes and four torpedoes. It was planned to arm this class with 5.5in deck guns, but these were in short supply, so four 3in mortars were substituted. Antiaircraft weapons included two twin and three

single 25mm guns. The number of torpedoes could be increased in lieu of aircraft torpedoes.

I-53 at Kure in October 1945. *I-53* was converted into a *kaiten* carrier in November 1944. Its *kaiten*s sank a destroyer escort, the biggest success of the war for that weapon. Beyond *I-53* is B3 Type boat *I-58*. (Naval History and Heritage Command)

Wartime service

This was the largest Japanese transport submarine completed. It completed one round trip to Singapore, returning to Japan with 132,000 gallons of aviation fuel. On its second trip it was torpedoed by a US submarine in the South China Sea en route to Japan.

STo (*Sen-Toku* or Special Submarine) Type

This class comprised the largest Japanese submarines built during the war; in fact, they were the largest submarines ever built until the introduction of the USN's Benjamin Franklin class of nuclear-powered ballistic missile submarines in 1965. The class took the Japanese fascination with operating aircraft from submarines to new levels, as they were designed to operate floatplane bombers against American cities. The original design called for space for two floatplanes, but this was later enlarged to carry three. The design was mainly an enlarged version of the AM design with a similar conning tower and catapult arrangement. The double hull design was unique and featured a figure eight configuration forward which turned into a horizontal figure eight amidships. In order to carry out its mission of long-range strikes, the class had sufficient fuel for a range of 37,500nm at 14 knots – unmatched until the advent of nuclear propulsion. Patrol endurance was 90 days.

STo (*Sen-Toku* or Special Submarine) Type Specifications

Units in class: 3 (*I-400* to *I-402*)
Displacement: 5,223 tons surfaced; 6,560 tons submerged
Dimensions: Length 400.25ft / beam 39.33ft / draft 23ft
Machinery: Four diesels with 7,700shp driving two shafts; electric motors with 2,400shp
Maximum speed: 18.75kt surfaced; 6.5kt submerged
Range: 30,000nm at 16kt surfaced; 60nm at 3kt submerged
Operating depth: 330ft
Crew: 144

I-401 pictured after its surrender to the USN. This profile shows the large combined hangar/conning tower with three 25mm triple antiaircraft guns. A 5.5in deck gun is fitted aft. The aircraft crane is shown in its upright position. (*Ships of the World* magazine)

Three boats were commissioned before the end of the war. The first was laid down in January 1943 and was not completed until almost two years later. The last boat was completed just before the war's end. Work on two other boats was stopped in March 1945 and several other units were canceled before construction began.

Armament

Eight 21in bow torpedo tubes and 20 torpedoes; one 5.5in deck gun, plus one single and three triple 25mm antiaircraft guns. Three bomber floatplanes could be accommodated in the hangar.

Wartime service

Despite the considerable resources devoted to this class and a number of design innovations, these boats contributed nothing to the Japanese war effort. Two of the three units completed were committed to Operation *Arashi*. While they were en route to attack Ulithi, the war ended. *I-400* surrendered on August 27 and *I-401* two days later. Both were later taken to Pearl Harbor by US crews for study and were sunk as targets in May and June 1946. The third boat, *I-402*, saw no action before Japan's surrender and was scuttled in April 1946 off Japan.

ST (*Sen-Taka* or High-speed Submarine) Type

The heavy submarine losses suffered during the first years of the war prompted the IJN to develop submarines with high submerged speeds to negate the effectiveness of American antisubmarine forces. From 1938–40, the Japanese had evaluated an experimental high-speed submarine designated *Vessel Number 71* for cover purposes. This was a small 213-ton unit that reached over 21 knots submerged, making it the fastest undersea craft of its day. These experiments formed the basis for the ST Type, 24 of which were ordered in the 1943–44 program.

The key components to the ST design resulted from extensive efforts to streamline the welded hull and sail; hull fittings were recessed, and even the deck guns were on retractable mounts. The electric motors were almost twice as powerful as the diesels and 4,192 high-capacity batteries provided a burst capability of up to 19 knots submerged. These were also the deepest-diving submarines built by Japan during the war. The boats were fitted with snorkels and possessed an endurance of 30 days. The first boat was laid down in March 1944; eight units were begun, but only three were finished before the war ended. Despite extensive use of prefabrication and welding, Japanese industry proved unable to get this potentially revolutionary class of submarine into service in time to affect the war.

ST (*Sen-Taka*) Type Specifications

Units in class: 3 (*I-201* to *I-203*)
Displacement: 1,291 tons surfaced; 1,450 tons submerged
Dimensions: Length 259ft / beam 19ft / draft 18ft
Machinery: Two diesels with 2,750shp driving two shafts; electric motors with 5,000shp
Maximum speed: 15.75kt surfaced; 19kt submerged
Range: 5,800nm at 16kt surfaced; 135nm at 3kt submerged
Operating depth: 360ft
Crew: 31

Armament

Four 21in bow torpedo tubes and ten torpedoes; two retractable single 25mm guns, one forward and one aft of the conning tower.

Wartime service

Although commissioned on February 2, 1945, *I-201* did not see operational service during the war. After the war, the boat was taken to Pearl Harbor for study and was later sunk in May 1946 during ordnance tests. *I-202*, also commissioned in February, was damaged by US carrier raids in July 1945. It was scuttled in Japanese waters in April 1946. *I-203* was completed in May 1945 and accompanied *I-201* to Pearl Harbor. In May 1946, it was expended as a target.

The modern streamlined appearance of the ST Type submarine is clearly shown in this photograph of *I-202*. These were the fastest submarines built during World War II, surpassing the German Type XXI U-boats. (Kure Maritime Museum)

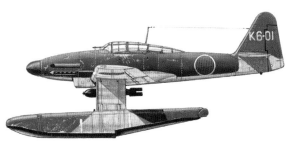

The IJN was the only navy to employ attack aircraft from submarines during the Pacific War. The top profile depicts the AM Type boat *I-14*. The bottom view shows a Special Submarine – similar to the AM Type, but much larger. The inset is the M6A1 Seiran bomber floatplane. Only a handful were completed before the end of the war.

D1/2 Type Specifications

Units in class: 13 (D1: *I-361* to *I-372*; D2: *I-373*)
Displacement: 1,779 tons surfaced (D2 1,926 tons); 2,215 tons submerged (D2 2,240 tons)
Dimensions: Length 248ft (D2 242.75ft) / beam 29.25ft / draft 15.5ft (D2 16.5ft)
Machinery: Two diesels with 1,850shp driving two shafts (D2 1,750shp); electric motors with 1,200shp
Maximum speed: 13kt surfaced; 6.5kt submerged
Range: 15,000nm at 10kt surfaced (D2 5,000nm); 120nm at 3kt (D2 100nm) submerged
Operating depth: 245ft (D2 330ft)
Crew: 75 (plus up to 110 troops) (D2 60)

D1/2 Type

The IJN had never been happy about using its combat submarines to carry out supply missions, but felt duty-bound to do all it could to support many increasingly isolated garrisons throughout the Pacific. Aside from removing these boats from their primary missions, losses on supply missions were heavy. To release combat submarines from supply duties, work on a special transport submarine design was begun in mid-1942. The D1 class could carry 22 tons of internal cargo plus 110 troops in cargo spaces in the former torpedo room and aft of the control room. External cargo included two 42ft landing craft and 60 additional tons of cargo. Of the 104 units projected, only 12 were completed, all between May and November 1944. The D2 design had its range reduced, as 150 tons of fuel were now used and total cargo capacity was increased to 110 tons. Only a single landing craft was carried.

Armament

The first unit completed had two 21in bow torpedo tubes, but these were removed after initial sea trials and were not carried in subsequent units. One 5.5in deck gun and two single 25mm guns were carried. In early 1945, *I-361, I-363, I-366, I-367, I-368,* and *I-370* had their deck guns and landing craft fittings removed to permit mountings for five *kaiten*s to be fitted.

Wartime service

For the loss of nine of the 13 D1/D2 boats, the IJN gained a dismal return. These boats proved to be easy targets. Four were sunk by US submarines,

During late 1944 and early 1945, most of the IJN's remaining submarines were converted to carry the *kaiten*s. Among these were five of the 12 D1 Type transport submarines. One of those, *I-370,* is shown here departing on February 21, 1945 on its first *kaiten* mission. *I-370* was later sunk during this mission by USS *Finnegan* (*DE-307*) south of Iwo Jima on February 26, 1945.

I-370 seen departing for a *kaiten* mission in 1945. The *kaiten* pilots are waving from atop their weapons. Despite their great promise, the *kaiten*s proved a major disappointment. (Kure Maritime Museum)

two on their first mission; *I-373*, sunk by a US submarine on August 14, was the last Japanese submarine lost during the war. The six boats converted into *kaiten* carriers accomplished nothing; two of these were lost to air-launched acoustic torpedoes and a third to US destroyers.

RO SERIES SUBMARINES

L4 Type

This was the oldest class of RO boat to see active service during the war. Older RO boats, if still in existence by 1941, were reduced to a training role only. Originally based on the British L class, the L4 boats were improved versions of the preceding L3 Type boats with two torpedo tubes added and the deck gun moved forward of the sail, a position kept on all subsequent RO boat designs.

Armament

Six bow 21in torpedo tubes and ten torpedoes; one 3in deck gun and one 13mm machine gun.

Wartime service

Despite their age, being completed between 1923 and 1927, they were used operationally during the initial phases of the war, though only committed to secondary areas. Six of the units were engaged in the attack on Wake Island where *RO-66* was lost in a collision with *RO-62*. Another was lost after running aground early in the war, and two more were lost in the Aleutians when six ships in the class were committed there in 1942. The only success of the class was scored when *RO-61* sank a seaplane tender in the Aleutians. In 1943, the five surviving boats were assigned to training duties. One of these was later lost to mines in the Inland Sea in 1945; four survived the war.

L4 Type Specifications

Units in class: 9 (*RO-60* to *RO-68*)
Displacement: 996 tons surfaced; 1,322 tons submerged
Dimensions: Length 250ft / beam 24.5ft / draft 12.33ft
Machinery: Two diesels with 2,400shp driving two shafts; electric motors with 1,600shp
Maximum speed: 16kt surfaced; 8kt submerged
Range: 5,500nm at 10kt surfaced; 80nm at 4kt submerged
Operating depth: 200ft
Crew: 60

K5 Type

These two units were the first medium submarines designed since the L4 Type dating from the early 1920s. They were intended to be prototypes of a medium submarine suitable for series production in wartime. With more powerful engines, they had a higher surface speed than the L4. The first unit was laid down in August 1933 and the second completed in May 1937.

Armament

Four 21in bow torpedo tubes and ten torpedoes; one 3in deck gun and one 13mm machine gun.

Wartime service

Both units were active supporting the invasion of the Dutch East Indies and then subsequently in the New Guinea/Solomons area. *RO-33* sank a small freighter in August 1942 in the Coral Sea with gunfire, then massacred the survivors in the water with machine-gun fire. Later in August, after *RO-33* torpedoed another freighter (which survived) off Port Moresby, it was sunk by the ship's Australian destroyer escort.

K5 Type Specifications

Units in class: 2 (*RO-33*, *RO-34*)
Displacement: 700 tons surfaced; 940 tons submerged
Dimensions: Length 239.5ft / beam 22ft / draft 10.5ft
Machinery: Two diesels with 3,000shp driving two shafts; electric motors with 1,200shp
Maximum speed: 19kt surfaced; 8.25kt submerged
Range: 8,000nm at 12kt surfaced; 90nm at 3.5kt submerged
Operating depth: 245ft
Crew: 75

RO-34 inflicted slight damage to a troop transport before being sunk by US destroyers in the Solomon Islands in April 1943.

KS (*Kaigun-Sho* or Small) Type

Submarines of this class were much smaller than earlier RO boats; they were more coastal than medium submarines. The design requirement set by the Naval General Staff called for a boat capable of conducting patrols around Pacific island bases, with an endurance of 21 days and a modest range of 3,500nm. Because of their small size, roughly comparable to the German Type VII units, they were not as vulnerable to detection by radar and sonar, could dive rapidly, and were maneuverable under water. They were built under the 1940–41 program, with the first units being laid down in June 1941. Six were completed in 1942, ten in 1943, and two in 1944.

KS Type Specifications

Units in class: 18 (*RO-100 to RO-117*)
Displacement: 601 tons surfaced; 782 tons submerged
Dimensions: Length 199.75ft / beam 19.5ft / draft 11.5ft
Machinery: Two diesels with 1,000shp driving two shafts; electric motors with 760shp
Maximum speed: 14.25kt surfaced; 8kt submerged
Range: 3,500nm at 12kt surfaced; 60nm at 3kt submerged
Operating depth: 245ft
Crew: 38

Armament

Four 21in bow torpedo tubes, each with one reload; the original plans called for a twin 25mm antiaircraft mount to be fitted but this was replaced with a 3in gun.

The two K5 Type boats were successful prototypes for the much larger K6 Type class built between 1941 and 1944. Note the 3in gun fitted forward of the conning tower. (Kure Maritime Museum)

Wartime service

KS boats saw service throughout the Pacific, from the Solomons area up to the Aleutians. Many of the patrols by these units were spent on supply runs, a questionable use given the amount of cargo that could be carried. Some units also conducted patrols in the Indian Ocean. Against the Americans, results were poor, with *RO-108* sinking a destroyer and *RO-103* sinking two cargo ships in convoy. Results in the Indian Ocean against less well-defended targets were somewhat better, with *RO-111* sinking two merchant ships, *RO-113* sinking one, and *RO-110* damaging two more. Not a single ship in the class of 18 survived the war. Eleven were sunk by surface forces, including five by destroyer escort *England* alone, two by the submarine *Batfish*, and two by aircraft. Another was mined and two more went missing.

The RO medium boats were an adjunct to the larger I-class fleet boats. The top profile shows the oldest RO boats to see service in the Pacific War, the L4 Type, derived from the Royal Navy's L class. The middle profile is of *RO-46*, a boat of the K6 Type. The smallest RO boats to see service during the war were the KS Type units, shown in the bottom profile. Their compact design actually made them more comparable to coastal defense submarines.

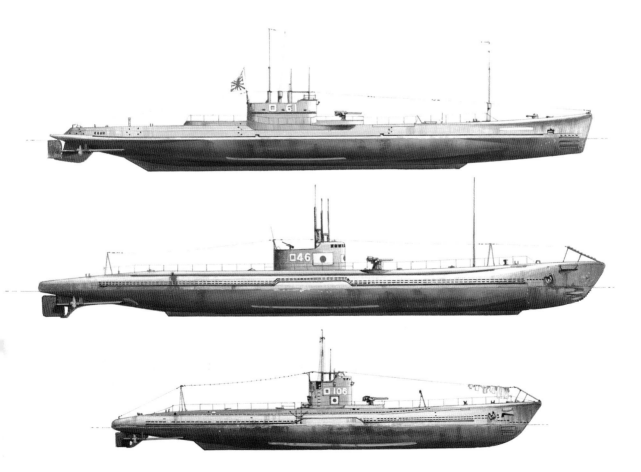

K6 Type

These ships were based closely on the K5 class. As almost the entire force of RO submarines was obsolete by 1940, this class was an attempt to fill the shortage of medium submarines. The first of the class was laid down in October 1941; ten were completed in 1943, with the final eight finished in 1944. The increase in size from the K5 translated into greater range as more fuel could be carried. Additionally, more powerful diesel engines were fitted and the submarine's operating depth was improved. These were the last RO boats built. Many other projected units in this class were canceled after they proved alarmingly vulnerable to USN antisubmarine forces.

Armament

Four 21in bow torpedo tubes and ten torpedoes; no guns were originally planned, but during construction a 3in deck gun and a twin 25mm cannon were added. These were the first RO boats capable of firing the Type 95 torpedo.

The KS Type was designed for coastal defense. These were the smallest RO boats to serve during the war. *RO-106*, pictured here, was destroyed north of Kavieng Island on May 22, 1944, one of five KS boats destroyed by USS *England* (*DE-635*).(Kure Maritime Museum)

Wartime service

The K6 class epitomized the wartime failure of the IJN's submarine force. Despite being well designed and fairly maneuverable and generally considered to be among the best of Japanese submarine designs, all but one (*RO-50*) were destroyed by the war's end. Of these, 13 were sunk by surface ships, two by air attack (one by an acoustic torpedo) and two went missing. In exchange, the K6 boats succeeded in sinking a single destroyer escort, an 800-ton yard oiler, and possibly a tank landing ship while damaging an attack transport. Most of the units in this class never even reported attacking the enemy, an utter condemnation of the over-cautious nature of their skippers. Their dismal record showed the futility of sending submarines to attack US fleet forces and the unsuitability of using submarines to defend islands against amphibious attack.

K6 Type Specifications

Units in class: 18 (*RO-35* to *RO-50*, *O-55*, *RO-56*)
Displacement: 1,115 tons surfaced; 1,447 tons submerged
Dimensions: Length 264ft / beam 23ft / draft 13.5ft
Machinery: Two diesels with 4,200shp driving two shafts; electric motors with 1,200shp
Maximum speed: 19.75kt surfaced; 8kt submerged
Range: 11,000nm at 12kt surfaced; 45nm at 5kt submerged
Operating depth: 265ft
Crew: 61

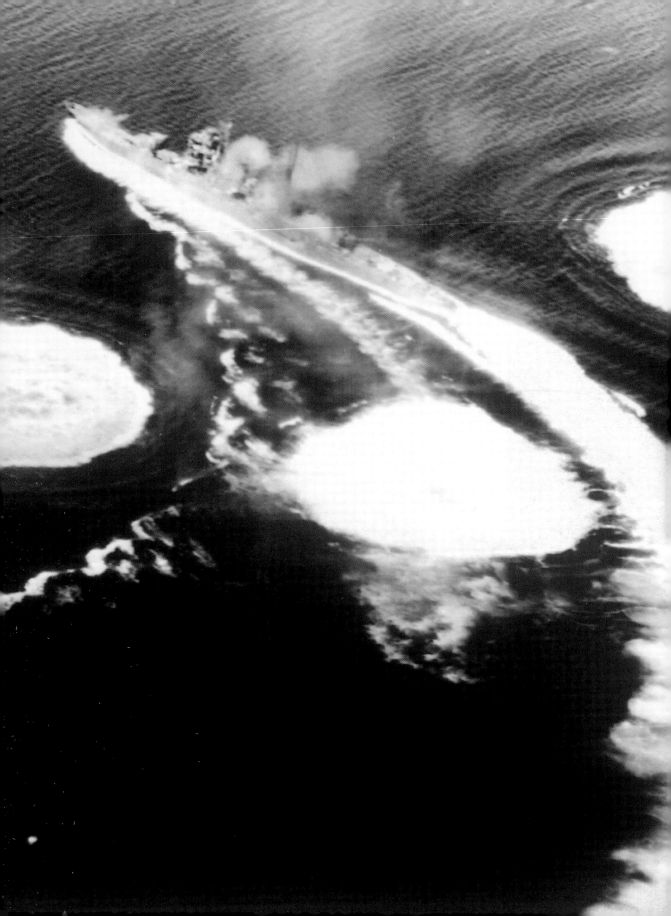

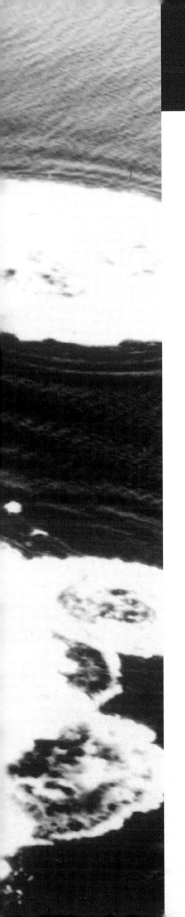

CONCLUSION AND ANALYSIS

The ultimate cause of the IJN's demise in the Pacific War was directly linked to two things. The first should have been easily foreseen by the Navy's leaders. When the Japanese initiated a war against the United States, they did not fully appreciate the nature of their opponent. While the Japanese knew the United States possessed many times the industrial potential of Japan, they failed to draw the appropriate conclusions. During the war, the USN commissioned 18 fleet, 9 light, 77 escort carriers, eight battleships, 13 heavy and 33 light cruisers, 349 destroyers, 420 destroyer escorts, 203 submarines, and a wealth of supporting amphibious and auxiliary ships. Against these overwhelming numbers, crewed by men able to adapt to the fast-changing pace of wartime technology, there was probably little the IJN could do to avoid defeat. However, by adhering to outdated and ill-suited strategies, the Japanese hastened their own demise.

The second factor crippling the IJN's wartime operations was its belief in the decisive battle concept which went unchallenged throughout the war. The first attempt to fight a decisive battle at Midway was defeated by extremely sloppy staff work at all levels and an American determination not to operate according to the Japanese script. Ironically, the closest the Japanese ever got to a decisive battle against the USN was the six-month death-struggle for Guadalcanal. This escalating battle for an insignificant island on the fringe of the Japanese perimeter did not meet the Japanese

Nachi under attack from carrier aircraft from US Navy Task Group 38.3 in Manila Bay on November 5, 1944. The ship was photographed by aircraft from the US carrier *Essex*. At this point in the attack, it remains undamaged. (Naval History and Heritage Command)

definition of decisive, so the opportunity went unrecognized. Accordingly, they never invested the resources required to defeat the USN while the two navies were still at rough numerical parity. Biding its strength until 1944, the IJN made two final attempts to conduct a decisive battle, and each ended in disaster.

Modern war between industrialized nations is decided not by a single battle, but by logistics, good intelligence, solid planning, technological innovation and adaptation, and industrial output – all the things the IJN gave short shrift to or did poorly. The Japanese were well aware that they could not compete with the Americans in these areas, so they planned to make up the difference with superior fighting spirit and determination. This was another indication that they simply did not understand the nature of modern war.

As flawed as Japanese naval strategy was, their tactics were often superior, at least in the initial stages of the war. The IJN trained intensively for war during peacetime under conditions as close to combat as could be devised. Though the decisive battle concept was a total bust, many of the tactics developed during training for the decisive battle were directly transferable for use by the IJN's cruiser and destroyer forces. This was easily demonstrated during 1942 when the two sides were equally matched numerically and both used prewar tactics. In the Pacific War's first large surface engagement, the Battle of the Java Sea in February 1942, an Allied naval force was shattered by Japanese cruiser-destroyer force using superior night-fighting doctrine, equipment and tactics.

The Guadalcanal campaign featured five major surface battles and two carrier actions. In the five surface actions, the Japanese were the clear winners in two, with two developing favorably for the USN and the fifth essentially ending in a draw. The results of these actions, and other smaller engagements, showed that both sides took heavy losses, but that the Japanese held an edge. In combatant ships, the USN's losses totaled 25 ships, while the IJN lost 18. Of these, 15 Allied and eight Japanese ships were sunk in surface actions, leading to the inevitable conclusion that the IJN was simply better in surface combat. The remainder of the losses were attributable to air power, proving that the Japanese navy was already showing its inability to defend against air attack and that its strategy of fighting a major battle under conditions of air inferiority was flawed.

The losses sustained by the Japanese, though less than the USN's, simply could not be sustained. The attrition to the IJN continued into 1943 during the fierce battles in the Central and Northern Solomons. From March–November 1943, 25 Japanese destroyers were lost in the Solomons and the

Bismarck Sea, and these losses were impossible to replace. Of the seven major battles fought during 1943 in the Solomons, several resulted in Japanese tactical victories, but overall the ratio of losses demonstrated that the Japanese had lost the tactical edge they held during 1942 off Guadalcanal. After this point, the growing numerical and technological (primarily evidenced by radar) superiority of the USN made Japanese tactics largely irrelevant.

Operations in 1944 featured the crippling of the IJN's carrier force and the reliance on their still-powerful surface force to fight yet another iteration of the long-sought decisive battle. The Japanese had carefully hoarded their carrier force since late 1942 for the next opportunity for a major carrier engagement in mid-1944. With nine carriers massed together, supported by land-based air, the Japanese had reason to believe that the Battle of the Philippine Sea would be decisive. Though this was a correct prediction, it was decisive in favor of the USN, which used radar and well-trained aviators flying superior fighters to destroy the Japanese carrier raids and cripple the IJN's carrier force for the remainder of the war.

Nothing shows the idiocy of Japanese wartime strategy more than the next attempt to fight a decisive battle when the Americans invaded Leyte in October 1944. The best that the IJN could devise was to mount an operation that would place the IJN's surviving heavy ships into Leyte Gulf in order to

The light carrier *Shoho* was attacked on the morning of May 7 1942 at the Battle of Coral Sea by a total of 93 aircraft from two American carriers. Within 15 minutes, the carrier was ripped apart by some 13 bombs and at least seven torpedo hits, sinking quickly with heavy loss of life. *Shoho* was the first IJN carrier lost during the war. (Naval History and Heritage Command)

attack whatever shipping remained there several days after the initial landings. It is hard to imagine that even the Japanese believed that an operation designed to sink empty or easily replaceable transports could provide a significant impact on the pace of the American advance toward Japan. Making the whole endeavor even more pointless is that if the fleet had followed its orders, it would almost certainly have been caught inside Leyte Gulf and totally destroyed. Even if it survived by some miracle and had actually gained a measure of success, there was insufficient fuel available to allow another follow-up operation for many weeks. The entire operation must be seen as reckless in the extreme and designed more as an opportunity for the ceremonial destruction of the IJN than as a serious operation designed to turn the tide of the war.

While the IJN searched vainly for its decisive battle, it totally disregarded the importance of protecting its own maritime trade. For an island nation dependent on moving raw materials into the home islands for survival, let alone to conduct a major war, such disregard can scarcely be believed. This weakness was concealed in 1942 by the extent of Japanese success and by the fact that problems with American torpedoes and tactics limited Japanese merchant losses to a survivable 900,000 tons. By 1944, the effect of the American submarine campaign and the introduction of American airpower into Japan's inner defense zones brought Japanese merchant losses to unsustainable levels. Of the 6.4 million tons of merchant shipping available to the Japanese before the war, only 1.5 million tons remained at the end of the war and these were pinned down in port and therefore unable to move raw supplies to the homeland. The only reasonable explanation for this neglect was that protection of merchant shipping could not contribute directly to the decisive battle, providing another example of the IJN's inability to comprehend the nature of modern war.

Even with this backdrop of overall defeat, there were clearly components of the IJN which fought well and earned the respect of their opponents. First among these was the IJN's carrier force, which opened the war with such a resounding note. When the Japanese concentrated their naval airpower into a single formation in April 1941 it was truly a revolutionary step. This pioneering move made the Kido Butai supreme in the Pacific, at least briefly. Japanese carrier doctrine, with its ability to mass airpower, at both the operational and tactical levels, was clearly superior to American carrier doctrine through 1942, which continued to rely on individual carrier air groups. However, American carrier doctrine developed rapidly and by late 1943 had eclipsed the Japanese. Even at its zenith, the Kido Butai was only a raiding force. When the American carrier force reached its peak, it had the capability to exert sustained power even against heavily defended targets, something the IJN never even contemplated.

The original Kido Butai comprised a mix of carriers which possessed great striking power at the expense of staying power. While *Akagi* and *Kaga* must also be seen as successful conversions, the Soryu class, which epitomized the IJN's desire to create a fast carrier with a large air wing at the expense of protection, proved unable to survive damage in its only clash with enemy carriers. In the Shokaku class, Japanese carrier design reached its peak. Both ships proved very tough and capable units in action and had very few foreign contemporaries.

The main problem with building ships as capable as the Shokakus was that they could not be produced in numbers during wartime. In fact, the Japanese completed only a single fleet carrier during the war in time to see action in a carrier engagement. This was the *Taiho* – certainly a fine design, but clearly not one that could be repeated in sufficient numbers to allow the IJN to sustain a campaign against the USN. The Unryu class was a design conceived with ease of construction in mind. However, it was actually a step back, as it possessed little protection, and by 1944 the size of its air group compared unfavorably with those of the new American fleet carriers already in service. The final fleet carrier, *Shinano*, was an anomaly but one that possessed considerable potential. However, by the time of its commissioning, it was irrelevant.

Japanese prewar plans for preparing merchant and auxiliary ships for conversion into carriers were also a mixed success. While the program was successful in providing 11 ships, these were generally not of a standard to be successful in fleet service. The most useful conversion was the Hiyo class. For the Japanese, these were important additions to their carrier force, as they came immediately after Midway. Generally, these ships offered the capability of the Soryu class but with a lower speed and reduced protection. Of the ships converted from merchants to act as fleet carriers during the war, they must be judged as the most successful in any navy. The five ships converted from auxiliaries into light carriers generally proved useful in service with the exception of *Ryuho*. However, even the more successful conversions could operate only a small number of aircraft, and, while maneuverable, were largely unprotected.

The IJN's five escort carriers rendered little useful service aside from acting as aircraft ferries. Not surprisingly, with no catapults and insufficient speed, they were a failure in their envisioned role as fleet units. Even used in a more suitable role as convoy escorts they proved a failure. The contributions of the IJN's five escort carriers contrast miserably with the key roles played by the over 125 escort carriers that entered service in the RN and USN.

The most unsuccessful component of the IJN was its battleship force. For all their prewar expectations, the Japanese battleship force contributed very little to Japan's war effort. While this failure can be largely attributed to the demise of the battleship in the dawning age of airpower, Japanese battleships never found a new role for which they were well suited, unlike their American counterparts.

In the opening stages of the war, only the Kongo class was active. Despite the speed of these ships, which permitted them to operate with the carrier force, they were basically unsuited to that role, since they lacked sufficient antiaircraft power to defend themselves, much less the carriers. Most of the IJN's battle line remained inactive during the initial stages of the war. All were committed at Midway, where they contributed nothing.

In the six-month struggle for Guadalcanal, the IJN's battleships had the potential to make significant contributions to a Japanese victory. Against American surface forces, or used against the pivotal airfield on Guadalcanal, their firepower would have been a significant addition. The Kongo class was committed to close action around the island, but none of the heavier battleships ever got close to it. Whether this was because of a lack of proper ammunition for shore bombardment, a lack of fuel in the forward areas, or a reluctance to commit what was still viewed as the IJN's most important assets, has not been fully explained. However, the USN did not share the same reluctance, and risked two of its most modern battleships at a key point in the battle. While *Yamato* sat at Truk, the battle for Guadalcanal was being decided in November 1942. Had the Japanese decided to risk their prestige battleship, the remaining American carriers and the small air force on Guadalcanal would not have possessed the killing power to handle it. By 1944, the Americans could commit literally hundreds of aircraft to pound even the most armored ships under the waves, but in 1942 this would have been problematic. In the end, the Guadalcanal campaign cost the Japanese two battleships, and the result was still a major defeat.

After Guadalcanal, the battleships were hoarded until late in 1944, when the American invasion of the Philippines forced the IJN to commit its last resources. Following Philippine Sea and the demise of the carrier force, the success of the Japanese plan to defend the Philippines was predicated on the firepower of its nine remaining battleships. Despite being committed with almost no air cover, this strategy placed the four remaining battleships of Force "A" in a favorable tactical position to inflict a sharp local defeat on the Americans. Even in this battle against unarmored, slow escort carriers and their weak escorts, the Japanese battleship force came out second with a display of poor gunnery and lack of aggression. The battle for Leyte cost another three battleships, and again resulted in a major defeat.

Leyte broke the back of the IJN and five of the remaining six battleships returned to Japan to sit idle for lack of fuel. Of the five, only one remained afloat at the end of the war. Three others had been sunk in harbor. The fate of *Yamato* symbolized the ineffectiveness of the entire Japanese battleship force. Built at great cost to the nation, it fired its main armament at a surface target once during the war. This was not during a great clash of battleships to decide control of the Pacific, but at an insignificant escort carrier. Unable to face the prospect of national defeat while leaving the symbol of the nation intact, the IJN recklessly committed *Yamato* on a virtual suicide mission in the face of waves of carrier aircraft. Its loss contributed nothing and epitomized the futility of Japan's battleship force.

Since the Japanese were reluctant to commit their battleships, the IJN's heavy cruiser force was forced to fill the gap. Japanese heavy cruiser designers produced a series of fast, well-armed and tough ships with considerable offensive capabilities. However, given this emphasis on offensive capabilities, Japanese heavy cruisers were not as well balanced as the later American treaty cruiser designs or those completed during the war.

The persistent issue of overweight designs resulted in several undesirable consequences. Instability was a problem that reached its zenith in the design of the Mogami class, which required a wholesale reconstruction to rectify it. Additional weight also reduced endurance and freeboard; the latter condition had the effect of pushing more of the main armor belt below the waterline, which increased the potential for damage from enemy shellfire. For all cruiser designs, underwater protection was inadequate, since the Japanese themselves had calculated that their passive torpedo defenses could only withstand 440lb of high explosive. Since the standard American air-launched torpedo during the war contained a warhead with 600lb of Torpex (50 percent more powerful than TNT), and the Mark 14 submarine-launched torpedo had a Torpex warhead with 643lb, Japanese cruisers were obviously vulnerable to torpedo damage.

The principal design difference between Japanese cruisers and American cruisers was the inclusion of a heavy torpedo armament. As predicted by some Japanese designers, inclusion of torpedoes proved to be a double-edged sword. As has been recounted, use of cruiser-fired torpedoes was decisive in several instances, namely during the battles of Java Sea and Savo Island. However, the loss of three cruisers (*Mikuma*, *Furutaka* and *Suzuya*) was directly attributable to detonations of onboard torpedoes, and two other cruisers (*Aoba* and *Mogami*) were severely damaged in the same way.

During the course of the war, the IJN's cruisers proved increasingly vulnerable to air attack, although this was not in itself due to a design flaw. Indeed, the primary cause for the destruction of the majority of the IJN's heavy cruisers (ten of 16 heavy cruisers lost) was air attack. The Japanese were not unaware of this vulnerability, but the continuing addition of growing numbers of light antiaircraft guns on the ships did nothing to lessen their vulnerability.

Nevertheless, heavy cruisers must be seen as one of the IJN's success stories. These ships spearheaded Japanese expansion into the critical Dutch East Indies, shattering all Allied opposition. Japanese heavy cruisers served with distinction during the Guadalcanal campaign, marked by the victory at Savo Island. By the end of the war, all but two had been sunk as the Americans exploited Japanese weaknesses in antiaircraft and antisubmarine warfare, but the fighting record of the IJN's heavy cruiser force was unmatched by the heavy cruisers of any other navy during World War II.

The IJN's light cruisers were underarmed compared to their foreign counterparts, carried almost no or limited antiaircraft protection, and possessed a mediocre torpedo armament. This translated into a record of steady, if unglamorous service. Overall, the IJN's 5,500-ton designs must be considered marginally successful given the undoubted success of the IJN's destroyer forces, which the light cruisers were responsible for leading.

In addition to their role as destroyer squadron flagships, Japanese light cruisers were employed in many other roles. They enjoyed no great success in any of these, but performed all adequately. However, as the war progressed, and American air and naval power penetrated deeply into Japanese-held areas, the weaknesses of the IJN's light cruisers became obvious. Of the 22 non-training light cruisers, only two survived; 11 were sunk by submarine attack, seven by air attack and two in surface engagements. Throughout the war they proved vulnerable to air attack. Unable to protect themselves and unable to take a great degree of damage, seven were sunk, and almost every ship damaged at least once, by air attack. Most apparent is their vulnerability to submarine attack. Since most light cruisers were not considered major fleet units, they were assigned secondary missions. In this capacity, they were not given adequate antisubmarine protection, and the results were evident. Japanese light cruisers did not possess dedicated antitorpedo defenses, so when they were torpedoed, one or two torpedoes were adequate to sink the ship.

The utility of the last generation of light cruisers, the Agano and Oyodo classes, must be questioned. The Japanese notion of using light cruisers to lead destroyers and submarines was deeply ingrained, and the design of the last light cruisers built reflected this specialized role. What resulted in the case of the Agano class was a beautiful ship, but one that was outclassed by foreign light cruiser designs in the areas of firepower and protection. The concept of using light cruisers as an operational flagship for submarine squadrons was never more than a fantasy, so this made the Oyodo nothing more than a white elephant. In the final analysis, the IJN's light cruiser ranks were a collection of overaged, underarmed, and marginally protected ships suited only for specialized roles.

The IJN's destroyer force went to war possessing some of the most powerful ships in the world. However, an assessment of its strengths and weaknesses reveals that these ships were suited for only a single mission: delivering torpedo attacks. Overall, Japanese destroyers were excellent torpedo boats, but were not well-balanced destroyers, since they were deficient in antiaircraft and antisubmarine warfare capabilities. In the early part of the war, with patchy Allied resistance and during the series of night battles in the Solomons against American surface ships, Japanese destroyers were well suited for the roles they were tasked to execute, and as a result performed excellently. However, as the war went on and the Americans

The fourth wave of attacking US aircraft, including torpedo bombers from the carrier *Lexington*, delivered a devastating attack on the immobile cruiser, *Nachi*. As many as five torpedoes hit the ship, blowing off the bow and the stern following the explosion of the aft magazine. The result of the attack is shown in this photo. Only 220 men survived the sinking and subsequent strafing by American aircraft; 807 were killed, including 74 from the embarked Fifth Fleet staff. (Naval History and Heritage Command)

brought increasing numbers of submarines into play and gained air superiority over the battle areas, the weaknesses of Japanese destroyers were ruthlessly exposed.

Japanese Destroyer Losses 1941–45 by Cause				
Surface	Submarine	Air	Other/Combination	Surviving
26	39	49	13	39

By far the leading causes of losses among the 166 Pacific War IJN destroyers were submarine and air attack. Losses in surface actions were relatively minor in comparison. Other causes of losses included mining, collisions, and a single loss to shore batteries. Losses increased throughout the war, with only four being lost in 1941, 17 in 1942, 33 in 1943, an astounding 58 in 1944, and 15 in 1945.

A review of each class supports this basic assessment of the strengths and weaknesses of the Japanese destroyer force. At the start of the war, the Minekaze class was considered obsolescent by the Japanese. Most were assigned to secondary commands and undertook general patrol and escort duties. In this capacity, the Minekaze class proved to be undistinguished submarine hunters, since its ships lacked modern sensors or antisubmarine weapons. Of the 13 ships, only five survived, and of the eight lost, seven were sunk by submarines.

The Kamikaze class formed two destroyer divisions at the beginning of the war and was briefly active in the forward areas before being assigned escort duties in rear areas. Of the nine ships, seven were lost, with submarines again being the primary agent of destruction.

The 12-ship Mutsuki class saw extensive service during the war, and all 12 were lost before the end of 1944. Unlike the previous two classes of older destroyers, they were employed in the forward areas, with almost the entire class seeing duty in the Solomons campaign. Ten units were lost to air attack, clearly demonstrating the inability of these ships to deal with concerted air assault. One ship was lost in surface action and, unusually, only a single ship was sunk by submarine attack.

After their stability faults had been addressed, the 19 Group I and II Special Type destroyers rendered good service. Fubuki-class units saw extensive action in the Solomons area, but were eventually assigned secondary duties as newer destroyers entered the fleet. Only one ship, *Ushio*, survived the war. Of the 18 ships sunk, six were lost to submarine attack, seven to air attack, three to surface action, and two were mined. Of the four Group III Special Type ships, only one survived.

The original Hatsuharu design also possessed severe stability problems that were corrected before the war. None of the six units survived, and four of these were sunk by air attack. The similar Shiratsuyu class also saw extensive service, with none of the ten ships surviving the war. Only one ship was sunk by air, but five were destroyed by submarine attack and three sunk in surface engagements.

The most telling statistic of all regarding the IJN's destroyer force is that, of the 48 ships that made up the Asashio and the Type A classes, comprising the most capable Japanese destroyers, only a single ship survived the war. This alone confirms the bitter nature of the combat that Japanese destroyers were forced to fight. The late-war destroyers of the Akizuki, Matsu, and Tachibana classes in many cases were not completed in time to see service beyond home waters. This explains the survival of 29 of these units.

The performance of the IJN's submarine force fell far short of Japanese expectations during the Pacific War. Originally designed to be an adjunct in the set-piece decisive battle, they were ill-suited to play a role in the war which developed.

The IJN had 64 submarines available at the start of the war. Of these, only 41 were modern fleet boats, two were modern medium submarines, and 21 were obsolete. The lackluster performance of the Japanese submarine force began immediately when 27 fleet submarines deployed off Hawaii in 1941 with very disappointing results. In 1942, the Japanese failed to develop a coherent submarine strategy. Linked to fleet operations, it did achieve some notable successes, but Japan's inability to supply garrisons demanded emergency measures and the submarine force was increasingly employed on supply missions.

The submarine force carried out various different missions, from attacking shipping off the US West Coast, to carrying midget submarines to targets in Australia and the Indian Ocean, and carrying out transport operations to Europe. However, most late-war operations were based on ill-coordinated responses to US attacks on Japanese-held islands. This typically featured setting up a submarine picket line against advancing US forces. Most often these lines were moved elsewhere when the deployment or timing of the original line was found to be faulty. In the face of US forces equipped with radar and superior intelligence, these tactics were suicidal. Throughout the war, the missions to supply cut-off garrisons increased, as did the losses.

Japanese submarines were generally much larger than any other navy's boats. Even the C1 Type boats, smallest of the A1/B1/C1 types, were significantly larger than US fleet boats. This large size was required to fulfill

The wreck of *Okinami* pictured in February 1945. *Okinami* was one of many Japanese destroyers lost during the Philippines campaign to American air attack because of insufficient air cover and inadequate antiaircraft capabilities. The ship was sunk on November 13, 1944 in Manila harbor, but only 14 crewmen were lost. (Naval History and Heritage Command)

their envisioned role as long-range, high-surface-speed torpedo platforms, but made them ill-suited to the type of antisubmarine war they were to experience. Being large, their diving time was excessive. Once detected, they were fairly easy to destroy because of their slow submerged speed, poor maneuverability, and limited diving depths. They were also noisy under water. To make things worse, Japanese boats were equipped with generally outdated radar and acoustic equipment. The increasing effectiveness of Allied antisubmarine measures was not appreciated by the Japanese until it was too late, partly because the IJN had neglected its own antisubmarine forces before the war and had no real idea what modern antisubmarine warfare had become.

The Japanese developed a multiplicity of designs during the war and never arrived at a standardized design adapted for mass production. During the war they added 126 submarines to their fleet, making a total of 190 used during the war. All told, 129 submarines were lost – 70 to surface forces, 19 to Allied submarines, 18 to air attack, and 22 others to unknown or various causes. In return, Japanese submarines accounted for some 185 merchant ships of just over 900,000 GRT (gross register tons) and a paltry total of warships sunk including two carriers, two cruisers, and ten smaller warships. Compared to the German U-boats' toll of over 2,500 merchant ships alone, this was a poor harvest. All considered, the exploits of the IJN's submarine force were among the more disappointing stories of the Pacific War.

The performance of the IJN's individual units, particularly during the early parts of the war, displayed the Japanese notion that quality would triumph over quantity. In a short, quick war, this core Japanese belief could have been correct, as it had been against the Russians in 1905. The lesson of the war against the Russians for the IJN was that reliance on a decisive battle was a viable strategy. When the Pacific War turned from a war of sweeping Japanese advances to one of attrition, the IJN was unable to adjust. The Japanese remained fixated on the development of a decisive battle. Against a modern opponent, with the industrial strength to sustain a war of attrition, this strategy, even if supported by excellent tactics, was disastrous. Most importantly, the decisive battle concept against the United States was totally void since no one battle could defeat a major industrial nation. More than anything else, the IJN's inability to comprehend, much less prepare for, total war led to its total and utter destruction.

BIBLIOGRAPHY

"Akizuki Class Destroyers," *Gakken Magazine*, vol. 23, Gakken Publishing (Tokyo, 1999)

Backer, Steve, *Japanese Heavy Cruisers*, Chatham Publishing, London (2006)

Bagnasco, Erminio, *Submarines of World War Two*, Sterling Publishing Co. Inc., New York (2000)

Breyer, Siegfried, *Battleships and Battle Cruisers 1905–1970*, Doubleday & Company Inc., Garden City, New York (1978)

Brown, David, *Aircraft Carriers*, Arco Publishing Company, New York, 1977

Campbell, John, *Naval Weapons of World War Two*, Naval Institute Press, Annapolis, Maryland (2002)

Carpenter, Dorr and Norman Polmar, *Submarines of the Imperial Japanese Navy*, Naval Institute Press, Annapolis, Maryland (1986)

Dickson, W. D., "The Shokakus," *Warship International*, vol. 1, International Naval Research Organization, Holden, Massachusetts, 1977

Dull, Paul, *A Battle History of the Imperial Japanese Navy (1941–1945)*, Naval Institute Press, Annapolis, Maryland (1978)

Evans, David C. and Mark R. Peattie, *Kaigun*, Naval Institute Press, Annapolis, Maryland (1997)

Friedman, Norman, *Naval Radar*, Conway Maritime Press (1981)

Fukui, Shizuo, *Japanese Naval Vessels at the End of World War II*, Naval Institute Press, Annapolis, Maryland (1991)

"Genealogy of Japanese Destroyers Part 1," *Warship Model Magazine*, 17, Model Art Co. (2005)

"Genealogy of Japanese Destroyers Part 2," *Warship Model Magazine*, 25, Model Art Co. (2007)

Goralski, Waldemar and Slawomir Lipiecki, *Japanese Heavy Cruiser Takao*, Kagero, Lublin, Poland (2007)

Goralski, Waldemar and Miroslaw Skwiot, *Heavy Cruiser Aoba*, Kagero, Lublin, Poland (2008)

Itani, Jiro, Hans Lengerer, and Tomoko Rehm-Takahara, "Anti-aircraft Gunnery in the Imperial Japanese Navy", *Warship 1991*, Conway Maritime Press, London (1991)

Itani, Jiro, Hans Lengerer, and Tomoko Rehm-Takahara, "Japanese Oxygen Torpedoes and Fire Control Systems," *Warship 1991*, Conway Maritime Press, London (1991)

Iwashige, Tashiro, *Visual Guide to Japanese Navy Small Combatants in WW2: Destroyers*, Dainippon Kaiga Co, Ltd, Tokyo (2012)

Januszewski, Tadeusz, *Japanese Submarine Aircraft*, Mushroom Model Publications, Redbourn, United Kingdom (2002)

Jentschura, Hansgeorg, Dieter Jung, and Peter Mickel, *Warships of the Imperial Japanese Navy 1869–1945*, Naval Institute Press, Annapolis, Maryland (1977)

Lacroix, Eric and Linton Wells II, *Japanese Cruisers of the Pacific War*, Naval Institute Press, Annapolis, Maryland (1997)

Lengerer, Hans, "*Akagi* and *Kaga*" (three parts), *Warship*, vol. VI, Conway Maritime Press, London (1982)

Lengerer, Hans and Tomoko Rehm-Takahara, "The Japanese Aircraft Carriers *Hiyo* and *Junyo*" (three parts), *Warship*, vol. IX, Conway Maritime Press, London (1985)

Marriot, Leo, *Treaty Cruisers*, Pen and Sword Maritime, Barnsley (2005)

"Matsu Class Destroyers," *Gakken Magazine*, vol. 18, Gakken Publishing, Tokyo (2003)

Mutsuki Class Destroyers, Gakken Publishing, Tokyo (2008)

Navy Yard Magazine, vol. 1, Dainippon Kaiga Co, Ltd, Tokyo (2005)

Navy Yard Magazine, vol. 3, Dainippon Kaiga Co, Ltd, Tokyo (2006)

Navy Yard Magazine, vol. 7, Dainippon Kaiga Co, Ltd, Tokyo (2008)

Navy Yard Magazine, vol. 19, Dainippon Kaiga Co, Ltd, Tokyo (2011)

O'Hara, Vincent, *The US Navy Against the Axis*, Naval Institute Press, Annapolis, Maryland (2007)

Preston, Anthony (ed.), *Super Destroyers*, Conway Maritime Press, London (1978)

Robbins, Guy, *The Aircraft Carrier Story 1908–1945*, Cassell, London (2001)

Skulski, Janusz, *The Heavy Cruiser* Takao, Naval Institute Press, Annapolis, Maryland (1994)

Skulski, Janusz, *The Battleship* Fuso, Naval Institute Press, Annapolis, Maryland (1998)

Skulski, Janusz, *The Battleship* Yamato, Naval Institute Press, Annapolis, Maryland (2000)

Special Type Destroyers, Gakken Publishing, Tokyo (2010)

Thornton, Tim, "The Sinking of the *Yamato*," *Warship 1989*, Conway Maritime Press, London (1989)

Thornton, Tim, "*Yamato*, the Achilles Heel," *Warship,* vol. XI, Naval Institute Press, Annapolis, Maryland (1990)

Thornton, Tim, "The Air Power Sinking of IJN Battleship *Musashi*," *Warship,* vol. XII, Naval Institute Press, Annapolis, Maryland (1991)

Warship Mechanism Picturebook Japanese Destroyers, Grand Prix Publishing, Tokyo (1995)

Warship Model Magazine, "Genealogy of Japanese Destroyers Part 3," no. 30, Model Art Co, Tokyo (2008)

Warship Model Magazine, "Genealogy of Japanese Destroyers Part 4," no. 37, Model Art Co, Tokyo (2010)

Watts, Anthony J. and Brian G. Gordon, *The Imperial Japanese Navy*, Macdonald, London (1971)

Wells, Linton, "Painting Systems of the Imperial Japanese Navy 1904–1945," *Warship International*, vol. 1, International Naval Research Organization, Holden, Massachusetts (1982)

Whitley, M. J., *Destroyers of World War Two*, Naval Institute Press, Annapolis, Maryland (1988)

Whitley, M. J., *Cruisers of World War Two*, Naval Institute Press, Annapolis, Maryland (1995)

Whitley, M. J., *Battleships of World War Two*, Naval Institute Press, Annapolis, Maryland (1998)

Wiper, Steve, *IJN Myoko Class Heavy Cruiser*, Classic Warships Publishing, Tucson, Arizona (2002)

Wiper, Steve, *IJN Takao Class Heavy Cruiser*, Classic Warships Publishing, Tucson, Arizona (2008)

Yoshihide, Yamamoto, Yoshiwara Kannari, Hara Katsuhiro, and Shibata Takehiko, *All About Japanese Naval Shipboard Weapons*, KK Bestsellers, Tokyo (2002)

www.combinedfleet.com

INDEX